Promoting Health for Working Women

Athena Linos · Wilhelm Kirch

Editors

Promoting Health
for Working Women

Foreword by Karen Messing

Springer

Editors

Athena Linos
Department of Hygiene, Epidemiology,
 and Medical Statistics
School of Medicine
National and Kapodistrian University
 of Athens
75 M. Asias Street
Goudi, Athens 115 27
alinou@cc.uoa.gr

Wilhelm Kirch
Research Association Public Health
Saxony and Saxony-Anhalt
Medical Faculty Carl Gustav Carus
Technische Universität Dresden
Fiedlerstr. 27
01307 Dresden, Germany
Wilhelm.Kirch@mailbox.tu-dresden.de

The HPROWOMEN project and the current publication received funding from the Stavros Niarchos Foundation and from the European Union/DG Health and Consumer Protection/Health Programme. The sole responsibility for the content of this book lies with the authors and not the European Commission. The European Commission is not responsible for any use that may be made of the information contained in the book.

ISBN: 978-0-387-73037-0   e-ISBN: 978-0-387-73038-7

Library of Congress Control Number: 2007933088

Printed on acid-free paper.

9 8 7 6 5 4 3 2 1

springer.com

This book is dedicated to all working women

Foreword

In general, women's health is better if they work, however this is not true for working-class women (Romito 1994). In fact, all women's health is at risk if their jobs expose them to risk factors such as toxic or infectious agents, infections, repetitive movements, awkward postures, and heavy time pressure (Vogel 2003, Messing & Mergler 2006). Therefore, health promotion for women involves two components: preventing workplace-induced damage to health, and using the workplace as a place to promote healthy behavior and detect illness (Karnaki et al., this volume). Research is lacking in both areas, and this book is, I hope, part of a serious European effort to fill the gaps.

Relatively little is known about women's occupational health. At least since the publication of *Women's Work, Women's Health* (Stellman 1978), occupational health researchers have been aware of a severe deficit in research on women, which continues to this day (McDiarmid & Gucer 2001, Messing & Mergler 2006). Not only are women often ignored, but the treatment of sex as a variable has not been appropriate (Niedhammer et al. 2000, Messing et al. 2003). This book presents a wealth of information that will be useful to those wanting to improve workplace-related health for women.

I hope it will inspire researchers and practitioners to increase efforts to understand the consequences of the sexual division of paid and unpaid labor in women's health, the interactions between biological sex differences and workplace conditions, and the health effects of women's social situation in the workplace. For example, with recent transformations in global labor-force practices and the increasing proportion of atypical and precarious jobs, especially for women (Cranford et al. 2003), we need to know a lot more about the health effects of such terms of employment. More broadly, we should know more about all the effects of sex discrimination in the labor market and on the job (Bond et al. 2004, Schmitt et al., this volume).

This book also presents several interesting case studies of health promotion for women, as well as important theory concerning health promotion. We need to know even more, however, about how to produce change in the workplace and more about how women's needs can be met in practice, given their position in the hierarchy, their social roles, and the constraints put on them. For example, we know that women in health care are exposed to many communicable diseases that can affect their health (Tsiodras, this volume). Carpentier-Roy [1991], however, tells us that nurses are reluctant to put physical barriers between themselves and their patients, especially when the patients are close to death. How can health protection be reconciled with the essential act of caring, which is fundamental to nursing and a recognized and valued part of women's social role? We ourselves have observed that cleaners are excluded from information about the health state of patients whose rooms they clean. How to reconcile health protection with confidentiality? We also learn from this book that the workplace is a good place to give women important information related to cessation of smoking (Merkur, this volume). We have observed that food servers and other women working under time pressure with very short breaks use cigarettes to transition between accelerated movements and relaxation. How can practitioners consult with employers to change working conditions to make the use of this unhealthy tool unnecessary? These and other puzzles must be resolved by talking to and observing women workers—to identify what is important to them about their jobs, and how they deal with the challenges in their working environments.

Unfortunately, we cannot assume that such things will be done just because they are a good idea. In a holistic consideration of health promotion, Chapter 9's section on breastfeeding (Geuskens & Burdorf) invites workers and practitioners to weigh the benefits of breastfeeding against the dangers of contamination of the infant by toxic substances present in the workplace. The authors propose that the workplace adapt to the presence of nursing women in a number of ways. Malenfant [1996] has shown in her study of the experiences of pregnant workers, however, that it can be dangerous to ask too loudly for the workplace to adjust to women's specific needs. It is unfortunately still true that, in most workplaces, even unionized women workers must avoid any act that marks them as a different group from male workers, who are seen as the norm (Messing et al. 2006). Researchers and practitioners must therefore collaborate to make workplaces more likely to adapt to the needs of all workers. This book should be an important step toward transforming research and practice in health promotion in Europe, so women can gain social and economic equality without endangering their health.

Karen Messing, Ph.D.
Professor, Department of Biological Sciences
CINBIOSE WHO-PAHO Collaborating Centre
Université du Québec à Montreal
CP 8888, Succursale Centre-ville
Montreal QC H3C 3P8 Canada

References

Bond MA, Punnett L, Pyle JL, Cazeca D, Cooperman M. (2004) Gendered work conditions, health, and work outcomes. *J Occup Health Psychol* 9: 28–45.
Carpentier-Roy MC. (1991) *Corps et Âme*. Montréal: Éditions Liber.

Cranford C, Vosko LF, Zukewich N. (2003) The gender of precarious employment in Canada. *Relations Industrielles/Industrial Relations* 58: 454–479.

Malenfant R. (1996) *Travail et grossesse. Peut-on laisser la maternité à la porte de l'entreprise?* Montréal: Éditions Liber.

McDiarmid MA, Gucer PW. (2001) The "GRAS" status of women's work. *J Occup Environ Med* 43: 665–669.

Messing K, Mergler D. (2006) Introduction: women's occupational and environmental health. *Environ Res* 101: 147–148.

Messing K, Stellman JM. (2006) Sex, gender and women's occupational health: the importance of considering mechanism. *Environ Res* 101: 149–162.

Messing K, Seifert AM, Couture V. (2006) Les femmes dans les métiers non-traditionnels: le général, le particulier et l'ergonomie. *Travailler* 15: 131–148.

Niedhammer I, Saurel-Cubizolles MJ, Piciotti M, Bonenfant S. (2000) How is sex considered in recent epidemiological publications on occupational risks? *Occup Environ Med* 57: 521–527.

Romito P. (1994) Work and health in mothers of young children. *Int J Health Serv* 24: 607–628.

Stellman JM. (1978) *Women's Work, Women's Health.* New York: Pantheon Books.

Vogel, L. (2003) *The Gender Workplace Health Gap in Europe.* Brussels: European Trade Union Institute.

Preface

In the past few decades, the European workforce has seen a substantial rise in the number of employed women. There is an increasing trend in women entering most occupations while still carrying the responsibilities of domestic labor. Professional and domestic demands can be overwhelming and difficult to balance, thus placing women in a very sensitive yet powerful position. Working women face increased risks as a consequence of their employment and domestic undertakings, yet they have the power to influence the health habits and behaviors of their family and, to a certain extent, of their social contacts. In addition, successful work-life balance constitutes an important health resource.

Understandably, the delivery of health promotion programs specifically addressing women is of utmost importance due to their multiplying effect. What better place to address women than the workplace—a setting where peer pressure can exercise an extremely positive influence. Occupational settings offer the possibility of reaching large numbers of women at regular intervals, which is a critical element in the success of any health promoting intervention.

Despite all this, health-related initiatives are limited and have not taken into account the potential of women for disseminating health-promoting messages. Such initiatives should stem from health authorities, public health professionals (including occupational safety and health services), employers, and employee associations. All these parties need to understand that investing in the health and welfare of their employees and their families has a direct positive impact on productivity and wealth.

Some might argue that health interventions addressing just women in the workplace constitute gender discrimination, yet one can easily find counter arguments by looking at recent data published by the World Health Organization (WHO) in 2004.* Part-time work is more common for women than men, women are underrepresented in permanent employment contracts, and female unemployment rates are much higher compared to men, indicating instability in professional life and higher exposure to health risks. Mental health problems, stress, burnout syndrome, work-related violence, and sexual harassment constitute important public health issues affecting more women than men, and are directly related to work.

---

*World Health Organization (2004) Gender, Health and Work. Geneva: Department of Gender, Women and Health (GWH).; http://www.who.int/gender/documents/en/

This book is an effort to provide public health professionals with background knowledge in organizing health-promoting programs, and enable them to address a series of health issues—some of which are exclusively relevant to women.

The book is divided into four parts. Part I provides an overview of the principles and concepts of health promotion for working women, and provides a methodological framework for the design and implementation of health promotion programs. The first part of the book also includes a review of the relevant European Union (EU) legislative framework.

Part II reviews specific health topics of particular interest to working women, namely, occupational diseases, mental health and work-life balance, musculoskeletal disorders, work-related violence, bullying and sexually harassment, and communicable diseases. In Part III, special emphasis is made on two particular health issues concerning working women—reproductive health and breastfeeding. The final part reviews lifestyle determinants such as smoking, alcohol, and nutrition from a woman's perspective, and in view of the special role women still have in most of today's family and societal structures.

Athena Linos
Wilhelm Kirch

Acknowledgments

The editors wish to express their sincere gratitude to the European Commission (DG SANCO) and the STAVROS NIARCHOS FOUNDATION for their most valuable support in the delivery of the HPROWOMEN project that led to the production of this book.

STAVROS NIARCHOS FOUNDATION

Contents

PART III   WOMEN'S REPRODUCTIVE HEALTH ISSUES

PART IV   LIFESTYLE DETERMINANTS

List of Figures

List of Tables

List of Contributors

Athena Linos, M.D., M.P.H., F.A.C.E.
Department of Hygiene, Epidemiology
and Medical Statistics
School of Medicine
National and Kapodistrian University
of Athens
Athens, Greece

Elena Riza, M.P.H., Ph.D.
Department of Hygiene, Epidemiology
and Medical Statistics
School of Medicine
National and Kapodistrian University
of Athens
Athens, Greece

Christos Chatzis, M.D., Ph.D.
Department of Hygiene, Epidemiology
and Medical Statistics
School of Medicine
National and Kapodistrian University
of Athens
Athens, Greece

Ioannis Polychronakis, M.D. M.Sc.
Department of Hygiene, Epidemiology
and Medical Statistics
School of Medicine
National and Kapodistrian University
of Athens
Athens, Greece

George Lazarou, M.D., Ph.D.
Orthopaedic Surgeon

Social Insurance Institute (IKA)
Oropos Branch
Athens, Greece

Ioanna Kotsioni, M.Sc.
Institute of Preventive Medicine
Environmental & Occupational Health
Athens, Greece

Pania Karnaki, M.H.S.
Institute of Preventive Medicine
Environmental & Occupational Health
Athens, Greece

Sotirios Tsiodras, M.D, M.Sc., Ph.D.
Instructor in Medicine and
Infectious Diseases
Medical School
University of Athens
Athens, Greece

Natalie M. Schmitt, M.D., M.P.H.
Research Association Public Health
Saxony and Saxony-Anhalt
Medical Faculty Carl Gustav Carus
Technische Universität
Dresden, Germany

Andreas Fuchs
Institute of Clinical Pharmacology
and Therapeutics
Medical Faculty Carl Gustav Carus
Technische Universität
Dresden, Germany

Professor Wilhelm Kirch M.D., D.M.D.
Research Association Public
Health Saxony and Saxony-Anhalt
Medical Faculty Carl Gustav Carus
Technische Universität
Dresden, Germany

Associated Professor Alex Burdorf, Ph.D.
Department of Public Health,
Erasmus MC, University Medical
Center Rotterdam
Rotterdam, Netherlands

Goedele Geuskens, M.A.
Department of Rheumatology,
Erasmus MC, University Medical
Center Rotterdam
Rotterdam, Netherlands

Sherry Merkur, M.Sc.
LSE Health London
School of Economics and
Political Science
London, UK

Professor Elias Mossialos, M.D., Ph.D.
LSE Health
London School of Economics
and Political Science
London, UK

Professor Manolis Kogevinas, M.D., Ph.D.
Centre for Research in Environmental
Epidemiology (CREAL) Municipal
Institute of Medical Research
(IMIM) Barcelona, Spain

Dept. of Social Medicine
Medical School
University of Crete
Heraklion, Greece

Gemma Janer, Ph.D.
Centre for Research in Environmental
Epidemiology (CREAL) Municipal
Institute of Medical Research (IMIM)
Barcelona, Spain

Professor Kaisa Kauppinen, Ph.D.
Finnish Institute of Occupational Health
Helsinki, Finland

Tarita Tuomola, M.So.Sc.
Finnish Institute of
Occupational Health
Helsinki, Finland

Verka Koytcheva, D.M.Sc.
Faculty of Public Health
Medical University of Sofia
Sofia, Bulgaria

Assistant Professor Alexander Zhekov
Faculty of Public Health
Medical University of Sofia
Sofia, Bulgaria

Teus Brand, M.D.
Occupational Physician KLM Health
Services at Schiphol Airport
Amsterdam, Netherlands

Netherlands Centre for Occupational
Diseases, Academic Medical
Centre, University of Amsterdam
Amsterdam, Netherlands

PART I
GENERAL PRINCIPLES
AND CONCEPTS

Chapter 1
Introduction to Health Promotion for Working Women: A Methodology

Pania Karnaki, Ioannis Polychronakis, Athena Linos and Ioanna Kotsioni

Introduction

The number of working women in the European Union (EU) and the United States has risen considerably in the course of the last few decades, constituting one of the major challenges facing labor forces in the Western world. Women currently comprise 42 percent of the employed population in the EU, and this figure is expected to rise in coming years.

The European labor market is characterized by strong gender segregation. As a consequence of horizontal segregation, men are mostly involved in manual and technical jobs (machine operation, construction, crafts engineering, etc.) and transportation jobs, while women are mostly occupied in sales and service jobs, including professions such as store assistants, nurses, secretaries, social workers, and so on. The EU labor force is also characterized by vertical segregation, with men holding the most senior managerial positions compared to women. Labor segregation means that men and women are exposed to different working conditions and face different occupational safety and health hazards.

Little has been done in terms of health promotion for working women. More specifically, prevention measures at the workplace have not addressed women as a separate group but have not taken into consideration factors such as gender segregation and the increased responsibilities of women at home. It is important for women to maintain a well-balanced life, both physically and mentally. Healthy female employees are important to the organization not only in terms of productivity, but most importantly for women's immediate environment—the family—and society at large, in which women hold vital and multiple roles. This critical role of women as promoters of health for society has been overlooked. Women can play an important role as leaders in health promotion because of their traditional roles in the family and community.

This chapter will provide an overview of the definitions and concepts of workplace health promotion (WHP) with a particular emphasis on women, and discuss issues of WHP program planning and implementation.

A. Linos, W. Kirch (eds), *Promoting Health for Working Women.*
© Springer 2008

Concepts and Definitions

Traditionally, the workplace was approached as a convenient setting for implementing health promotion programs. Currently, the approach to WHP is more comprehensive, and the workplace is seen as a setting where people bring along and act out their behaviors as well as a setting that alone influences employee health in the traditional sense of health and safety and in terms of how work is organized, exercised, and managed.

WHP according to the Centre of the Health Communication Unit at the University of Ontario is defined as: *"an approach to protecting and enhancing the health of employees that relies and builds upon the efforts of employers to create a supportive management under and upon the efforts of employees to care for their own well-being"* (The Health Communication Unit, 2004a). Comprehensive WHP is exercised on the following three levels, which constitute the main components of this practice:

I. **Occupational Health and Safety Level** This level refers to traditional occupational health and safety activities aimed at minimizing environmental and chemical hazards that threaten employee health, such as controlling exposure to toxic substances, removing dangerous equipment, and improving or alleviating health- and life-threatening working conditions.

Even though women's health is affected differently by occupational hazards and working conditions, women are under-represented in occupational health and safety studies in favor of men. Professions that are traditionally mostly represented by women, like nursing, have been studied extensively, leaving a gap in the current knowledge of other women's occupations such as hairdressers, domestic workers, and so on (Messing & Mergler 2006).

II. **Individual Health-Related Behaviors** Employee health-related practices refer to behaviors that employees bring with them to the workplace that have the potential to influence their health and may create problems in productivity—although ill health is a combination of many different factors other than lifestyle. The workplace is indeed a convenient location for addressing health-related behaviors and for implementing health promotion programs.

Targeting health-endangering behaviors specifically for women in the workplace has an additional advantage because women are excellent carriers or multipliers of healthy behaviors for the family and society at large. The workplace has been used as a setting not only for the promotion of employee health, but also as a means to promote the health of employees' families—especially their children (Eastman, Corona & Schuster 2006).

III. **Organizational Change Initiatives** The working environment in which people spend a significant part of their adult lives affects employee health and well-being through the way the organization functions, which is often referred to as the "organizational culture." Important issues which have an impact on the well-being of employees are management style, work organization, work overload, work control, and autonomy (Shain & Krmaer 2004). The way work is organized and the philosophy of the company (in terms of how workload is structured and dealt with), influences the balance between life and work. These factors have become increasingly important, especially for women, and are recognized as having a dramatic impact on their health, both mentally and physically. Women are affected more than men by the imbalance caused between their professional and domestic work, such as family demands and responsibilities like child care, the care of the elderly, and housekeeping responsibilities—all of which have a great impact on mental well-being. In the EU, for example, it has been found that[1]

- 16 percent of women are involved in caring for elderly or disabled relatives at least once or twice a week, compared with 8 percent of men
- 41 percent of women are involved in caring and educating children for one hour or more every day, compared with 24 percent of men
- 63 percent of women are involved in housework for one hour or more every day, compared with 12 percent of men
- 85 percent of women take responsibility for shopping and contributing to other household duties, compared with just 25 percent of men

From the above statistics, it becomes evident that an approach to workplace health promotion needs to combine strategies to combat:

a. Life- and health-threatening working conditions—monitored by Occupational Health and Safety (OSH)
b. Harmful individual lifestyle behaviors
c. Stressful organizational procedures—or work environments that cause anxiety and conflict with responsibilities outside of work

The Case for Women: Health Promotion for Working Women (HPWW)

The changing nature of work has fueled health inequalities among already disadvantaged populations (including women) through phenomena such as widespread long-term unemployment, job insecurity, short-term employment, downsizing, and work overload, caused primarily by economic globalization and the restructuring of economic activities worldwide and regionally. New types of employment that have attracted a large number of women are temporary or casual jobs, working from home, or working remotely using the Internet (Ziglio, Hagard & Griffiths 2000). These new forms of employment have not been studied adequately and the impact they have on health is, to a large extent, still unknown.

---

[1] European Agency for Safety and Health at Work 2003, 2005

In 2003, the European Agency for Safety and Health at Work published a report examining gender differences in the workplace that questioned the validity of the gender-neutral approach in policy and legislation followed by the EU. There is ample evidence to show that men and women are affected differently by work, and that interventions need to be gender-sensitive and based on an examination of real work situations (European Agency for Safety and Health at Work 2003, 2005).

There has been enough evidence to support the theory that women's occupational health problems are not dealt with adequately and that prevention measures are less common in women's jobs in comparison to men's jobs (Messing & Mergler 2006; Lippel 1999, 2003). Women have very different needs and face very different problems in the workplace than men. The case for workplace health promotion programs tailored for women is supported by evidence showing that

- Women in many countries have a higher rate of absence due to sickness and disability pensions compared to that of men
- Women, more often than men, occupy inferior positions that lack autonomy and control with fewer possibilities of influencing work content, career opportunities, and salaries. Consequently, this group has a higher incidence of depression, stress, and anxiety
- A high percentage of women are involved in low-paying, casual, or part-time work—i.e., domestic cleaners, teachers, and child care workers—making this population more vulnerable to poverty, social exclusion, and ill health, especially when taking into account that in these occupations migrant workers (and often undocumented migrant workers) are overrepresented. It is also well-known that casual or part-time domestic cleaners work in inadequate conditions with inadequate working schedules (early morning or late at night)
- Women are more exposed to sexual discrimination at work
- At the end of an 8-hour working day, women continue to hold the main responsibility for bearing and raising children and caring for elderly relatives and friends, creating a life-work imbalance
- Musculoskeletal disorders are more prevalent among women because of their segregation into sedentary, repetitive, and routine types of work and because of more involvement in domestic work at home (Strazdins & Bammer 2004).
- Many women are unable to advance their careers because many organizations base their promotion policy on the ability of their employees to frequently work overtime go on business trips, and attend business meals.

On the contrary, women

- Are more *health sensitive*
- Have the responsibility for health-related activities such as immunizations, hygiene issues, food and beverage choices for the family, housing conditions, and so on.

Planning Health Promotion Interventions
for Working Women - A Methodology

The methodology described in this section does not apply strictly to working women. It can be applied to all employees regardless of gender. It is only suggested as a useful tool for women because, through the planning process, issues of particular importance to women have been highlighted, such as women's dual roles in society.

The Ecological Approach

The work setting has been identified as an optimal venue to carry out health promotion because a large segment of the population can be reached and accessed for a significant part of their everyday life. Until recently, WHP intervened primarily on an individual lifestyle level, targeting harmful behaviors and single illnesses or risk factors following the traditional biomedical approach to health promotion (Arneson & Ekberg 2005; Chu et al. 2000). Programs that focused on individual-based interventions have proved insufficient in improving the health and well-being of workers (Arneson & Ekberg 2005; Schulte et al. 2007). Inevitably, such approaches carry the inherent notion of self-responsibility, which might be largely inappropriate because the wider social and environmental parameters that influence women's health are, in most cases, beyond their control and therefore neglected and underexamined.

Comprehensive HPWW should address the plethora of complex factors that influence women's health, and integrate strategies on individual, organizational, and community levels (McMahon et al. 2002; Nutbeam 1998; Wilson, Holman & Hammock 1996). Health as a final outcome is largely dependent on complex and interrelated factors that need to be considered in unison when addressing health promotion. Focusing on single causative factors will provide only small-scale and short-term changes. HPWW should aim at creating and promoting health through a comprehensive and holistic approach, and not focus on single issues, single problems, or single diseases. The chances of maintaining protective behaviors and promoting these in women's wider social environments would thus be increased.

The ecological perspective of health promotion focuses on the concept of a health-promoting environment that enhances and promotes well-being (Green & Kreuter 1999; National Cancer Institute 2005; Sparling et al. 2000; Stokols 1992; McLeroy et al 1988). The ecological model is widely used in health promotion as a comprehensive framework for project planning. The concept underlining this approach holds that humans act, interact, and shape their personalities and beliefs through the direct influence with their surrounding environment (ecology). Health behavior is perceived as being influenced at different levels namely on an individual/personal, social, community, and environmental level (Campbell et al. 2002; Nutbeam 1998).

Interventions developed according to the ecological perspective take into consideration that behavior is affected at multiple levels and action is directed not only towards the individual and her/his personal health-related behavior, but also towards the social, environmental, and economic contexts of society that affect health. The ecological perspective has been suggested as an important and necessary framework—especially for designing workplace health promotion interventions (Arneson & Ekberg 2005) among women (Campbell et al. 2002).

McLeroy and his colleagues (1988) identified five levels of influence for health-related behaviors and conditions:

1. **Intrapersonal Level:** Individual characteristics that can affect health behavior such as knowledge, prior personal experience, views, and attitudes.
2. **Interpersonal Level:** Health behavior is influenced and shaped by various social groups (family, education, work environment, other acquaintances).
3. **Community Level:**

   a. *Institutional Factors*—Health behaviors are influenced by the rules, regulations, or policies of institutional structures such as schools and workplaces.
   b. *Community Factors*—Formal or informal social networks, norms, and behavioral models of social groups or individuals.
   c. *Policy Factors*—The legal policy framework that supports specific health behaviors (i.e., population-based screening or vaccinations).

Within the framework of the ecological perspective, a widely used approach to WHP is the *settings* approach (Arneson & Ekberg 2005; Chu et al. 2000; McMahon et al. 2002; Noblet 2003; Paton, Sengupta & Hassan 2005; Whitelaw et al. 2001). The *settings* approach focuses on the physical, social, and organizational environments in which people live, and tries to create settings (workplaces) that support and enhance health (Baric 1993; Chu et al. 1997; Noblet 2003). For health promotion, a setting is considered a context (either physical or social) in which people go about their daily activities and in which factors stemming from environmental, personal, and organizational circumstances interact and affect health (Nutbeam 1998; Paton Sengupta & Hassan 2005). Health professionals who adopt a settings approach when designing their interventions aim at creating or building a health-promoting workplace instead of conducting health promotion in the workplace.

For example, the settings approach for dealing with workplace stress would strive to:

- Eliminate sources of stress rising from poor organizational structure or inadequate organizational policies and procedures, such as unplanned work or overtime, or lack of control over work
- Eliminate sources of hazardous work-related activities that endanger health and cause additional stress for employees
- Equipping workers with knowledge, skills, and supportive resources to better cope with stressful working conditions and balance work and life demands

Theories Underlining Health Promotion for Working Women

Planning WHP programs for women requires a deep understanding of health behaviors and the mechanisms involved in producing change. This understanding is facilitated through theories of health behavior that provide a framework for program planning and evaluation (Green & Kreuter 1999). Theories guide program planning by addressing all the known health determinants that cause ill health or influence the uptake of healthy behaviors. Theories are valuable for assessing and interpreting a situation, and for guiding the design of interventions, the strategies to be implemented, and the indicators to be measured. According to the National Cancer Institute (2005), theory is defined as:

> "A systematic way of understanding events or situations. It is a set of concepts, definitions, and propositions that explain or predict these events or situations by illustrating the relationships between variables."

The theory underlining the program design may determine the success or failure of the intervention (Goetzel & Ozminkowski 2002), therefore it is important that the theory reflects the unit that the project addresses (group, individuals, organization, community) and the nature of the identified health problem (National Cancer Institute 2005).

Some theories are defined as *explanatory theories* and others as *change theories*. *Explanatory theories* describe the causes of a problem and try to determine the factors that need to be addressed to bring about the desired change (e.g., lack of knowledge, self-efficacy, social support, or resources). Examples of explanatory theories are the Health Belief Model (HBM), the Theory of Planned Behavior, and the Precaution Adoption Process Model (Green 2000; National Cancer Institute 2005). *Change theories* are primarily used to guide the development of health interventions. They propose the elements on which interventions should be constructed, and offer guidance for program evaluation. Good examples of change theories include Community Organization and the Diffusion of Innovations (Green 2000; National Cancer Institute 2005).

Women's health is largely dependent on the environment, including family and social circumstances, responsibilities, and demands of everyday life. Programs that focus on providing information about certain health conditions through classical awareness-raising theories, therefore, could leave out important institutional and societal determinants of health. For example, a program aimed at increasing the knowledge of cervical or breast cancer screening among women employees may fail to have an impact on screening participation because 1) the majority of women do not have adequate insurance to cover the cost of screening or 2) they do not have time to visit free public health centers. Women's refusal to adhere to screening recommendations may also stem from social, religious, or other beliefs that prevent them from exposing their body to a male physician. Health promotion professionals have supported that a single theory as an underlying framework for health-promotion planning is not adequate (Eastman, Corona & Schuster 2006; Green 2000; Dishman et al. 1998; National Cancer Institute 2005; Sparling et al. 2000). Many programs have combined strategies from different theoretical backgrounds to construct comprehensive health promotion interventions (Hunt et al. 2005; Sorensen et al. 2002; Tessaro et al. 2000). When combining different theories to guide interventions, the use of planning models is suggested, such as PRECEDE-PROCEED and social marketing, which can facilitate practitioners throughout the many phases of the planning process (National Cancer Institute 2005).

We now present widely used theories in health promotion derived from the three levels of the ecological perspective of health—namely, the intrapersonal, the interpersonal, and community level.

Intrapersonal Level: The Health Belief Model (HBM)

The HBM was formulated in the 1950s by a group of U.S. Public Health Service social psychologists. The HBM was one of the first theories of health behavior and continues to be widely used in health research. It is an explanatory theory that enables researchers to identify intrapersonal factors influencing health-related behavior. The HBM (as seen in Fig. 1.1) advocates that health-protective behavior is a result of the following factors:

- Perceived susceptibility to a particular disease
- Perceived severity of the disease
- Perceived benefits in changing one's behavior
- Perceived barriers to changing one's behavior
- Cues to action
- Self-efficacy

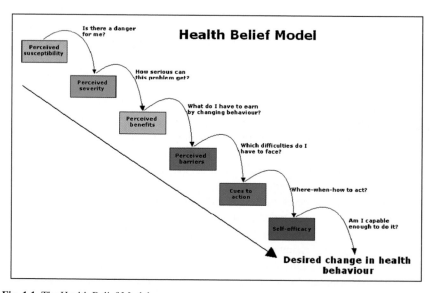

Fig. 1.1 The Health Belief Model

According to these components, people will act to protect their health if they perceive that they are personally at risk of a particular illness and that a particular preventive action will help them to deal with this risk. Before deciding to act, people contemplate their decision by measuring the recommended benefits of a certain behavior against the barriers of the action—for example, financial barriers (Hyman & Guruge 2002).

An application of the HBM in violence towards women in the workplace is presented in Table 1.1.

Interpersonal Level: The Social Cognitive Theory

The social cognitive theory is widely used in health promotion and is considered more comprehensive because it addresses socio-cultural and personal determinants of health (Bandura 1998; Dishman et al. 1998; Hyman & Guruge 2002; Sparling et al. 2000; Wallston & Armstrong 2002; Whitehead 2001). The richness of the theory makes it especially valuable in dealing with women's workplace health promotion and guiding relevant health promotion programs. It provides a framework for guiding interventions and deals with health at the interpersonal level (National Cancer Institute 2005).

The theory was developed by Bandura (1986) and is a contemporary version of the earlier social-learning theory. According to Bandura, there is an ongoing dynamic relationship between personal factors and the social and physical environment (National Cancer Institute 2005; Wallston & Armstrong 2002). This process has been named *reciprocal determinism* and refers to the continuous interaction and influence between behavior and environment (Sparling et al. 2000).

According to the social-cognitive theory, the causal structure in health-related behavior (and consequently the important aspects for health promotion) include:

- *Self-efficacy*—the belief that changes can be brought about through ones' own actions. If this belief is absent, it is considered a personal barrier
- Type of *goals* people set for themselves
- Anticipated *outcome expectations* of a behavior
- Perceived *environmental barriers and enablers*

The various constructs that derive from social cognitive theory on which interventions can be planned are seen in Table 1.2 using nutrition as an example.

Community Level: Community Organization

Health promotion initiatives at this level of the ecological perspective shift the emphasis of interventions from the individual to the wider social system that includes a) the community in which a person lives, b) the formal or informal institutions that surround people, and c) public policy (government and state institutions). Community-level theories offer a framework for implementing multi-dimensional interventions that can be effective in a number of settings, including workplaces

Table 1.1 Violence towards women in the workplace—the Health Belief Model

Influence Level	Effect On	Possible Intervention
Perceived Susceptibility	The degree to which each woman feels that she may face occurrences of violence in her working environment	– After careful evaluation, health professionals could raise the issue of violence in the working environment through statistical data or personal accounts of how susceptible women are to violence in the workplace
Perceived Severity	Awareness of the extent and seriousness of the phenomenon of violence towards women in the workplace	– Show evidence of how serious violent treatment of women in the workplace is. – Provide information on physical and psychological consequences of violence in the workplace
Perceived Benefits	Knowledge concerning the personal benefits to be gained from not tolerating violence in the workplace, or the value of reacting to incidents of violence	– Explain where, when and how to take action – Present what the personal benefits for women employees when working in a violence-free workplace environment are
Perceived Barriers	Psychological, material, or other barriers women believe are obstacles in dealing with work related violence (i.e., being strong enough, feeling that their job is at risk)	– Use strategies to change beliefs about certain barriers (i.e., provide reassurance that employment is not jeopardized) – Provide information on the legal framework supporting women who face violence in the workplace
Cues to Action	The degree of readiness of women to act against violence in the workplace	– Remind through frequent communication that the problem does exist and does have serious consequences – Present personal success stories of dealing with violence in the workplace – Provide practical information on how to deal with violence in the workplace – Provide self-defense classes – Provide information on women's organizations that deal with the prevention of violence – Use leaflets, e-mails, etc., and other reminders to change passive behavior towards violence in the workplace
Self-efficacy	Women's confidence and their sense of personal potential for taking action against violence in the workplace	– Forwarding messages to strengthen self-esteem in reacting to acts of violence in the workplace – Adoption of small, realistic targets for each working woman to gradually build her mental and physical defenses against incidents of violence

Table based on "Theory at a Glance" A Guide for Health Promotion Practice

Table 1.2 Nutrition interventions in the workplace—The Social Cognitive Theory

Theory Constructs	Influence On	Possible Intervention
Reciprocal Determinism	The ongoing interaction between women employees and their working environment	– Adjustments to the working environment could include making healthy food available in canteens or labeling the nutritional value of foods – Smaller companies could provide refrigerators where healthy food items can be easily stored (i.e., fruit, vegetables, milk, etc.) – Personal attitudes towards nutrition could be influenced through demonstrations about the benefits of a healthy diet for women and their families
Behavioral Capability	Women's abilities and skills in adopting and following a healthier diet and promoting this to her home and larger environment	– Cooking demonstrations and classes – Exchange of recipes – Food coupons from health stores – Personalized information and feedback – Time management strategies as a way of enabling women to have time for preparing healthy meals
Expectations	Women's expectations that changing their diets will have a positive effect on a physical, social and personal level	– Provide concrete and tangible information about enhanced physical, social and emotional health which comes as a result of improved nutrition
Self-efficacy	Beliefs and confidence that one has the ability to change harmful nutritional habits	– Use behavior change strategies such as problem-solving discussions both with the presence of experts and also among women themselves – Present examples of situations including difficult environmental situations and present solutions – Give personalized solutions to particular situations
Observational Learning	Learning that comes through observing both positive and negative outcomes on behaviors	– Show success stories of women who have followed a healthy diet and also show the negative side of the story and the consequences of not following a healthy diet – Identify issues of interest to women, like appearance factors for young employees, benefits to be gained for all the family
Reinforcements	Maintaining positive behavior by rewarding achievements	– Present examples of self-initiated rewards and incentives for achieving a desired outcome. Improved physical appearance, etc.

Table based on "Theory at a Glance" A Guide for Health Promotion Practice

(National Cancer Institute 2005). Theories of community organization have been of particular importance to workplace health promotion, especially for women, because they incorporate concepts of social support, social networking, and communication widely used in the workplace setting (Arneson & Ekberg 2005; Campbell et al. 2002; Chu et al. 2000; Sorensen et al. 1996; Tessaro et al. 2000). To a great extent, community organization theories encompass the ecological perspective recognizing multiple levels of influence and therefore can easily be integrated with social cognitive theory.

In Table 1.3, we present constructs of the community organization theory and how these influence behavior change through the example of workplace stress for women. Strategies developed within the context of this theory will be further analyzed in this chapter when examining interventions for women employees.

The Planning Process

Planning health promotion programs for working women involves a number of steps.

Obtaining Commitment

The first step in planning any workplace health-promotion program is *obtaining management support* (The Health Communication Unit 2004a). In particular, obtaining the support of senior management and supervisors is considered particularly valuable for a number of reasons:

- The approval of senior management guarantees funding and the human resources necessary for program implementation
- Senior management approval creates a feeling of trust among employees that their problems and work-related issues are being addressed, increasing the number of persons participating in the programs

Apart from senior management, many more *players* are involved in the operation of an organization, and obtaining their support and commitment increases the chances that the intervention will have an impact. According to the Health Communication Unit of the University of Toronto, the key stakeholders whose support needs to be secured (apart from senior management) before proceeding with planning interventions are:

- Employee associations or unions
- Employees
- Health and safety officers, occupational physicians, human resource officers
- Other key stakeholders

Table 1.3 Workplace stress—community organization

Theory Constructs	Rationale	Possible Intervention
Empowerment	The aim of empowerment is through various strategies to enable women employees to develop the necessary skills to influence their working environment in reducing work related stress	– Show stress-management techniques – Provide individualized solutions – Allow opportunities for re-scheduling work shifts by women according to work load
Community Capacity	The ability of women to identify problems and address these, at the same time mobilizing their colleagues	– Arrange discussion groups to identify problems – Allow monthly or six-month updates to management concerning problems related to workplace stress
Participation	Through participation, women are able to take part in the process of changing the sources of workplace stress	– Adopt a "lay" helpers strategy where influential members of the workforce help each other by creating their own personal social networks
Relevance	Emphasis is on the real sources of the problems and interventions are focused on the women and not "around the women"	– Women workers indicate that workplace related stress is increased because of often unplanned overtime
Issue Selection	Emphasizing the real issues that cause workplace stress and setting tangible and measurable real targets	– Company management urges detailed weekly work organization to avoid frequent unplanned overtime
Critical Consciousness	Being aware of company or public policy that contributes to workplace stress or instituting relevant changes that could contribute to solving workplace stress	– Changing the company policy or the "organizational culture" that bases promotion policy only on frequent overtime and business trips

Table based on "Theory at a Glance" A Guide for Health Promotion Practice

Health Promotion Team or Committee

Once support is obtained, it is important to create a team or committee of the most important decision makers and representatives of the interest groups and experts who will be responsible for planning and implementing activities. The participation of women on this committee, especially female representatives of employees and women senior managers, is important to spread the message and obtain commitment and acceptance from fellow employees. Examples of successful WHP programs emphasize the importance of involving the workforce in the process of identifying problems and suggesting intervention plans (Arneson & Ekberg 2005; Aust & Ducki 2004; Elo & Leppaenen 1999; Saksvik et al. 2002; Tessaro et al. 2000).

One of the functions of a WHP team or committee is to ensure cooperation between WHP and OSH. WHP is an important complement of OSH, therefore it is important to maintain cooperation between the two fields and work closely with OSH officers on issues of health promotion. This cooperation may become complex because traditional health and safety measures (in most cases, the legislative responsibility of companies obliged by law to protect the health and safety of their employees) is confused with health promotion. The line that separates OSH and WHP can become hazy, as in the case of smoking (Hawe, Degeling & Hall 1993). In this example, it is not clear where OSH ends and where WHP begins. Smoking is a health-threatening lifestyle behavior, and a number of activities can be introduced for female employees who are interested in quitting smoking. At the same time, in many countries measures for a smoke-free workplace have become mandatory and are legislatively imposed on companies as a way of protecting employees who do not smoke as well as those who do (Hawe, Degeling & Hall 1993). Workplace health promotion should build on and complement existing OSH measures, and integrate different approaches and different strategies to have an effect on many different levels. WHP should, under no circumstances, be seen as replacing OSH, but as a set of complementary actions for protecting the organizations' interests and its employees' health.

Research has shown that integrated WHP and health and safety interventions have been more successful in meeting their objectives, as in the case of blue-collar workers. Workers may perceive that their health is more jeopardized by hazardous working conditions and less by behavioral factors, such as nutrition or screening. Failure to address obvious dangers in the working environment will doom any attempts to address health behavior determinants such as smoking (Hunt et al. 2005; Sorensen et al. 2002).

Needs Assessment

The third step in the planning process of a WHP program is to conduct a thorough needs or situational assessment. If workplace health promotion programs are to be tailored to the needs of women, it is important to first acknowledge the fact that women workers have different needs than those of male employees, and that there are differences between men and women in terms of work setting and working conditions.

The purpose of needs assessment is to construct a comprehensive picture of the health problems women face in the workplace and define the sort of interventions that should be planned to combat the identified problems (current or foreseeable). In short, needs assessment is about determining needs, defining priorities and health problems, and understanding their determinants and causes.

A health need is defined as *"states, conditions, or factors which, if absent, prevent people from achieving the optimum of physical, mental and social well being"* (Hawe, Degeling & Hall 1993). For example, an identified problem or health need might be low numbers of cervical cancer screenings or poor oral health. Caution should be taken not to confuse health needs with the need for an intervention. For example, the need for more dentists and the need to increase cervical cancer screening are considered to be solutions and not health needs (Hawe et al. 1993).

A needs assessment includes two major stages: a) Identifying priority health problems among women employees, and b) Analyzing the health problem.

A. Identifying Priority Health Issues Among Women Employees

The purpose of the first stage of needs assessment is to determine priority areas for intervention from a range of data and opinions.

There are a number of methods for assessing the workplace situation and the profile of female employees. No method alone will yield the information needed to acquire a comprehensive picture of a workplace. The best way to reach this goal is to combine and integrate needs assessment methods.

A needs assessment usually starts by utilizing existing information relating to the company's employees—for example, statistics on sick leave, long-term disability rates, compensation claims, absenteeism, turn-over rates, and so on. Important insight concerning priority areas for intervention can also be gained through informal discussions or focus groups with employees, employee representatives, management, and more formal bodies like unions and employee associations, which allow for fruitful discussions and rigorous exchange of ideas.

In most work settings, health needs are identified solely by the professionals in charge of the intervention who base their judgments primarily on population or company mortality or morbidity data. Such practices have become the focus of feminist critiques, which stress that women's voices are often ignored during program planning and emphasize the importance of allowing women to determine their own health priorities (Belenky 1986; Hunt 2000). Women have different life experiences compared to men that need to be taken into consideration, especially during this stage of program planning. Allowing women to determine their own health priorities is a method referred to as *biographical health promotion* (Hunt 2000; Hunt 1998). The method supports self help, which facilitates the *"sharing of personal experiences and gives authority to the voice of each woman rather than to health professionals"* as a way of identifying health needs (Hunt 2000; Hunt 1998). The value of asking women to identify their own health problems and voice their own concerns is that issues that traditionally have not been the focus of mainstream health promotion interventions, such as menstruation and pre-menstruation problems, post-natal depression, breastfeeding, and sexual harassment, will have a chance of being adequately addressed (Hunt 2000; Hunt 1998).

Valuable information about employee problems can also be obtained through surveys with the use of questionnaires. There are many examples of assessment tools used in various work settings for identifying health problems. An excellent selection of questionnaires with a detailed description of applicability factors has been published by the Health Communication Unit of the University of Toronto (2006). Biomedical examinations such as body mass index (BMI), blood pressure, and biochemical data, will also yield important information in identifying priority areas for intervention.

A needs assessment has to also include an examination of the so-called *organizational culture* (Health Communication Unit 2004b)—in other words, the special circumstances that exist in every company in terms of job satisfaction, job control, management of overtime, extra pay, management of deadlines, promotions, and so on.

Until recently, WHP was the target of large scale enterprises and multinational companies which had the resources and the means to implement relevant programs. It has recently become evident that to realize the potential that WHP has for society at large, it is imperative that health promotion professionals target workers from work settings such as Small Medium Enterprises (SMEs) and small family retail and other businesses that attract large numbers of female workers. Employment settings that attract large numbers of women employees and have been identified as priority areas for WHP by the International Forum of the West Pacific Region are

- Workers in isolated conditions or areas
- Migrant workers
- Small businesses and workplaces
- Rural industry and the informal sector
- High-risk industries
- Joint-venture businesses (Chu et al. 2000)

This stage of needs assessment should also yield a profile of female employees and their position in the organization, including working conditions and circumstances and how these interrelate to influence health, well-being, and productivity. At the end of this stage, and based on the information gathered, the following points have to be determined:

- The target group experiencing the problem (i.e., married women with young children)
- Problems and priority areas
- The extent or magnitude and seriousness of the identified problems

B. Analyzing the Health Problem

The focus of the second phase of needs assessment is on developing a thorough analysis of why, and under what circumstances, women are experiencing the problems identified during the first stage.

The first step of this phase is to conduct a detailed literature review on the identified problems. The review should include evidence that the problem does exist and is indeed serious, the causative factors contributing to the emergence of the condition, and the types of interventions implemented in the past to deal with those specific problems.

Identifying good research on women's occupational safety and health and workplace health promotion may prove to be a tedious task (Messing & Mergler 2006). Until recently, occupational research focused mainly on men and—excluded or under-represented women in study designs (Zahm & Blair 2003). Women's health issues during the last few decades have mostly been defined by men, leading to scientific inaccuracies and leaving out important health issues for women (Zeytinoglu et al. 1999). In a recent publication, Messing and Mergler (2006) reviewed the scientific literature to determine how gender is being tested in studies and find the gaps in occupational health research regarding women. The findings listed below show the important points that should be taken into consideration when researching women's health problems identified in the workplace:

- The most common professions and sectors in which women work are not systematically examined, so there is a lack of information about the risks women face in these professions. Numerous workplaces dominated by women (hairdressers, textile industries, domestic help employees, garment workers) have not been adequately studied (Hatch & Moline 1997)
- Women in occupational health studies are often under-represented or excluded from the study design, and thus the conclusions drawn are not applicable to women
- Occupational health problems that most commonly are given attention to, such as accidents, noise and vibrations, chemicals, and personal protective equipment are more relevant for professions dominated by men—i.e., in engineering occupations, construction, road works, and others
- Exposure parameters associated with gender are often not taken into consideration when male-female comparisons are being made. This allows for erroneous assumptions to be made—like for example, that the characteristics of the female sex alone causes women to be more vulnerable to specific health risks
- When hypotheses are being made about health-related phenomena observed among women in the workplace, close attention needs to be paid to the wider social and psychological context of women's lives that is often ignored. Research should reflect women's position in the society and their health concerns over the life cycle (Hunt 2000; Hunt 1998). Health professionals also need to address women's life circumstances—their roles as mothers, wives, and caretakers of their elders, and the effect these have on their health and their work (Hunt 2000; Hunt 1998).

- When it comes to women and their health profile, it is suggested that the health profiles of people whom women feel responsible for in their family and larger environment be taken into consideration. Not addressing the needs of these people might cause feelings of anxiety in women, or a sense of inadequacy or injustice. For example, women may feel guilty taking care of their own health but not that of their children.

Health professionals planning a WHP program need to be able to associate the identified health problems to causes not only related to lifestyle behaviors, but to causes originating in the organizational and management culture of the company.

Given the limitations in gender specific occupational health research, the knowledge gaps in the causation of the identified problems, as well as the verification of the identified health problems, should be made through the women themselves. Women should have a voice in issues concerning their own health, and projects need to address health problems as identified by women.

An in-depth understanding of the identified problems includes a description of the factors that contribute to the problem. A complete needs assessment requires a health professional to list all those factors associated with the occurrence of the problem. Once these factors are identified and understood, implementation strategies can be built around them. This phase of needs assessment also includes a detailed description of the target group, including details about women's age, ethnic composition, socioeconomic and educational level, marital status, and so on.

By the end of this stage, a complete needs assessment report should be prepared. The elements of this report are presented here and are based on the work by Hawe et al. (2003), tailored to the needs and characteristics of WHP programs for women:

- A description of the health issue—the priority of which has been agreed to by the women of the target group
- Evidence (including statistical, biomedical, and qualitative evidence) that supports the magnitude and seriousness of the identified problem
- A description of the target population, explaining its characteristics in relation to the identified health problem
- A list of risks and contributing factors that have been identified to be the cause of the health problem. Caution needs to be taken here to base causation on relevant literature review or previous relevant studies, but also on personal accounts of the women themselves. In this way, it is certain that issues associated to the organizational culture and wider social context are taken into consideration

In summary, before proceeding with the intervention plan the following must be taken care of:

1. Management commitment secured
2. Workplace health-promotion committee established
3. Comprehensive needs assessment completed

The focus and the purpose of this stage of program planning should be to create a sound and comprehensive knowledge base about the causal pathways of ill health, on which interventions should be structured. The failure of many health promotion interventions can be traced to the fact that activities were based only on weak research findings that did not take into consideration the complex multifaceted causes of health (Dean and McQueen, 1996).

Developing a Program Plan

The information collected during needs assessment has to be translated into a WHP program plan. This is the next step in which the health professional (with the support of the WHP committee) needs to engage is. The devised program should:

- Be appropriate for the health problem and the identified target group
- Be realistic in terms of the available resources
- Utilize the most effective strategies to bring about the desired change (Hawe, Degeling & Hall 1993)

The health of female employees is influenced by multiple factors on both the interpersonal and intrapersonal levels. Workplace health-promotion interventions tailored to the needs of women therefore have to be based on an integrative multi-level approach addressing all the possible causes of ill health among female employees. Research has shown that interventions focusing on individual traits are insufficient in stimulating health enhancing behaviors (Arneson & Ekberg 2005). Furthermore, from a feminist perspective, the focus on individual behavior change carries with it a notion of self-responsibility—and ignores the other social and environmental circumstances that may influence the development of an ill condition (Hunt 2000; Hunt 1998). For example, an obese or overweight woman may be viewed as self-responsible for her condition, and interventions to change her weight may simply focus on persuading the woman to eat healthier or to exercise more. This emphasis on self care ignores the context of this woman's life, who may live in an underprivileged inner city neighborhood or have increased responsibilities towards a family or an elderly relative, allowing no time for exercise or for cooking healthy meals. Overeating may also be a response, a reaction, or a way out of too much stress (Hunt 2000; Hunt 1998).

The health professional planning a WHP program targeting women is faced with a complex situation that calls for combined interventions on multiple levels of influence. WHP strategies need to implement change on three levels, namely

- Implementing healthy and safe working conditions
- Changing individual harmful behaviors by taking into consideration the social, environmental, and psychological barriers and demands that may hinder the adoption of a healthy lifestyle and make change difficult
- Changing the organizational *culture* of the working environment so the demands of the workplace do not clash with women's responsibilities away from the workplace. This also means that the working environment takes women's social position into account, and allows equal opportunities for career enhancement, promotion, and salary increase

With all this information taken into consideration, the next step is to actually devise a program plan. A comprehensive program plan should include

- Key findings identified during needs assessment
- Program goals describing the desired end result, from running the program and the time frame to achieve this (Hawe et al. 1993)—i.e., *to reduce sources of unnecessary stress in the workplace like unplanned overtime by the end of 2008, or change the policy of promoting employees who work long hours* or *a reduction in the number of women with high cholesterol levels by June 2007*
- Program objectives that describe the specific changes one wishes to bring about in the target group (Hawe et al. 1993). In other words, what the program will achieve—i.e., *to decrease by 20 percent the proportion of women who are absent from work because of "stress related" problems* or *increase by 20 percent the percentage of women who eat daily portions of fruit and vegetables*
- The recommended intervention strategies (educational campaign on nutrition, new company policy concerning overtime) and the materials, tools, and methods to be used (nutrition pamphlets, discussion groups with women and senior management concerning overtime, focus groups). Activities have to be implemented across the three components of WHP—i.e., OSH, individual behaviors, and the *organizational culture*—keeping in mind the wider context of women's lives
- What resources are needed and available to implement the activities
- Indicators of success and evaluation metrics that are tied to the stated goals and objectives. Thus, goals and objectives need to be clearly defined and measurable
- Benefits to be gained by the organization—e.g., *decreased sick leave, decreased compensation costs, improved productivity*

The success of a WHP program tailored for women depends not only on the approval of the plan by senior management, but most importantly by the women themselves who can provide valuable insight and feedback concerning the suggested strategies and the possible barriers (such as time issues).

It is valuable to do a pilot test of the intervention through a small-scale or short-term application before implementation begins. Pilot testing may show that some of the strategies chosen are inadequate for the specific target group, resulting in low participation, or that they are time-consuming or costly.

Implementation: Examples of Strategies

The Literature has shown that successful health promotion programs for women have used strategies derived from community theories and, most specifically, empowerment and participatory strategies (Campbell et al. 2002; Zeytinoglu 1999; Tessaro et al. 2000; Munn-Giddings, Hart & Ramon 2005).

Many times, health-related problems identified through the needs assessment procedure will reveal problems or health needs that are not easily addressed through traditional health-promotion interventions. For example, a needs assessment may reveal that women are frequently absent from work because of work-related stress. Further examination may reveal that the cause of stress is the high demand placed on women for working overtime, which clashes with women's responsibilities to their families. In this case, improving the situation has to do with changing the culture of the organization and working closely with top management to bring this about. Likewise, a needs assessment may reveal that women are experiencing high levels of depression or anxiety because of their inability to occupy higher positions in the company because they are not able to work overtime or to engage in many business trips due to high demands outside the workplace (their families, for example). This calls for a change in the company's policy and philosophy of only rewarding employees devote personal overtime to the company. Change is brought about by interventions targeted at senior management and less on women employees themselves.

Furthermore, changing the culture of an organization is, in most cases, closely dependent on policy change at the governmental level. Some strategies implemented to address problems related to work-life balance include initiatives such as integrating the development of all work-life balance policies and activities, publicly promoting work-life balance through awards programs, supporting employers, and developing projects to reduce work-related stress. In April 2003, the U.K. government enacted legislation to help parents cope with work while caring for children. Parents with children under six years old or disabled children under 18 have the right to apply for work flexibility, and employers have a statutory duty to consider these requests seriously. Other arrangements that can be made include flexible working patterns such as annualized hours, compressed hours, flex time, job-sharing, shift-working, unpaid leave during school holidays, and staggered hours (Todd 2004).

Successful interventions for WHP have focused on a few key factors in the design of strategies for WHP, including programs directed at women employees. These factors include social support, empowerment, and participation.

Social Support—these are strategies that utilize the strength of interpersonal networks emphasizing peer support (Israel 1985). One such intervention strategy is the natural (lay) helpers' strategy, which trains women in the workplace to diffuse information and provide their fellow female employees with support for healthy behavior changes (Campbell et al. 2002; Zeytinoglu et al. 1999; Tessaro et al. 2000). The lay helpers' strategy aims at enhancing the ability of women to help each other through their personal social networks (Israel 1985). This method may prove valuable for spreading health promotion messages outside the workplace because women will continue to diffuse information about healthy living in the wider community (Tessaro et al. 2000).

Empowerment and Participation—Empowerment has been identified as crucial and essential for health, and has driven the science of health promotion since the Ottawa charter (WHO 1986). Empowerment aims at strengthening the ability of vulnerable individuals or groups to influence the environment in which they live with the goal of improving their health and overall conditions of life. It is a process that enables the making of decisions and active participation in events that shape people's lives (Arneson & Ekberg 2005).

Empowerment is a way through which vulnerable groups can gain control, efficacy, and a sense of social justice (Peterson et al. 2005). According to WHO, this approach enables and mobilizes people by strengthening their skills and influencing the social and economic contexts of their everyday lives. For example, a problem-based learning (PBL) intervention was implemented in a number of workplace settings that formed employee work groups, which, with the help of a facilitator, identified problems and suggested solutions. Solutions involved organizational changes such as hiring a manager to facilitate the work load or activities such as rearrangement of furniture or organizing several social events (Arneson & Ekberg 2005).

Empowerment also requires active participation. The participatory process allows women to actively engage in the development of the project, and in generating shared solutions to shared problems (Munn-Giddings et al. 2005). An example of a successful workplace health intervention project that combined participation and empowerment aspects was the "Healthy Circles" project. With "Healthy Circles," employees were regarded as experts and experts in identifying the working conditions that caused problems and stress. Consequently, they were the most appropriate source of identifying the best strategies for interventions (Aust & Ducki 2004). "Healthy Circles" were discussion groups formed at the workplace to identify problems and suggest solutions involving employees in the decision-making process, which increased their control and therefore their sense of empowerment.

Program implementation must ensure continuous communication between the WHP committee and the target group. The program needs to be promoted both internally and externally, and feedback should be continuously requested by the target group and responded to. Finally, the process of creating a supportive and healthy working environment for women requires long-term commitment and a long-term implementation period of activities to enhance learning and allow time for reflection (Arneson & Ekberg 2005).

Evaluation

The final stage of program implementation is evaluation. Evaluation is an ongoing process through which health promotion professionals decide whether or not the program met the predefined criteria, its objectives and goals. Active participation of women employees throughout the evaluation is necessary and crucial to determine the effect of the project and its weaknesses, limitations, and strengths. Furthermore, evaluation metrics should include measuring changes in the overall organization function. There are four stages of evaluation: formative, process, impact, and outcome.

> **Formative evaluation**—Formative evaluation is conducted during program implementation for the purpose of improving the program. Through this process, health professionals ensure that the needs of the target group are met

and that the materials used are appropriate. Formative evaluation should be ongoing, frequent, and set correct and valuable indicators.

Process evaluation—Process evaluation is the first level of evaluation conducted to measure if the program was implemented as initially planned—in other words, measuring how the program performed. According to Hawe et al., (2003), the answers to the following questions comprise process evaluation:

- *Has the program reached the intended audience?*
- *Are the participants satisfied?*
- *Have the program activities been implemented as planned?*
- *Were the materials used adequate?*
- *Was there ongoing quality assurance?*

Impact and Outcome evaluation—Impact evaluation measures the immediate effects of the program—measuring the extent to which the stated objectives or the short-term indicators have been met. Outcome evaluation is the final stage of the evaluation process, and is conducted to test whether the health problem has been eliminated or if its negative impact has at least been reduced. It involves testing to see if the predetermined goals or the long-term indicators have been met. Impact and outcome evaluation involve measuring knowledge, attitudes, health status, social support, quality of life, and workplace organizational factors such productivity, job satisfaction, job turnover, and so on. A variety of designs can be utilized for impact and outcome evaluation such as pre- and post-testing, randomized controlled trials, and more (Hawe et al. 2003).

Evaluation (and especially outcome evaluation) should be an ongoing, long-term process in need of continuous monitoring that extends beyond the workplace to the wider context of women's lives to include the family and social environments. A good example of what constitutes a comprehensive evaluation procedure is mammography screening.

According to the European guidelines for quality assurance in mammography screening (2001), a distinction can be made between evaluating the performance of a screening program (short-term indicators) and the impact of the program on long-term indicators such as mortality (Broeders, Codd, Nystrom, Ascunce & Riza 2001). Performance evaluation looks at provision of health services, service utilization, and coverage. Performance indicators that should be measured when evaluating a screening program include the following:

- Participation rate
- Recall rate
- Benign-to-malignant biopsy ratio
- Surgical procedures performed
- Interval between screening test and final assessment/surgery
- Proportion of women who are invited within the specified screening interval
- Rate of invasive investigations (cytology, core biopsy, open biopsy)
- Specificity of the screening test

Measuring the impact indicators of a screening program is a long-term process (Broeders, Codd, Nystrom, Ascunce & Riza 2001) requiring the application of epidemiological and statistical methodologies to show any impact on mortality and morbidity of breast cancer. Measuring impact indicators of screening programs also requires access to data sources often not easily accessible, such as medical records of regional physicians and hospitals, pathology registries, and so on. (Broeders, Codd, Nystrom, Ascunce & Riza 2001).

Useful Internet Links on Workplace Health Promotion Methodology

- The Health Communication Unit—Workplace Health Promotion Project; http://www.thcu.ca/Workplace/Workplace.html
- BKK: http://www.bkk.de
- Turning Point—Public Health Foundation: www.turningpointprogram.org
- European Agency for Safety and Health at Work: http://osha.europa.eu/OSHA
- European Network of Workplace Health Promotion: http://www.enwhp.org
- National Cancer Institute—USA: http://www.cancer.gov/
- Health Canada—Environmental and Workplace Health: http://www.hc-sc.gc.ca/ewh-semt/index_e.html
- National Public Health Partnership—Australia: www.nphp.gov.au
- Public Health Agency of Canada— Work Life Conflict: http://www.phac-aspc.gc.ca/publicat/work-travail/index.html
- Public Health Agency of Canada—Workplace Health—http://www.phac-aspc.gc.ca/new-e.html
- Australian Women's Health Network: www.awhn.org.au

References

Arneson H, Ekberg K (2005) Evaluation of empowerment processes in a workplace health promotion intervention based on learning in Sweden. *Health Promotion International 20*(4), 351–359

Aust B, Ducki A (2004) Comprehensive health promotion interventions at the workplace: experiences with health circles in Germany. *Journal of Occupational Health Psychology, 9*(3), 258–270

Ballard TJ, Corradi L, Lauria L, Mazzanti C, Scaravelli G, Sgorbissa F, Romito P, Verdecchia A (2004). Integrating qualitative methods into occupational health research: a study of women flight attendants. *J Occupational and Environmental Medicine, 61,* 163–166.

Bandura A (1986) *Social foundations of thoughts and action: A social cognitive theory.* W.H. Freeman, New York

Bandura A (1998) Health promotion from the perspective of social cognitive theory. *Psychology and Health, 13,* 623–649

Baric L (1993) The settings approach: implications for policy and strategy. *Journal of the Institute of Health Education, 31,* 17–24

Belenky M, Clinchy B, Goldberger N, Tarule J (1986) *Women's ways of knowing. The development of self, voice and mind.* Basic Books, New York

Broeders M, Codd M, Nystrom L, Ascunce N, Riza E (2001) Epidemiological guidelines for quality assurance in breast cancer screening. In Perry N, Broeders M, de Wolf, Tornberg S,

Schouten J (eds) European guidelines for quality assurance in mammography screening. Office for Official Publications of the European Communities, Luxembourg

Campbell MK, Tessaro I, DeVellis B, Benedict S, Kelsy K, Belton L, Sanhueza A (2002) Effects of a tailored health promotion program for female blue-collar workers: health works for women. *Preventive Medicine 34*, 313–323

Chu C, Breucker G, Harris N, Stitzel A, Xingfa G, Gu X, Dwyer S (2000) Health –promoting workplaces – international settings development. *Health Promotion International, 15*(2), 155–167

Dean K, McQueen D (1996) Theory in health promotion. Introduction. *Health Promotion International, 11*(1), 7–9

Dishman RK, Oldenburg B, O'Neil H, Shephard RJ (1998) Worksite physical activity interventions. *American Journal of Preventive Medicine 15*(4), 344–361

Eastman KL, Corona R, Schuster MA (2006) Talking parents, healthy teens: a worksite-based program for parents to promote adolescent sexual health. *Preventing Chronic Disease 3*(4), 1–10

Elo AL, & Leppaenen A (1999) Efforts of health promotion teams to improve the psychosocial work environment. *Journal of Psychosocial Work Environment, 4*, 87–94

European Agency for Safety and Health at Work (2003) *Gender issues in safety and health at work — A review*. Luxembourg: Office for Official Publications of the European Communities

European Agency for Safety and Health at Work (2005) *Mainstreaming gender into occupational safety and health*. Luxembourg: Office for Official Publications of the European Communities

Goetzel RZ, Ozminkowski RJ (2002) Program evaluation. In O'Donnell (ed.). *Health Promotion in the Workplace*. Delmar Thompson Learning, New York

Green J (2000) The role of theory in evidence-based health promotion practice (Editorial). *Health Education Research, 15*(2), 125–129

Green LW, & Kreuter MW (1999) *Health Promotion Planning: An Educational and Ecological Approach (3rd ed)*. Mayfield Publishing Company, Mountain View (California) Hatch M, Moline J (1997) Women, work and health. *American Journal of Industrial Medicine, 32*(3). 303–308

Hawe P, Degeling D, Hall J (1993) *Evaluating health promotion: a health worker's guide.* MacLennan and Petty, Sydney

Hunt L (2000) *Promoting Women's Health*. Better Practice Series, South, West Population Health Unit, Banbury, Western Australia

Hunt, L (1998) The principles and practice of women's primary healthcare. In C. Rogers-Clark and A.Smith (eds) Women's Health: A Primary Health Care Approach. Sydney: MacLennan & Petty. 278–297

Hunt MK, Lederman R, Stoddard AM, LaMontagne AD, McLellan D, Combe C, Barbeau E, Sorensen G (2005) Process evaluation of an integrated health promotion/occupational health model in WellWorks-2. *Health Education and Behaviour, 32*(1), 10–26

Hyman IH, Guruge S (2002) A review of theory and health promotion strategies for new immigrant women. *Canadian Journal of Public Health, 93*(3), 183–187

Ioannou S (2005) Health logic and health-related behaviors *Critical Public Health, 15*(3), 263–273

Israel BA (1985) Social networks and social support: implications for natural helper and community level interventions. *Health Education Quarterly, 12*(1), 311–351

Krantz G, Ostergen PO (2000) Common symptoms in middle aged women: their relation to employment status, psychological work conditions and social support in a Swedish setting. *Journal of Epidemiol. Community Health, 54*, 192–199

Lippel K (1999) Workers' compensation and stress: gender and access to compensation. *International Journal of Law Psychiatry 22*(1), 79–89

Lippel K (2003) Compensation for musculo-skeletal disorders in Quebec: systematic discrimination against women workers? *International Journal of Health Services 33*(2), 253–282

McLeroy KR, Bibeau D, Steckler A, Glanz K (1988) An ecological perspective of health promotion programs. *Health Education Quarterly, 15*, 351–378

McMahon A, Kelleher CC, Helly G, & Duffy E (2002) Evaluation of workplace cardiovascular health promotion program in the Republic of Ireland. *Health Promotion International, 17*(4), 297–308

Messing K, Mergler D (2006) Women's Occupational and Environmental Health (Editorial). *Environmental Research 101*, 147–148

Messing K, Stellman Mager J (2006) Sex, gender and women's occupational health:The importance of considering mechanism. *Environmental Research*(101), 149–162

Messing K, Punnett L, Bond M, Alexanderson K, Pyle J, Zahn S, Wegman D, Stock SR de Grosbois S (2003) Be the fairest of them all: challenges and recommendations for the treatment of gender in occupational health research. *American Journal of Industrial Medicine, 43*, 618–629

Munn-Giddings C, Hart C, Ramon S (2005) A participatory approach to the promotion of well-being in the workplace: lessons from empirical research. *International Review of Psychiatry, 17*(5), 409–417

National Cancer Institute (2005) *"Theory at a Glance" A Guide for Health Promotion Practice*; http://www.cancer.gov/PDF/481f5d53-63df-41bc-bfaf-5aa48ee1da4d/TAAG3.pdf, accessed on 28 March 2007

Noblet A (2003) Building health promoting work settings: identifying the relationship between work characteristics and occupational stress in Australia. *Health promotion International, 18*(4), 351–359

Nutbeam D (1998) Evaluating health promotion – progress, problems and solutions. *Health Promotion International, 13*(1), 27–44

Paton K, Sengupta S, Hassan L (2005) Settings, systems and organization development: the Healthy Living and Working Model. *Health Promotion International, 20*(1), 81–89

Peipert JF, & Ruggiero L (1998) Use of the transtheoretical model for behavioural change in women's health. *Women's Health Issues, 8*(5), 304–309

Peterson NA, Lowe JB, Aquilino ML, Schneider JE (2005) Linking social cohesion and gender to intrapersonal and interactional empowerment: support and new implications for theory. *Journal of Community Psychology, 33*(2), 233–244

Rangan VK, Karim S, Sandberg SK (1996) Doing better at doing good. *Harvard Business Review,* May-June: 42–54

Saksvik PO, Nytro K, Dahl-Jorgensen C, Mikkelsen A (2002) A process evaluation of individual and organisational occupational stress and health interventions. *Work and Stress, 16*, 37–57

Schulte PA, Wagner GR, Ostry A, Blanciforti LA, Cutlip RG. Krajnak KM, Luster M, Munson AE, O'Callaghan JP, Parks CG, Simeonova PP, Miller DB (2007) Work, obesity and occupational safety and health. *American Journal of Public Health, 97*(3), 428–436

Shain M, & Krmaer DM (2004) Health promotion in the workplace: framing the concept; reviewing the evidence. *Occupational and Environmental Medicine 61*, 643–648

Sorensen G, Stoddard AM, LaMontagne AD, Emmons K, Hunt MK, Youngstrom R, McLellan D, & Christiani DC (2002) A comprehensive worksite prevention intervention: behaviour change results from a randomized controlled trial (United States)

Sorensen G, Thompson B, Glanz K, Feng Z, Kinne S, DiClemente C, Emmons ., Heimendinger J, Probart C, Lichtenstein E (1996) Work site – based cancer prevention: primary results from the working well trial. *American Journal of Public Health, 86*(7), 939–947

Sparling PB, Owen N, Lambert EV, Haskell WL (2000) Promoting physical activity: the new imperative for public health. *Health Education Research, 15*(3), 367–376

Stokols D (1992) Establishing and maintaining healthy environments: Towards a social ecology of health promotion. *American Psychologist, 47*(1), 6–22

Strazdins L, Bammer G (2004) Women, work and musculoskeletal health. *Social Science and Medicine 58*(6), 997–1005

Tessaro IA, Taylor S, Belton L, Campbell MK, Benedict S, Kelsey K De Vellis B (2000) Adapting a natural (lay) helpers model of change for worksite health promotion for women. *Health Education Research, 15*(5), 603–614

The Health Communication Unit (2004a) *An Introduction to Comprehensive Workplace Health Promotion.* Centre for Health Promotion, Un. of Toronto; http://www.thcu.ca/workplace/documents/intro_to_workplace_health_promotion_v1.1.FINAL.pdf, accessed on 28 March 2007

The Health Communication Unit (2004b) *Influencing the organizational environment to create healthy workplaces.* Centre for Health Promotion, Un. of Toronto; http://www.thcu.ca/workplace/documents/influencing_org_envir_infopackv_1.1.FINAL.pdf, accessed on 28, March 2007.

The Health Communication Unit (2006) *Comprehensive Workplace Health Promotion: Recommended and Promising Practices for Situational Assessment Tools.* Centre for Health Promotion, University of Toronto; http://www.thcu.ca/Workplace/sat/pubs/sat_v102.pdf, accessed on 28, March 2007

Todd S (2004) *Improving work – life balance – what are other countries doing.* Labor Program. Human resources and skills development – Canada. http://www.hecol.ualberta.ca/Courses/2007%20Winter/HECOL550/%5B%20Presentations%20%5D%20Improving-work-life-balance,%20other%20countries.pdf, accessed on 27 March 2007

Wallston KA, Armstrong C (2002) Theoretically-based strategies for health behaviour change. In O'Donnell (ed.). *Health Promotion in the Workplace.* Delmar Thompson Learning, New York

Whitelaw S, Baxendale A, Bryce C, Machardy L, Young I, Witney E (2001) "Settings" based health promotion: a review. *Health Promotion International, 16*(4), 339–353

Wilson MG, Holman PB, Hammock A (1996) A comprehensive review of the effects of worksite health promotion on health-related outcomes. *The Science of Health Promotion 10*, 429–435

Witehead D (2001) A social cognitive model for health education/health promotion practice. *Journal of Advanced Nursing 36*(3), 417–425

World Health Organization (1986) *The Ottawa Charter for Health Promotion,* http://www.who.int/hpr/NPH/docs/ottawa_charter_hp.pdf, accessed on 28 March 2007

Zahm SH, Blair A (2003) Occupational cancer among women: where have we been and where are we going? *American Journal of Industrial Medicine, 44*(6), 565–575

Zeytinoglu IU, Denton M, Hajdukowski-Ahmed M, O'Connor M, Chambers L (1999) Women's work, women's voices: from invisibility to visibility. In Denton M, Hajdukowski-Ahmed M, O'Connor M, Zeytinoglu IU (eds) *Women's voices in health promotion.* Canadian Scholars' Press, Toronto

Ziglio E, Hagard S, Griffiths J (2000) Health promotion developments in Europe: achievements and challenges. *Health Promotion International 15*(2), 143–154

Chapter 2
The Legal Context for Workplace Safety and Health Promotion: Thinking of Women

Ioannis Polychronakis, Christos Chatzis, Ioanna Kotsioni, Elena Riza, Teus Brand and Athena Linos

Introduction

The main focus of this chapter is to describe the current legislative and policy context of Occupational Safety & Health (OSH) and Workplace Health Promotion (WHP) for women workers across the European Union (EU).

Since the foundation of the European Community, numerous directives and amendments concerning OSH have been issued. The directives are mandatory and in their majority have been fully incorporated into the national legislations of member states, with the exception of cases where national legislation is even more stringent. Furthermore, there are a number of nonmandatory resolutions or communication documents addressed to member states, that are aimed at harmonizing the European regulatory environment on OSH issues.

Most directives pertaining to specific workplace conditions and hazards do not refer specifically to male or female workers, because the relevant risk factors can affect both sexes and therefore there is no legitimate reason to consider either of them as more vulnerable. The only exception is Council Directive 92/85/EEC, which refers to the protection of pregnant and breast-feeding working women.

It is therefore important to investigate whether the EU legal context concerning OSH sufficiently covers the needs of female workers. In the next section, the most important EU directives are discussed in that respect, and the specificities of female workers regarding OSH are highlighted.

The Legal Context of Occupational Health and Safety in the European Union

General Framework

Most EU directives regarding OSH derive from Article 118A and Articles 136 and 137 of the "Treaty Establishing the European Community" (as it was amended by the Treaty of Nice and the "Single European Act" of 1987), which mandate the

Table 2.1 Articles 118A, 136, and 137 of the "Treaty establishing the European Community"

Article 136 EC (of the Treaty establishing the European Community)

"The EC and the Member States... shall have as their objectives the promotion of employment, improved living and **working conditions...**"

Article 137 EC (of the Treaty establishing the European Community)
*Amended by the Treaty of Nice

"With a view to achieving the objectives of Article, 136 the Community shall support and complement the activities of the Member States in the following fields:

(a)   improvement of the working environment to protect workers' health and safety

(b)   working conditions

　　　...

(e)   the information and consultation of workers

　　　...

(i)   equality between men and women with regard to labour market opportunities and treatment at work"

Article 21 of the "Single European Act" (amending Article 118A EC)

1.   "Member states... encouraging **improvements** especially in the **working environment** ...health and safety of workers..."

2.   "...the Council... shall adopt, by means of directives, **minimum requirements** for gradual implementation, having regard to the conditions and technical rules..."

3.   "The provisions adopted... not prevent any member state from maintaining or introducing **more stringent measures for the protection of working conditions...**"

---

implementation of measures towards the improvement of OSH status in all EU countries. The specific provisions of these articles concerning OSH are included in Table 2.1.

Article 118A has constituted the main statute upon which the body of European legislation on OSH has been based. The overall legislative framework concerning the safety and health of the working population in Europe is described in the European Council (EC) directives included in Table 2.2, following the codification by thematic category established by the European Commission (European Commission 2007):

The general context of OSH is summarized in Council Directive 89/391/EEC (Official Journal L 183, 1989), the key points of which are presented in Table 2.3:

Since 2002, the EU has also adopted a new approach towards health and safety at the workplace, initiating a new policy entitled: "Adapting to Change in Work and Society: A New Community Strategy on Heath and Safety at Work 2002–2006" (COM 2002 118 final).

An innovative component of this new strategy, according to the Commission, is "a global approach to well-being at work." This stipulation embraces more extensively the factors contributing to the individual worker's overall health status, attributing a wider concept to the term *worker's health* than just the absence of occupational illness and accidents in the workplace.

Table 2.2 Legal context of occupational health and safety

Code of E.E.C. Directive	Topic
Council Directive **89/391/EEC**	General framework for the amelioration of working conditions
Council Directive **89/654/EEC**	Generic regulatory framework for workplace environment
Council Directive **89/655/EEC**	Specifications and requirements for the safe use of equipment by workers
Amendment	
Directive **95/63/EC**	
Directive **2001/45/EC**	
Council Directive **89/656/EEC**	Specifications and requirements for the use of personal protective equipment by workers
Council Directive **92/29/EEC**	Medical treatment of personnel in board vessels (Official Journal L 113, 1992)
Council Directive **93/103/EC**	General regulatory guidelines for the occupational safety and health of workers in fishing vessels
Council Directive **1999/92/EC**	Specifications and requirements for the safety of workers in explosive workplace environment (Official Journal L 23, 2000)
Council Directive **92/58/EEC**	Specifications and requirements for the proper use of safety signs at the workplace
Council Directive **92/57/EEC**	Specifications and requirements for the safety of workers in mobile construction sites
Council Directive **92/91/EEC**	Specifications and requirements for the safety of workers in mineral extracting industries
Council Directive **92/104/EEC**	Specifications and requirements for the safety of workers in surface and underground mineral extracting industries
Council Directive **90/269/CEE**	General safety guidelines for the protection of workers handling heavy loads
Council Directive **90/270/CEE**	General safety guidelines for the protection of video display unit operators
Council Directive **04/37/CE**	OSH context for carcinogenic substances used at the workplace
Council Directive **98/24/EC**	General safety guidelines for handling chemical substances and tabulation of chemical agents
Council Directive **91/322/EEC**	Index of indicative limit values for chemical agents (Official Journal L 177, 1991)
Council Directive **2000/39/EC**	Index of indicative limit values for occupational exposure to chemical agents(Official Journal L 142, 2000)
EP and Council Directive **2000/54/EC**	General framework for the protection from exposure to biological agents. Index of occupational biological hazards
Council Directive **86/188/EEC**	General regulatory guidelines for occupational exposure to noise (Official Journal L 137, 1986)
Council Directive **2003/10/EC**	
EP and Council Directive **2002/44/EC**	General regulatory guidelines for occupational exposure to vibrations
Council Directive **04/40/CE**	General regulatory guidelines for occupational exposure to vibrations
Council Directive **83/477/EEC**	General regulatory guidelines for occupational exposure to asbestos (Official Journal L 97, 2003)
Modification	
Council Directive **91/382/EEC**	
Council Directive **2003/18/EC**	
Council Directive **92/85/EEC**	General regulatory guidelines for the protection of women workers during pregnancy and breastfeeding
Council Directive **94/33/EC**	General regulatory guidelines for the protection of young workers

Table 2.3 Council Directive 89/391

SECTION I- General Provisions	
Article 1, Object Paragraph 2	"Training of workers and their representatives"
	Training of workers, even if not strictly defined, includes among others the concept of health education and training, which are 2 of the key-elements of WHP activities.
SECTION II- Employers Obligations	
Article 6, General Obligations on Employers Paragraph 1	"Provision of information and training"
	Information and training refers to prevention of occupational risks, and therefore implies the obligation of employers to implement activities pertinent to the scopes WHP
Article 6, General Obligations on Employers Paragraph 2 (d)	"Adopting the work to the individual…design of workplaces…equipment"
	This subparagraph underlines the necessity to adopt working conditions to the individual characteristics of workers, justifying the basic argument of HPROWOMEN for a "gender specific" approach to employees needs
Article 6, General Obligations on Employers Paragraph 3 (a)	"Evaluate the risks to the safety and health of workers… workplaces"
	The assumption of a "default" working population, without taking account of specific gender characteristics and differences, may over- or under-estimate the risks involved
Article 6, General Obligations on Employers Paragraph 3 (c) & Article 11, Consultation and Participation of Workers Paragraph 2.3	"…planning and introduction of new technologies are the subject of consultation with the workers and/or their representatives…"
	Women workers should be represented at the decision-making process concerning OSH issues, even in if they are outnumbered by men workers in a specific sector.
Article 9, Various Obligations on Employers Paragraph 1 (a)	"…assessment of the risks… groups of workers exposed to particular risks;"
	This subparagraph recognizes the need for a more "comprehensive" risk assessment process, taking account of the particular needs of certain groups of workers (e.g. female workers & reproductive hazards in a chemical industry)

Article 12, Training of Workers Paragraph 1

"…each worker receives adequate safety and health training…"
Safety and health training in this article refers mostly to occupational hazards, but in a wider sense, establishes the basic concept of health education for the working population. Health education topics may include health issues which even if not directly associated with occupational hazards, affect employee's health and consequently compromise the safety status of their employment [e.g. smoking cessation and reducing risk for occupationally induced C.O.P.D.(Chronic Pulmonary Obstructive Disease)]

Article 14 Health Surveillance Paragraph 1

"…health surveillance appropriate for the health and safety risks they incur at work"
Health surveillance algorithms for occupational diseases should be updated to include hazards which specifically affect certain bodily functions of female workers (e.g. reproductive disorders following prolonged occupational exposure to endocrine disruptors)

Article 15, Risk Groups

"Particularly sensitive groups must be protected against the dangers which specifically affect them."
Women should not be considered collectively as a particularly sensitive group, but rather as a part of the working population which is entitled to the right of being protected according to their own individual needs and special gender characteristics. The only circumstance where female workers **should** be provided with extra protection, is during **pregnancy** and **breast-feeding**, not only because of the physiological changes they sustain during this period, but mainly due to the fact that occupational exposures at that stage may seriously affect a non-involved person (fetus or infant).

This acceptance provides a stepping stone for the inclusion of WHP concepts and practices into the wider context of OSH, as it becomes clear that a more comprehensive approach is needed to deal with issues that may affect the health of the working population beyond their everyday occupational activities.

Furthermore, the Commission identifies—within the context of the 2002–2006 strategy—the need to adopt OSH. policies across Europe to meet the changing needs of society in respect to the characteristics of the working population, the types of employment, and the emerging new risks for employees. Some of the topics referred to as priorities of the EU within this action plan are cited in Table 2.4.

Many of the issues brought up by "Community Strategy 2002–2006" included in Table 2.4—are highly pertinent to the scope, content, and concerns of the WHP agenda. Moreover, employed women in particular are regarded as a high priority population for OSH interventions by EU authorities.

Since 1994, the European Agency for Safety and Health at Work has also been established (Council Regulation 2062/94), with the primary objective to provide the European Commission, member states and other interested stakeholders (policymakers, scientific institutions, trade unions) with "technical, scientific and economic information of use in the field of safety and health at work" and to raise awareness on OSH issues (European Agency for Safety and Health at Work 2007).

Workplace Conditions and Equipment

Workplace

The legal provisions concerning workplace conditions are laid down by Council Directive 89/654/EEC (Official Journal L 393, 1989a), which is presented in Table 2.5.

This Council Directive (especially with reference to paragraph 16 of Annex I, concerning restrooms for employees) includes no specific provision for facilities appropriate for the storage and preparation of food for workers.

The above-mentioned legislative insufficiency, however, constitutes a hindrance at the policy level for interventions preventing major current health threats such as obesity and metabolic syndrome. If legislation would address the issue of workplace facilities for food storage and preparation, it could lead to a conducive workplace environment (with the support of the employer) and feed the individual willingness of workers to adopt healthy dietary habits.

Equipment Design

The required specifications for the equipment used in the workplace are outlined by Council Directive 89/655/EEC (Official Journal L 393, 1989b), and especially Article 1 of the Directive, which is presented in Table 2.6.

Table 2.4 Priority issues of Community Strategy 2002–2006

I. Increasing participation in women to the labor force - Job and Risk Segregation

COM (2002) 118 final), 2.1 Changes in Society (2.1.1 *An increasingly feminised society*)

Par.1: "83% of employed women work in services, which explains why they suffer a much lower rate of accidents and occupational illness. . . "

Par.2: a) ". . . **kind of work in which women predominate** is generating a growing accident rate, including fatal accidents. . . "

b) ". . . the proportion was much higher in **certain groups**: 45% of allergies, 61% of infectious illnesses, 55% of neurological complaints, 48% of hepatitic and dermatological complaints. . . "

Par.3: ". . . specific account of the growing proportion of women in the workforce, and of the risks to which women are **particularly liable**. These measures must be based on research covering the ergonomic aspects, workplace design, and the effects of exposure to physical, chemical and biological agents, and pay heed to the physiological and psychological differences in the way work is organised."

II. Change in Forms of Employment (increased participation of women in part-time employment, night work)
COM (2002) 118 final), 2.2 Changes in forms of employment

Par.1: a) "The labour market is seeing increasingly diversified forms of employment, with particularly strong growth in **temporary employment relationships**."

b) "People who have been employed for **less than two years are more likely to suffer an accident** at work than the average. . . "

Par.2: ". . . new forms of work, **part-time work** and non-standard working times (e.g. **shift work or night work**) are likewise factors which add to the degree of risk"

III. Emerging Occupational Risks (high prevalence among women workers)

COM (2002) 118 final), 2.3 Changes in the nature of risk

Par.2: ". . . emerging illnesses such as **stress, depression, anxiety, violence at work, harassment and intimidation** are responsible for 18% of all problems associated with health at work. . . "

IV. Comprehensive Approach to Worker's Health (consideration for extra-occupational factors contributing to ill health)
COM (2002) 118 final), 3.1 For a global approach to well-being at work

Par.2: "Mainstreaming the **gender dimension into risk evaluation, preventive measures** . . . specific characteristics of women in terms of health and safety at work."

Par.3: "Prevention of social risks. Stress, harassment at the workplace, depression and anxiety, and risks related to dependence on alcohol drugs and medicines, should all be the subject of specific measures. . . "

V. Prevention and Health Promotion
COM (2002) 118 final), 3.2 Strengthening the prevention culture (3.2.1. *Education, awareness, anticipation: improving people's knowledge of risks*)
". . . developing an approach which is both global and preventive, geared to promoting well-being at work, and going beyond the mere prevention of specific risks"

Par.1: ". . . **continuing vocational training**. . . geared to the realities of day-to-day work, with a view to impacting directly on the work environment."

VI. Multidisciplinary Approach to Worker's Health and Gender Perspective of OSH

COM (2002) 118 final), 3.2 Strengthening the prevention culture (3.2.2. *Better application of existing law*)
Par.3: ". . . prevention services should be **multi-disciplinary, embracing social and psychological risks, and the gender** factor;"

Table 2.5 Council Directive 89/654

ANNEX I- Minimum Safety and Health Requirements for Workplaces Used for the First Time, as Referred to in Article 3 of the Directive 1

Par.16: Restrooms	16.3 "... protection of non-smokers against discomfort caused by tobacco smoke..."
	This paragraph refers to the obligation of employers to protect their staff from passive smoking. Even though restrictive measures may appear somewhat "hostile," in certain cases smoking bans within the premises of the workplace may prove to be a useful tool for WHP initiatives for smoking cessation.
Par.18: Sanitary Equipment	18.1.3 "... separate changing rooms ... for men and women"
	18.2.3 "... washbasins must be separate for... men and women"
	18.3 "... separate lavatories... for men and women"
	This paragraph mandates that employers must take into account the practical issues arising from the coexistence of men and women workers at the workplace, concerning the provision of sanitary facilities.
	Example
	An effective workplace intervention for the prevention of exposure to chemical or biological hazards must, apart from instructing workers to properly clean their body or remove their clothes after work, provide some practical solutions on how to implement those guidelines. No matter how simple the problem may seem though, the lack of separate facilities for male and female employees is an important barrier for the effective implementation of any similar program.

The context of this article was amended by the provisions of Council Directive 95/63/EC (Official Journal L 335, 1995) and Council Directive 2001/45/EC (Official Journal L 195, 2001), included in Tables 2.7 and 2.8, respectively.

These articles dictate that work equipment should be designed using ergonomic principles to provide workers with the ability to perform their tasks according to

Table 2.6 SECTION II—EMPLOYER'S OBLIGATIONS: Article 1

SECTION II - EMPLOYER'S OBLIGATIONS Article 1,

General Obligations - Paragraph 1	"... work equipment... suitable for the work to be carried out or properly adapted for that purpose..."
	*This article establishes the provision of proper equipment to the employees according to the tasks they perform, as an obligation of the employers

Table 2.7 Council Directive 95/63

Article 1, Amendment of 89/655/EEC, Paragraph 3

Article 5a – Ergonomics and Occupational Health	"The working posture... work equipment and ergonomic principles ... minimum health and safety requirements "
	*This article establishes the introduction of ergonomic principles to the design of equipment and tools.

Table 2.8 Council Directive 2001/45

Article 1, Addition of Annex to Annex II, of 89/655/EEC	
Annex 4 Provisions concerning the use of work equipment provided for temporary work at a height **Par:** 4.1.1.	"The dimensions of the work equipment must be appropriate to the nature of the work to be performed and to the foreseeable stresses..." *This subparagraph of the annex, also dictates that equipment used at the workplace has to be selected according to the nature of the specific tasks to be performed (e.g. women workers in the cleaning industry)

the requirements of their position and without risk of injury due to inappropriate body posture or exposure to extreme loads. These statutes introduce the concept of specifically designed tools and equipment to fit the somatometric characteristics of individual workers (e.g., different average body dimensions of women workers) rather than the *one-size-fits-all* model that has been applied up to now. This Directive is therefore a useful tool for women-centered WHP interventions towards the prevention of musculoskeletal diseases.

Personal Protective Equipment

Even though Council Directive 89/656/EEC (Official Journal L 393, 1989c), which is presented in Table 2.9, refers specifically to different means of protection from exposure to hazardous agents at work, it also brings up the issue of the appropriate design and use of personal protective equipment (PPE), which is a major concern for the safety of female workers. According to this Directive, women should not use protective equipment that is designed for the average male worker because the variation in size, body shape, and muscular strength could make the equipment ineffective (Han DH 2000), or even sometimes hazardous for their health (e.g., musculoskeletal strain resulting from prolonged use of heavy protective gear).

Safe Use of Equipment

Both Paragraphs 1 and 3 of Article 6 of Council Directive 89/655/EEC (Official Journal L 393, 1989b) presented in Table 2.10 introduce the subject of safe use of equipment for the prevention of occupational accidents.

One of the issues of concern for employed women, as well as men, is also the existence of communication (language) barriers among immigrant workers.

Table 2.9 Council Directive 89/656

SECTION II: Employer's Obligations Article 4, General provisions, Paragraph 1	
Subparagraph (a)	"...appropriate for the risks"
Subparagraph (c)	"...ergonomic requirements and the worker's state of health..."
Subparagraph (d)	"...fit the wearer correctly..."

Table 2.10 Council Directive 89/655

SECTION II - Employer's Obligations

Article 6, Informing of Workers

Par. 1	"…adequate information… written instructions on the work equipment "
Par. 3	"…instructions must be comprehensible to the workers concerned"

ANNEX: Minimum Requirements referred to in Article 4(1) (a) (ii) and (b) 1

2. General minimum requirements applicable to work equipment

Par. 2.11	"Warning devices on work equipment must unambiguous and easily perceived and understood."
Par. 2.15	"Work equipment must bear the warnings and markings essential to ensure the safety of workers"

Therefore, special care should be taken to protect this part of the working population, using pictograms, translation of safety instructions, or personalized training of workers whenever it is considered necessary (in accordance with the meaning of Paragraphs 2.11 and 2.15 of the Annex of Directive 89/655 cited in Table 2.10).

Safety Signs

The Subparagraph of Annex VIII of Council Directive 92/58/EEC (Official Journal L 245, 1992b) cited in Table 2.11, underlines the significance of effective communication at the workplace for the protection of the health and safety of workers and the avoidance of exposure to occupational hazards. Furthermore, it introduces the legal context for the promotion of the health and safety of employees with inadequate language skills—especially **immigrants**—which, in certain professions, constitute a significant part of female employees (i.e., service industry, textile industry).

Work in Temporary or Mobile Construction Sites

Council Directive 92/57/EEC (Official Journal L 245, 1992a), some key points of which are cited in Table 2.12, does raise some practical issues concerning the employment of both male and female workers in the same workplace (e.g., provision of hygienic facilities for cleaning and disposal of clothes after work, facilities for pregnant workers, etc.).

Table 2.11 Council Directive 92/58

Annex VIII, Minimum Requirements for Verbal Communication

2. Specific Rules Governing Use Par. 2.1	"persons involved must have a good knowledge of the language… understand the spoken message correctly"

Table 2.12 Council Directive 92/57

ANNEX IV

Minimum Safety and Health Requirements for Construction Sites (Referred to in Article 9(a) and Article 10 (1) (a) (i) of the Directive Preliminary Remarks)

Paragraph 14, Sanitary Equipment	14.1.3. "… separate changing rooms or separate use of changing rooms for men and women" 14.2.1. "… separate shower rooms or separate use of shower rooms for en and women " 14.3 "… separate lavatories or separate use of lavatories for men and women"
Paragraph 15, Restrooms and/or Accommodation Areas	15.5 "… protection of non-smokers against discomfort caused by tobacco smoke…" This subparagraph, even if not specific for women workers, identifies the necessity for the protection of nonsmokers at the workplace, and provides the context for the implementation of prevention programs to protect employees from passive smoking
Paragraph 16, Pregnant Women and Nursing Mothers	"Pregnant women and nursing mothers must be able to lie down to rest in appropriate conditions" Paragraph 16 grants special provision for pregnant women and nursing mothers concerning available facilities at the workplace, acknowledging the fact that this subgroup of the working population needs a more "sensitive" approach, as more liable to occupational risks than their colleagues

Mineral Extracting Industries: Drilling, Surface and Underground

The OSH context in these sectors of activity is stipulated by Council Directive 92/91/EEC and Council Directive 92/104/EEC (Official Journal L 348, 1992b; Official Journal L 404, 1992).

Although the mineral-extracting industry is one of the sectors with the lowest participation of women workers, specific legal provisions on certain issues concerning female employees still do exist—some of which are listed in Tables 2.13 and 2.14.

The sections of Directives 91/91/EEC and 92/104/EEC cited in Tables 2.13 and 2.14 outline practical issues concerning the use of hygienic facilities by workers of different sexes. The regulation of such minor issues, however, could help women employees comply with the guidelines and safety regulations introduced by prevention programs at the workplace (example of Par.18: Sanitary equipment, Annex I of Council Directive 89/654/EEC) and increase their sense of security through reducing chances of sexual harassment and mobbing.

Furthermore, both these directives refer to the training of workers on safety and health issues. Even though WHP does not confine itself to the prevention of occupational diseases, the training of employees on OSH topics constitutes an important component of health promotion in the workplace, especially in this sector that involves certain major occupational hazards. The specific references are cited in Tables 2.15 and 2.16.

Table 2.13 Council Directive 92/91—Hygienic facilities

ANNEX : Minimum Safety and Health Requirements (as referred to in Article 10 of the Directive)

PART A, Common minimum requirements applicable to the on-shore and off-shore	Paragraph 19. Pregnant women and nursing mothers "Pregnant women and nursing mothers must be able to lie down to rest in appropriate conditions"
PART B, Special minimum requirements applicable to the on-shore sector	7. Sanitary equipment 7.1.3. "...separate changing rooms or separate use of changing rooms for men and women" 7.2.1. "...separate shower rooms or separate use of shower rooms for men and women"
PART C, Special minimum requirements applicable to the off-shore sector	8. Sanitary equipment 8.1.3. "...separate changing rooms or separate use of changing rooms for men and women" 10.Accomodation 10.3. "...separate shower rooms or separate use of shower rooms for men and women"

Manual Handling of Loads

Council Directive 90/269/CEE (Official Journal L 156, 1990a) refers to the prevention of musculoskeletal disorders (MSDs) in the workplace, providing specific measures for the safe handling of loads.

Table 2.14 Council Directive 92/104—Hygienic facilities

ANNEX : Minimum Safety and Health Requirements (as Referred to in Article 10 of the Directive)

PART A, Common minimum requirements applicable to surface and underground mineral-extracting industries and to ancillary surface installations	14.Sanitary installations 14.1.3. "...separate changing rooms or separate use of changing rooms for men and women" 14.2.1. "...separate shower rooms or separate use of shower rooms for men and women" 14.3. "...separate lavatories or separate use of lavatories for men and women"

Table 2.15 Council Directive 92/91—Training of workers

ANNEX : MINIMUM SAFETY AND HEALTH REQUIREMENTS AS REFERRED TO IN ARTICLE 10 OF THE DIRECTIVE

PART A, Common minimum requirements applicable to the on-shore and off-shore sectors	2.5. Information, instructions and training "Workers must be given the necessary information, instructions, training and retraining to ensure their health and safety." 2.6. Written instructions "Written instructions specifying rules to be observed to ensure the safety and health of workers..." 2.7. Safe working methods "...applied at each workplace or in respect of each activity"

Table 2.16 Council Directive 92/104—Training of Workers

ANNEX: Minimum Safety and Health Requirements as Referred to in Article 10 of the Directive	
PART A, Common minimum requirements applicable to surface and underground mineral-extracting industries and to ancillary surface installations	1.5. Information, instructions and training "Workers must be given the necessary information, instructions, training and re-training to ensure their health and safety." 1.6. Written instructions "Written instructions specifying rules to be observed to ensure the safety and health of workers…" "…must include information on the use of emergency equipment and action to be taken in the event of an emergency…" 1.7. Safe working methods "…applied at each workplace or in respect of each activity"

MSDs are very commonly encountered in certain occupational sectors that employ predominantly women (e.g., nursing, assembly lines) and are considered to be one of the major causes of absenteeism and morbidity among the female working population. Although this condition may manifest through a variety of syndromes (lower-back pain, carpal tunnel syndrome, shoulder bursitis, etc.), it is well-known that a number of factors related to activities in the workplace, or specific tasks, are highly associated with the development of musculoskeletal disorders in different parts of the body.

The manual handling of loads is not the only occupational risk factor for MSDs, but the legal context introduced by the specific Directive includes some generic prevention principles that apply more or less to all potential sources of risk for similar disorders. The key points of concern for the implementation of a tailored prevention program are listed in Table 2.17.

According to the references in Table 2.17, the Directive presents the minimum safety standards for the protection of workers from musculoskeletal injuries, and provides a nonexhaustive list of measures to be taken by the employers in that direction, including:

- Provision of appropriate means (e.g., lifting devices for patients in the case of nursing personnel, and proper tools for production line workers)
- Introduction of ergonomic design into the workplace and individual workstations (e.g., adjusting the level of an assembly line to the height of female workers)
- Provision of adequate instructions and training for workers (e.g., safe lifting techniques, avoiding exertion and awkward body posture during the handling of loads or equipment)
- Modification of the working process to allow for adequate bodily rest of workers (e.g., work pace must be regulated by workers and not imposed by an automatic system, use of rotating shifts to provide workers with adequate time to rest)
- Adjustment of tasks to the physical ability of workers (e.g., women should not handle loads that exceed their physical capability by performing tasks originally designed for the physical strength of male workers)

Table 2.17 Council Directive 90/269

SECTION II: Employer's Obligations	
Article 3, General Provision	Paragraph 1, "…use the appropriate means, in particular mechanical equipment in order to avoid the need for manual handling" Paragraph 2, "…take the appropriate organizational measures, use the appropriate means or provide workers with such means in order to reduce the risk"

Article 4,
  Organization of
  Workstations
	"…organize workstations in such a way as to make such handling as safe and healthy as possible …"

Article 6,
  Information for,
  and Training of,
  Workers
	Paragraph 1,
	"…workers and/or their representatives shall be informed of all measures to be implemented…"
	"…workers and/or their representatives receive general indications…weight of a load…centre of gravity…"
	
	Paragraph 2,
	"..proper training and information on how to handle loads correctly, and the risks they might be open to…"

ANNEX I: (*)Reference Factors (Article 3(2), Article 4 (a) and (b), and Article 6(2))	
4. Requirements of the Activity	"…over-frequent or over-prolonged physical effort " "…insufficient bodily rest" "…rate of work imposed by a process"
ANNEX II: (*) Individual Risk Factors	
Articles 5 and 6 (2)	"…physically unsuited to carry out the task…" "…does not have adequate or appropriate knowledge or training"

Table 2.18 Council Directive 90/270

SECTION II: Employer's Obligations	

Article 3,
  Analysis of
  Workstations
	Paragraph 1,
	"…analysis of workstations…risks to eyesight, physical problems and problems of mental stress."

Article 6,
  Information for,
  and Training
of,   Workers
	Paragraph 1,
	"…workers shall receive information on all aspects of safety and health relating to their workstation…"
	
	Paragraph 2,
	"…every worker shall also receive training in the use of the workstation…"

Article 7, Daily Work Routine	"…breaks or changes of activity reducing the workload at the display screen."

Article 9,
  Protection of
  Workers' Eyes
  and Eyesight
	Paragraph 1,
	"…appropriate aye and eyesight test…"
	
	Paragraph 2,
	"…ophthalmologic examination…"

Work with Display Screen Equipment

Working with video display units (VDU) is widespread nowadays across the tertiary sector, especially in workplaces with high participation of women (call-centers, receptions, secretarial posts, airport terminals), and is often associated with musculoskeletal and eyesight disorders, as well as mental exhaustion, the effects of poor ergonomic design, and stressful working conditions.

Council Directive **90/270/CEE** (Official Journal L 156, 1990b) does not refer specifically to female employees but the list of workplace interventions it mentions, contributes to the improvement of working conditions for a significant number of employed women in positions involving similar tasks.

Legislation Addressing Significant Exposure Factors

Carcinogens

The general OSH context regarding the use of this category of compounds is stipulated by Council Directive 2004/37/EC (Official Journal L 158, 2004), parts of which are presented in Table 2.19. This Directive has repealed previous Directives: 90/394/EC (Official Journal L 196, 1990), 97/42/EC (Official Journal L 179, 1997) and 1999/38/EC (Official Journal L 138, 1999)

Even though the Directive does not refer to women workers specifically, it has been acknowledged that no *safe level* of exposure can be established because carcinogenic substances can harm both male and female workers. Furthermore, Paragraph 13 of the Introduction states that more scientific research needs to be carried out in the future to identify further potential harmful effects that we do not already acknowledge.

One should also keep in mind that this directive refers to agents with mutagenic effect (i.e., potential genetic damage to germ cells) and, besides carcinogenicity, it is therefore pertinent to the protection of the reproductive health of workers regardless of gender.

These two points cited in Table 2.20 could be considered as an argument in favor of a gender-specific risk assessment approach concerning issues of OSH, implying that there is no way to establish an exposure safety limit that is protective for men but not for women and vice versa. In a practical sense, this means that safety standards should be stringent enough to protect the most susceptible individuals

Table 2.19 Council Directive 2004/37—Introduction

Introduction: The European Parliament and the Council of the European Union **Whereas:**	
Par. 11	"Although current scientific knowledge is not such that a level can be established below which risks to health cease to exist…"
Par. 13	"…limit values must be revised whenever this becomes necessary in the light of more recent scientific data."

Table 2.20 Council Directive 2004/37—Provisions

CHAPTER II: **Employer's Obligations**	
Article 3 Scope -Determination and Assessment of Risks	"… employers shall give particular attention to any effects concerning the health or safety of**workers at particular risk** and shall, inter alia, take account of the desirability of not employing such workers in areas where they may come into contact with carcinogens or mutagens."
Article 11, Information and Training of Workers	Par.1 "Appropriate measures… in the form of information and instructions, concerning: (a) potential risks to health, including the additional risks due to tobacco consumption; (b) precautions to be taken to prevent exposure; (c) hygiene requirements; (d) wearing and use of protective equipment and clothing; (e) steps to be taken by workers, including rescue workers, in the case of incidents and to prevent incidents."

among workers, with introduction of exposure limit values at least as low as the Non-Observed Adverse Effects Level (NOAEL) for either men or women, because the lack of scientific evidence does not allow assumptions regarding a *harmless* level of exposure for the rest of the working population.

Furthermore, Article 3 of the Directive cited in Table 2.21 refers to the identification and protection of high-risk groups of workers, recognizing that the distribution of occupational risk among the working population is not uniform. One should note that the Article does not deal with specific worksites, sectors, or tasks involving a high risk of exposure, but rather to the individual susceptibility of certain groups of workers.

Risk assessment activities and preventive measures should therefore take into consideration certain characteristics that affect the level of risk of each individual worker (health status, gender, age, specific tasks) and adjust the implemented prevention policy accordingly. At this point, we should mention that there is a slight inconsistency in Article 3 (in the introductory part of the Directive) regarding which groups of workers should be regarded as more susceptible to exposure to mutagenic factors, whereas:

- Many of the chemical agents mentioned need to be further examined because little is known about their potential effects on health
- There is no concentration level that can be regarded as *safe for all workers* because all assumptions for exposure below a certain limit are based on extrapolation and are therefore subject to bias

It should be stressed here that the misinterpretation of the term *workers at particular risk* could potentially provoke discriminatory behavior against the female working population, excluding women from positions and tasks on the basis of their presumed susceptibility. According to this Directive, it is debatable whether one can adequately document this kind of *gender susceptibility* however, given the lack of evidence, because exposure to such agents (no matter how low) cannot be consid-

Table 2.21 Council Directive 98/24

SECTION II: Employer's Obligations	
Article 5 General Principles for Prevention of Risks...	Par. 2. Risks to the health and safety … shall be eliminated… by: "… design and organisation of systems of work at the workplace"… "… provision of suitable equipment for work with chemical agents …" "… reducing to a minimum the number of workers exposed…" "… reducing to a minimum the duration and intensity of exposure…" "… appropriate hygiene measures…" "… reducing the quantity of chemical agents… to the minimum required…" "… suitable working procedures including… safe handling, storage and transport…"
Article 8 Information and Training for Workers	Par. 1. "… employer shall ensure that workers and/or their representatives are provided with: "… the data obtained… and further informed whenever a major alteration at the workplace leads to a change in these data" "… information on the hazardous chemical agents… such as the identity… the risks to safety and health, relevant occupational exposure limit values and other legislative provisions…" "… training and information on appropriate precautions and actions …" "… access to any safety data sheet provided by the supplier…" "

*Annexes I, II and III of the Directive concerning occupational exposure limit values, biological limit values, and prohibitions, refer to both male and female workers.
*In Commission Directive 91/322/EEC (Official Journal L 177, 1991) and Commission Directive 2000/39/EC (Official Journal L 142, 2000) laying down exposure limit values do not refer particularly to gender.

ered absolutely safe for either sex. Furthermore, Article 11 of the Directive that is included in Table 2.20 provides a framework for the training of workers on practices and procedures to protect themselves from exposure to carcinogenic compounds.

Each of the following directives provide a general context for the protection of the OSH of workers concerning specific exposures, introducing an array of preventive measures and practices that involve both employers and employees.

Chemical Agents

The OSH context concerning exposure to chemical agents is laid down by Council Directive 98/24/EC (Official Journal L 131, 1998)—certain points of which are presented in Table 2.21.

Biological Agents

European Parliament (EP) and Council Directive 2000/54/EC (Official Journal L 262, 2000) refers to exposure to biological agents in the workplace. Some key issues of the Directive pertaining to prevention and health protection of workers are cited in Table 2.22.

We should stress at this point that Article 14 of the Directive brings out the issue of immunization of workers against biological agents, especially for workers involved in tasks where specific agents or employment settings dictate special protective measures.

This provision greatly pertains to the protection of pregnant workers or women of childbearing age working in sectors where the risk of exposure to biological agents

Table 2.22 Council Directive 2000/54/EC

CHAPTER II: **Employer's Obligations**

Article 6 Reduction of Risks	Par.2 "…risk of exposure must be reduced to as low a level as necessary…by the following measures…: (a) "keeping as low as possible the number of workers exposed…" (b) "design of work processes and engineering control measures so as to avoid or minimise the release of biological agents…" (c) "collective protection measures and/or, where exposure cannot be avoided by other means, individual protection measures…" (d) "hygiene measures… prevention or reduction of the accidental transfer…" (e) "use of the biohazard sign…" (f) "drawing up plans to deal with accidents …" … (h) "means for safe collection, storage and disposal of waste …" (i) "arrangements for the safe handling and transport of biological agents…""
Article 8 Hygiene and Individual Protection	Par.1. Employers shall be obliged…to take appropriate measures to ensure that: (a) "workers do not eat or drink in working areas …risk of contamination …" (b)"…provided with appropriate protective clothing…special clothing…" (c) "…appropriate and adequate washing and toilet facilities…" (d) "any necessary protective equipment …" (e) "procedures are specified for taking, handling and processing samples of human or animal origin"
Article 9 Information and Training of Workers	Par.1 "…employer to ensure that workers and/or any workers' representatives …receive sufficient and appropriate training… in the form of information and instructions, concerning: (a) potential risks to health; (b) precautions to be taken to prevent exposure; (c) hygiene requirements; (d) wearing and use of protective equipment and clothing; (e) steps to be taken by workers in the case of incidents and to prevent incidents."

CHAPTER III: **Miscellaneous Provisions**

Article 14 Health Surveillance	Par.3. "…identify those workers for whom special protective measures may be required…" "When necessary, effective vaccines should be made available for those workers who are not already immune to the biological agent to which they are exposed or are likely to be exposed."

*ANNEX I of indicative activities pertinent to the Directive refers, among others, to healthcare, agriculture, and food production plants—sectors employing a significant female working population

is high (e.g., vaccination of women working in education and health-care sectors against rubella or other viruses).

Physical Agents

Noise—The OSH context concerning exposure to noise is stipulated by the EP and Council Directive 2003/10/EC (Official Journal L 42, 2003), parts of which are cited in Table 2.23

Vibrations—The legal context concerning exposure to vibrations is laid down by the EP and Council Directive 2002/44/EC (Official Journal L 177, 2002), certain key-points of which are presented in Table 2.24.

Electromagnetic Fields—Certain provisions of the EP and Council Directive 2004/40/EC (Official Journal L 159, 2004) concerning protection of workers' health from electromagnetic fields are listed in Table 2.25

Table 2.23 Council Directive 2003/10

SECTION II: **Employer's Obligations**	

Article 5
Provisions Aimed at
    Avoiding or
    Reducing
Exposure
	"Risks arising from exposure to noise shall be eliminated at their source or reduced to a minimum."
	"The reduction of such risks shall... take into account in particular:
	(a) other working methods that require less exposure to noise
	(b) the choice of appropriate work equipment...
	(c) the design and layout of workplaces and work stations;
	(d) adequate information and training to instruct workers...
	(e) noise reduction by technical means:
	i. reducing airborne noise, e.g. by shields, enclosures...
	ii. reducing structure-borne noise, e.g. by damping or isolation;
	(f) appropriate maintenance programmes for work equipment...
	(g) organisation of work to reduce noise
	(i) limitation of the duration and intensity of the exposure;
	(ii) appropriate work schedules with adequate rest periods."

Article 8 Worker Information and Training	"...employer shall ensure that workers who are exposed to noise at ... and/or their representatives, receive information and training... in particular: (a) the nature of such risks; (b) the measures taken... in order to eliminate or reduce to a minimum the risks from noise, (c) the exposure limit values and the exposure action values... (d) the results of the assessment and measurement of the noise... (e) the correct use of hearing protectors; (f) why and how to detect and report signs of hearing damage; (g) the circumstances in which workers are entitled to health surveillance... (h) safe working practices to minimize exposure to noise."

Table 2.24 Council Directive 2002/44

SECTION II: **Employer's Obligations**	
Article 5 Provisions Aimed at Avoiding or Reducing Exposure	Par. 2. "On the basis of the risk ... the employer shall establish and implement a programme of technical and/or organisational measures... taking into account in particular: (a) other working methods that require less exposure to mechanical vibration; (b) the choice of appropriate work equipment of appropriate ergonomic design... (c) the provision of auxiliary equipment that reduces the risk of injuries... (d) appropriate maintenance programmes for work equipment... (e) the design and layout of workplaces and work stations; (f) adequate information and training to instruct workers to use work equipment correctly and safely in order to reduce their exposure... (g) limitation of the duration and intensity of the exposure; (h) appropriate work schedules with adequate rest periods; (i) the provision of clothing to protect exposed workers from cold and damp."
Article 6 Worker Information and Training	"... the employer shall ensure that workers who are exposed ... and/or their representatives receive information and training... concerning in particular: (a) the measures taken... in order to eliminate or reduce... the risks... (b) the exposure limit values and the exposure action values; (c) the results of the assessment and measurement of the mechanical vibration... (d) why and how to detect and report signs of injury; (e) the circumstances in which workers are entitled to health surveillance; (f) safe working practices to minimize exposure to mechanical vibration."

Artificial Optical Radiation—EP and Council Directive 2006/25/EC (Official Journal L 114, 2006) includes certain provisions for the protection of workers' safety and health, which are listed in Table 2.26.

As far as employers are concerned, this set of Directives lays down a number of technical and organizational measures for the protection of workers, including:

- Modification of production methods to minimize exposure to the lowest possible level
- Improved design of facilities, equipment, tools, and procedures
- Introduction of safety procedures and hygienic practices
- Utilization of collective protective systems for workers
- Provision of personal protective and auxiliary equipment
- Organizational measures to minimize the number of exposed persons and the duration and intensity of exposure (isolation of processes involving specific risks, automation, rotating shifts)
- Performance of regular maintenance procedures on equipment

Table 2.25 Council Directive 2004/40

SECTION II: **Employer's Obligations**	
Article 5 Provisions Aimed at Avoiding or Reducing Risks	Par.2 "On the basis of the risk assessment...the employer...shall devise and implement an action plan ... to prevent exposure exceeding the exposure limit values, taking into account in particular: (a) other working methods that entail less exposure to electromagnetic fields; (b) the choice of equipment emitting less electromagnetic fields... (c) technical measures to reduce the emission of electromagnetic fields... (d) appropriate maintenance programmes for work equipment... (e) the design and layout of workplaces and workstations; (f) limitation of the duration and intensity of the exposure; (g) the availability of adequate personal protection equipment."
Article 6 Worker Information and Training	"...the employer shall ensure that workers who are exposed to risks...and/or their representatives receive any necessary information and training...concerning in particular: (a) measures taken... (b) the values and concepts of the exposure limit values and action values and the associated potential risks; (c) the results of the assessment, measurement...of the levels of exposure... (d) how to detect adverse health effects of exposure and how to report them; (e) the circumstances in which workers are entitled to health surveillance; (f) safe working practices to minimize risks from exposure."

There is also a reference made within each of these Directives to measures that need to be taken concerning the workers themselves. *Information and Training* of personnel is considered an essential component of prevention, and is therefore incorporated into the context of all OSH issues. Information and training of workers refers to:

- Information on the nature, source, and magnitude of the potential risk to their health
- Training on a) recognizing the sources of risk, and b) taking adequate protective actions (through labeling of substances, interpretation of signs, and readings of instruments)
- Information on the measures taken by the employer to reduce the risk, as well as their personal contribution to their effective implementation
- Training on proper techniques, safety procedures, and hygienic practices
- Training on safe use of tools, and personal protective equipment
- Training on how to identify detrimental effects on health induced by the specific occupational hazard

Table 2.26 Council Directive 2006/25

SECTION II : **Employer's Obligations**	
Article 5 Provisions Aimed at Avoiding or Reducing Risks	Par. 2 "... the employer shall devise and implement an action... to prevent the exposure exceeding the limit values, taking into account in particular: (a) other working methods that reduce the risk from optical radiation; (b) the choice of equipment emitting less optical radiation... (c) technical measures to reduce the emission of optical radiation... (d) appropriate maintenance programmes for work equipment... (e) the design and layout of workplaces and workstations; (f) limitation of the duration and level of the exposure; (g) the availability of appropriate personal protective equipment; (h) the instructions of the manufacturer of the equipment..."
Article 6 Worker Information and Training	"... the employer shall ensure that workers who are exposed to... and/or their representatives receive any necessary information and training... concerning in particular: (a) measures taken... (b) the exposure limit values and the associated potential risks; (c) the results of the assessment, measurement... of the levels of exposure to artificial optical radiation... together with an explanation of their significance and potential risks; (d) how to detect adverse health effects of exposure and how to report them; (e) the circumstances in which workers are entitled to health surveillance; (f) safe working practices to minimize risks from exposure; (g) proper use of appropriate personal protective equipment."

Legislation Specific to Female Workers

Pregnant Workers and Workers who are Breastfeeding

It should be stressed that Council Directive 92/85/EEC (Official Journal L 348, 1992a), that stipulates the context for the protection of pregnant and breast-feeding workers, is the only statute at the European level that refers specifically to female workers.

It is clearly stated in Paragraphs 9, 10, and 11 of the introductory part of the Directive (which are cited in Table 2.27), that legislators consider this category of workers (pregnant and breastfeeding women) as a high-risk population who should be provided with additional protection against tasks and agents in the workplace that may pose a threat to the fetus or the infant. It is also stressed in the same Directive (Paragraph 10 of the introductory part), however, that the provisioned extra protection for pregnant and breast-feeding workers should not occur at the expense of their occupational rights. Related legal provisions should not pose restrictions to

Table 2.27 Council Directive 92/85—Introduction

Introduction	
Par.9	"Whereas pregnant workers, workers who have recently given birth or who are breastfeeding must be considered a specific risk group in many respects"
Par.10	"Whereas the protection of the safety and health of pregnant workers, workers who have recently given birth or workers who are breastfeeding should not treat women on the labour market unfavorably nor work to the detriment of directives concerning equal treatment for men and women"
Par.11	"Whereas some types of activities may pose a specific risk, for pregnant workers, workers who have recently given birth or workers who are breastfeeding, of exposure to dangerous agents, processes or working conditions;"

women's opportunities to pursue their own career goals (equal treatment with male workers).

Furthermore, a number of specific provisions within this Directive are listed in Table 2.28 for the protection of women workers during the period of pregnancy and breastfeeding.

The Directive provides an array of specific measures for the protection of this category of workers, including:

- Identification and characterization of sources of risk for pregnant and breastfeeding workers, which should be performed according to the individual characteristics of each workplace (in this way, EU legislation avoids exhaustive listings of hazardous factors)
- Modification of working conditions or *temporary* reassignment of tasks only in the case that modification is not feasible, to minimize exposure of female workers to the hazardous factor
- Maternity leave of at least 14 weeks (this must include at least 2 weeks compulsory leave before or after delivery)

Apart from the protection of the embryo and the newborn infant from exposure to hazardous agents, the scope of this statute is to facilitate the working mother's ability to breastfeed her baby. Maternity leave gives mothers the opportunity to commence breastfeeding after birth and adapt to the feeding patterns of the newborn before their return to work. Furthermore, the reassignment of breastfeeding mothers to day tasks instead of night work aims to support their efforts to continue breastfeeding at least till the infant reaches the age of six months.

Thus, Directive 92/85/EEC lays down the provisions for the context of WHP interventions to promote breastfeeding among working mothers. There are no specific provisions, however, for facilities at the workplace for breastfeeding workers (even though something like that is beyond the scope of the Directive). Paragraph 17.1 of Council Directive 89/654/EEC refers to restrooms for *nursing mothers*, however there is no provision for specific facilities for workers who are breastfeeding to express and store expressed milk.

Table 2.28 Council Directive 92/85—Provisions

SECTION II: General Provisions

Article 3 Guidelines	Par. 1 "…Commission shall draw up guidelines on the assessment of the chemical, physical and biological agents and industrial processes considered hazardous for the safety or health of workers…" "…guidelines…shall also cover movements and postures, mental and physical fatigue and other types of physical and mental stress connected with the work done by workers…"
Article 4 Assessment and Information	Par. 1 "For all **activities liable to involve a specific risk** of exposure to the agents, processes or working conditions…the employer shall assess the nature, degree and duration of exposure…assess any risks to the safety or health and any possible effect on the pregnancy or breastfeeding of workers…"
Article 5 Action Further to the Results of the Assessment	Par. 1 "…the employer shall take the necessary measures to ensure that, by **temporarily adjusting the working conditions** and/or the **working hours** of the worker concerned, the exposure of that worker to such risks is avoided." Par. 2 "If the adjustment of her working conditions and/or working hours is not…feasible…the employer shall take the necessary measures to **move the worker** concerned **to another job**." Par. 3 "If moving her to another job is not…feasible…the worker concerned shall be **granted leave**…for the whole of the period necessary to protect her safety or health."
Article 7 Night Work	Par. 1 "…workers…are **not obliged to perform night work** during their pregnancy and for a period following childbirth…" Par. 2 "The measures…entail the possibility…of: (a) transfer to daytime work; or (b) leave from work or extension of maternity leave where such a transfer is not technically and/or objectively feasible"
Article 8 Maternity Leave	"…workers…are entitled to a continuous period of maternity leave of at least 14 weeks allocated before and/or after confinement…"

*Annex I of the Directive 92/85 lists agents, processes, and working conditions potentially harmful during pregnancy and breastfeeding

*Annex II of Directive 92/85 lists agents and conditions where exposure is prohibited during pregnancy and breastfeeding

Legislation Relevant to Work Culture and Organization

Harassment in the Workplace

Commission Recommendation 92/131/EEC (Official Journal L 049, 1992) is the first statute at the European level to identify harassment as an issue of concern for the working population, although it does not have a mandatory character. Some of the key points of the Directive pertaining to the context of harassment prevention are cited in Table 2.29.

The recommendation does not make particular reference to men or women employees (Article 1, paragraph (a), (b), and (c)) because this problem may affect both sexes at the workplace. Nevertheless, in Paragraph 5 of the introduction, it is acknowledged that women constitute a high-risk group among the working population for experiencing harassment, and therefore they should be the focus of interventions that tackle harassment in the workplace.

Furthermore, the Recommendation sets forth an array of practices and measures to prevent harassment, which apply some of the principles of WHP methodology, including:

- Improvement of women's position within the job hierarchy. Equal access to the decision-making process
- Establishment of a workplace environment that is intolerant to harassment through attitude and behavioral change among employees
- Involvement of companies' administration in the prevention of harassment (training of managers and supervisors)
- Introduction of clearly-defined procedures for dealing with the problem (reporting cases of harassment, designated persons, investigation)
- Practical guidelines for employees
- Involvement of employees' representatives. Raising awareness among the working population on the specific issue

Working Time

EP and Council Directive 2003/88/EC (Official Journal L 299, 2003), amending Council Directive 93/104/EC (Official Journal L 307, 1993), lays down the context for the organization of working time, as well as certain aspects of employment (night work, rotating shifts, and patterns of employment) cited in Table 2.30.

This Directive can be highly relevant for female workers who experience significant work-life balance problems, trying to apportion their limited time between demanding jobs and household chores.

Parental Leave

Council Directive 96/34/EC (Official Journal L 145, 1996) establishes the workers' right to parental leave when family obligations concerning their children force their absence from work—especially in cases of health-related problems that demand their immediate attention. While it is not within the scope of this Directive to be exhaustive, further issues concerning conditions and terms of parental leave, as well as alternative forms of parental leave (part-time, time-credit system), are to be regulated by national laws and collective agreements. The main provisions of this Directive are cited in Table 2.31.

Table 2.29 Council Recommendation 92/131 EEC

Article 1	
Par. (a)	"...such conduct is unwanted, unreasonable and offensive to the recipient"
Par. (b)	"...a person's rejection of, or submission to, such conduct on the part of employers or workers (including superiors or colleagues) is used explicitly or implicitly as a basis for a decision which affects that person's access to vocational training, access to employment, continued employment, promotion, salary or any other employment decisions"
Par. (c)	"...conduct creates an intimidating, hostile or humiliating work environment..."
ANNEX: Protecting the Dignity of Women and Men at Work	
A code of practice on measures to combat sexual harassment	
1. Introduction **Par. 5**	"Some specific groups are particularly vulnerable to sexual harassment... divorced and separated women, young women and new entrants to the labor market and those with irregular or precarious employment contracts, women in non-traditional jobs, women with disabilities, lesbians and women from racial minorities are disproportionately at risk..."
3. The Law and Employers' Responsibilities	**Par. 4** "As sexual harassment is often a function of women's status in the employment hierarchy, policies to deal with sexual harassment are likely to bemost effective where they are linked to a broader policy to promote **equal opportunities and to improve the position of women**." **Par. 5** "The prime objective should be to **change behaviour and attitudes**, to seek to ensure the prevention of sexual harassment"
5. Recommendations to Employers (iv) Training	"...provision of **training for managers and supervisors**. Such training should aim to identify the factors which contribute to a working environment free of sexual harassment and to familiarize participants with their responsibilities under the employer's policy and any problems they are likely to encounter. In addition, those playing an official role in any formal complaints procedure in respect of sexual harassment should receive specialist training, such as that outlined above..."
5. Recommendations to Employers B. Procedures	"The development of **clear and precise procedures** to deal with sexual harassment once it has occurred is of great importance. The procedures should ensure the resolution of problems in an efficient and effective manner. **Practical guidance** for employees on how to deal with sexual harassment when it occurs and with its aftermath will make it more likely that it will be dealt with at an early stage. Such guidance should of course draw attention to an employee's legal rights and to any time limits within which they must be exercised. "
6. Recommendations to Trade Unions	"...It is recommended as good practice that trade unions formulate and issue clear policy statements on sexual harassment and take steps to **raise awareness** of the problem of sexual harassment in the workplace, in order to help create a climate in which it is neither condoned nor ignored. For example, trade unions could aim to give all officers and representatives **training on equality issues**, including dealing with sexual harassment, and include such information in union-sponsored or approved training courses, as well as information on the union's policy. Trade unions should consider declaring that sexual harassment is inappropriate behaviour and educating members and officials about its consequences is recommended as good practice..."

Table 2.30 EP and Council Directive 2003/88/EC—Provisions

CHAPTER 2: Minimum Rest Periods—Other Aspects of the Organization of Working Time	
Article 3 Daily Rest	"…measures necessary to ensure that every worker is entitled to **a minimum daily rest period of 11consecutive hours** per 24-hour period…"
Article 4 Breaks	"…where the working day is longer than six hours, every worker is entitled to a **rest break**…"
Article 5 Weekly Rest Period	"…per each seven-day period, every worker is entitled to a minimum uninterrupted rest period of 24 hours plus the 11 hours' daily rest…"
Article 6 Maximum Weekly Working Time	"…the **average working time** for each seven-day period, including overtime, does not exceed **48 hours**."
CHAPTER 3: Night Work/Shift Work Patterns	
Article 8 Length of Night Work	"…normal hours of work for night workers do not exceed an average of eight hours in any 24-hour period…"
Article 13 Pattern of Work	"…an employer…takes account of the general principle of **adapting work to the worker**, with a view, in particular, to alleviating monotonous work and work at a predetermined work rate …"

Table 2.31 Council Directive 96/34/EC

ANNEX: Framework Agreement on Parental Leave	
Clause 1: Purpose and Scope	"…lays down minimum requirements designed to facilitate the **reconciliation of parental and professional responsibilities** for working parents."
Clause 2: Parental Leave	Par.1 "…grants…men and women workers an individual right to parental leave on the grounds of the birth or adoption of a child to enable them to take care of that child, for at least three months, until a given age up to 8 years…"
	Par.3 "…conditions of access and detailed rules for applying parental leave shall be defined by law and/or collective agreement in the Member States…in particular:
	(a) decide whether parental leave is granted on a **full-time** or **part-time** basis, in a **piecemeal way** or in the form of a **time-credit system**;
	(b) make entitlement to parental leave subject to a period of work qualification and/or a length of service qualification which shall not exceed one year;
	(c) adjust conditions of access and detailed rules for applying parental leave to the special circumstances of adoption;
	(f) …arrangements to meet the operational and organizational requirements of small undertakings."
	Par.5 "At the end of parental leave, workers shall have the right to return to the same job or, if that is not possible, to an equivalent or similar job consistent with their employment contract or employment relationship."
Clause 3: Time Off from Work on Grounds of Force Majeure	"…necessary measures to entitle workers to time off from work…on grounds of force majeure for **urgent family reasons** in cases of sickness or accident making the immediate presence of the worker indispensable…"

Taking into account that women, despite their often over-demanding jobs, are still the ones who carry the greatest share of responsibility for raising and nurturing children in a family, it is obvious how significant the provisions of the following Council Directive are for working mothers.

Part-time and Self-employed Workers

Given the increasing participation of women in more flexible forms of employment—part-time jobs (retail, restaurants) and unregulated self-employed work (cleaners, care-givers for elderly persons)—the following statutes pertaining to the legal status of these categories of workers are highly important.

Part-time Workers

The legal context for this category of workers is laid down by Council Directive 97/81/EC (Official Journal L 14, 1997). Some of the provisions of this Directive pertaining to WHP are listed in Table 2.32.

Within Clause 5, the Directive provides measures to promote the *opportunities* for transfer of workers from full-time to part-time work and vice versa. This transfer upon request from the workers may contribute significantly to the flexibility of employment that is desirable in certain cases (e.g., temporary transfer to part-time work of a working mother and reassignment to her initial position when circumstances become more favorable), especially when the conflicting demands arising from the dual role of women professionals force them sometimes to leave work.

Furthermore, Clause 4 stipulates that part-time workers should be granted the same employment rights as the rest of the working population. Consequently, this

Table 2.32 Council Directive 97/81/EC

ANNEX: Framework Agreement on Part-time Work	
Clause 4: Principle of Nondiscrimination	"…part-time workers shall not be treated in a less favourable manner than comparable full-time workers solely because they work part time…"
Clause 5: Opportunities for Part-time Work	Par.3 "…employers should give consideration to: (a) requests by workers to transfer from full-time to part-time work… (b) requests by workers to transfer from part-time to full-time work… should the opportunity arise; (c)…provision of timely information on the availability of part-time and full-time positions in the establishment… (d) measures to facilitate access to part-time work at all levels of the enterprise, including skilled and managerial positions… facilitate access by part-time workers to vocational training to enhance career opportunities …"

also refers to OSH provisions and access to health promotion programs and services. One should stress at this point that part-time workers have been among those categories of workers with little or no access to WHP interventions, and therefore this reference is significant because it lays down the context for their participation in similar activities.

Self-employed Workers

Even though Council Recommendation 2003/134/EC (Official Journal L 53, 2003) does not have the mandatory power of a Council Directive, it depicts the increasing concern of EU authorities for the self-employed working population, especially with regard to issues of OSH, some of which are cited in Table 2.33.

Legislators acknowledge the fact that self-employed individuals sustain the same level of occupational risk as the rest of the workforce when performing similar tasks. Furthermore, sometimes they are subjected to further unidentified occupational hazards as a result of activities that are not even recorded due to the lack of a specific legal context.

While the lack of OSH awareness of the self-employed population entails excess occupational risk, both for them and for the rest of the workers employed at the same workplace, this recommendation communicates that further actions should be taken in that direction. Therefore, in Paragraphs 1, 2, 3 and 6 of the Recommendation, the Directive lays down an array of available interventions for the improvement of the health and safety status of this category of workers.

Table 2.33 Council Directive 97/81/EC

Introduction Whereas:	
Par.6	"Self-employed workers...may be subject to health and safety risks similar to those experienced by employees..."
Par.14	"...necessary to improve access of self-employed workers to training and information with a view both to improving their own health and safety and that of the persons working at the same workplace."
Recommendations	
Par.1	"...promote, in the context of their policies on preventing occupational accidents and diseases, the safety and health of self-employed workers, while taking account of the special risks existing in specific sectors..."
Par.2	"...when promoting health and safety for self-employed workers, choose the measures they deem to be most appropriate, such as one or more of the following: legislation, incentives, information campaigns and encouragement of relevant stakeholders..."
Par.3	"...necessary measures, including **awareness-raising campaigns**, so that self-employed workers can obtain ...useful information and advice on the prevention of occupational accidents and diseases;"
Par.6	"...allow self-employed workers who so wish to have access to **health surveillance** appropriate to the risks to which they are exposed;"

European Schedule of Occupational Diseases

The main statute at the European level that provides an exhaustive categorization of recognized occupational hazards and diseases, is the "European Schedule of Occupational Diseases" adopted by the Commission in 2003 (Official Journal L 238, 2003).

This Schedule includes an index of the ailments for which an occupational causality has been well-established (Annex I of the European Schedule of Occupational Diseases), and a second index of diseases potentially related to occupation (Annex II of the European schedule of Occupational Diseases). Annex II, however, needs to be further substantiated to be included in the first list. The outline of the Schedule is shown in Figures 2.1 and 2.2.

Among the recognized occupational diseases reported in Annex I of the European Schedule of Occupational Diseases, there is no particular reference to women as being more seriously affected or more frequently exposed in comparison to male workers. Furthermore, in the categorization of certain diseases according to target organs, no female-specific risk factor is identified, because both genders are equally affected by the specific agents.

On the other hand, one could argue that some of the occupational diseases included in this list are highly associated with specific occupational sectors, or tasks with predominantly female participation, and may, therefore, be more prevalent among women employees. They are not, however, considered as female-specific occupational diseases because male workers holding the same positions could be affected in the same way (if all other factors including somatometric characteristics are controlled for).

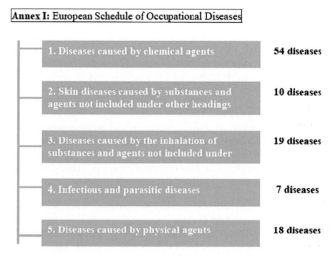

Fig. 2.1 Annex I of the European Schedule of Occupational Diseases

> **Annex II:** Additional list of diseases suspected of being occupational in origin which should be subject to notification and which may be considered at a later stage for inclusion in Annex I to the European Schedule

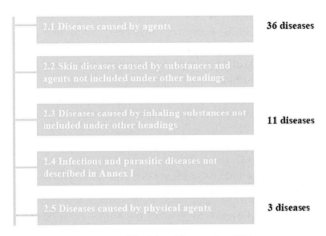

2.1 Diseases caused by agents	**36 diseases**
2.2 Skin diseases caused by substances and agents not included under other headings	
2.3 Diseases caused by inhaling substances not included under other headings	**11 diseases**
2.4 Infectious and parasitic diseases not described in Annex I	
2.5 Diseases caused by physical agents	**3 diseases**

Fig. 2.2 Annex II of the European Schedule of Occupational Diseases

Example

> Carpal tunnel syndrome (Code 506.45 in the European Schedule of Occupational Diseases) is considered to be a very prevalent disease among women working in the tertiary sector (secretaries, typists, VDU operators, production line workers), primarily because these tasks involve small, precise, repetitive movements of the wrist and fingers during an 8-hour shift.
>
> Women are generally considered more predisposed to this kind of musculoskeletal injury, because the prevalence among women is higher compared to men with the same job title. There is scientific evidence, however, that attributes this variability to the existing segregation of tasks even within the same job. Men are found equally affected as women by carpal tunnel syndrome for jobs with more narrowly defined tasks (e.g., data-entry keyers) (McDiarmid, Oliver, Ruser & Gucer 2000).
>
> Even in this case, however, the excess occupational risk to women depends on further differences arising from workers' body size, workstation design, ergonomy of tools, protective equipment, and so on.

The same applies for ailments listed in Annex II of the European Schedule, shown in Figure 2.2, because no reference exists for occupational diseases of specific interest to female workers.

The approach of the International Labour Organisation (ILO) concerning similar issues should be mentioned at this point. There is also no specific reference to women workers' health issues in regard to recognized occupational hazards and diseases within the "R194 List of Occupational Diseases Recommendation" (International Labour Organization, 2002).

It has to be stressed, however, that the ILO has raised the issue of occupationally induced mental disorders, such as depression and post-traumatic stress disorder, for possible inclusion in the list of occupational diseases (MEULOD/2005/10, 2005) for the first time—two problems that women might face more frequently than men. Specific reference was also made to mobbing and harassment at work as a potential source of mental ill-health of employees that needs additional consideration in the future. The European Schedule of Occupational Diseases does not yet consider mobbing and harassment at the workplace (which predominantly affect women employees) as occupational hazards.

Conclusion

Reviewing the existing legal context regarding OSH and health promotion interventions for working women, two main conclusions have been reached:

1. There is *no specific legal provision* to mandate the implementation of health promotion programs that address risk factors or health determinants not directly related to working environmental conditions for employers and management. The current context only refers to employer's obligations towards the promotion of employee's health in a generic and indirect way, through a number of OSH directives (e.g.,**89/391/EEC**). These, in turn, communicate available practices and measures for the safeguarding of employee's health and safety in a non-exhaustive way, which may, however, provide an effective legislative tool for health professionals in this area.

   Example

   > The prevention of musculoskeletal disorders among female workers is a concern for both OSH and WHP interventions. Musculoskeletal problems like lower-back pain, carpal tunnel syndrome, osteoarthritis and osteoporosis may affect the occupational activity of female workers (job performance, ability to work), on the one hand, or be induced or aggravated as a result of certain work-related factors (poor ergonomics, manual handling, repetitive strain, slippery floors, etc.) on the other.
   >
   > The current legal context does not dictate specific health promotion activities, but introduces certain preventive practices (e.g., use of lifting devices, ergonomic design of workplaces and tools, training of workers on safe lifting techniques) providing the regulatory environment (at the company policy level) for the practical implementation of health promotion programs regarding the prevention of musculoskeletal disorders.
   >
   > It should be stressed, though, that such disorders could be induced or aggravated by more general life conditions or practices of women, such as domestic work (Strazdins & Bammer 2004), inadequate leisure time, and lack of exercise, and therefore should not be attributed in a strict sense to working conditions.

> The role of WHP professionals in this case, is not to monitor the application of EU legislation, but rather to communicate the rationale and scopes of these guidelines (regardless of their obligatory character) to the company's management to ensure their maximum cooperation and commitment towards the objectives of the prevention program.

2. There is *no specific consideration for the individual needs of female employees* in any of the existing EU directives referring to OSH issues. All related legislation has been based on the *principle of equal treatment of men and women* regarding their employment status and working conditions, as dictated by Council Directive 76/207/EEC. The only exception to this gender-neutral approach has been Council Directive 92/85/EEC, which imposes protective measures for pregnant women and women who are breastfeeding. This example of legislative *partiality* for female workers, even though it is both ethically and scientifically justifiable in this specific case (protection of the fetus *in utero* from environmental exposures has been the legislator's major concern), brings focus to a major issue for discussion regarding future trends in current EU policies.

Considering the existing differences between men and women with a number of health issues, there is disagreement among stakeholders on whether the European OSH legislation should include further provisions focusing specifically on female employees, or not.

It is rather doubtful that an *overprotective* legal context in the form of directives designating specific obligations for employers for the specific health promotion of working women would be in the best interest of the employees themselves.

It is most likely that such arrangements and regulations would induce the preferred employment of men in certain professions and the reduction of female employees in occupational sectors where they are already underrepresented. Furthermore, women themselves may object to the implementation of *protective* policies jeopardizing their right to equal access to employment (professions or tasks considered hazardous for female workers) or to equal payment (e.g., exclusion of women employees from *more difficult* tasks with higher salaries). Two very instructive examples of legal cases dealing with gender-related OSH policies, and a case study presenting a European company's policy for the protection of pregnant workers, are offered in Appendix I and Appendix II, respectively.

Appendix I

Legal Case: Example I

> In 1991, the United States Supreme Court (Case 89-1215) commented (in an unanimous 9-0 decision) that the policy of a battery manufacturing firm that excluded women of reproductive age (apart from those who were infertile according to medical documentation) from particular tasks that involved exposure to lead,

on the basis of the potential detrimental effect of metal to the developing fetus, contravened the principle of equal rights of men and women workers (Cornell Law School).

After 1982, Johnson Controls Inc. had implemented an exclusion policy for all women "capable of bearing children" from jobs involving exposure in any way to lead (an ingredient of batteries). This company regulation was induced after the detection of a number of cases of women employees who had conceived while having blood concentrations of lead that exceeded the specifications of the Occupational Health and Safety Administration (OSHA).

The court held the company responsible for discrimination based on sex, because:

a. The exclusion policy did not apply for men employees as well, despite the existing scientific evidence of potential hazardous effects of lead to the male reproductive system.

b. Women employees' ability to perform their tasks (Bona Fide Occupational Qualification standard), which would be the only legitimate cause for such an exclusion policy, was not affected by maternity issues.

The Supreme Court's decision finally mandated the abolishment of the specific policy by Johnson Controls as a violation of the Pregnancy Discrimination Act (PDA).

Legal Case: Example II

On July 25th 1991, the European Court pronounced judgment in favor of Alfred Stoeckel (European Court reports 1991 Page I-04047) concerning the employment of women workers in night work.

Mr. Stoeckel was an executive of the company Suma SA, who was prosecuted by the local Tribunal of the Police (Illkirch) in 1988 (26/10) after employing 77 women employees on night shifts contrary to the national legislation and (specifically) Article L 213-1 of the French Labor Code.

To avoid downsizing the company (this option included the layoff of 200 employees in their factory in Obenheim) as a result of the economic recession and foreign competition, the management of Suma SA made an agreement with trade unions to adopt an alternative employment schedule. This included a continuous shift-work system for all employees to contain the economic loss of the company, which involved night work as well. Considering the fact that women employees were equally capable of performing these tasks, both parties (management and trade unionists) agreed that men and women should be given equal opportunities to ensure their post by participating in the new system, hence employing both male and female workers in night work.

Article L.213-1 of the French Labor Code (till then) banned the employment of women in industry night work (between 22:00 and 05:00) with certain exemptions (e.g., technical or managerial positions). The European Court resolved that this ban contravened the "principle of equal treatment of men and women as regards access to employment, vocational training and promotion, and working conditions" provided by Council Directive 76/207/EEC. Given that European directives prevail over all national legislation, the European Court's decision over the Stoeckel case invalidated the provisions of French Labor Code concerning the exclusion of women from night work.

In 1994, the European Commission proceeded against France (European Court Reports 1997, page I-01489) as well as other member countries of the European Union (Belgium, Greece, Portugal, and Italy), on the basis of their failure to harmonize their national legal context regarding exclusion of women from night work with existing European Directives. Such bans—apart from conflicting with the gender-neutral approach applied within the EU in occupational health and safety issues—restricted women's opportunities for employment in sectors where night work was a common practice.

Most of these countries finally incorporated the directives in their national legislation, with the exception of France (Case C-197/96) and Italy (European Court Reports 1997, page I-06869), where further measures for noncompliance with the dictates of the Commission of European Communities were imposed. Moreover, the Commission asked the European Court of Justice to impose a financial penalty of 142.425 € / day to France (European Commission) for nonimplementation of the Court's judgement on women's night work.

Appendix II

Case Study: Company Policies and Protection of OSH of Pregnant Workers

T. Brand,[1,2] T. Smid,[3] N.P. Wildenborg, and H. Hlobil[1]

[1] Occupational physician KLM Health Services at Schiphol Airport, The Netherlands

[2] Netherlands Centre for Occupational Diseases, Academic Medical Centre, University of Amsterdam

[3] Occupational hygienist KLM Health Services and Professor in Working Conditions at the Free University Medical Centre, Amsterdam

Cabin Attendants and Pregnancy

Recently, new insights regarding the negative effect of certain working conditions on pregnancy have emerged. A major airline company employing 10.000 cabin attendants asked its occupational health service to conduct an analysis of the presence of these risk factors in the work of cabin attendants. The ultimate goal was to provide advice on safe working conditions for pregnant cabin attendants.

Each year, approximately 600 cabin attendants of this airline company report to be pregnant. Until 2007, cabin attendants had been allowed to continue their work on the plane during the first 26 weeks of their pregnancy. During this period, approximately 69 percent chose to continue flying, 26 percent chose a job accommodation and stayed on the ground, and the remaining 4-5 percent chose unpaid leave. This policy contrasted with most other large airline companies, where cabin attendants were not permitted to continue flying duties when they reported to be pregnant.

Recently, the risks were reassessed by reviewing the relevant literature. It is clear that cabin attendants are at higher risk of negative pregnancy outcomes, such as preterm birth or low birth weight, than the general population. This is due to shift work, time shifts, high stress levels, risk of injury due to turbulence, and increased risks of infection. From the literature, it is not clear whether the physical workload of cabin attendants is also too high. No relevant risks were described for cosmic radiation, low air pressure, noise, vibrations, or climate conditions at the destinations.

Next, the workload was compared with health and safety legislation. For most of the risk factors, the policy of the airline was in line with the legislation because cabin attendants were allowed to choose to continue their work during the first 26 weeks of their pregnancy or to stop flying when they become pregnant. The total dose of cosmic radiation is kept well below the norm (<1 mSv additional radiation during pregnancy) by restricting the airtime of pregnant employees to a maximum of 200 hours during their pregnancy. A turbulence incident during the first 26 weeks of pregnancy may have a negative effect on pregnancy outcome, as well as on flight safety. A few years ago, guidelines limiting physical workload were incorporated into the legislation. During pregnancy, for example, cabin attendants should not lift loads totaling more than 10 kg, and once they are 20 weeks along in their pregnancy, they are advised not to lift weights heavier than 5 kg more than 10 times per day. From a comparison of the workload with the current legislation, it is likely that the physical workload of cabin attendants exceeds the limits and may have negative effects on their pregnancy outcome.

In conclusion, turbulence can not be prevented, and may have negative effects on flight safety and pregnancy outcome. Secondly, it is likely that the physical workload of pregnant cabin attendants exceeds the limits mentioned in the legislation. Restricting these risks during flights as well as during their stays abroad—although theoretically possible—was considered not feasible for airline operations. Therefore, the occupational health service advised that cabin attendants should stop flying when they report to be pregnant to prevent negative pregnancy outcomes.

This resulted in the decision at this airline that, from Jan 1st, 2007 onward, cabin attendants are no longer considered fit for flying duty once they have reported to be pregnant to prevent negative pregnancy outcomes.

References

COM (2002) 118 final. COMMUNICATION FROM THE COMMISSION: Adapting to change in work and society: a new Community strategy on health and safety at work 2002—2006

Cornell Law School. Supreme Court collection: Syllabus, INTERNATIONAL UNION, UNITED AUTOMOBILE,AEROSPACE & AGRICULTURAL IMPLEMENTWORKERS OF AMERICA, UAW, et al. v. JOHNSON CONTROLS, INC. certiorari to the United States Court of Appeals for the Seventh Circuit No. 89-1215. Argued October 10, 1990 – Decided March 20, 1991. Retrieved 28/02/2007, from http://www.law.cornell.edu/supct/html/89-1215.ZS.html

European Agency for Safety and Health at Work (2007). Introduction to the Agency. Retrieved 09/01/2007, http://osha.europa.eu

European Commission. The Commission asks the European Court of Justice to impose a daily fine of 142.425 euros on France for non-implementation of an earlier judgment on nightwork by women (electronic version). Retrieved 14/02/2007 from http://ec.europa.eu/employment_social/equ_opp/news/infring_en.htm

European Commission (2007). Legislation - Directives by theme. *Employment, Social Affairs & Equal Opportunities: Health and Safety at Work* Retrieved 07/03/2007, http://ec.europa.eu/employment_social/health_safety/legislation3_en.htm

European Court Reports (1991) Judgment of the Court of 25 July 1991. Criminal proceedings against Alfred Stoeckel. Reference for a preliminary ruling: Tribunal de police d'Illkirch, France. Equal treatment for men and women - Legislation prohibiting nightwork by women - Case C-345/89, page I-04047

European Court Reports (1997) Judgment of the Court (Fifth Chamber) of 13 March 1997 Commission of the European Communities v French Republic. Failure of a Member State to fulfil its obligations. Equal treatment for men and women. Prohibition of nightwork. Case C-197/96, page I-01489

European Court Reports (1997) Judgment of the Court (Fifth Chamber) of 4 December 1997. Commission of the European Communities v Italian Republic. Failure of a Member State to fulfil its obligations. Equal treatment for men and women. Prohibition of nightwork. Case C-207/96, page I-06869

Han DH (2000) Fit factors for quarter masks and facial size categories. *Ann Occup Hyg*(44), 227–234

International Labour Organization (2002) R194 List of Occupational Diseases Recommendation, (electronic version). Retrieved 28/3/2007 from http://www.ilo.org/public/english/protection/safework/health/expmtg05/english/list_e.pdf

McDiarmid M, Oliver M, Ruser J, Gucer P (2000) Male and female rate differences in carpal tunnel syndrome injuries: personal attributes or job tasks? *Environ Res, 83*(1), 23–32

MEULOD/2005/10 (2005). INTERNATIONAL LABOUR ORGANIZATION: Report of Meeting of Experts on Updating the List of Occupational Diseases, Geneva13–20 December 2005 (electronic version) from http://www.ilo.org/public/english/standards/relm/gb/docs/gb295/pdf/meulod.pdf

Official Journal L 14 (1997) COUNCIL DIRECTIVE 97/81/EC of 15 December 1997 concerning the Framework Agreement on part-time work concluded by UNICE, CEEP, and the ETUC. 9–14

Official Journal L 23 (2000) DIRECTIVE 1999/92/EC OF THE EUROPEAN PARLIAMENT AND OF THE COUNCIL of 16 December 1999 on minimum requirements for improving the safety and health protection of workers potentially at risk from explosive atmospheres (15th individual Directive within the meaning of Article 16(1) of Directive 89/391/EEC). 57–64

Official Journal L 42 (2003) DIRECTIVE 2003/10/EC OF THE EUROPEAN PARLIAMENT AND OF THE COUNCIL of 6 February 2003 on the minimum health and safety requirements regarding the exposure of workers to the risks arising from physical agents (noise) (Seventeenth individual Directive within the meaning of Article 16(1) of Directive 89/391/EEC). 38–44

Official Journal L 049 (1992) 92/131/EEC: Commission Recommendation of 27 November 1991 on the protection of the dignity of women and men at work. 1–8

Official Journal L 53 (2003) COUNCIL RECOMMENDATION of 18 February 2003 concerning the improvement of the protection of the health and safety at work of self-employed workers (2003/134/EC). 45–46

Official Journal L 97 (2003) DIRECTIVE 2003/18/EC OF THE EUROPEAN PARLIAMENT AND OF THE COUNCIL of 27 March 2003 amending Council Directive 83/477/EEC on the protection of workers from the risks related to exposure to asbestos at work (Text with EEA relevance). 48–52

Official Journal L 113 (1992) Council Directive 92/29/EEC of 31 March 1992 on the minimum safety and health requirements for improved medical treatment on board vessels. 19–36

Official Journal L 114 (2006) DIRECTIVE 2006/25/EC OF THE EUROPEAN PARLIAMENT AND OF THE COUNCIL of 5 April 2006 on the minimum health and safety requirements regarding the exposure of workers to risks arising from physical agents (artificial optical radiation) (19th individual Directive within the meaning of Article 16(1) of Directive 89/391/EEC). 38–59

Official Journal L 131 (1998) COUNCIL DIRECTIVE 98/24/EC of 7 April 1998 on the protection of the health and safety of workers from the risks related to chemical agents at work (fourteenth individual Directive within the meaning of Article 16(1) of Directive 89/391/EEC). 11–23

Official Journal L 137 (1986) Council Directive 86/188/EEC of 12 May 1986 on the protection of workers from the risks related to exposure to noise at work. 28–34

Official Journal L 138 (1999) COUNCIL DIRECTIVE 1999/38/EC of April 1999 amending for the second time Directive 90/394/EEC on the protection of workers from the risks related to exposure to carcinogens at work and extending it to mutagens 66–69

Official Journal L 142 (2000) COMMISSION DIRECTIVE 2000/39/EC of 8 June 2000 establishing a first list of indicative occupational exposure limit values in implementation of Council Directive 98/24/EC on the protection of the health and safety of workers from the risks related to chemical agents at work (Text with EEA relevance). 47–50

Official Journal L 145 (1996) Council Directive 96/34/EC of 3 June 1996 on the framework agreement on parental leave concluded by UNICE, CEEP and the ETUC. 4–9

Official Journal L 156 (1990a) Council Directive 90/269/EEC of 29 May 1990 on the minimum health and safety requirements for the manual handling of loads where there is a risk particularly of back injury to workers (fourth individual Directive within the meaning of Article 16 (1) of Directive 89/391/EEC). 9–13

Official Journal L 156 (1990b) Council Directive 90/270/EEC of 29 May 1990 on the minimum safety and health requirements for work with display screen equipment (fifth individual Directive within the meaning of Article16 (1) of Directive 89/391/EEC). 14–18

Official Journal L 158 (2004) DIRECTIVE 2004/37/EC OF THE EUROPEAN PARLIAMENT AND OF THE COUNCIL of 29 April 2004 on the protection of workers from the risks related to exposure to carcinogens or mutagens at work (Sixth individual Directive within the meaning of Article 16(1) of Council Directive 89/391/EEC) (codified version) (Text with EEA relevance). 50–76

Official Journal L 159 (2004) DIRECTIVE 2004/40/EC OF THE EUROPEAN PARLIAMENT AND OF THE COUNCIL of 29 April 2004 on the minimum health and safety requirements regarding the exposure of workers to the risks arising from physical agents (electromagnetic fields) (18th individual Directive within the meaning of Article 16(1) of Directive 89/391/EEC). 1–26

Official Journal L 177 (1991) Commission Directive 91/322/EEC of 29 May 1991 on establishing indicative limit values by implementing Council Directive 80/1107/EEC on the protection of workers from the risks related to exposure to chemical, physical and biological agents at work. 22–24

Official Journal L 177 (2002) DIRECTIVE 2002/44/EC OF THE EUROPEAN PARLIAMENT AND OF THE COUNCIL of 25 June 2002 on the minimum health and safety requirements regarding the exposure of workers to the risks arising from physical agents (vibration) (sixteenth individual Directive within the meaning of Article 16(1) of Directive 89/391/EEC). 13–19

Official Journal L 179 (1997) Council Directive 97/42/EC of 27 June 1997 amending for the first time Directive 90/394/EEC on the protection of workers from the risks related to exposure to carcinogens at work (Sixth individual Directive within the meaning of Article 16 (1) of Directive 89/391/EEC). 4–6

Official Journal L 183 (1989) Council Directive 89/391/EEC of 12 June 1989 on the introduction of measures to encourage improvements in the safety and health of workers at work. 1–8

Official Journal L 195 (2001) DIRECTIVE 2001/45/EC OF THE EUROPEAN PARLIAMENT AND OF THE COUNCIL of 27 June 2001 amending Council Directive 89/655/EEC concerning the minimum safety and health requirements for the use of work equipment by workers at work (second individual Directive within the meaning of Article 16(1) of Directive 89/391/EEC) (Text with EEA relevance). 46–49

Official Journal L 196 (1990) Council Directive 90/394/EEC of 28 June 1990 on the protection of workers from the risks related to exposure to carcinogens at work (Sixth individual Directive within the meaning of Article 16 (1) of Directive 89/391/EEC). 1–7

Official Journal L 238 (2003) COMMISSION RECOMMENDATION of 19 September 2003 concerning the European schedule of occupational diseases (notified under document number C(2003) 3297) (Text with EEA relevance) (2003/670/EC). 28–34

Official Journal L 245 (1992a) Council Directive 92/57/EEC of 24 June 1992 on the implementation of minimum safety and health requirements at temporary or mobile construction sites (eighth individual Directive within the meaning of Article 16 (1) of Directive 89/391/EEC). 6–22

Official Journal L 245 (1992b) Council Directive 92/58/EEC of 24 June 1992 on the minimum requirements for the provision of safety and/or health signs at work (ninth individual Directive within the meaning of Article 16 (1) of Directive 89/391/EEC). 23–42

Official Journal L 262 (2000) DIRECTIVE 2000/54/EC OF THE EUROPEAN PARLIAMENT AND OF THE COUNCIL of 18 September2000 on the protection of workers from risks related to exposure to biological agents at work (seventh individual directive within the meaning of Article 16(1) of Directive 89/391/EEC). 21–45

Official Journal L 299 (2003) DIRECTIVE 2003/88/EC OF THE EUROPEAN PARLIAMENT AND OF THE COUNCIL of 4 November 2003 concerning certain aspects of the organisation of working time. 9–19

Official Journal L 307 (1993) Council Directive 93/104/EC of 23 November 1993 concerning certain aspects of the organization of working time. 18–24

Official Journal L 335 (1995) Council Directive 95/63/EC of 5 December 1995 amending Directive 89/655/EEC concerning the minimum safety and health requirements for the use of work equipment by workers at work (second individual Directive within the meaning of Article 16 (1) of Directive 89/391/EEC). 28–36

Official Journal L 348 (1992a) Council Directive 92/85/EEC of 19 October 1992 on the introduction of measures to encourage improvements in the safety and health at work of pregnant workers and workers who have recently given birth or are breastfeeding (tenth individual Directive within the meaning of Article 16 (1) of Directive 89/391/EEC). 1–8

Official Journal L 348 (1992b) Council Directive 92/91/EEC of 3 November 1992 concerning the minimum requirements for improving the safety and health protection of workers in the mineral- extracting industries through drilling (eleventh individual Directive within the meaning of Article 16 (1) of Directive 89/391/EEC). 9–24

Official Journal L 393 (1989a) Council Directive 89/654/EEC of 30 November 1989 concerning the minimum safety and health requirements for the workplace (first individual directive within the meaning of Article 16 (1) of Directive 89/391/EEC). 1–12

Official Journal L 393 (1989b) Council Directive 89/655/EEC of 30 November 1989 concerning the minimum safety and health requirements for the use of work equipment by workers at work (second individual Directive within the meaning of Article 16 (1) of Directive 89/391/EEC). 13–17

Official Journal L 393 (1989c) Council Directive 89/656/EEC of 30 November 1989 on the minimum health and safety requirements for the use by workers of personal protective equipment at the workplace (third individual directive within the meaning of Article 16 (1) of Directive 89/391/EEC). 18–28

Official Journal L 404 (1992) Council Directive 92/104/EEC of 3 December 1992 on the minimum requirements for improving the safety and health protection of workers in surface and underground mineral-extracting industries (twelfth individual Directive within the meaning of Article 16 (1) of Directive 89/391/EEC). 10–25

Strazdins L, Bammer G (2004) Women, work and musculoskeletal health. *Soc Sci Med, 58*(6), 997–1005

PART II
SPECIFIC HEALTH TOPICS

Chapter 3
Workplace Health Promotion Interventions Concerning Women Workers' Occupational Hazards

Ioannis Polychronakis, Elena Riza, Pania Karnaki and Athena Linos

Introduction

In the European labor market, women today constitute an increasing part of the working population, equaling about 42 percent of the European workforce (European Agency for Safety and Health at Work 2003a) as a result of their dynamic entrance in the labor market during the last few decades. While women have occupied posts even in professions that so far have been considered as "traditionally male," the European labor market retains a high degree of segregation regarding women's participation rates in certain occupational sectors (European Agency for Safety and Health at Work 2003a; 2005).

The European Union (EU) has so far applied a *gender-neutral* approach (European Agency for Safety and Health at Work 2003a; 2005) to policies and legislation concerning Occupational Safety and Health (OSH) to comply with World Health Organization (WHO) guidelines for equality in health standards and access to health service. However, this approach does not seem to suffice for effectively meeting gender-specific issues of occupational hygiene and safety that have emerged concerning female workers in particular.

The female working population carries certain characteristics that have to be taken into consideration through the process of design and implementation of OSH policies, because their interaction with the occupational environment may produce additional hazardous effects for women employees:

Women at work: Points to consider

The Double Role of Female Workers

Women's workday concerns arising from their roles as mothers, spouses, or carers for the elderly, add an extra load on the mental and physical fatigue they sustain in their workplace (Artazcoz et al. 2004; Artazcoz, Borrell & Benach 2001). Everyday household tasks amount to hours of unpaid overtime on top of the 8-hour working day, increasing their total physical and psychological strain. As a consequence,

A. Linos, W. Kirch (eds), *Promoting Health for Working Women.*
© Springer 2008

women workers are more easily affected by *burnout effect* or suffer more frequently from work-related stress than their male colleagues, who continue to participate significantly less than women in house tasks.

Task Design

Working conditions in terms of ergonomics, working pace, managing heavy work-loads, and using tools or personal protective equipment (PPE) (Tapp 2003; Murphy, Patton, Mello, Bidwell, & Harp 2001) are often designed according to the size and the physical strength of an average male worker.

This is a consequence of the fact that many occupational sectors were, until recently, almost exclusively staffed by men, and even today employ an overwhelming majority of male workers. Despite the increase in the participation of female workers in many professional fields, the high cost of adequate interventions still constitutes a forceful barrier to adjusting the modern workplace to female employee's needs for health and safety.

Female Reproductive Health

Because women of child-bearing age constitute a significant part of the female workforce, the protection of women's reproductive health is an issue of great concern for EU policymakers, in terms of legislation. This applies to factors and working conditions that both directly and indirectly influence the female reproductive system, including fertility (biological, physical, or chemical hazards-e.g., endocrine disruptors that affect women's ability to conceive), pregnancy (detrimental factors for the foetus during intrauterine development), and lactation. One also has to underline the fact that pregnant women are in need of specially designed ergonomic work-places (Niedhammer, Saurel-Cubizolles, Piciotti & Bonenfant 2000), that consider changing physical and biological conditions and needs throughout the gestation and post-partum period.

Physical Strength

Biological predisposition determines that women employees have reduced physical strength in comparison with their male colleagues (Hooftman, van der Beek, Bongers, & van Mechelen 2005). This fact creates a comparatively higher burden for female workers who perform the same tasks as men, and creates a greater risk for musculoskeletal strain. Furthermore, women's reduced average muscle force places them in an unfavorable position in cases of bullying and physical violence at their workplace, both from co-workers or the public (e.g., psychiatric ward nurses).

Male Predominance in the Workplace

Women workers are still a minority group in certain professional fields (e.g., construction, mineral extraction, heavy industry), and in most cases they remain in lower managerial positions in comparison with men. Under these circumstances, women employees have limited control over administrative decisions (European Agency for Safety and Health at Work 2005) concerning occupational health and safety, and often lack access to the appropriate communication channels to report cases of bullying, mobbing, or even sexual harassment-especially when superiors are involved.

Immigrant Workers

In certain areas of industrial production (e.g., the textile industry), the female working population consists predominantly of immigrant workers with poor literacy skills, or difficulty communicating. This language barrier may, in some situations, cause work-related accidents, as well as expose workers to occupational hazards due to misconception or ignorance of safety instructions or warning labels and signs.

Part-time Employment

Women in Europe present higher percentages of part-time employment than men, as shown in Figures 3.1 and 3.2.

In many occupational sectors (e.g., cleaning industry, cashiers), the overwhelming majority of women work part time. In addition, female employees show a higher turnover rate during their career and seem to spend shorter periods, on average, in the same position (McDiarmid & Gucer 2001). Because of this effect, women's occupational diseases are, in many cases, significantly underreported, introducing a systematic bias in many studies on occupational hazards and creating the misperception that female workers generally occupy *safer* jobs. To make matters even worse, women in this kind of unstable employment pattern have, in most cases, only limited access to occupational health services and workplace health promotion activities, even though they constitute a high-priority group for similar interventions.

It should be underlined, however, that under no circumstance does this gender-specific approach lead to the false conclusion that women workers constitute a

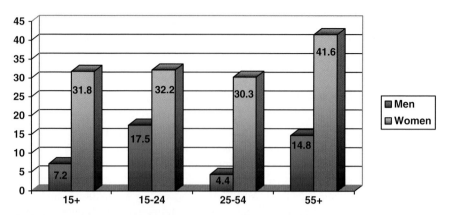

Fig. 3.1 Part-time employment as a percentage (%) of the working population of men and women for different age groups in EU 25 (Romans & Hardarson 2006)

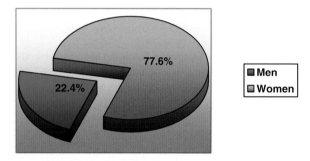

Fig. 3.2 Percentage of men and women employees working part-time in EU 25 (Total: 36.2 million employees/Source: EUROSTAT) (Jouhette & Romans 2006)

high-risk group requiring preferential treatment over issues of occupational safety and health in comparison to male workers. Such a misinterpretation could cause unacceptable discrimination against women and, in some cases, their exclusion from occupational sectors where female workers have for a long time now proven their worthiness as employees.

Occupational hazards and gender differences— The epidemiological evidence

Even though available research data in the literature may suggest that certain traits or characteristics connected with gender could possibly influence the occupational risk of female employees, they fail to identify occupational hazards that are *selectively* or *exclusively* harmful to women.

At this point, it is useful to categorize all gender-related parameters that have been identified as distinguishing occupational health and safety issues between male and female workers. According to previous studies, three fields of possible gender influence (Kennedy & Koehoorn 2003) on estimated occupational risk can be identified.

Difference in the Source of Occupational Hazards

Workforce Segregation

Because of job and task segregation observed among the European workforce, OSH studies based on occupational categorization alone have been insufficient in assessing potential health risks for women, because their tasks may vary significantly from men's even if they carry the same professional title (Östlin 2000). Women follow different time patterns of exposure through part-time or shift work, and usually carry out tasks requiring more precise, repetitive movements than male workers (Hooftman et al. 2005; Stellman 2000).

Gender Characteristics Affecting the Exposure to Hazardous Factors and its Impact on Working Population

Differences in Exposure

- Female workers have smaller (on average) body dimensions (Hooftman et al. 2005), which differentiates their occupational exposure:
  a. In professions involving manual handling, greater physical workload may be required by women to perform the same tasks as men.
  b. In cases of chemical exposure through the skin, the female body provides smaller available surface for absorption.
  c. Protective equipment is often ineffective for women employees (protective clothing, gloves, masks, and respirators) (Han DH 2000). Protective equipment originally designed for male workers does not fit appropriately to the shape and size of the female body and does not fully prevent exposure to hazardous agents.

Biological Differences in Absorption-Metabolism

- Under normal conditions, women present lower alveolar ventilation rate and cardiac output (Brown, Shelley & Fisher 1998), which reduces the input rate of volatile chemicals into their body

- In the case of benzene (a proven carcinogen) and other volatile organic compounds (VOCs), it has been experimentally demonstrated that women present higher blood/air partition coefficients (Brown et al. 1998) (greater blood / air concentration fraction), increasing the amount of chemicals diffused from alveoli to the blood compartment
- Concerning the metabolism of chemical compounds, potential gender-related disparities in enzymic activity (Gandhi, Aweeka, Greenblatt & Blaschke 2004) (e.g., cytochromes P450, transporting enzymes) have been reported, although research results are contradictory
- In the case of exposure to metals, women appear to absorb greater amounts of cadmium through digestion, possibly due to a common absorption pathway for iron and cadmium (Vahter, Berglund, Åkesson & Lidén 2002) (especially for menstruating women with low body-iron storage)

Differences in Body Distribution-Retention of Chemicals

- Chemicals absorbed into the bodies of women workers are distributed in a relatively smaller body mass than men, because their body mass index (BMI) is lower (Gandhi et al. 2004). As a further consequence:

  a. Women present a relatively higher organ blood flow, which increases the rate at which chemical substances circulating in blood compartment are delivered to the tissues.

  b. Women's renal clearance (Gandhi et al. 2004) (a parameter that is directly related to body weight) is slower in comparison with men's, and therefore their capacity to excrete toxic compounds, as well as their metabolites, through daily production of urine is low.

- Bodily distribution of chemicals in women also differs in regard to their concentration in plasma. Experiments on gender influence on the distribution of certain drugs, indicate that (Gandhi et al. 2004):

  a. Plasma volume is generally lower in females (the same total-body chemical burden may produce more toxic plasma concentrations in women).

  a. The concentration of certain binding proteins for drug metabolites or other chemicals in plasma depends heavily on hormonal status—especially estrogens (e.g., pregnancy, menstrual phase, and menopause).

- The female body carries a greater proportion of adipose tissue than that of males (Brown et al. 1998; Gandhi et al. 2004), and as a result it demonstrates a different pharmacokinetic response to lipophilic metabolites (e.g., prolonged retain and increased metabolism of benzene).
- In professions involving exposure to inorganic lead, blood concentrations do not provide a reliable criterion of chronic exposure in the case of female employees. As the metal gradually accumulates in the bone tissue, demineralization of women's skeleton during periods of increased bone turnover (as in pregnancy

or menopause) releases significant quantities of lead into their bloodstream (Vahter M et al. 2002).

Modifying Factors (Nonoccupational)

- Women present different social and dietary habits, such as smoking (e.g., cadmium absorption) (Vahter M et al. 2002) and alcohol or coffee consumption (McGovern 2003), which may act as modifiers to environmental exposures
- The use of chemical substances for household tasks (e.g., cleaning products), hobbies (e.g., fertilizers in gardening), or other activities involving application of potentially harmful agents (including cosmetics and artificial hair dyes) may subject women to further exposure outside their daily work hours
- Wearing jewelery is an additional nonoccupational source of skin exposure to metals for women (e.g., nickel) (Vahter M et al. 2002), increasing the burden of metal-induced occupational dermatitis for women employees
- Female employees in occupations involving manual tasks may also have to sustain additional workloads arising from family demands, especially in large families with children under 15 years old, or elderly persons over 65 years old (Artazcoz et al. 2001), which may contribute to producing symptoms of physical fatigue or musculoskeletal strain.
- Increased family demands of female workers, combined with strenuous job tasks may also have a serious impact on women's mental health (disturbed work-life balance, inadequate leisure time, lack of personal life) (Artazcoz et al. 2001)

Differences in Response

- Besides the immediate toxic effects of certain metals such as cadmium on humans (affecting both men and women), there is ongoing research on possible estrogen-like activity as well as its potential association with breast cancer through the activation of estrogenic receptors (Brama M et al. 2007)
- The manifestation of certain gender-specific cancers (e.g., breast cancer, which occurs almost exclusively in women) seems to involve among others, interaction between genetic expression (e.g. Atm tumor suppressors) (McGovern 2003) and environmental exposures
- The manifestation of autoimmune diseases (highly frequent among the female population) might be triggered or accelerated by substances or agents commonly used in certain professions (as in the case of lupus erythematosus and mercury exposure) (McGovern 2003)

Gender-related Methodological Implications in Assessment of Occupational Risk

- The varying composition of the labor force in different occupational sectors may have introduced a significant bias in epidemiological studies concerning occupational hazards for women:

a. Especially in the heavy industry and construction sectors, which employ almost exclusively male employees, the small minority of women who work alongside their male co-workers in various positions may have been overlooked (Niedhammer et al. 2000) in OSH studies, introducing *exclusion bias* (concerning women workers) because of the difficulties researchers had in finding women employees to participate in their studies.

b. On the other hand, women-focused OSH research has concentrated on the relatively small number of professions that master the majority of the female work-force. This fact probably explains the relatively large volume of studies on health-care professions (which are easily accessible to research), while women workers remain heavily underrepresented in OSH studies in other sectors (Messing & Stellman Mager 2006)

c. The majority of studies that focus exclusively on women workers deal with mental health issues and psychological parameters (Messing & Stellman Mager 2006; Niedhammer et al. 2000), while other work-related hazards such as exposure to chemicals, radioactive material, biological factors, electromagnetic fields, noise, or ergonomic factors are either indirectly examined by surveys on mixed working populations (where results are adjusted for gender), or even worse, by generalizing epidemiological evidence of OSH conducted among male employees.

- The segregation of tasks performed within the same job department or even under the same occupational title, may introduce *misclassification* bias when the influence of gender on occupational risk is under study. Any observed excess risk among women workers (e.g. musculoskeletal injuries) in comparison with men, should not necessarily be attributed to the role of gender, especially when such results are based only on job title (Hooftman et al. 2005). In such cases, further quantification of exposure (job exposure matrices, stratification according to tasks) is essential in determining whether the declination in study results arises from differences in performed tasks, or is truly related to gender—e.g., the excess risk for developing carpal tunnel syndrome in female workers seems to be eliminated in professions with strictly defined tasks (McDiarmid, Oliver, Ruser & Gucer 2000).

- Other forms of bias related to gender have been identified in the design of clinical, as well as OSH, studies:

a. An observer error due to adopting "male perspective and way of thinking"(Pinn 2003) in interpreting epidemiological data.

b. The "male norm" bias, arising from the use of male workers as *standard* (Pinn 2003), even for occupational health and safety issues where both sexes are affected (e.g., occupational cancer).

- There are indications that many of the existing studies on women workers—especially those concerning occupational musculoskeletal injury—may suffer from *perceptual bias* (the increased likelihood of employees to report injuries), or overrating the severity of related symptoms in questionnaire surveys according to the way they perceive their working environment or their degree of job satisfaction (Strazdins & Bammer 2004). Taking into account that female workers are generally occupied in less satisfactory, underpaid jobs with repetitive-monotonous tasks (Hooftman et al. 2005), over-reporting may contribute significantly to the excess risk found by many relevant studies for female employees.

- For the majority of female workers employed outside the *dangerous* industrial or construction sectors, there is little public awareness of the occupational exposures they sustain from their working environment because they usually do not face immediate danger of acute toxic effects or death. This fact may introduce a significant *recall bias* in relative studies because women workers are either unable to identify potentially harmful agents they have been exposed to, or tend to underestimate the extent of such exposures (e.g., unawareness of types of agents involved in their tasks that may constitute reproductive hazards) (Bauer, Romitti & Reynolds 1999).

- In mixed working populations, the *healthy worker effect* appears stronger for male than female employees (Lea et al. 1999), which is possibly attributable to the fact that men are hired to perform more physically demanding tasks than women and are therefore subjected to more rigorous selection during the hiring process.

Summary

The existing research evidence indicates a widely accepted false sense of safety in many of the professional sectors employing predominantly women, which has been recognized in earlier occupational health and safety studies in the United States as the so-called *Generally Recognized as Safe* (GRAS) status (McDiarmid & Gucer 2001) for most of the *female* professions. This is partially due to the fact that male workers, especially in heavy industry (construction workers, miners, welders, heavy machinery operators), are expected to face a higher number of severe or even fatal incidents or occupational diseases (Niedhammer et al. 2000), than those in the *safe* tertiary sector. GRAS reflects the commonly held belief that certain drugs and chemicals are *safe* if empirical knowledge obtained by their wide use over a period of years does not indicate they are detrimental to the population. As a consequence, this approach is also adopted in occupational sectors, where such materials have been widely used—the majority of which involve female-dominated professions where, until recently, OSH research has been considered nonessential.

Contemporary *evidence-based medicine*, however, requires more solid epidemiological data to conclude whether this group of occupations is as *safe* as is currently presumed. In addition, there is an increasing need to study the possible side-effects on health from exposure to thousands of chemical compounds present in jobs generally considered as nonhazardous (cleaning agents, drugs, cosmetics, food preservatives).

The latter translates as a need to expand the field of occupational health and safety research and place the so-called *female* professions under a more thorough and systematic investigation.

Female professions and their corresponding occupational hazards

According to official statistics of the European Agency for Safety and Health at Work, certain occupational sectors (health professionals, education workers) employ mostly females while the percentage of women in other professions (construction workers, heavy industry) (European Agency for Safety and Health at Work 2005) remains relatively low. Figure 3.3 presents the distribution of the female working population in different occupational activities, in the European Union.

For many of the professions where women are highly represented, research has explored specific occupational hazards. In Tables 3.1 through 3-13, reference

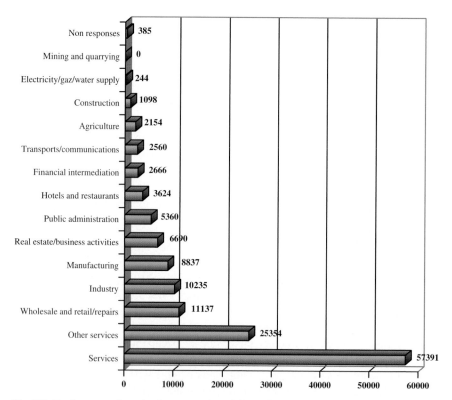

Fig. 3.3 Employment of women by economic activity in EU 15, in thousands of workers (Total: 70.165.000 employed women/ Source: EUROSTAT; Eurostat 2002)

Table 3.1 Health service sector workplace hazards

- **Violent behavior** (M. Denton, Zeytinoglu, & Webb, 2000; Kindy, Petersen, & Parkhurst, 2005; McPhaul & Lipscomb, 2004; Presley & Robinson, 2002) from patients or relatives
- **Sexual harassment** (Chuang & Lin, 2006; M. A. Denton, Zeytinoglu, & Davies, 2002)
- **Intense psychological stress** (Artazcoz Lazcano, Cruz i Cubells, Moncada i Lluis, & Sanchez Miguel, 1996; Stordeur, Vandenberghe, & D'Hoore, 1999) (decreased sense of control of work pace, low degree of job satisfaction)
- **Musculoskeletal problems** (Ando et al., 2000; Nathenson, 2004) (patient lifting(De Castro, 2004; De Castro, Hagan, & Nelson, 2006; Edlich et al., 2004), manual handling of heavy loads)
- **Exposure to ionizing radiation** (x-ray & computed tomography departments, nuclear laboratories, patients treated with radioactive drugs)
- **Reproductive hazards** (volatile compounds (Smith & Wang, 2006; Takigawa & Endo, 2006; Xelegati, Cruz Robazzi, Palucci Marziale, & Haas, 2006), anaesthetic gases, cytotoxic drugs(Krstev, Perunicic, & Vidakovic, 2003; Polovich, 2004; Tomioka & Kumagai, 2005; Undeger, Basaran, Kars, & Guc, 1999b; Weaver, McDiarmid, Guidera, Humphrey, & Schaefer, 1993), viruses(Ku, Liu, & Christian, 2005))
- **Infectious diseases** (Cesana, Arduca, Latocca, & Sirtori, 1998; Chandra & Gupta, 2001; Gurubacharya, Mathura, & Karki, 2003) (airborne, blood borne (Parra Madrid, Romero Saldana, Vaquero Abellan, Hita Fernandez, & Molina Recio, 2005; Porta, Handelman, & McGovern, 1999))
- **Dermatitis** (allergic, irritative)
- **Disturbance of the regular circadian -metabolic rhythm** (shift work)
- **Exposure to inhaled chemicals** (Cesana et al., 1998; Gimeno, Felknor, Burau, & Delclos, 2005) and micro particles(Biggins & Renfree, 2002; Lea et al., 1999)

is made to some of the sources of occupational risk by profession, according to existing literature. Tables 3.1 through 3-13 follow the codification of the European Agency for Safety and Health at Work concerning gender and occupational risk assessment (European Agency for Safety and Health at Work 2003b).

Health Service Sector

In the health services sector, women are employed in various positions (e.g., nurses, laboratory technicians, emergency room technicians) and face a multitude of occupational risks, some of which are cited in Table 3.1.

Educative—Pedagogic Sector

Women are also often employed in the education sector, especially in nursery and primary education, and therefore face diverse occupational risks, some of which are specific to the profession (e.g., voice disorders). Table 3.2 presents some of the related occupational hazards for this category of workers.

Cleaning Industry

While affected by many occupational hazards, some of which are cited in Table 3.3, women working in the cleaning industry are also disadvantaged due to the fact that

Table 3.2 Educative—Pedagogic sector workplace hazards

- **Exposure to infectious diseases** (Gavana, Tsoukana, Giannakopoulos, Smyrnakis, & Benos, 2005; Gyorkos et al., 2005; Nakazono, Nii-no, & Ishi, 1985; Skillen, Olson, & Gilbert, 2001; Valeur-Jensen et al., 1999)
- **Vascular problems** (Kovess-Masfety, Sevilla-Dedieu, Rios-Seidel, Nerriere, & Chee, 2006) **of the lower extremities** due to extended standing(Sandmark, Wiktorin, Hogstedt, Klenell-Hatschek, & Vingard, 1999) in upright position
- **Voice disorders** due to overuse of vocal chords (De Jong et al., 2006; Duff, Proctor, & Yairi, 2004; Kooijman et al., 2006; Kosztyla-Hojna, Rogowski, Ruczaj, Pepinski, & Lobaczuk-Sitnik, 2004; Roy, 1999; Sliwinska-Kowalska et al., 2006; Sulkowski & Kowalska, 2005; Thibeault, Merrill, Roy, Gray, & Smith, 2004; Williams, 2003)
- **Exposure to increased levels of noise** (Behar et al., 2004)
- **Musculoskeletal problems** (Fjellman-Wiklund, Brulin, & Sundelin, 2003; Sandmark, 2000; Yamamoto, Saeki, & Kurumatani, 2003) (handling and lifting small children in day care centres, physical education teachers, inadequate body posture)
- **Work-related stress** (Fjellman-Wiklund et al., 2003; Zidkova & Martinkova, 2003)
- Children's or adolescent's **violent behavior** (Lawrence & Green, 2005)

Table 3.3 Cleaning industry workers workplace hazards

- Exposure to **infectious agents**
- Dermatitis due to direct skin contact with **irritating substances** (Weisshaar et al., 2006)
- **Dermal infections** (staphylococcus, fungi) (McBryde, Bradley, Whitby, & McElwain, 2004)
- Inhalation of irritating **vapours and airborne micro-particles** containing dust or other allergens (J. J. Jaakkola & Jaakkola, 2006)
- **Musculoskeletal disorders** due to handling or lifting heavy objects, inadequate body posture (Balogh et al., 2004; Mondelli et al., 2006)
- **Fall injuries** (stairs, slippery floors) (Kines, Hannerz, Mikkelsen, & Tuchsen, 2007)
- **Workplace violence** (Chen & Skillen, 2006)
- **Sexual harassment**

Table 3.4 Food production industry workers workplace hazards

- Inhalation of **airborne allergens** emitted from food processing (e.g., artificial dyes, flour, animal proteins)
- **Dermal infections** (staphylococcus, b-haemolytic streptococcus, bacillus anthracis, fungi)
- **Dermatitis** (allergic or irritating) from skin contact to foods themselves or substances used for their processing (Jappe, Bonnekoh, Hausen, & Gollnick, 1999; Kanerva, Estlander, & Jolanki, 1996)
- Exposure to **zoonoses** (processing animal products)
- **Musculoskeletal disorders** (handling and lifting excessive loads, inappropriate body postures, poor ergonomic design of workstations, repetitive strain) (Chyuan, Du, Yeh, & Li, 2004)
- **Injuries** (falls due to slippery floors, burns, lacerations from knives or used tools) (Courtney et al., 2006)
- Exposure to **extreme temperatures** (cold in refrigerators, excessive heat in kitchens)

their occupation is often unregulated, and thus no occupational safety and health services are available to them.

Food Production Industry

The food production sector involves various types of work, from food preparation to packaging, storing, and more, involving mainly biological and chemical hazards due to immediate contact with food. Table 3.4 presents a non-exhaustive lists of related occupational hazards.

Hospitality Services Industry—Restaurant Workers

A large number of women are employed in the sector of hospitality services (e.g., waitresses, cooks, bar attendants) and are subject to a number of risks, some of which are listed in Table 3.5.

Textile Industry—Clothing Manufacturing

The textile sector is heavily industrialized, and women working in this sector face many and serious risks, some of which are cited in Table 3.6.

Laundry Workers

Laundry workers are also faced with heavy tasks such as long hours on their feet, exposure to extreme temperatures, and lifting heavy loads, as can be seen in Table 3.7.

Table 3.5 Hospitality services industry—restaurant workers' workplace hazards

- Exposure to **extreme temperature conditions** (excessive heat in cookers)
- **Musculoskeletal injury** due to handling or lifting heavy objects–repetitive movements–strenuous workload (Chyuan et al., 2004; Dempsey & Filiaggi, 2006)
- **Dermatitis** induced by skin contact with foods or cleaning agents (Jappe et al., 1999; Kanerva et al., 1996)
- **Dermal infections** (skin contact to infected food surfaces, development of fungal infections due to extended exposure to humidity)
- **Injuries** (falls due to slippery floors, falling objects, skin lacerations from sharp objects, burns from heat- emitting objects or appliances) (Courtney et al., 2006; Horwitz & McCall, 2004)
- **Inhalation of micro-particles** (food-cooking, passive smoking, poor ventilation) (Svendsen, Jensen, Sivertsen, & Sjaastad, 2002)
- Workplace **violence** (Graham, Bernards, Osgood, & Wells, 2006)
- **Sexual harassment**
- **Work-related stress** (low levels of job satisfaction, stressful working conditions)

Table 3.6 Textile industry-clothing manufacture workplace hazards

- Exposure to **increased levels of noise** (weaving machines) (Bedi, 2006; Cardoso, Oliveira, Silva, Aguas, & Pereira, 2006)
- Increased concentration of **fibres, micro-particles and organic solvents** (artificial dyes, chemicals used in textile processing) in workplace environment (Bakirci et al., 2006; Ghio et al., 2006)
- **Musculoskeletal injury** (poor ergonomic design (Choobineh, Lahmi, Hosseini, Shahnavaz, & Jazani, 2004) of the production line, repetitive movements (Bjorksten, Boquist, Talback, & Edling, 1996), lifting and handling heavy objects)
- **Visual fatigue**
- Injuries (entanglement in moving parts of equipment, skin lacerations by sharp objects)
- Intense work-related stress (strenuous workload, intense work pace in production lines, low level of job satisfaction)

Table 3.7 Laundry workers' workplace hazards

- Exposure to **infectious agents** (e.g. infectious biological material in hospital linen) (Keeffe, 2004)
- Exposure to **extreme heat** (in combination with high humidity) (Belinda Thielen, 2003; Brabant, 1992)
- **Musculoskeletal injury** (poor ergonomic design of equipment, repetitive muscle strain, handling and lifting heavy objects) (Nemecek & Buchberger, 1987)
- **Injuries** (e.g., slippery floors) (Kines et al., 2007)
- Exposure to **volatile cleaning chemical agents** (Belinda Thielen, 2003; Hruska, Furth, Seifer, Sharara, & Flaws, 2000) (e.g., tetrachlorethylene)

Ceramics Industry and Pottery

Ceramic and pottery workers face a series of specific occupational risks connected with the nature of their profession, as presented in Table 3.8.

Light Manufacturing

Light manufacturing includes many types of industries, employing mainly non-specialized workers and therefore involving diverse types of exposure. Table 3.9 presents some of the hazards involved in these occupational activities.

Table 3.8 Ceramics industry and pottery workers' workplace hazards

- Exposure to **inhaled lead dust, silica fibres and solvents** (poor ventilation design) (Plovets'ka, 2000a, 2000b)
- Exposure to **extreme heat and fumes** emitting from blast-furnaces (Dorevitch & Babin, 2001)
- **Musculoskeletal injury** due to poor ergonomic design, handling heavy loads, repetitive muscle strain, vibrations (Martinelli & Carri, 1996)
- **Stressful working conditions** – strenuous work pace in production lines

Table 3.9 Light manufacture workers' workplace hazards

- **Musculoskeletal injury** due to poor ergonomic design (equipment, tools and workstations that don't fit the physical dimensions of female workers), handling and lifting heavy loads, repetitive movements (Bjorksten et al., 1996; Roquelaure et al., 2002)
- **Visual fatigue** (Untimanon et al., 2006)
- **Exposure to chemical agents** (e.g., metals & solvents in electronic circuits manufacture, drug by-products in the pharmaceutical industry) (Clapp, 2006; LaDou, 2006)
- **Stressful working conditions** in production lines

Call Center and Computer Workstations

Call center work is a newly developed sector that employs mostly women who are faced with risks such as visual fatigue, musculoskeletal disorders, and other hazards as presented in Table 3.10.

Hairdressers and Beauticians

Hairdressing is a female-dominated sector that, until recently, has been regarded as a safe occupation. However, current literature associates this profession with various hazards, some of which are included in Table 3.11.

Office Employees

The tertiary sector—especially office workers—are faced with hazards arising mainly from poor ergonomic design and poor indoor air quality, as shown in Table 3.12.

Agriculture & Livestock-farming

Hazards in agriculture are linked mainly to a high risk of injuries and to the use of chemical substances such as pesticides, herbicides, and others, as shown in Table 3.13.

Table 3.10 Call center and computer workstation workers' workplace hazards

- **Musculoskeletal injury** from inadequate body postures during work, poor ergonomic design of workstations, repetitive movements (Hush, Maher, & Refshauge, 2006; Iwakiri et al., 2004)
- Hearing impairment induced by continuous **exposure to increased levels of noise**
- Dysphonia due to **overuse of vocal chords** (telephone operators) (Lehto, Alku, Backstrom, & Vilkman, 2005)
- **Visual fatigue** in computer screen users (poor ergonomic design, inadequate lighting) (Ustinaviciene & Januskevicius, 2006)
- **"Sick building syndrome"** (inadequate ventilation, high concentration of micro-particles) (Abbritti & Muzi, 2006; M. S. Jaakkola, Yang, Ieromnimon, & Jaakkola, 2007)
- **Sexual harassment** at the workplace
- **Job related stress** (strenuous working conditions, low job satisfaction)

Table 3.11 Hairdressers and beauticians' workplace hazards

- **Musculoskeletal injury** (Best et al., 2002) (inadequate body postures (Osteras, Ljunggren, Gould, Waersted, & Bo Veiersted, 2006), poor ergonomic design(Boyles, Yearout, & Rys, 2003))
- **Vascular problems of the lower extremities** due to prolonged standing in upright position
- **Dermal infections** (Ballas, Psarras, Rafailidis, Konstantinidis, & Sakadamis, 2006; Schroder, Merk, & Frank, 2006) (skin lacerations from scissors or other sharp tools (Moghadam, Mazloomy, & Ehrampoush, 2005), dermal fungi from continuous exposure to humidity)
- **Dermatitis** (Khrenova, John, Pfahlberg, Gefeller, & Uter, 2006; Perkins & Farrow, 2005) (irritating or allergic) (Cavallo et al., 2005; Doutre, 2005) induced by contact to cosmetics (Amado & Taylor, 2006; Iorizzo, Parente, Vincenzi, Pazzaglia, & Tosti, 2002; Katugampola et al., 2005; Sosted, Hesse, Menne, Andersen, & Johansen, 2005), artificial hair dyes (Belinda Thielen, 2003; Rastogi, Sosted, Johansen, Menne, & Bossi, 2006) or even protective gloves (Foti et al., 2005)
- **Allergic asthma** (Akpinar-Elci, Cimrin, & Elci, 2002; Allmers, Nickau, Skudlik, & John, 2005; Macchioni et al., 1999; Moscato et al., 2005) induced by exposure to volatile substances (Baur, 1999; Berges & Kleine, 2002; Gala Ortiz et al., 2001; Hoerauf, Funk, Harth, & Hobbhahn, 1997; Hollund & Moen, 1998; Labreche, Forest, Trottier, Lalonde, & Simard, 2003; Piipari & Keskinen, 2005) and particles (cosmetics, hair sprays(Albin et al., 2002; Montomoli, Cioni, Sisinni, Romeo, & Sartorelli, 2004), dryers
- **Job-related stress** (strenuous working conditions, low job satisfaction)

Table 3.12 Office employees' workplace hazards

- **Musculoskeletal injury** from inadequate body postures during work, poor ergonomic design of workstations, repetitive movements (Hush et al., 2006)
- **Inhalation of volatile chemical compounds and micro-particles** emitted form various office-work activities (computer's electronic circuits, photocopying equipment, cleaning agents, dust)
- **Poor air quality** (insufficient ventilation system, indoor plants) (Abbritti & Muzi, 2006; M. S. Jaakkola et al., 2007)
- **Visual fatigue** (extended use of VDUs , poor illumination)
- **Job related stress** (monotonous-repetitive work, low job satisfaction)
- **Violence** (verbal or physical abuse) at the workplace
- **Sexual harassment**

Table 3.13 Agriculture and livestock-farming workplace hazards

- **Injuries** (falls, accidents due to inappropriate use of equipment e.g. tractors or chainsaws, injuries from domestic animals) (Hard, Myers, & Gerberich, 2002; Pryor, Carruth, & LaCour, 2005)
- **Musculoskeletal injuries** (strenuous work, repetitive movements, handling heavy loads, poor design of equipment) (McCoy, Carruth, & Reed, 2002)
- Prolonged skin exposure to **solar radiation** (dermal cancers)
- Exposure to **noise** (McBride, Firth, & Herbison, 2003; Perry & May, 2005)
- Exposure to **zoonoses** due to close contact with animals or animal products (bacillus anthracis, mycobacterium, brucellosis, viral infections e.g. avian influenza)
- Exposure to **chemical compounds** during transportation, storage, mixing or application of fertilizers, pesticides or herbicides (Buranatrevedh & Roy, 2001; Garcia, 2003)
- **Exposure to allergens** through inhalation or direct skin contact (pollen, animal proteins, fungi) (Linaker & Smedley, 2002)
- **Exposure to natural phenomena** (extreme heat, frost, thunderstorms, floods)
- **Job related stress** (stressful working conditions, job insecurity, low income, low job satisfaction)
- **Violence at the workplace** (verbal or physical abuse)
- **Sexual harassment**

Workplace Health Promotion and Women's Occupational Hazards

The Case of Reproductive Health of Female Workers

This section will focus on how theories and models of health promotion can be put into practice for the design and implementation of workplace interventions concerning OSH issues targeted at female workers. The example that will be used is *work-related reproductive disorders.*

The specific health topic has been selected as an example for three primary reasons:

- Reproductive disorders have been associated with a wide range of occupational hazards (e.g. physical, chemical, biological agents)
- A large number of professions employing women involve exposure to hazards such as those mentioned in the above point
- Further research is needed on this topic because many of the *traditionally female* professions considered generally safe may involve unidentified risks for women's reproductive health

Identification of the Problem

Literature Search

Reproductive hazards constitute a field of increasing interest for occupational hygienists and health professionals across the world. There is little or no information at all about the possible effects on female reproductive health of the vast majority of chemical substances introduced by the thousands every year in industrial production (Lawson et al. 2006).

Even in cases of widely used chemicals, the existing literature of their possible detrimental effects on women's reproductive physiology is relatively poor. For most of the agents considered as hazardous for the reproductive system, their causal relationship to problems in human reproduction has not been adequately documented and gender differences in exposure or toxicity have not been thoroughly examined.

Because female workers constitute a nonhomogenous population of diverse occupational categories, various physical, chemical, and biological exposures are under examination concerning their potential risks on the reproductive health of women. A non exhaustive list of factors under investigation concerning their potential harmful effects on female reproductive health is presented in Table 3.14.

Table 3.14 Occupational hazards and potential effects on female reproductive system

Hazard	Reproductive Health Effects	High Risk Occupations
Chemical Hazards		
Smoking		
Active and passive smoking(60% of non smokers)(Hruska et al., 2000; Mlynarcikova, Fickova, & Scsukova, 2005)	• Infertility • Reduced fecundity	• All occupational categories (e.g. office workers)
Volatile pharmaceutical compounds		
Nitrous Oxide (anaesthetic gases)	• Reduced fecundity (Hruska et al., 2000) • Mutagenicity in experimental animals (Burm, 2003)	• Operating room personnel
Cytotoxic drugs (e.g., methotrexate) (Dranitsaris et al., 2005; Undeger, Basaran, Kars, & Guc, 1999a)	• Infertility • Fetal loss • Congenital defects, mutagenesis • Low birth weight	• Health care workers • Hospital cleaners • Pharmacists
Metals		
Lead and compounds (HAZ-MAP, 2006f)	• Spontaneous abortions • Premature birth • Developmental disorders	• Battery manufacturing industry workers • Ceramics industry workers • Semi-conductors manufacturing industry workers • Painters • Jewelry workers • Passive smokers
Cadmium and compounds (HAZ-MAP, 2006b)	• Increased fetal loss and congenital defects in experimental animals	• Battery manufacturing industry workers • Ceramics industry workers • Semi-conductors manufacturing industry workers • Painters • Jewelry workers • Passive smokers
Nickel and compounds (HAZ-MAP, 2006g)	• Congenital defects in highly exposed experimental animals	• Battery manufacturing industry workers • Ceramics industry workers • Semi-conductors manufacturing industry workers • Painters • Jewelry workers

Table 3.14 (continued)

Hazard	Reproductive Health Effects	High Risk Occupations
		• Oil refinery workers • Hair dressers • Passive smokers
Solvents Perchlorethylene (HAZ-MAP, 2006h; Hruska et al., 2000)	• Increased time to conception • Increased spontaneous abortion rates (HAZ-MAP, 2006h)	• Dry cleaning industry workers • Metal degreasing • Occupations exposed to glues and adhesives (HAZ-MAP, 2006h)
Toluene	• Reduced fecundity (Hruska et al., 2000) • Increased incident of spontaneous abortions (HAZ-MAP, 2006i)	• Printing industry workers • Semiconductor manufacturing (HAZ-MAP, 2006i)
Carbon disulfide CS_2	• Menstrual disorders • Increased incident of spontaneous abortions (HAZ-MAP, 2006c)	• Textile manufacturing industry workers (HAZ-MAP, 2006c) (Viscose- rayon)
Ethylene glycol ethers (HAZ-MAP, 2006e)	• Fetal loss • Increased risk for congenital defects	• Electronic industry workers • Lithography(after 1990 they are being replaced by PMGEA) (HAZ-MAP, 2006e)
Fumigants Ethylene oxide (HAZ-MAP, 2006d)	• Menstrual disorders (Makowiec-Dabrowska, Hanke, Sprusinska, Radwan-Wlodarczyk, & Koszada-Wlodarczyk, 2004) • Increased risk for spontaneous abortions (limited data)(congenital defects in experimental animals)	• Health care workers (equipment sterilization procedures) (HAZ-MAP, 2006d)
Plastic Monomers Beta- Chloroprene (HAZ-MAP, 2006a)	• Increased incident of spontaneous abortions	Synthetic rubber industry (neoprene)

Table 3.14 (continued)

Hazard	Reproductive Health Effects	High Risk Occupations
Pesticides (Hanke & Jurewicz, 2004)		
Dicamba	• Prolonged time to pregnancy • Spontaneous abortions	• Agriculture industry workers • Pesticide production workers
Gluposate	• Prolonged time to pregnancy • Spontaneous abortions • Congenital defects • Preterm delivery	• Agriculture industry workers • Pesticide production workers
Phenoxy herbicides	• Prolonged time to pregnancy • Spontaneous abortion	• Agriculture industry workers • Pesticide production workers
Triazines	• Spontaneous abortions • Preterm delivery	• Agriculture industry workers • Pesticide production workers
Organophosphate pesticides	• Infertility • Fetal loss • Preterm delivery	• Agriculture industry workers • Pesticide production workers
Perythroids	• Prolonged time to pregnancy • Low birth weight • Fetal loss	• Agriculture industry workers • Pesticide production workers
Mankozeb & Maneb	Congenital defects	Agriculture industry workersPesticide production workers
Physical Hazards		
Ionizing radiation	• Infertility • Foetal loss • Congenital defects-mutagenesis • Low birth weight • Developmental disorders	• Health care workers • Hospital cleaners
Strenuous labor (prolonged standing, handling heavy loads)	• Fetal loss • Premature birth	• Health care workers • Production line workers • Occupations that demand prolonged standing and manual handling

Table 3.14 (continued)

Hazard	Reproductive Health Effects	High Risk Occupations
Shift work (especially working at nights)	• Disturbance of menstrual circle	• Occupations that demand 24h rotating shifts (e.g. nurses, police women)
Biological Hazards		
Cytomegalovirus CMV	• Fetal loss • Congenital defects-developmental disorders • Low birth weight	• Health care personnel • Teachers-educative personnel • Nursery workers
Hepatitis B (Yavuz et al., 2005)	• Low birth weight • Congenital infection	• Health care workers • Sexual workers
HIV	• Low birth weight • Congenital infection	• Health care workers • Sexual workers
Rubella	• Fetal loss • Congenital defects • Low birth weight	• Health care personnel • Teachers-educative personnel • Nursery workers
Parvovirus B19	• Fetal loss	• Health care personnel • Teachers-educative personnel • Nursery workers
Varicella zoster virus VZV	• Congenital defects Low birth weight	• Health care personnel • Teachers-educative personnel • Nursery workers
Toxoplasmosis	• Fetal loss • Congenital defects-developmental disorders • Low birth weight	• Livestock-farming workers • Veterinarians

NOTE: Table adapted and modified from "The Effects of Workplace Hazards on Female Reproductive Health" DHHS (NIOSH) Publication No. 99-104.

Diagnostic Procedure

Using the PRECEDE-PROCEED Model

The PRECEDE-PROCEED model of planning will be used as a framework to guide the diagnostic phase of the suggested intervention (Gielen & McDonald 1997; Green & Kreuter 1991; Green, Kreuter, Deeds & Partridge 1980; National Cancer Institute 2005b; Ransdell. 2001). The outline of this theoretical model is presented in Figure 3.4.

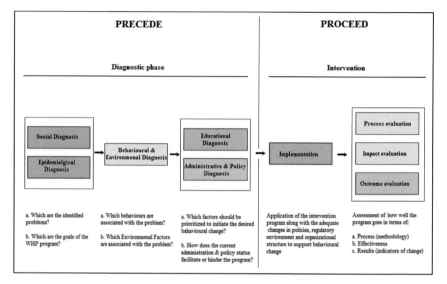

Fig. 3.4 The PRECEDE-PROCEED model

- PRECEDE provides the methodological framework for the design of tailored educational interventions targeting specific populations. It is based on the medical model, involving an initial diagnostic approach to the needs of a patient, before prescribing a specific treatment. As an analogy, PRECEDE constitutes a tool to design a specific educational plan, according to the identified needs of the target group.
- PROCEED has been an addition to the original model, to further include environmental determinants (e.g., policies, managerial and economic issues) that influence human attitudes towards specific health behaviors. This model follows a reverse course, towards the origin of certain health behaviors to target interventions for the causal factors themselves, rather than just the symptoms. The outline of the process that takes place in nine stages is presented in Figure 3.4.

For our example, only the diagnostic part of the model will be analyzed.

Social Diagnosis

Despite the fact that we have already chosen occupational reproductive hazards as our intervention subject in this case, the stage of social diagnosis is supposed to have taken place before making our choice.

For any workplace health promotion effort to be effective, the key issue must be tailored according to the needs of the predefined target population. Even though women's reproductive health may seem like a scientifically important field of intervention, our target group of women employees *may not* consider it to be a high-priority issue-either because they consider having more important health problems or because they are not adequately informed on the possible impact of similar disorders on their personal health status.

The main focus of health professionals at this stage is to investigate:

- The target group's perception of their quality of life
- The most important determinants of their quality of life (e.g., career, family, health)
- Their expectations and concerns about their health status
- Whether reproductive health issues are considered an important enough factor for women that an intervention through a WHP program is valuable

Epidemiological Diagnosis

The focus of health professionals during this phase is to identify—through analyzing epidemiological evidence—the impact of the specific problem on the predefined target group (e.g., female workers in a factory, women employed in a specific profession). Furthermore, this procedure aims at prioritizing the specific subgroups that face the highest risk of exposure to reproductive hazards and need more immediate preventive measures. This stage includes:

- Identification of work-related parameters, as well as individual behaviors that may influence the reproductive health status of women employees
- Evaluation of specific indicators of reproductive health disorders in our target population. Some of these indicators are listed in Table 3.15

One of the specific interests of health professionals at this stage is to locate groupings of reproductive disorder indicators in certain subgroups (specific job tasks, worksite-specific reproductive hazards) of the population, to prioritize them as intervention groups (e.g., focusing a WHP program for the prevention of reproductive disorders on oncology unit nurses in case they present higher incidence of congenital defects compared to the rest of health care personnel)

Table 3.15 Potential indicators of reproductive disorders (Lawson et al. 2006)

1. **Increased infertility rates** among women of a specific industry
2. A **prolonged conception period** among female workers
3. Frequent reports of **menstrual disorders** and early menopause by female employees in the company's medical files
4. **Male/female ratio of births**
5. Reported **pregnancy complications** among employed pregnant workers (e.g., diabetes, hypertension, pre-eclampsia, etc.)
6. Reduced (or increased) **average birth-weight** of infants
7. Increased rates of **pre-term deliveries** (and miscarriages)
8. Number of **sick-leave days** among pregnant employees (for problems related to pregnancy)
9. Increased rates of **congenital defects** among infants of female workers
10. Increased incidence of **neoplasms of reproductive organs** among employed women

Behavioural and Environmental Diagnosis

It is imperative during the initial design of a tailored WHP intervention program for the prevention of occupation-induced female reproductive disorders, to incorporate a set of behavioral and environmental change indicators that serve as general objectives for the program. WHP professionals, prior to the development of an intervention plan, should conduct behavioral and environmental diagnosis to identify existing key issues concerning OSH attitudes and beliefs and practices in the organization (employees, executives, and company administration) and the safety status of facilities, procedures, and equipment. These key issues may include (State of Alaska 2003):

- **Personal accountability**: This parameter is crucial for the success or failure of any prevention program, both on worksites and in the general population. It is important to adjust the program's aims and methods according to women's perceptions of its personal influence on their health status. Female employees should be able to recognize their personal responsibility and contribution to the effective implementation of the preventive measures and practices by the completion of the WHP intervention.
- **Attitude towards change**: A key component for the design of an effective intervention prevention program is taking into account the degree to which women agree with the proposed changes (safety behavior, practices, OSH regulatory environment), so that invention methods can be modified accordingly. At this stage, therefore, health professionals should evaluate the awareness status and the ability of female employees to adopt the desired safety practices introduced by the WHP program on both personal and collective levels to determine the kind of messages and strategies appropriate for the specific population.
- **Participation:** One of the primary targets of the WHP intervention is to achieve a high degree of participation in the program's activities, as it is one of the key elements that significantly influences results. It is important at this stage to recognize and alleviate barriers that are driving women to abstain from similar programs. Furthermore, there is a need to identify the subgroups of female workers where the focus of the intervention needs to be to promote their involvement.
- **Occupational hazard identification**: Apart from recognizing that female workers are at a high risk for reproductive disorders, the WHP program should also concentrate on specific protective measures and proposals for these groups of employees. It is essential, therefore, to identify and record existing working conditions of women in the specific organization in detail, to determine their possible detrimental effect on the reproductive physiology of those same women, and assess the existent OSH status of their job tasks. This process includes recording:

1. **Procedures** (production line, manual tasks, strenuous work pace, extreme climate conditions, emission of fumes/particles, and stressful conditions)
2. **Hazardous agents** (physical, chemical, and biological) involved in female workers' tasks or working environment
3. **Equipment used** in specific tasks (radiation sources, vibrating parts, electromagnetic fields)

4. **Existing protective measures** (ventilation systems, separate mixing chambers for chemicals, lifting devices for manual handling, radiation shields, PPE, rotation of night shift workers, etc.) for women employees
5. **Potential for OSH improvement** (substitution of procedures or agents, automatization of tasks, amelioration of working conditions, change of job post, or rotation of workers)

Education and Organizational Diagnosis

This part of the diagnostic process involves the identification of the educational needs of female employees, as well as the structural changes that are needed in the specific organization to effectively introduce the WHP interventions for the protection of women worker's reproductive health. This process will be used to shape our strategic approach towards the target population, through the analysis of determinants of compliance with safety practices at individual, collective, and organizational levels. Three categories of such factors may be identified—namely, *Predisposing*, *Enabling*, and *Reinforcing* factors, that will be further analyzed:

Predisposing Factors:

Health professionals may recognize multiple potential fields of intervention on which to focus the WHP program:

Individual Level—

- Lack of sensitization concerning female reproductive disorders because of limited access to information (limited media coverage, GRAS (McDiarmid & Gucer 2001) status of female employment, limited research on the specific topic)
- Low literacy among the population of female workers that causes difficulties in comprehending scientific literature on reproductive hazards
- Lack of adequate prevention skills (recognizing types of substances, interpretation of MSDS or safety labeling, use of PPE, existing best practices, emergency safety procedures)

Collective Level—

- Negative example of non-compliance with safety practices by peers (co-workers, supervisors)
- Widely accepted misbeliefs, and false sense of safety among female workers

Organizational Level—

- Lack of strict company policies and regulations on OSH practices for positions putting women at risk of exposure to reproductive hazards
- Inadequate surveillance of reproductive disorders for women employed in job tasks generally considered *safe*

Enabling Factors:

The WHP program may introduce certain interventions to promote the desirable change to compliance in OSH practices.

Individual Level—

- Personalized information on female reproductive system and occupational risks involved
- Health awareness building on reproductive health issues and their importance

Collective Level—

- Wide dissemination of existing scientific evidence on reproductive hazards for women employees (population awareness)
- Creation of peer support systems among groups of women workers to promote compliance with safety procedures

Organizational Level—

- Detailed recording of job tasks for female employees and identification of sources of exposures to known or potential reproductive hazards
- Introduction of specific safety guidelines and policies for the prevention of reproductive disorders
- Establishment of clear communication channels between employees and administration to report their concerns or personal experience on relative issues
- Improvement of the existing surveillance system for reporting suspicious cases among women workers

Reinforcing Factors

WHP program officials may utilize numerous tactics to support the desired prevention strategy at this field.

Individual Level—

- Provision of access to supplementary information resources on reproductive health issues and available prevention methods to the population of women employees
- Application of periodic follow-up sessions and use of frequent reminders (letters, telephone calls, e-mail messages) to retain an increased awareness level among female workers
- Dispensation of easily accessible screening services for exposure of employees to reproductive hazards

Collective Level—

- Building a support network for the compliance of individuals with occupational safety practices by appointing safety committees that include female workers at risk for reproductive hazards
- Organization of group discussions among workers of specific occupational categories to share common experiences and concerns on related issues
- Projection of specific employees as models of good conduct in OSH issues involving reproductive hazards prevention
- Presentation of statistics on results of exposure level reduction, or outcomes, if available (e.g., reduction on rate of miscarriages)

Organizational Level—

- Active participation of women employees in the decision-making process concerning applied safety policies in the company
- Representation of female workers from different occupational sectors within the organization in administrative issues regarding the design of workstations and job tasks, and the introduction of new technologies, materials, and procedures
- Introduction of incentives for the compliance of employees with safety policies

Administrative and Policy Diagnosis

WHP professionals should conduct this final diagnostic procedure before the implementation of the prevention program, to determine whether the program's scope and activities are compatible with the administrative and policy framework of the organization. The main issues to be identified at this stage are:

- Whether the policies and safety regulations related to potential reproductive hazards are in accordance with the program's requirements and the existence of requisite modifications or complementary arrangements
- Whether the program introduces any interventions that are in conflict with the organization's operational framework
- Whether the selected form of intervention (information campaign, skill building sessions, group activities) is appropriate for the existing *company culture* in OSH issues
- Which of the existing structures and activities in the organization are useful to the program's strategic planning. Some examples of similar structures and activities are presented in Table 3.16.
- Whether the company's administration is sufficiently flexible to adopt the participatory decision model proposed by the program for the resolution of OSH issues
- Whether the organization's field of activities and operational status allows for alternative practices, procedures, and materials. Table 3.17 sites an indicative list of similar practices and procedures.

Table 3.16 Structures and activities useful to the strategic planning of WHP for the prevention of reproductive disorders

1. Systematic **record of occupational medical history** of workers
2. **Safety committees** appointed by company's employees
3. **Trade-union department specialized in OSH** issues for female employees
4. **Registry** of recognized occupational reproductive disorders
5. **Official forms for reporting** employees remarks on working conditions and related hazards
6. **Detailed registry of materials, substances and processes** utilized in each department of the organization (toxicity, carcinogenicity, potential for endocrine disrupting activity)
7. **Regular group meetings among workers** and administration representatives
8. **Periodic screening of working population** for hazardous occupational exposures

Table 3.17 Examples of alternative solutions

1. Partial **automatization** of procedures
2. **Isolation of procedures** involving hazardous exposures
3. Use of **alternative materials** and chemical compounds
4. **Design modification** of production lines and workstations
5. Use of **ancillary equipment**
6. Change in **time schedule, staff rotation**

- Whether the WHP program's focus of interest conforms to the health priorities identified by the company's administration
- Whether the segregation of tasks among different departments blocks the desired dissemination of the program and excludes certain categories of employees

Identification of the Target Population's Needs

The primary concern of WHP professionals in the design of an educative intervention for women workers is to provide a tailored program according to the specific target population and its educational needs. The selection of a specific approach for this *educational needs assessment* depends heavily on the available resources (staff, time, expenditure limitation) of the program. Listed below are some of the available techniques, and the form in which they may be employed, to obtain related information from the female workers' population (National Cancer Institute 2005a; Pfizer 2004; Younger, Wittet, Hooks & Lasher 2001):

Surveys

Women employees can be accessed individually, either at their worksite or through telephone or Internet surveys, to fill in specifically designed questionnaires. Some of the questions that may be included in such a questionnaire are listed in Table 3.18.

Focus Groups

This approach involves two-hour sessions of small work groups of six to ten women employees who testify their individual concerns, experiences, and percep-

Table 3.18 Outline of questionnaires

Demographic Data:	Age Marital status
Subgroups:	Ethnicity (Native, immigrant, ethnic minority) Religious groups (beliefs, attitudes)
Occupational Category:	Blue collar worker (manual handling, machine operator) Clerical employees Administrative-executive level
Awareness Level:	Previous participation to similar programs (sensitization) Existing knowledge on reproductive health issues Perception of personal susceptibility to reproductive disorders
Required Practical Skills:	Identification of occupational risk sources (MSDS, properties of chemical compounds) Training in safe practices (proper use of PPE, facilities)Identification of early warning symptoms of reproductive disorders Appropriate use of screening and other medical services
Literacy Skills:	Level of education

tions on work-related reproductive health issues. The activity takes place under the continuous supervision of an expert facilitator (health professional). The workgroup is selected on the basis of common socioeconomic and ethnic characteristics (e.g., representation of low literate immigrant female workers) as well as their specific job tasks. The application of this technique offers the WHP program a more comprehensive insight into the target population profile (Younger et al. 2001), as well as the specific needs of certain special subgroups of womens workers (e.g., effective approach and training techniques, use of appropriate educative material).

Individual Interviews

Women employees are interviewed in the form of open-ended questions, where they are encouraged to identify themselves and their educational needs by trained professionals (instead of being guided by specific queries). Even though this technique is the most time-consuming, it offers the most in-depth needs identification (Younger et al. 2001).

Advisory Boards

These committees are formed by women employee representatives of specific at-risk populations, and consult WHP professionals on specific issues related to reproductive health disorders among certain categories of workers, contributing their own experiences and concerns.

Available Actions

The Ecological Model (McLeroy, Bideau, Steckler & Glanz 1988) that was presented in the first chapter of this book offers the opportunity to identify the determinants of individual behavior within the wider context of social groups or organizations to which a person belongs. This perspective can therefore be useful for implementing comprehensive WHP programs addressing specific health issues.

Analyzing the profile of a specific organization according to the five individual levels of the ecological perspective model-*intrapersonal*, *interpersonal*, *institutional*, *community*, and *policy*—one can identify multiple and multi-component potential interventions for the protection of female workers from the main categories of reproductive hazards recognized in the existing literature.

Intrapersonal Level Interventions

At the intrapersonal level, workplace health promotion activities focus on individual skill building for female workers in the form of personal counseling on issues of reproductive health. The general scope of these interventions, some of which are presented in Table 3.19, is the introduction of a number of issues including:

- Identification of occupational reproductive hazards, personal risk factors, and related symptoms
- Requested behavioral changes towards prevention
- Skill-building in the correct use of equipment, materials, and safety practices
- Access to scientific resources and specialized health services

Interpersonal Level Interventions

Workplace health promotion interventions at this level appeal to groups of working women instead of individuals. This stage of WHP involves skill-building sessions, team collaboration and support activities, and health education, which may vary in group size or duration according to the educational needs of a specific working population. These groups can be selected according to common epidemiological or social characteristics of the workers (e.g., age, education, ethnicity) to adequately tailor any intervention. Table 3.20 presents some of the group activities that may take place within the context of WHP:

Institutional Level Interventions

Cited in Table 3.21 is a list of available interventions at the institutional (or *company*) level concerning organizational measures, practices, and policies that may be implemented for the protection of women worker's reproductive health.

Table 3.19 Intrapersonal level interventions

Potential Hazard	Intervention Opportunities
Hazardous Chemical Agents (solvents, inhaled vapors, liquid substances)	• Education of female employees in potential hazardous effects of chemicals on reproductive health • Education of employees on identification of chemicals, labeling, and proper use of M.S.D.S. (Material Safety Data Sheets) • Provision of definite safety guidelines for handling, storing, mixing and applying chemical substances • Training in proper use of PPE (Personal Protective Equipment)
Smoking (active & passive)	• Education of female employees on the detrimental effects of smoking on female fertility and pregnancy • Implementation of smoking cessation programmes
Ionizing Radiation	• Education of female employees about the hazardous effects of ionizing radiation • Provision of definite safety guidelines for operating equipment which emit radiation • Supply, and training in the use of personal radiation dosimeters • Training in proper use of PPE (Personal Protective Equipment)
Strenuous Work – Manual Handling	• Training of female personnel in stress management techniques and psychological consultation • Education on methods for preventing occupational fatigue (adequate lifestyle and nutritional changes, early recognition of warning symptoms of physical strain, proper clothing) • Personal training in basic principles of ergonomics and safe manual handling techniques
Infectious Diseases	• Education of female employees on hazardous effects of infectious agents on reproductive health and pregnancy • Provision of prevention guidelines for infectious agents (vaccination, transmission pathways) • Training in proper use of PPE (gloves, goggles, safe sexual practices for sexual workers)

Community Level Interventions

To implement effective workplace health promotion programs for the protection of female reproductive health, health professionals should not neglect the fact that the female working population in a specific worksite acquires certain characteristics that

Table 3.20 Interpersonal level interventions

Potential Hazard	Intervention Opportunities
Hazardous Chemical Agents	• Group sessions on safety procedures for handling chemical substances, to enhance acceptance of safety regulations and team-building
Smoking	• Group education on the detrimental effects of tobacco on female reproductive health • Smoking cessation groups for employees
Ionizing Radiation	• Group training sessions on radioactive material safe handling, and protective measures against ionizing radiation
Strenuous Work – Manual Handling	• Group skill-building on stress management techniques, workplace design for the protection of pregnant women employees, safe manual handling methods
Infectious Diseases	• Group education on infectious agents hazardous for female reproductive health, their transmission pathways, methods for prevention

Generic:

• Creation of employee's groups to constitute models of "best practice" and provide a supportive environment for the adoption of safety techniques (or "healthy behaviour") among women workers

• Creation of idea-exchanging groups, for identification of specific workplace reproductive hazards and special issues of concern for women workers

define a *community*. The main focus of a successful WHP project at this level is to incorporate the issue of reproductive health in the *safety culture* of female workers.

This involves organizing targeted group activities for female workers that addresses the problem of reproductive hazard prevention through the community's system of "group norms, inner rules and beliefs"(Edlich, Winters, Hudson, Britt & Long 2004), and create a *climate* of awareness on issues related to female employees.

Policy Level Interventions

At this level, workplace health promotion programs involve contacts with stakeholders (trade union members, employee representatives, company executives) and policymakers to propose measures, policies, and legal provisions for the protection of female workers' reproductive health, some of which are listed in Table 3.22.

Communication Strategy

WHP programs may utilize multiple channels of communication to deliver messages related to women's reproductive health protection. The approach may take various forms (Prevention 2003):

Table 3.21 Institutional level interventions

Potential Hazard	Intervention Opportunities
Hazardous Chemical Agents	• Proposals (by health professionals) for specific changes in the production line – substitution of chemical factors which are detrimental for female reproductive health with "safer" compounds • Proposals for specific design changes in facilities, to isolate chemical procedures • Frequent measurements by health technicians in the workplace to record concentration of chemicals, and identification of high risk population • Training of occupational physicians and nurses in: a) identification of chemical reproductive hazards b) available preventive measures c) early diagnosis of reproductive disorders • Re-positioning of pregnant employees to reduce potential exposure to chemicals • Provision to all staff members of specific company's guidelines on occupational safety and reproductive hazards prevention (official forms, leaflets, electronic mail), as well as standard operating procedures for using chemicals • Rotation of workers to reduce potential exposure
Smoking	• Definition of a strict company's policy on health protection for non-smokers • Placement of warning signs to prohibit smoking in the company • Provision of adequate outdoor spaces, and time-breaks for smokers • Funding of campaigns and incentives on smoking cessation for employees
Ionizing Radiation	• Proposals for specific design changes (e.g. armoring improvement, isolation of radioactive material) to avoid exposure of personnel to radiation • Frequent radiation measurements in the workplace environment to identify potential sources of exposure and high risk employees • Provision (to all staff) of specific directives on safe use of radiation emitting equipment (instruction sheets, official forms, leaflets, electronic mail) • Re-positioning of pregnant employees to reduce potential exposure. Rotation of workers to reduce potential exposure
Strenuous Work – Manual Handling	• Proposals to administration to conduct adequate modifications in ergonomic design and provision of special equipment

Table 3.21 (continued)

Potential Hazard	Intervention Opportunities
	• Proposals to administration for the introduction of specific safety regulations concerning female employees (especially during pregnancy): a) time-schedule modification, b) maximum working hours, c) mandatory time-breaks, d) provision of sick-leave days, e) maximum allowed weight for manual handling, f) re-positioning of pregnant employees, g) zero-tolerance policy on aggressive behavior against employees
	• Providing staff with the organization's safety guidelines for preventing physical strain (instruction sheets, official forms, leaflets, electronic mail). Rotation of workers to reduce physical strain
Infectious Diseases	• Provision to all staff of educative material on potential effects of infectious agents to female reproductive health
	• Introduction of collective safety guidelines for all health-care personnel
	• Provision of adequate safety equipment to prevent accidental transmission of infectious agents (safety syringe mechanisms, syringe disposal vessels, goggles, masques, gloves)
	• Extensive vaccination program for child-bearing age personnel (health care workers, teachers, nursery workers)

Lectures

Lectures constitute single courses or one-shot education interventions (Prevention 2003) providing general information on the topic of occupational reproductive hazards for women (risk factors, generic preventive measures). Presentations and lectures may be used as well to carry health messages among the staff in an effort to establish general acceptance and support for the company's pertinent safety regulations and policies.

Table 3.22 Policy level interventions

Intervention Opportunities
• Prioritization of systematic research on suspected reproductive toxicants
• Collaboration between experts in industrial toxicology, human reproductive biology, epidemiologists and industry representatives (Lawson et al., 2006)
• Systematic occupational exposure assessment to identify high risk female employees
• Proposal for legislative regulation to substitute hazardous agents with "safer" chemical compounds
• Promotion of scientific research on gender specific reproductive issues for female workers
• Obligatory reproductive health surveillance of women workers in high risk for reproductive disorders
• Systematic registry of birth defects according to maternal occupational exposures
• Production of specifically designed protective equipment for female workers

Print Material

This form of communication is able to provide wide-scale access to the population of working women (e.g., access to agricultural workers in distant areas, low-literacy skill employees) through billboards, magazines, and newspapers published by the company, or items of special interest to certain professional sectors, such as leaflets referring to reproductive safety issues. Health professionals may utilize this channel to address generic guidelines for prevention on issues of reproductive health either to female workers themselves or to their coworkers, which may effect women employees through their tasks or behavior (e.g., men employees smoking indoors, safe storage or handling of hazardous chemicals in the workplace).

Clearinghouse

This form of health promotion is based on establishing an interactive information service for the prevention of occupational reproductive disorders (Prevention 2003). This service should incorporate a telephone center with the ability to provide personal telephone counseling to women employees, as well as a hotline for answering women's questions concerning reproductive health issues. Furthermore, this service should develop an electronic library, accessible through the Internet, for all female workers and the general public, providing official safety guidelines for reproductive hazards and answers to related questions. Finally, it enables continuous sensitization of high-risk female employees through frequent electronic reminders and their activation in safeguarding their reproductive health.

Media

Media has proven to be one of the most effective communication channels for many health issues and health promotion activities. It can be utilized to address messages on a larger scale, mostly by health professionals who work in workplace health promotion programs on community, national, or European level. It uses public announcements, short messages, and commercials to address reproductive health hazard prevention issues through radio, television, and newspapers. In some cases, this form of health promotion may be useful for approaching female workers who are not easily accessible by other workplace health promotion programs, such as occupations in small enterprises, part-time employment, and female agricultural workers in remote areas.

References

Abbritti G, and Muzi G (2006) Indoor air quality and health in offices and other non-industrial working environments. *Med Lav*, *97*(2), 410–417

Akpinar-Elci M, Cimrin A H, and Elci OC (2002) Prevalence and risk factors of occupational asthma among hairdressers in Turkey. *J Occup Environ Med*, *44*(6), 585–590

Albin M, Rylander L, Mikoczy Z, Lillienberg L, Hoglund AD, Brisman J, et al. (2002) Incidence of asthma in female Swedish hairdressers. *Occupational and Environmental Medicine*, 59(2), 119–123

Allmers H, Nickau L, Skudlik C, and John SM (2005) Current findings about the development of obstructive airway diseases in hairdressers (BK numbers: 4301/4302). *Allergologie*, 28(5), 172–176

Amado A, and Taylor JS (2006) Women's Occupational Dermatologic Issues. *Dermatologic Clinics*, 24(2), 259–269

Ando S, Ono Y, Shimaoka M, Hiruta S, Hattori Y, Hori F, et al. (2000) Associations of self estimated workloads with musculoskeletal symptoms among hospital nurses. *Occup Environ Med*, 57(3), 211–216

Artazcoz L, Artieda L, Borrell C, Cortes I, Benach J, and Garcia V (2004) Combining job and family demands and being healthy: what are the differences between men and women? *Eur J Public Health*, 14(1), 43–48

Artazcoz L, Borrell C, and Benach J (2001) Gender inequalities in health among workers: the relation with family demands. *J Epidemiol Community Health*, 55(9), 639–647

Artazcoz Lazcano L, Cruz i Cubells JL, Moncada i Lluis S, and Sanchez Miguel A (1996) Stress and work-related tension in the nurses and clinical aides of a hospital. *Gaceta sanitaria / S.E.S.P.A.S*, 10(57), 282–292

Bakirci N, Kalaca S, Fletcher AM, Pickering CA, Tumerdem N, Cali S, et al. (2006) Predictors of early leaving from the cotton spinning mill environment in newly hired workers. *Occup Environ Med*, 63(2), 126–130

Ballas K, Psarras K, Rafailidis S, Konstantinidis H, and Sakadamis A (2006) Interdigital pilonidal sinus in a hairdresser. *Journal of Hand Surgery*, 31(3), 290–291

Balogh I, Orbaek P, Ohlsson K, Nordander C, Unge J, Winkel J, et al. (2004) Self-assessed and directly measured occupational physical activities–influence of musculoskeletal complaints, age and gender. *Appl Ergon*, 35(1), 49–56

Bauer EP, Romitti PA, and Reynolds SJ (1999) Evaluation of reports of periconceptual occupational exposure: maternal-assessed versus industrial hygienist-assessed exposure. *Am J Ind Med*, 36(5), 573–578

Baur X (1999) Work-related obstructed airway diseases by irritative noxae in the low concentration range. *Arbeitsmedizin Sozialmedizin Umweltmedizin*, 34(1), 9–14

Bedi R (2006) Evaluation of occupational environment in two textile plants in Northern India with specific reference to noise. *Ind Health*, 44(1), 112–116

Behar A, MacDonald E, Lee J, Cui J, Kunov H, and Wong W (2004) Noise Exposure of Music Teachers. *Journal of Occupational and Environmental Hygiene*, 1(4), 243–247

Thielen B (2003) Laundry Workers: Cleaning Up an Industry. *We Can Do It: Protecting Women Workers*, 2006, from http://www.occupationalhazards.com/articles/10725

[I can't move this reference, but it needs to be relocated to the correct alphabetical spot in the list.]

Berges M, and Kleine H (2002) Hazardous substances in the air at hairdressers' workplaces. *Gefahrstoffe Reinhaltung der Luft*, 62(10), 405–409

Best M, French G, Ciantar J, Didzys D, Fitzgerald C, Moore K, et al. (2002) Work-related musculoskeletal disorders in hairdressers. *Journal of Occupational Health and Safety - Australia and New Zealand*, 18(1), 67–76

Biggins J, and Renfree S (2002) The hazards of surgical smoke. Not to be sniffed at! *British journal of perioperative nursing : the journal of the National Association of Theatre Nurses*, 12(4), 136–138, 141

Bjorksten MG, Boquist B, Talback M, and Edling C (1996) Neck and shoulder ailments in a group of female industrial workers with monotonous work. *Ann Occup Hyg*, 40(6), 661–673

Boyles JL, Yearout RD, and Rys MJ (2003) Ergonomic scissors for hairdressing. *International Journal of Industrial Ergonomics*, 32(3), 199–207

Brabant C (1992) Heat exposure standards and women's work: equitable or debatable? *Women Health*, 18(3), 119–130

Brama M, Gnessi L, Basciani S, Cerulli N, Politi L, Spera G, et al. (2007) Cadmium induces mitogenic signaling in breast cancer cell by an ERalpha-dependent mechanism. *Mol Cell Endocrinol*.(264(1-2)), 102–108

Brown EA, Shelley ML, and Fisher JW (1998) A pharmacokinetic study of occupational and environmental benzene exposure with regard to gender. *Risk Anal, 18*(2), 205–213

Buranatrevedh S, and Roy D (2001) Occupational exposure to endocrine-disrupting pesticides and the potential for developing hormonal cancers. *J Environ Health, 64*(3), 17–29

Burm AG (2003) Occupational hazards of inhalational anaesthetics. *Best Pract Res Clin Anaesthesiol, 17*(1), 147–161

Cardoso AP, Oliveira MJ, Silva AM, Aguas AP, and Pereira AS (2006) Effects of long term exposure to occupational noise on textile industry workers' lung function. *Rev Port Pneumol, 12*(1), 45–59

Cavallo D, Ursini CL, Setini A, Chianese C, Cristaudo A, and Iavicoli S (2005) DNA damage and TNF(alpha) cytokine production in hairdressers with contact dermatitis. *Contact Dermatitis, 53*(3), 125–129

Cesana G, Arduca A, Latocca R, and Sirtori G (1998) [Risk evaluation and health surveillance in hospitals: a critical review and contributions regarding experience obtained at the S. Gerardo dei Tintori Hospital in Monza]. *Med Lav, 89*(1), 23–46

Chandra H, and Gupta S (2001) Health care providers and professional hazards. *International Journal of Medical Toxicology and Legal Medicine, 3*(2), 13–15

Chen SI, and Skillen DL (2006) Promoting personal safety of building service workers: issues and challenges. *AAOHN journal : official journal of the American Association of Occupational Health Nurses., 54*(6), 262–269

Choobineh A, Lahmi M, Hosseini M, Shahnavaz H, and Jazani RK (2004) Workstation design in carpet hand-weaving operation: guidelines for prevention of musculoskeletal disorders. *Int J Occup Saf Ergon, 10*(4), 411–424

Chuang SC, and Lin HM (2006) Nurses confronting sexual harassment in the medical environment. *Stud Health Technol Inform, 122*, 349–352

Chyuan JY, Du CL, Yeh WY, and Li CY (2004) Musculoskeletal disorders in hotel restaurant workers. *Occup Med (Lond), 54*(1), 55–57

Clapp RW (2006) Mortality among US employees of a large computer manufacturing company: 1969–2001. *Environ Health, 5*, 30

Courtney TK, Huang YH, Verma SK, Chang WR, Li KW, and Filiaggi AJ (2006) Factors influencing restaurant worker perception of floor slipperiness. *J Occup Environ Hyg, 3*(11), 592–598

De Castro AB (2004) Handle with care: The american nurses association's campaign to address work-related musculoskeletal disorders. *Online Journal of Issues in Nursing, 9*(3)

De Castro AB, Hagan P, and Nelson A (2006) Prioritizing safe patient handling: The American Nurses Association's Handle With Care campaign. *Journal of Nursing Administration, 36*(7–8), 363–369

De Jong FICRS, Kooijman PGC, Thomas G, Huinck WJ, Graamans K, and Schutte HK (2006) Epidemiology of voice problems in Dutch teachers. *Folia Phoniatrica et Logopaedica, 58*(3), 186–198

Dempsey PG, and Filiaggi AJ (2006) Cross-sectional investigation of task demands and musculoskeletal discomfort among restaurant wait staff. *Ergonomics, 49*(1), 93–106

Denton M, Zeytinoglu I, and Webb S (2000) Work-related violence and the OHS of home health care workers. *Journal of Occupational Health and Safety - Australia and New Zealand, 16*(5), 419–427

Denton MA, Zeytinoglu IU, and Davies S (2002) Working in clients' homes: the impact on the mental health and well-being of visiting home care workers. *Home health care services quarterly, 21*(1), 1–27

Dorevitch S, and Babin A (2001) Health hazards of ceramic artists. *Occup Med, 16*(4), 563–575, iii

Doutre MS (2005) Occupational contact urticaria and protein contact dermatitis. *Eur J Dermatol, 15*(6), 419–424

Dranitsaris G, Johnston M, Poirier S, Schueller T, Milliken D, Green E, et al. (2005) Are health care providers who work with cancer drugs at an increased risk for toxic events? A systematic review and meta-analysis of the literature. *J Oncol Pharm Pract, 11*(2), 69–78

Duff MC, Proctor A, and Yairi E (2004) Prevalence of voice disorders in African American and European American preschoolers. *Journal of Voice, 18*(3), 348–353

Edlich RF, Winters KL, Hudson MA, Britt LD, and Long WB (2004) Prevention of disabling back injuries in nurses by the use of mechanical patient lift systems. *Journal of Long-Term Effects of Medical Implants, 14*(6), 521–533

European Agency for Safety and Health at Work (2003a) *Gender issues in safety and health at work — A review.* Luxembourg: Office for Official Publications of the European Communities

European Agency for Safety and Health at Work (2003b) Including gender issues in risk assessment [Electronic Version]. *FACTS.* Retrieved 25/8/2006 from http://osha.europa.eu/publications/factsheets/43/facts-43_en.pdf/file_view

European Agency for Safety and Health at Work (2005) *Mainstreaming gender into occupational safety and health.* Luxembourg: Office for Official Publications of the European Communities

Eurostat (2002) *European social statistics: Labour force survey results 2002*: Office for Official Publications of the European Communities

Fjellman-Wiklund A, Brulin C, and Sundelin G (2003) Physical and psychosocial work-related risk factors associated with neck-shoulder discomfort in male and female music teachers. *Medical Problems of Performing Artists, 18*(1), 33–41

Foti C, Scrimieri V, Corazza M, Gola M, Giusti F, Seidenari S, et al (2005) Prevalence of sensitivity to rubber additives and latex in hairdressers with hand and/or forearm contact dermatitis. *Annali Italiani di Dermatologia Allergologica Clinica e Sperimentale, 59*(2), 77–84

Gala Ortiz G, Gancedo SQ, Ordonez RF, Camo IP, Mancebo EG, Agustin MC, et al. (2001) Diagnostic approach and management of occupational asthma by persulfate salts in a hairdresser. *Allergy and asthma proceedings : the official journal of regional and state allergy societies, 22*(4), 235–238

Gandhi M, Aweeka F, Greenblatt RM, and Blaschke TF (2004) Sex differences in pharmacokinetics and pharmacodynamics. *Annu Rev Pharmacol Toxicol, 44*, 499–523

Garcia AM (2003) Pesticide exposure and women's health. *Am J Ind Med, 44*(6), 584–594

Gavana M, Tsoukana P, Giannakopoulos E, Smyrnakis E, and Benos A (2005) Adequacy of vaccination coverage at school-entry: Cross-sectional study in schoolchildren of an urban population. *Archives of Hellenic Medicine, 22*(4), 358–369

Ghio AJ, Funkhouser W, Pugh CB, Winters S, Stonehuerner JG, Mahar AM, et al. (2006) Pulmonary fibrosis and ferruginous bodies associated with exposure to synthetic fibers. *Toxicol Pathol, 34*(6), 723–729

Gielen AC, and McDonald EM (1997) The PRECEDE-PROCEED planning model. In K. Glanz, F.M Lewis & B. K. Rimmer (Eds.), *Health Behavior and Education (2nd ed.)* (pp. 359–383). San Francisco: Jossey-Bass

Gimeno D, Felknor S, Burau KD, and Delclos GL (2005) Organisational and occupational risk factors associated with work related injuries among public hospital employees in Costa Rica. *Occup Environ Med, 62*(5), 337–343

Graham K, Bernards S, Osgood DW, and Wells S (2006) Bad nights or bad bars? Multi-level analysis of environmental predictors of aggression in late-night large-capacity bars and clubs [Electronic Version]. *Addiction*, 101, 1569-1580. Retrieved Nov from http://www.ncbi.nlm.nih.gov/entrez/query.fcgi?cmd=Retrieve&db=PubMed&dopt=Citation& list_uids=17034436

Green LW, and Kreuter MW (1991) *Health Promotion Planning: An Educational and Environmental Approach. (2nd ed.)* Mayfield Publishers

Green LW, Kreuter MW, Deeds SG, and Partridge KB (1980) *Health Education Planning: A Diagnostic Approach*: Mayfield Publishers

Gurubacharya DL, Mathura KC, and Karki DB (2003) Knowledge, attitude and practices among health care workers on needle-stick injuries. *Kathmandu Univ Med J (KUMJ), 1*(2), 91–94

Gyorkos TW, Beliveau C, Rahme E, Muecke C, Joseph S, and Soto JC (2005) High rubella seronegativity in daycare educators. *Clinical and Investigative Medicine, 28*(3), 105–111

Han DH (2000) Fit factors for quarter masks and facial size categories. *Ann Occup Hyg*(44), 227–234

Hanke W, and Jurewicz J (2004) The risk of adverse reproductive and developmental disorders due to occupational pesticide exposure: an overview of current epidemiological evidence. *Int J Occup Med Environ Health, 17*(2), 223–243

Hard DL, Myers JR, and Gerberich SG (2002) Traumatic injuries in agriculture. *J Agric Saf Health*, 8(1), 51–65

HAZ-MAP (2006a) Beta-Chloroprene. *Occupational Exposure to Hazardous Agents* Retrieved 20-9-2006, from http://hazmap.nlm.nih.gov/cgi-bin/hazmap_generic?tbl=TblAgents&id=357

HAZ-MAP (2006b) Cadmium and compounds. *Occupational Exposures to Hazardous Agents* Retrieved 25-9-2006, from http://hazmap.nlm.nih.gov/cgi-bin/hazmap_ generic?tbl= TblAgents&id=2

HAZ-MAP (2006c) Carbon disulfide. *Occupational Exposure to Hazardous Agents* Retrieved 20-9-2006, from http://hazmap.nlm.nih.gov/cgi-bin/hazmap_generic?tbl=TblAgents&id=52

HAZ-MAP (2006d) Ethylene Oxide. *Occupational Exposure to Hazardous Agents*, from http://hazmap.nlm. nih.gov/cgi-bin/hazmap_generic?tbl=TblAgents&id=21

HAZ-MAP (2006e) Glycol-ethers. *Occupational Exposure to Hazardous Agents* Retrieved 20-9-2006, from http://hazmap.nlm.nih.gov/cgi-bin/hazmap_generic?tbl=TblAgents&id=688

HAZ-MAP (2006f) Lead. *Occupational Exposure to Hazardous Agents* Retrieved 25-9-2006, from http://hazmap.nlm.nih.gov/cgi-bin/hazmap_generic?tbl=TblAgents&id=10

HAZ-MAP (2006g) Nickel and compounds. *Occupational Exposures to Hazardous Agents* Retrieved 25-9-2006, from http://hazmap.nlm.nih.gov/cgi-bin/hazmap_generic?tbl= TblAgents&id=50

HAZ-MAP (2006h) Perchlorethylene. *Occupational Exposure to Hazardous Agents* Retrieved 20-9-2006, from http://hazmap.nlm.nih.gov/cgi-bin/hazmap_ generic?tbl=TblAgents&id=432

HAZ-MAP (2006i) Toluene. *Occupational exposure to Hazardous Agents* Retrieved 20-9-2006, from http://hazmap.nlm.nih.gov/cgi-bin/hazmap_generic?tbl=TblAgents&id=83

Hoerauf K, Funk W, Harth M, and Hobbhahn J (1997) Occupational exposure to sevoflurane, halothane and nitrous oxide during paediatric anaesthesia. Waste gas exposure during paediatric anaesthesia. *Anaesthesia*, 52(3), 215–219

Hollund BE, and Moen BE (1998) Chemical exposure in hairdresser salons: effect of local exhaust ventilation. *Ann Occup Hyg*, 42(4), 277–282

Hooftman WE, van der Beek AJ, Bongers PM, and van Mechelen W (2005) Gender differences in self-reported physical and psychosocial exposures in jobs with both female and male workers. *J Occup Environ Med*, 47(3), 244–252

Horwitz IB, and McCall BP (2004) Quantification and risk analysis of occupational burns: Oregon workers' compensation claims, 1990 to 1997. *J Burn Care Rehabil*, 25(3), 328–336

Hruska KS, Furth PA, Seifer DB, Sharara FI, and Flaws JA (2000) Environmental factors in infertility. *Clin Obstet Gynecol*, 43(4), 821–829

Hush JM, Maher CG, and Refshauge KM (2006) Risk factors for neck pain in office workers: a prospective study. *BMC Musculoskelet Disord*, 7, 81

Iorizzo M, Parente G, Vincenzi C, Pazzaglia M, and Tosti A (2002) Allergic contact dermatitis in hairdressers: Frequency and source of sensitisation. *European Journal of Dermatology*, 12(2), 179–182

Iwakiri K, Mori I, Sotoyama M, Horiguchi K, Ochiai T, Jonai H, et al. (2004) [Survey on visual and musculoskeletal symptoms in VDT workers]. *Sangyo Eiseigaku Zasshi*, 46(6), 201–212

Jaakkola JJ, and Jaakkola MS (2006) Professional cleaning and asthma. *Curr Opin Allergy Clin Immunol*, 6(2), 85–90

Jaakkola MS, Yang L, Ieromnimon A, and Jaakkola JJ (2007) Office work, SBS and respiratory and sick building syndrome symptoms. *Occup Environ Med*, 64(3), 178–184

Jappe U, Bonnekoh B, Hausen BM, and Gollnick H (1999) Garlic-related dermatoses: case report and review of the literature. *Am J Contact Dermat*, 10(1), 37–39

Jouhette S, and Romans F (2006) *EU Labour Force Survey,Principal results 2005* (No. KS-NK-06-013-EN-N)

Kanerva L, Estlander T, and Jolanki R (1996) Occupational allergic contact dermatitis from spices. *Contact Dermatitis*, 35(3), 157–162

Katugampola RP, Statham BN, English JSC, Wilkinson MM, Foulds IS, Green CM, et al. (2005) A multicentre review of the hairdressing allergens tested in the UK. *Contact Dermatitis*, 53(3), 130–132

Keeffe EB (2004) Occupational risk for hepatitis A: a literature-based analysis. *J Clin Gastroenterol, 38*(5), 440–448

Kennedy MS, and Koehoorn M (2003) Exposure Assessment in Epidemiology: Does Gender Matter? *American Journal of Industrial Medicine*(44), 576–583

Khrenova L, John SM, Pfahlberg A, Gefeller O, and Uter W (2006) Development of hand eczema in hairdressers, 8 to 10 years after the start of training - A follow-up study of "POSH-Studie" participants. *Dermatologie in Beruf und Umwelt, 54*(1), 25–33

Kindy D, Petersen S, and Parkhurst D (2005) Perilous work: nurses' experiences in psychiatric units with high risks of assault. *Arch Psychiatr Nurs, 19*(4), 169–175

Kines P, Hannerz H, Mikkelsen KL, and Tuchsen F (2007) Industrial sectors with high risk of women's hospital-treated injuries. *Am J Ind Med, 50*(1), 13–21

Kooijman PGC, De Jong FICRS, Thomas G, Huinck W, Donders R, Graamans K, et al. (2006) Risk factors for voice problems in teachers. *Folia Phoniatrica et Logopaedica, 58*(3), 159–174

Kosztyla-Hojna B, Rogowski M, Ruczaj J, Pepinski W, and Lobaczuk-Sitnik A (2004) An analysis of occupational dysphonia diagnosed in the north-east of Poland. *International Journal of Occupational Medicine and Environmental Health, 17*(2), 273–278

Kovess-Masfety V, Sevilla-Dedieu C, Rios-Seidel C, Nerriere E, and Chee CC (2006) Do teachers have more health problems? Results from a French cross-sectional survey. *BMC Public Health, 6*(-)

Krstev S, Perunicic B, and Vidakovic A (2003) Work practice and some adverse health effects in nurses handling antineoplastic drugs. *Med Lav, 94*(5), 432–439

Ku CH, Liu YT, and Christian DC (2005) Case report: Occupationally related recurrent varicella (chickenpox) in a hospital nurse. *Environmental Health Perspectives, 113*(10), 1373–1375

Labreche F, Forest J, Trottier M, Lalonde M, and Simard R (2003) Characterization of Chemical Exposures in Hairdressing Salons. *Applied Occupational and Environmental Hygiene, 18*(12), 1014–1021

LaDou J (2006) Printed circuit board industry. *Int J Hyg Environ Health, 209*(3), 211–219

Lawrence C, and Green K (2005) Perceiving classroom aggression: The influence of setting, intervention style and group perceptions. *British Journal of Educational Psychology, 75*(4), 587–602

Lawson CC, Grajewski B, Daston GP, Frazier LM, Lynch D, McDiarmid M, et al. (2006) Workgroup report: Implementing a national occupational reproductive research agenda–decade one and beyond. *Environ Health Perspect, 114*(3), 435–441

Lea CS, Hertz-Picciotto I, Andersen A, Chang-Claude J, Olsen JH, Pesatori AC, et al. (1999) Gender differences in the healthy worker effect among synthetic vitreous fiber workers. *Am J Epidemiol, 150*(10), 1099–1106

Lehto L, Alku P, Backstrom T, and Vilkman E (2005) Voice symptoms of call-centre customer service advisers experienced during a work-day and effects of a short vocal training course. *Logoped Phoniatr Vocol, 30*(1), 14–27

Linaker C, and Smedley J (2002) Respiratory illness in agricultural workers. *Occup Med (Lond), 52*(8), 451–459

Linda Tapp A, CSP, (2003) Making Manufacturing a Safe Work Environment for Women Workers. *We Can Do It: Protecting Women Workers*, 2006, from http://www.occupationalhazards.com/articles/10725

Macchioni P, Kotopulos C, Talini D, De Santis M, Masino E, and Paggiaro PL (1999) [Asthma in hairdressers: a report of 5 cases]. *Med Lav, 90*(6), 776–785

Makowiec-Dabrowska T, Hanke W, Sprusinska E, Radwan-Wlodarczyk Z, and Koszada-Wlodarczyk W (2004) [Menstrual disorders. Is this a problem to be handled by occupational medicine physician?]. *Med Pr, 55*(2), 161–167

Martinelli M, and Carri MG (1996) [Evaluation of the exposure to biomechanical overload of the upper limbs and clinical investigation in a female population employed in the manual loading of production lines in 2 ceramics factories]. *Med Lav, 87*(6), 675–685

McBride DI, Firth HM, and Herbison GP (2003) Noise exposure and hearing loss in agriculture: a survey of farmers and farm workers in the Southland region of New Zealand. *J Occup Environ Med, 45*(12), 1281–1288

McBryde ES, Bradley LC, Whitby M, and McElwain DL (2004) An investigation of contact transmission of methicillin-resistant Staphylococcus aureus. *J Hosp Infect*, 58(2), 104–108

McCoy CA, Carruth AK, and Reed DB (2002) Women in agriculture: risks for occupational injury within the context of gendered role. *J Agric Saf Health*, 8(1), 37–50

McDiarmid M, Oliver M, Ruser J, and Gucer P (2000) Male and female rate differences in carpal tunnel syndrome injuries: personal attributes or job tasks? *Environ Res*, 83(1), 23–32

McDiarmid MA, and Gucer PW (2001) The "GRAS" status of women's work. *J Occup Environ Med*, 43(8), 665–669

McGovern V (2003) Sex matters: exploring differences in responses to exposures. *Environ Health Perspect*, 111(1), A24–25

McLeroy Bideau D, Steckler A, and Glanz K (1988) An ecological perspective of health promotion programs. *Health Education Quarterly*(15), 351–378

McPhaul KM and Lipscomb JA (2004) Workplace violence in health care: recognized but not regulated. *Online J Issues Nurs*, 9(3), 7

Messing K and Stellman Mager J (2006) Sex, gender and women's occupational health:The importance of considering mechanism. *Environmental Research*(101), 149–162

Mlynarcikova A, Fickova M and Scsukova S (2005) Ovarian intrafollicular processes as a target for cigarette smoke components and selected environmental reproductive disruptors. *Endocr Regul*, 39(1), 21–32

Moghadam MHB, Mazloomy SS and Ehrampoush MH (2005) The effect of health education in promoting health of hairdressers about hepatitis B based on health belief model: A field trial in Yazd, Iran. *Acta Medica Iranica*, 43(5), 342–346

Mondelli M, Grippo A, Mariani M, Baldasseroni A, Ansuini R, Ballerini M, et al. (2006) Carpal tunnel syndrome and ulnar neuropathy at the elbow in floor cleaners. *Neurophysiol Clin*, 36(4), 245–253

Montomoli L, Cioni F, Sisinni AG, Romeo R and Sartorelli P (2004) Occupational asthma among hairdressers. *Giornale Italiano di Medicina del Lavoro ed Ergonomia*, 26(4 SUPPL.), 299–301

Moscato G, Pignatti P, Yacoub MR, Romano C, Spezia S and Perfetti L (2005) Occupational asthma and occupational rhinitis in hairdressers. *Chest*, 128(5), 3590–3598

Murphy MM, Patton J, Mello R, Bidwell T and Harp M (2001) Energy cost of physical task performance in men and women wearing personal protective clothing. *Aviation Space and Environmental Medicine* 72(1), 25–31

Nakazono N, Nii-no M, and Ishi K (1985) Rubella infections of the school teachers in Sapporo municipal schools after their employment. *Japanese Journal of Hygiene*, 40(5), 855–861

Nathenson P (2004) Adapting OSHA ergonomic guidelines to the rehabilitation setting. *Rehabil Nurs*, 29(4), 127–130

National Cancer Institute (2005a) *Theory at a glance: A Guide for Health Promotion Practice* (2nd ed.)

National Cancer Institute (2005b) *"Theory at a Glance" A Guide for Health Promotion Practice*

Nemecek J, and Buchberger J (1987) [Occupational health-related organization of work in large laundry facilities]. *Soz Praventivmed*, 32(4-5), 261–263

Niedhammer I, Saurel-Cubizolles MJ, Piciotti M, and Bonenfant S (2000) How is sex considered in recent epidemiological publications on occupational risks? *Occup Environ Med*, 57(8), 521–527

Osteras N, Ljunggren AE, Gould KS, Waersted M, and Bo Veiersted K (2006) Muscle pain, physical activity, self-efficacy and relaxation ability in adolescents. *Advances in Physiotherapy*, 8(1), 33–40

Östlin P (2000) *GENDER INEQUALITIES IN OCCUPATIONAL HEALTH*: Harvard School of Public Health

Parra Madrid AC, Romero Saldana M, Vaquero Abellan M, Hita Fernandez A and Molina Recio G (2005) Accidental exposure to biological risk among health care workers of a sanitary area. *Mapfre Medicina*, 16(2), 106–114

Perkins JB and Farrow A (2005) Prevalence of occupational hand dermatitis in U.K. hairdressers. *International Journal of Occupational and Environmental Health*, 11(3), 289–293

Perry MJ and May JJ (2005) Noise and chemical induced hearing loss: special considerations for farm youth. *J Agromedicine, 10*(2), 49–55

Pfizer (2004) Pfizer Principles for Clear Health Communication2nd Edition. Retrieved June 6, 2006

Piipari R and Keskinen H (2005) Agents causing occupational asthma in Finland in 1986-2002: Cow epithelium bypassed by moulds from moisture-damaged buildings. *Clinical and Experimental Allergy, 35*(12), 1632–1637

Pinn, VW (2003). Sex and Gender Factors in Medical Studies: Implications for Health and Clinical Practice. *JAMA, 289*(4), 397–400

Plovets'ka IA (2000a) [Epidemiologic characteristics of bronchopulmanory diseases in workers in the porcelain industry]. *Lik Sprava*(6), 109–111

Plovets'ka IA (2000b). [Morbidity patterns among workers in the porcelain industry]. *Lik Sprava*(7-8), 112–114

Polovich M (2004). Safe handling of hazardous drugs. *Online J Issues Nurs, 9*(3), 6

Porta C, Handelman E and McGovern P (1999) Needlestick injuries among health care workers. A literature review. *Aaohn J, 47*(6), 237–244

Presley D and Robinson G (2002) Violence in the emergency department: nurses contend with prevention in the healthcare arena. *Nurs Clin North Am, 37*(1), 161–169, viii-ix

Prevention DoHA (2003) Designing and Evaluating Intervention Plans *Evaluating CDC-Funded Health Department HIV Prevention Programs* Retrieved 25-9-2006, from http://www.cdc.gov/hiv/aboutdhap/perb/hdg/3deip.pdf

Pryor SK, Carruth AK and LaCour G (2005) Occupational risky business: injury prevention behaviors of farm women and children. *Issues Compr Pediatr Nurs, 28*(1), 17–31

Ransdell LB (2001) Using the PRECEDE-PROCEED Model to Increase Productivity in Health Education Faculty [Electronic Version]. *The International Electronic Journal of Health Education*, 4, 276–282

Rastogi SC, Sosted H, Johansen JD, Menne T and Bossi R (2006) Unconsumed precursors and couplers after formation of oxidative hair dyes. *Contact Dermatitis, 55*(2), 95–100

Romans F and Hardarson Ó (2006) *Labour Market Latest Trends - 3rd quarter 2005 data* (No. KS-NK-06-006-EN-N)

Roquelaure Y, Mariel J, Fanello S, Boissiere JC, Chiron H, Dano C, et al. (2002) Active epidemiological surveillance of musculoskeletal disorders in a shoe factory. *Occup Environ Med, 59*(7), 452–458

Roy DR (1999) Histology and pathology laboratories. Chemical hazard prevention and medical/health surveillance. *Aaohn J, 47*(5), 199–205

Sandmark H (2000) Musculoskeletal dysfunction in physical education teachers. *Occupational and Environmental Medicine, 57*(10), 673–677

Sandmark H, Wiktorin C, Hogstedt C, Klenell-Hatschek EK and Vingard E (1999) Physical work load in physical education teachers. *Applied Ergonomics, 30*(5), 435-442

Schroder CM, Merk HF and Frank J (2006) Barber's hair sinus in a female hairdresser: Uncommon manifestation of an occupational dermatosis. *Journal of the European Academy of Dermatology and Venereology, 20*(2), 209–211

Skillen DL, Olson JK and Gilbert JA (2001) Framing personal risk in public health nursing. *West J Nurs Res, 23*(7), 664–678

Sliwinska-Kowalska M, Niebudek-Bogusz E, Fiszer M, Los-Spychalska T, Kotylo P, Sznurowska-Przygocka B, et al. (2006) The prevalence and risk factors for occupational voice disorders in teachers. *Folia Phoniatrica et Logopaedica, 58*(2), 85–101

Smith DR and Wang RS (2006) Glutaraldehyde exposure and its occupational impact in the health care environment. *Environmental Health and Preventive Medicine, 11*(1), 3–10

Sosted H, Hesse U, Menne T, Andersen KE and Johansen JD (2005) Contact dermatitis to hair dyes in a Danish adult population: an interview-based study. *Br J Dermatol, 153*(1), 132–135

State of Alaska, D. o. L. W. D., Division of Labor Standards and Safety, Occupational Safety and Health (2003) *The Manager's Handbook: A Reference for Developing a Basic Occupational Safety and Health Program for Small Businesses.* Retrieved November 13, 2006 from http://www.labor.state.ak.us/lss/forms/mgrhandbook.pdf

[what is "D. o. L. W. D." in the above reference? This needs to be spelled out with a comma after it, if it was a co-author of this Handbook]

Stellman JM (2000) COMMENTARY,Perspectives on Women's Occupational Health. *JAMWA Vol.55*, *55*(2), 69–72

Stordeur S, Vandenberghe C, and D'Hoore W (1999) [Predictors of nurses' professional burnout: a study in a university hospital]. *Rech Soins Infirm*, *59*(59), 57–67

Strazdins L, and Bammer G (2004) Women, work and musculoskeletal health. *Soc Sci Med*, *58*(6), 997–1005

Sulkowski WJ and Kowalska S (2005) Occupational voice disorders: An analysis of diagnoses made and certificates issued in 1999-2004. *International Journal of Occupational Medicine and Environmental Health*, *18*(4), 341–349

Svendsen K, Jensen HN, Sivertsen I and Sjaastad AK (2002) Exposure to cooking fumes in restaurant kitchens in norway. *Ann Occup Hyg*, *46*(4), 395–400

Takigawa T and Endo Y (2006) Effects of glutaraldehyde exposure on human health. *Journal of Occupational Health*, *48*(2), 75–87

Thibeault SL, Merrill RM, Roy N, Gray SD and Smith EM (2004) Occupational risk factors associated with voice disorders among teachers. *Annals of Epidemiology*, *14*(10), 786–792

Tomioka K and Kumagai S (2005) Health risks of occupational exposure to anticancer (antineoplastic) drugs in health care workers. *Sangy eiseigaku zasshi = Journal of occupational health.*, *47*(5), 195–203

Undeger U, Basaran N, Kars A and Guc D (1999a) Assessment of DNA damage in nurses handling antineoplastic drugs by the alkaline COMET assay. *Mutat Res*, *439*(2), 277–285

Undeger U, Basaran N, Kars A and Guc D (1999b) Assessment of DNA damage in nurses handling antineoplastic drugs by the alkaline COMET assay. *Mutation Research - Genetic Toxicology and Environmental Mutagenesis*, *439*(2), 277–285

Untimanon O, Pacharatrakul W, Boonmeepong K, Thammagarun L, Laemun N, Taptagaporn S, et al. (2006) Visual problems among electronic and jewelry workers in Thailand. *J Occup Health*, *48*(5), 407–412

Ustinaviciene R and Januskevicius V (2006) Association between occupational asthenopia and psycho-physiological indicators of visual strain in workers using video display terminals. *Med Sci Monit*, *12*(7), CR296–301

Vahter M, Berglund M, Åkesson A and Lidén C (2002) *Metals and Women's Health*: Institute of Environmental Medicine, Division of Metals and Health, Karolinska Istitutet, Sweden; and † Occupational and Environmental Dermatology, Department of Medicine, Karolinska Institutet and Stockholm County Council, Sweden

Valeur-Jensen AK, Pedersen CB, Westergaard T, Jensen IP, Lebech M, Andersen PK, et al (1999) Risk factors for parvovirus B19 infection in pregnancy. *Journal of the American Medical Association*, *281*(12), 1099–1105

[the first author in the above reference is incorrect. There is an extra "M" that is out of place. Please put this in the proper format and move this reference to its alphabetical place in the "P's"]

Weaver VM, McDiarmid MA, Guidera JA, Humphrey FE and Schaefer JA (1993) Occupational chemical exposures in an academic medical center. *J Occup Med*, *35*(7), 701–706

Weisshaar E, Radulescu M, Soder S, Apfelbacher CJ, Bock M, Grundmann JU, et al. (2006) Secondary individual prevention of occupational skin diseases in health care workers, cleaners and kitchen employees: aims, experiences and descriptive results. *Int Arch Occup Environ Health*

Williams NR (2003) Occupational groups at risk of voice disorders: A review of the literature. *Occupational Medicine*, *53*(7), 456–460

Xelegati R, Cruz Robazzi MLDC, Palucci Marziale MH and Haas VJ (2006) Chemical occupational risks identified by nurses in a hospital environment. *Revista Latino-Americana de Enfermagem*, *14*(2), 214–219

Yamamoto N, Saeki K and Kurumatani N (2003) Work-related musculoskeletal disorders and associated factors in teachers of physically and intellectually disabled pupils: A self-administered questionnaire study. *Journal of Nara Medical Association*, *54*(2), 83–101

Yavuz T, Ozdemir I, Sencan I, Arbak P, Behcet M and Sert E (2005) Seroprevalence of varicella, measles and hepatitis B among female health care workers of childbearing age. *Jpn J Infect Dis*, 58(6), 383–386

Younger E, Wittet S, Hooks C and Lasher H (2001) *Immunization and Child Health Materials Development Guide*

Zidkova Z and Martinkova J (2003) Psychic load in teachers of elementary schools. *Ceske Pracovni Lekarstvi*, 4(3), 122–126

Chapter 4
Mental Health Disorders and Work-life Balance

Natalie M. Schmitt, Andreas Fuchs and Wilhelm Kirch

Introduction

Job segregation is one of the key influences on the gender differences seen in the exposure to occupational hazards and diseases suffered. Men and women are strongly segregated into different work sectors, and hold different positions in corporate hierarchy. Women, for example, predominate in the healthcare sector. Women are more likely than men to be in lower-paid jobs, and less likely to hold supervisory or managerial positions. In addition, women still carry out a greater proportion of unpaid work in the home. If paid and unpaid work is added together, women work much longer hours than men. As a result, women are more likely to suffer work-related stress (OSHA 2003a; OSHA 2005).

The prevalence of mental illness (e.g., depression, anxiety) and psychological distress is higher in women in comparison with men. Mental illness accounts for almost 25 percent of early retirements in German women (BMFSFJ, 2001). Major depression will be the primary cause of disability in developed countries by the year 2020. These are only some reasons why the prevention of mental disorders in women is a major public health concern (COHSM 2005). Mental health indicators are *prevalence* and *incidence* of anxiety and depression, disability pensions, and the number of sick leave days due to psychiatric disorders, suicide, and dementia.

Gender differences in mental health seem to be primarily due to socioeconomic disparities. Other explanations may be related to different help-seeking behavior, biological differences, and the different ways men and women acknowledge and deal with distress (Schmitt & Kirch 2006; WHO 2000b). Women have higher rates of depression and anxiety (internalizing disorders) and men have higher rates of substance abuse and antisocial disorders (externalizing disorders) (DGHCP 2004).

The multiple roles that women fulfil in society (wife, mother, homemaker, employee, caregiver to an elderly parent) render them at greater risk of experiencing mental health problems compared to other members of society. In addition to the many pressures placed on women, they must contend with significant gender discrimination and the associated factors of poverty, malnutrition, and overwork. An extreme, but common, expression of gender inequality is sexual and domestic violence perpetrated against women. Sociocultural violence contributes to the high prevalence of mental health problems experienced by women (WHO 2000b).

A. Linos, W. Kirch (eds), *Promoting Health for Working Women.*
© Springer 2008

Due to the recognition of women's high level of education, the necessity of a double income, and women's increased wish for autonomy and social recognition, the employment rate of women has increased worldwide. The double workload of family duties and workplace duties may result in health and safety concerns. Consequently, work-life balance is critically important for working women to sustain their mental health. Work-related mental health problems can occur at any age, and are distinguished by thought and perception disorders and emotional problems (COHSM 2005).

Work-life balance pertains to the balance between occupational and personal obligations. Leading a balanced life contributes to working healthier and more successfully. Issues concerning the balance of family life, private life, and work have attracted increased attention in Europe as more and more women have entered the workforce. Due to changes in technology, which have offered greater flexibility in the structure of work while also eroding the distinction between work and personal life (e.g., the opportunity to telecommute or work nonstandard work hours), work-life balance has gained further relevance for both men and women. Providing employees with the option of balancing their work and private life has become an important managerial exercise. As more and more skilled women are entering the labor market, organizations have become aware of the necessity to support work-life balance. It is not only employees who suffer from an imbalance between working and private life, and the negative impacts it often has on their health, but also the success of the organization in which women work (ENWHP 2007).

Women who work and successfully balance work and private life experience great variation in everyday life and profit from additional possibilities of compensation and increased resources. Work-life balance may be a challenge for women, but it is also a chance to increase women's quality of life and satisfaction. Many women prefer to work outside the home because it gives them a greater sense of life satisfaction. For others (e.g., single parents), employment is not an option but a necessity.

Needs Assessment of Women's Mental Health

At the present time, an accurate needs assessment of women's mental health (an essential element in effective health promotion) remains hampered by inadequate sources of data and an overly biological, individual focus on research and theoretical models that often neglect to consider how women's low social status and material circumstances intersect with their family roles and their participation in paid employment in determining mental health outcomes. The omission of these social factors from studies of women's *vulnerability* to mental health problems amounts to a form of selection bias that precludes the very possibility of examining how gender inequalities might determine women's emotional well-being. (WHO 2000a)

Until now, research on biopsychological and socioenvironmental risk factors for stress has been primarily focused on working conditions, and gender variables, family work, and women's everyday lives have rarely been taken into consideration.

So far, biological and hormonal causes have been considered as the main causes of depression in women. Knowledge of the various risk factors in women's mental health is critical for improving suitable prevention strategies. One study has already shown that increased family work may be a risk factor for the development of mental pathologies in women (Reale, Sardelli & Giffoni 1998)

Safety and health problems suffered by men are generally more visible and more likely to be directly linked to a single cause. Because risks to male workers are often more evident than those faced by women, attention has been focused on male workers and the traditional industries in which they work, rather than on the health and safety of women workers. To redress this balance, gender needs to be systematically mainstreamed into all areas concerning mental health risk factors in the workplace. Data on occupational health and work-related illness always needs to be collected and analyzed by gender. (OSHA 2003a; OSHA 2005)

There is a lack of research concerning work-related risk factors that affect women's health. It is critical, however, to assess risk factors specific to women. (Kuhlmann & Kolip 2005) Psychological trauma, as a common outcome of violent incidents, has not received nearly enough attention or study.

Although the psychological demands and stress in the workplace have been increasing over the last few decades, techniques to effectively assess and measure psychological demands have only been tested and approved recently. The Copenhagen Psychosocial Questionnaire (COPSOQ), which was developed at the Danish National Institute of Occupational Health in 2001, is an example of such a tool. The COPSOQ is used for assessing the psychosocial work environment. There are three versions of the COPSOQ—the long version (141 questions; used by researchers), the medium version (95 questions; for work environment professionals), and the short version (44 questions; for workplaces). (Kristensen et al. 2005; Nübling, Stößel & Green 2005)

The Current Situation

Ten percent of workers are at risk of suffering from mental health problems that lead to unemployment or hospitalization. Costs arising from work-related stress are estimated at around €20 billion annually within the EU. The International Labour Organization (ILO) states that the cost of work-related mental health problems, including stress, represents 3 percent of the EU's gross domestic product (GDP) (ILO 2000)

In general, studies undertaken in different countries and settings do not reveal inconsistencies in the findings that women suffer more often from mental illness than do men. (WHO 2000b) Mental illness, such as anxiety and depression, is twice as frequent in professions in which the majority of workers are typically female—i.e., education, social and health services, and client-oriented jobs.

Men have consistently higher scores than females for positive mental health. Differences between men and women are constant across countries. Women show higher levels of psychological distress, and higher probability of mental ill-health, than men in most European countries (exception: Austria, Netherlands, Luxembourg). In most of the countries where the psychological distress is the highest (France, Portugal and Italy), the female-male rates are the highest. Conversely, in the country with the lowest psychological distress (the Netherlands), there is no difference. Thus, female psychological distress contributes substantially to the differences between countries. Sweden is an exception with a low rate of psychological distress and a high female-male ratio.

In Europe, women consistently score higher than men for any 12-month mood disorder. There seems to be no difference across countries, even though women in southern European countries seem to carry a slightly higher risk. Women generally suffer from poorer mental health than men across many different European countries and regions. This trend holds true for most mental health problems. When all disorders are put together, including alcohol disorders, women still have a higher risk, except in Belgium. Italy and Spain carry more relative mental health risks for women than Germany and Belgium. (DGHCP 2004)

Serious consequences of stress in organizations include decreased presenteeism, higher rates of absenteeism, staff turnover, and lower productivity. Therefore, the direct and indirect costs of workplace stress are considerable. Mental health problems account for greater numbers of workdays lost in comparison to other health problems such as heart disease and back pain. In Europe, workplace stress is responsible for more than 50 percent of all workdays lost, is the second most common occupational health problem (following musculoskeletal disorders), significantly reduces economic performance, and costs EU member states more than 20 billion € every year (COHSM 2005; Paoli & Merllié 2000). Due to their multiple roles as well as to their changing psychological and physical conditions, pregnant workers, women workers who have recently given birth, and women who are

Table 4.1 Prevalence rates of depressive disorders in selected major European studies (period: 12 months / 6 months)

Country	Study	Year	Sample (n)	Prevalence: All— Male (M)—Female (F)
Spain, Italy, Germany, France, Belgium and Netherlands	MHEDEA/ ESEMeD	2000–2002	21425	3.90% – 2.60% (M) – 5% (F)
Finland	Finland 2000	2000	8028	N.A. – 4% (M) – 6% (F)
France	Sante des BN	1998	1445	3.4% – N.A. – N.A.
Germany	TACOS	1998	4075	2.1% – 1.1% (M) – 3% (F)
Germany	GHS	1999	4181	8.30% – 5.50% (M) – 11.20% (F)
Netherlands	NEMESIS	1996	7076	5.80% – 4.10% (M) – 7.50% (F)
France	Paris/Sardinia	1994–96	2260	5.9% – n/a – n/a
France	Santé des F	1998	1183	5.8% – n/a – n/a
Italy	Sardinia	1994–96	1040	6.5% – n/a – n/a

(adapted from Paykel, Brugha, & Fryers, 2005) (reprinted from European Neuropsychopharmacology, 15(4), Paykel, E. S., Brugha, T., & Fryers, T., Size and burden of depressive disorders in Europe, 411–23, 2005, with permission from Elsevier BV & European College of Neuropsychopharmacology)

Table 4.2 Psychological distress in ten European countries

Country	Prevalence
Netherlands	10.9%
Sweden	12.4%
Spain	17.6%
Luxembourg	18.7%
Belgium	19.1%
Austria	19.5%
Germany	20.1–23.4%
France	25.9%
Portugal	29.3%
Italy	30.2%

(Percentage with a score of 52 or less on MHI-5 (Mental Health Inventory) scale of SF36 (short-form health survey) (DGHCP, 2004)

breastfeeding, are considered a specific risk group concerning work-related mental illness. Tables 4.1 and 4.2 and Figs. 4.1 and 4.2 show European data on mental health and psychological distress, as well as on sick leave days and disability pensions related to psychiatric disorders.

In European studies, prevalence rates of depressive disorders vary between 2.1 and 8.3 percent. In these studies, women consistently are more likely to suffer from depressive disorders in comparison to men (see Table 4.1) (Paykel, Brugha, & Fryers 2005).

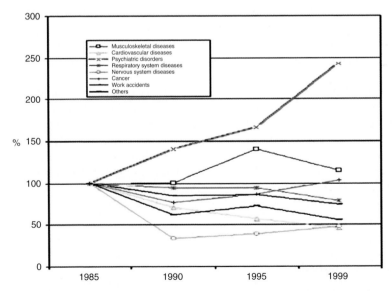

Fig. 4.1 Changes in the frequencies of new disability pensions (1985–1999) (1985 = 100%), Austria (Hrabcik, 2003)
(permission granted from Dr. Hubert Hrabcik, Bundesministerium für Gesundheit, Familie und Jugend, Vienna)

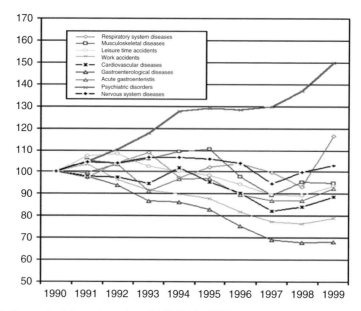

Fig. 4.2 Changes in sickness leave days (1990-1999) (1990 = 100%), Austria (Hrabcik, 2003) (permission granted from Dr. Hubert Hrabcik, Bundesministerium für Gesundheit, Familie und Jugend, Vienna)

Table 4.2 shows the percentage of persons with psychological distress as defined by a score of 52 or less on the Mental Health Inventory 5 (MHI-5) scale of the Short-Form (SF) Health Survey SF36. People scoring 52 or less are considered to have high psychological distress and to consequently be at risk of suffering from mental health problems. As Table 4.2 clearly demonstrates, the prevalence of psychological distress is significantly different between countries.

Figures 4.1 and 4.2 show data on trends of causes of new disability pensions and sickness leave days in Austria. Unfortunately, we do not know of any more recent data. There is no reason, however, for any substantial change in the conspicuous trend. The percentage of sickness leave days and disability pensions that are due to psychiatric disorders increases significantly, while other causes remain more stable over time. In 1999, 19 percent of new disability pensions were granted because of psychiatric disorders in Austria. Psychiatric conditions were second to musculoskeletal diseases (39 percent of new disability pensions).

Problem Analysis

In general, occupational stress is caused by a mismatch of demands relating to work and the individual's resources and ability to cope. Work overload, lack of recognition by peers, a poor relationship with one's supervisor, lack of participation in decision-making, and lack of information are the most important sources of stress in the work environment. Insufficient participation at work may cause psychological tension, dissatisfaction, alcohol abuse, depression, anxiety, and low self esteem. Levels of responsibility that are either too low or too high have an impact on women's mental health. In addition, women in client-oriented jobs—particularly women who have to deal with angry clients—are at increased risk of anxiety and depression (COHSM 2005).

Compared with men, women are more likely to hold jobs with little autonomy and responsibility. Women are also more involved in occupations that are both intellectually demanding and involve helping others, such as teaching and nursing (COHSM 2005). Decreased presenteeism and increased absenteeism due to mental health disorders may compromise job security and, consequently, women's socioeconomic position.

There is evidence that even after controlling for occupational grade, perceived work conditions, and gender roles, women still suffer significantly more from mental health problems in comparison with men, which is not true for physical symptoms (DGHCP 2004).

Workplace stress is increasingly becoming a concern for both individuals and organizations. In 2000, about one-third of European workers claimed to be affected by stress. The number of workers reporting high levels of workplace stress doubled in the last decade. Workplace stress is related to mental health problems such as depression, anxiety, sleep disorders, mood and affective disorders, post traumatic stress and adjustment disorders, and behavioral disorders like drug abuse, sexual disorders, and eating disorders. In addition, working women increasingly complain about problems concentrating, irritability, mood swings, personal conflicts in the workplace, being burnt out, isolation, and lack of social activities. Intense, prolonged, or frequent feelings of occupational stress are major risk factors of psychological disorders (COHSM 2005). Figure 4.3 shows a model of the development of psychological complaints.

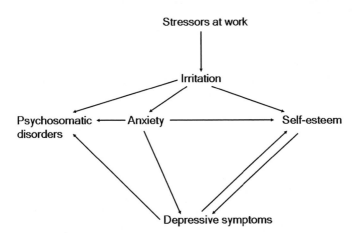

Fig. 4.3 The development of psychological complaints
(adapted from Dormann & Zapf, 2002)

There are various causes of work-related mental health problems on the individual, organizational, and societal levels. Stress seems to be caused primarily by working conditions. It is often difficult, however, to separate the personal life from the work life. Personality, gender, and age are critically influential in the way workers cope with difficult situations, and consequently in the development of mental health disorders. Young and middle-aged workers are more susceptible to workplace stress than older people. In terms of differences based on gender, women are more likely to suffer from anxiety, depression, and psychological distress in comparison with men. Because women typically have to play multiple roles, and shoulder the weight of various responsibilities as wives and mothers, their psychological demands add up. Even women who work full time spend more time than their spouses do meeting family obligations. Personalities who adopt good time-management and problem-solving strategies, and are able to express needs, take advantage of social support, and maintain a healthy lifestyle, are more likely to successfully combat mental health problems. Additional causes of stress common to women include decreased time to rest and relax, victimization, assertiveness, and physical unattractiveness (Friedrich 2006). Work overload, lack of participation in decision-making, and lack of recognition of the individual and his work by peers may cause mental health problems (COHSM 2005).

Shift work, irregular work schedules, and long working hours are particularly harmful to women's mental health because women have to fulfill multiple roles and these working conditions complicate work-life balance. Women who spend most of their time at the workplace or have irregular working hours may experience difficulties balancing their personal, family, and work lives. In addition, an unhealthy environment at work with high levels of noise, pollution, and poor lighting and air quality is harmful to women's health (COHSM 2005).

Call center agents are at risk of being exposed to disturbing background noise generated by the high amount of work-related talk of colleagues on the phone, or by the ringing of telephones. Exposure to high levels of noise leads to mental fatigue. Good room acoustics and adequate headsets may reduce these stresses. In addition, call center workplaces are typically characterized by higher stress levels related to interactions with clients, decreased job control, and higher time pressure than in other occupations. All these factors were found to correlate with mental health disorders and psychosomatic symptoms.

Violent, abusive, or threatening incidents in the workplace are more prevalent for women than for men, and often result in serious and disabling psychological damage. Emotional problems resulting from violent incidents include depression, fear, posttraumatic stress syndrome, loss of sleep, disturbed relationships with family, friends, and co-workers, decreased ability to function at work (presenteeism), and increased absenteeism.

Women who are at an increased risk for experiencing workplace violence include employees who work in homes or out in the community, persons working late or at irregular hours (e.g., healthcare workers), and persons who provide care and advice (e.g., healthcare workers, mental health workers, emergency room technicians, and hospital admissions workers) (AFSCME 2007).

Mental health in working women, and issues related to work-life balance are a significant public health concern. Gender-based differences concerning women's susceptibility to work-related mental health problems are not necessarily due to biology, but rather are due to the combination of low educational levels and poor working conditions. Additionally, due to conflicts resulting from work-life balance and women's commitment to multiple roles, women are more likely to suffer from mental illness (COHSM 2005). Women's risk factors for mental illness are consequently mostly preventable and need to be focused on more intensively in prevention programs.

Promotion of Work-Life Balance and the Prevention of Mental Illness and Work-Related Stress in Women

Effects of Good Mental Health and Work-Life Balance

Knowledge of the various risk factors in the development of mental illness enables women to recognize and avoid situations and behavior that may be harmful in everyday life, including working life. Prevention of mental illness in women increases the individual's—and the whole family's—quality of life and decreases significant disability in both. All relationships women have may be strengthened and positively influenced.

Prevention of mental illness requires constant time and effort on the part of the working woman. Although the results of prevention efforts may not be visible in the short term, women need unreserved family support from the beginning of any behavior change. Family members have to get used to the fact that responsibilities concerning family life need to be distributed more equally. Successful prevention of women's mental health disorders will compensate for increased efforts on the part of the family.

Investments in work-life balance benefits both the individual employee and the company. Satisfaction, motivation, and feelings of well-being may be increased. Availability of in-house child care facilitates women's acceptance of educational programs and flexible working hours and increases women's attachment to the organization (ENWHP 2007).

Practical Advice: Worker-Related Issues

Direct efforts specific to primary prevention of mental disorders, and behavioral, psychosocial, and neurological disorders, would survey the scientific knowledge base, examine primary prevention activities around the world, address the cross-cultural relevance of prevention programs, and define training needs and related activities. Successful prevention programs call for the integration of biological and psychosocial factors, and the active promotion of proven preventive programs. Models taking account of the co-morbidity of many disorders—the clusters of psychiatric disorders and psychosocial distress—must be developed to encourage interventions for supporting individuals who are afflicted with mental illness. In addition, prevention programs require an understanding of indigenous protective factors, such as the activities of caretakers of those who are ill and those local practices that enhance the mental and physical health and well-being of individuals and of communities. Listening to women with and without professional activity should help to identify these factors (WHO 2000a).

Women first need to recognize that the current situation compromises mental health before they will be willing to participate in prevention strategies, invest in efforts to cope with the problems, and be susceptible to behavior change. Successfully coping with stress requires that women learn to identify symptoms of stress, such as increased heart rate, clammy hands, and difficulty concentrating. Good support networks, participation in leisure activities and physical exercise, as well as reduction of the consumption of stimulating foods and beverages, are critically important in the prevention of workplace stress and its consequences—they strengthen mental resources and increase resistance to psychological distress (COHSM 2005).

Women should be encouraged to improve communication in the workplace, communicate problems and expectations, and play an active role within the organization. Social isolation, as well as social conflicts at work (trouble with the boss, subordinates, or customers), is positively related to depression (Dormann & Zapf 2002).

Continuous education on pedagogical skills is most important in the prevention of mental health problems in teachers. Role-playing is a method that may help teachers to conceive reactions and develop problem-solving strategies (OSHA 2003b). In addition, training in violence avoidance and self defense may help women in the prevention of mental health disorders.

Choice of Occupation and Workplace

Women may select a workplace in an organization that offers child care and flexible working hours. Working in an organization with family-friendly policies reduces stress and promotes work-life balance. Organizations that provide a mentor system, psychological support systems, and that support communication should be chosen first to prevent mental health problems.

Choice of profession should be unrestricted for women. Women should choose their education and occupation on their own so that they will be motivated at work. If women already know about family planning early on, they should prioritize professions that allow work-life balance more easily.

Whether women should avoid jobs in which male workers are overrepresented, or whether gender mainstreaming should be accomplished in all fields to maximize mental health prevention in the workplace needs to be discussed.

Interventions at the Organizational Level

Primary Prevention

Primary prevention of mental health disorders within organizations should focus on the reduction of work-related stress. Indicators of high levels of stress at the organizational level may include increased injuries and absenteeism, increased staff turnover, decreased productivity and quality of work, and decreased use of vacation time. Action should aim to reduce the work load, improve communication, and enhance workers' participation in decision-making processes within the organization. Suggestions and requests of individuals may be gathered, analyzed, and applied within the work environment with the participation of these workers. In addition, data on long- and short-term leave may be analyzed to diagnose the scope of the problem and its possible causes. Although primary prevention strategies reduce problems at their source, and considerably reduce resulting costs, they are used less often. Strategies for increasing workers' participation in decision-making processes require significant time and effort, support by upper management, and may not immediately show positive effects. On the other hand, these actions may have lasting effects and may be integrated into daily management activities. There are various other primary prevention strategies:

- Regular group meetings are a chance to give recognition, social support, and feedback, share information concerning the organization, discuss individual expectations, problems, and desired solutions, and stimulate dialog with supervisors and colleagues
- Employee training enables employees to assume more responsibilities and autonomy and helps to avoid qualitative work overload
- Analysis of positions and tasks may avoid work overload, clarify roles und responsibilities related to the position, specify expectations and objectives, and reduce risks linked to the work environment and working conditions (COHSM 2005)

Secondary and Tertiary Prevention

Secondary and tertiary prevention of mental health problems aims at limiting the consequences of workplace stress. The idea is to give workers the tools needed to better recognize their reactions to stress and deal more effectively with stress. In organizations, individuals may be taught how to better manage problems concerning their professional lives. Secondary prevention strategies include information and awareness activities and skills development programs that allow a worker to strengthen her (mental) resources and to develop new ones—to combat stress more effectively and increase resistance to it. All prevention strategies, however, leave the responsibility of developing personal resources to the individual. Specific secondary prevention strategies may be:

- Publication of articles on mental health at work in internal newsletters and on bulletin boards
- Providing sessions and seminars on causes, symptoms, and prevention of work-related mental health problems
- Organizing workshops on change management
- Promotion and development of healthy eating programs in the staff restaurant
- Promotion of physical exercise (e.g., disposal of an exercise room or organizational memberships at fitness centers)
- Training on stress and time management, conflict and problem management, and balancing personal and professional obligations (COHSM 2005)

Tertiary prevention strategies aim to treat, avoid chronification of the disease, and rehabilitate workers, as well as facilitate the return-to-work and the follow-up to reduce the risk of relapse. These activities are centered on the individual rather than on the work situation, and therefore must be voluntary, confidential, and available at all times. Examples of tertiary prevention strategies are:

- Peer-help networks and employee assistance programs for active listening, information, needs assessment, support, and referrals to specialized resources (doctors, psychologists, psychiatrists, social workers, lawyers)
- Return-to-work programs for maintenance of employment relationships, development of return-to-work plans, and employment support measures such as progressive return to work, temporary assignments, and medical follow-up (COHSM 2005)

Prevention strategies must be integrated into the daily operation of the organization. The prevention of work-related mental health problems must be an integral part of the daily life of all members of the organization. Child care should be provided for seminars that take place outside regular working hours.

An in-depth analysis of the situation within the organization is essential for the development and implementation of effective prevention strategies that have to take place within a planned and structured approach to obtain lasting results. Support of workers and their representatives is a prerequisite to effective organizational prevention programs.

Clear, realistic, and quantifiable goals need to be established prior to the implementation of prevention strategies. To ensure program effectiveness, interventions have to be evaluated and updated regularly (COHSM 2005).

Prevention of Workplace Violence

Risk of workplace violence may be decreased with engineering and administrative controls. Engineering controls include entrance controls in the building, closed circuit TV cameras, restricted entrance to a facility after dark, and cell phones for field personnel. If possible, workplaces should be open and lucid. Examples of administrative controls are additional staffing, a ban on working alone, recording accidents, verbal abuse, and *near misses*, and training in self-defense.

People trained in treating people exposed to violent incidents should intervene immediately after an incident has taken place, because early intervention may reduce the long-term impact of trauma. The Critical Incident Stress Debriefing (CISD) model that includes immediate emotional support, education about normal stress reactions, symptom reduction, and appropriate referrals to specialists, may be used (Antai-Otong 2001). Counseling should include coworkers and colleagues as well as family members (AFSCME 2007).

Promotion of Work-life Balance

There is an increasing amount of research that provides good reasons for the implementation of strategies to improve work-life balance and invest in appropriate initiatives. The company's ability to compete and perform successfully is increased if work-life balance is increased. A healthy balance between work life and private life benefits the health of both the employees and their companies. Investments in work-life balance may increase employee satisfaction and motivation, raise employees' levels of health and feelings of well-being, raise customer satisfaction and customer loyalty, improve the image and public reputation of the enterprise, and increase its productivity and business performance. Work-life balance activities primarily fall within the scope of work design, personnel, and health policies, and primarily serve to achieve work flexibility (ENWHP 2007).

Work-life balance policies help women to effectively combine work and family responsibilities, as well as those in their personal life. Work-life balance on the work side includes flexible working hours arrangements (e.g., annualized working hours), flexible leave arrangements (e.g., paternity leave, leave during school holidays), reduced working time and flexible design of work processes (e.g., job sharing, job rotation, work sharing, part-time work), and flexible location (e.g., telecommuting) (ENWHP 2007; WLB 2005). Provision of financial and social support (e.g., child care) and offering of reintegration programs, stress management, and physical activity programs for women may benefit work-life balance and personal development.

The availability of child care within the organization or in the neighborhood is crucial in enabling women to balance work and life. Organizations that offer child care help reduce effort and time spent on the road, and create flexible time schedules. The operating hours of child care facilities must be long and flexible to enable women to attend seminars and educational programs after work. Planning of vacation and shift arrangements have to take into account that mothers may have to be on vacation during school holidays and may not be able to organize child care in the short term (ENWHP 2007).

Organizations may establish mentor systems and offer support by trained specialists who serve as contact persons for women who experience problems in balancing working and family life. These employees may help to organize child care or a substitute in the event that the female worker is not able to work in the short term.

Practical Advice for Public Health Professionals

Women who suffer from mental health problems or work-related stress, or who do not manage to balance their private and working lives should be motivated to invest in behavior change and prevention. Although prevention of mental illness requires constant time and effort on women's part, it increases the quality of life for both the individual and the family, at least in the long term. Spouses and close family members of affected women should also be motivated to participate in prevention programs.

The various risk factors for the development of mental illness should be explained to women so that they may better recognize and avoid possibly harmful situations and behavior. Women who are working in jobs in which there is an increased risk of violent incidents should be enlightened about the effectiveness of early intervention. A list of persons trained in treating people exposed to violent incidents should be provided in advance. In addition, training in violence avoidance and self defense may prevent mental health disorders.

Women should be advised to select a workplace in an organization with family-friendly policies (e.g., concerning the availability of child care, flexible working hours), mentor systems, psychological support systems, and that supports communication. Organizations with family-friendly policies should be identified and promoted. Their products should be promoted as well. Women should be taught the symptoms of stress, such as increased heart rate, clammy hands, and difficulties in concentrating (COHSM 2005).

Women should further be advised to participate in leisure activities and physical exercise, have a balanced, healthy diet, and avoid consumption of stimulating foods and beverages to increase resistance to stress (COHSM 2005).

Women should also be encouraged to improve communication at the workplace, communicate problems and expectations, and play an active role within the organization because social isolation, as well as social conflicts at work, is positively related to depression (Dormann & Zapf 2002). Continuous education plays a critical role in the primary prevention of mental illness. Its importance must be emphasized.

To promote the organizational changes necessary for the prevention of workplace stress and mental health disorders, the management of local businesses and organizations should be contacted. Suggestions for organizational changes must be communicated to them.

Public campaigns (e.g., in local newspapers) should be launched to fight against the tenacious prejudices that working women have to face. Women who have to balance family and working life are esteemed *less productive*. Studies comparing the productivity of female workers without children and those with children should be conducted. Collected data and results of data analysis should be published and explained to those concerned. Positive images of working women must be promoted.

Local politicians should be encouraged to adopt laws that ensure financial and social support, such as the availability of child care for women who are willing to work. Positive examples of women who successfully balance family and working life, and whose families profit from the women working, should be integrated into soap operas and other telecasts.

Barriers and Problems

The barriers and problems which working women have to face are manifold:

- Due to their multiple responsibilities in work, family, and private life, women may not be able to spend additional time at the workplace for job training, prevention programs, and continuing education
- Part-time work may enable women to better balance working and family life. On the other hand, part-time work results in decreased salary, which may restrict women in getting support in family responsibilities (e.g., hiring maids and babysitters). Working women may need support while engaging in leisure activities or educational programs that are essential in the prevention of mental health disorders
- If child care is not available, women may not be able to engage in prevention programs
- Child care is still primarily referred to women in society. Mothers have to care for their children. Therefore, women may have a guilty conscience about engaging in additional activities after work
- The prejudice that women who have to balance family and working life are less productive and show increased absenteeism is tenacious
- Even though the situation has improved over the last few decades, gender stereotypes still exist in the workplace. Mothers are especially still facing negative stereotypes. Mothers are held to stricter employment standards than women without children. Mothers seem to have lower promotion rates compared to childless workers with the same qualifications (Fuegen et al. 2004)

Framework of the Prevention of Mental Illness

Figure 4.4 shows the ecological framework that can be applied to the prevention of mental health disorders.

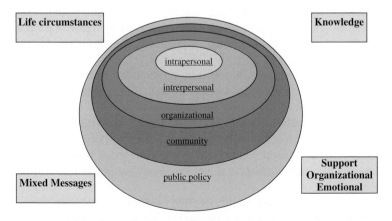

Fig. 4.4 Ecological framework on the prevention of mental health disorders

Stakeholders in the prevention of mental health disorders in women in the workplace are the female worker herself, her colleagues, other female workers, her supervisors, the boss, the organization, the family, friends, physicians in general as well as psychiatrists, policy makers, and society.

Causes of mental illness may be events in the private lives of women, in the organization where they work, or in the society in which they live. Personal, interpersonal, organizational, and societal (including the healthcare system) issues influence women's well-being, health, and their behavior change concerning mental health. The framework applies to behavior change as it captures intra- and interpersonal factors, as well as environmental factors that are external to the family level—e.g., the healthcare system, community factors, societal norms, and public policies (Fig. 4.4).

Self-efficacy, the personal resistance to work-related stress, and the female worker's believe in the ability to prevent mental health problems and successfully balance family and working life may be the most important factors on the intrapersonal level. Women's problem-solving approach is also closely related. Women who actively seek support and information are more likely to prevent mental health problems than women with a passive problem-solving approach. Attitudes of the family, and especially the spouse, about working women, and their emotional support are other important factors that influence women's behavior.

Workplace policies that should be implemented to promote women's mental health and work-life balance are described in the previous section, "Interventions at the Organizational Level." Organizational policies should primarily focus on the reduction of work-related stress—one of the causes of work-related illness—and flexible working hours. Family-friendly policies benefit both the female worker and the organization. Data on the causes of mental health disorders have to be collected and analyzed. Organizational programs have to be evaluated and adapted on a regular basis. All businesses must be trained to better adapt their health and safety policies so that health and safety is sensitive, targeted, and inclusive. Awareness training must become more tailor-made for each specific situation, because the needs of small- and medium-sized organizations will naturally differ from those of a large multinational company.

Adherence to legislation concerning maternity leave and pregnant workers must be enforced by all means. Certainty on the adherence to rights (e.g., protection against unlawful dismissal) of pregnant women may significantly reduce stress in the workplace.

A positive image of women who are working should be cultivated in the community to reduce women's necessity to fight against common prejudices and social norms. Feeling the need to defend the decision to go back to work after childrearing may negatively influence women's mental well-being. Positive examples of women who successfully balance family and work life, and whose families profit from the women working, should be integrated into soap operas and other telecasts to increase acceptance and encourage women to invest in work-life balance.

Policies concerning the availability of child care and the healthcare system (e.g., promotion of prevention programs, availability of healthcare providers, utilization of healthcare, unmet needs assessment) play a critical role in the prevention of mental health disorders. Physicians and therapists have to take into account the various roles women play, the importance placed on these roles, and how closely those roles are tied to women's self-identity (Friedrich 2006). All psychosocial aspects of working have to be integrated in public policies. Gender mainstreaming has to be enforced, as well as equality in health policy, organizational policy, and social and economic policies (OSHA 2003a; OSHA 2005).

Factors from different levels of the framework on prevention of mental health disorders interact and aggregate with the following key influences: women's knowledge of mental health, women's life circumstances, support, and mixed messages (Fig. 4.4). In addition, the later factors determine women's susceptibility to mental health disorders. Women's understanding of how to best prevent mental health disorders can significantly reduce the risk of mental illness, and is primarily influenced by the mother's personality, her problem-solving approach, her family and significant other, and educational programs on the organizational level. Organizational and emotional support is important for women in the workplace—particularly for mothers. All levels of the described framework play an important role in women's support systems.

Mixed messages about the cultural and societal acceptance of working women, work-life balance, and the importance for mothers to continue working, are sent out from the family and the community. Women's (private) life circumstances (e.g., marital status, number of children, influence of family members, social network, housing conditions), as well as their career circumstances (e.g., employment status, promotion prospects), modify their risk of mental health disorders and their self efficacy primarily on the intrapersonal, interpersonal, and societal levels of the framework.

References

American Federation of State, County, and Municipal Employees (AFSCME) (Accessed 2007) Fact Sheet: Workplace Violence. *American Federation of State, County, and Municipal Employees*. Washington DC. Available from http://www.afscme.org/issues/1293.cfm (accessed February 21st, 2007)

Antai-Otong D (2001) Critical Incident Stress Debriefing: A Health Promotion Model for Workplace Violence. *Perspectives in Psychiatric Care, 37*, 125–139

Bundesministerium für Familie, Soziales, Familie und Jugend (BMFSFJ) (2001) Bericht zur gesundheitlichen Situation von Frauen in Deutschland. *Bundesministerium für Familie, Soziales, Familie und Jugend*. Berlin. Available from http://www.bmfsfj.de/Politikbereiche/gleichstellung,did=4122.html (accessed February 21st, 2007)

Chair in Occupational Health and Safety Management (COHSM) (2005) A Series: Mental Health at Work. From Defining to Solving the Problem. Québec: Université Laval

Directorate General for Health and Consumer Protection (DGHCP) (2004) The State of Mental Health in the European Communion. *European Commission*. Luxembourg. Available from http://ec.europa.eu/health/ph_projects/2001/monitoring/fp_monitoring_2001_frep_06_en.pdf (accessed February 21st, 2007)

Dormann C, Zapf D (2002) Social stressors at work, irritation, and depressive symptoms: Accounting for unmeasured third variables in a multi-wave study. *Journal of Occupational and Organizational Psychology, 75*, 33–58

European Agency for Safety and Health at Work (OSHA) (2003a) Gender issues in safety and health at work—A review. *Office for Official Publications of the European Communities.* Luxembourg. Available from http://osha.europa.eu/publications/reports/209/reportgenderen_en.pdf (accessed February 21st, 2007)

European Agency for Safety and Health at Work (OSHA) (2003b) Prévention des risques psychosociaux et du stress au travail au pratique. *Office for Official Publications of the European Communities.* Luxembourg. Available from http://agency.osha.eu.int/publications/reports/104/stress_fr_fr.pdf (accessed February 21st, 2007)

European Agency for Safety and Health at Work (OSHA) (2005) Mainstreaming gender into occupational safety and health. *Office for Official Publications of the European Communities.* Luxembourg. Available from http://agency.osha.eu.int/publications/reports/6805688/full_publication_en.pdf (accessed February 21st, 2007)

European Network for Workplace Health Promotion (ENWHP) (Accessed 2007). Work-Life-Balance: A balanced life working healthily and more successfully. *Federal Association of Company Health Insurance Funds.* Essen. Available from http://www.enwhp.org/index.php?id=69&no_cache=1&sword_list[]=work&sword_list[]=life&sword_list[]=balance (accessed February 21st, 2007)

Friedrich SL (2006) Gender issues in mental health. Encyclopedia of mental disorders. Available from http://www.minddisorders.com/Flu-Inv/Gender-issues-in-mental-health.html (accessed February 21st, 2007)

Fuegen K, Biernat M, Haines E, Deaux K (2004) Mothers and Fathers in the Workplace: How Gender and Parental Status Influence Judgments of Job-Related Competence. *Journal of Social Issues,* 60(4), 737–754(18)

Hrabcik H (ed) (2003) Mental Health in Austria. Selected annotated statistics from the Austrian mental health reports 2001 and 2003. *Federal Ministry of Health and Women.* Vienna. Available from http://www.bmgf.gv.at/cms/site/attachments/8/5/0/CH0026/CMS1038920009809/mental_health_in_austria.pdf (accessed February 21st, 2007)

International Labour Organization (ILO) (2000) Study of Mental Health in the Workplace in Germany, the United States, Finland, Poland and the United Kingdom. *International Labour Organization,* Geneva

Kristensen TS, Hannerz H, Hogh A, Borg V (2005) The Copenhagen Psychosocial Questionnaire—a tool for the assessment and improvement of the psychosocial work environment. *Scand J Work Environ Health,* 31(6), 438-449

Kuhlmann E, Kolip P (2005) Gender und Public Health. Weinheim, München: Juventa

The Irish Work Life Balance Website (WLB) (2005) Work Arrangements. *National Framework Committee for Work Life Balance Policies.* Ireland. Available from http://www.worklifebalance.ie/index.asp?locID=40&docID=-1 (accessed February 21st, 2007)

Nübling M, Stößel U, Hasselhorn HM (2005) Methoden zur Erfassung psychischer Belastungen. *Bundesanstalt für Arbeitsschutz und Arbeitsmedizin.* Dortmund, Bremerhafen: Wirtschaftsverlag NW

Paoli P, Merllié (2000) Third European Study on Conditions at Work. *European Foundation for the Improvement of Living and Working Conditions.* Dublin

Paykel ES, Brugha T, Fryers T (2005) Size and burden of depressive disorders in Europe. *Eur Neuropsychopharmacol,*15(4), 411–23

Reale E, Sardelli V, Giffoni P (1998) Stress e vita quotidiana della donna [Stress and women's everyday life: Experimental research on psychological and social risk factors in female prevalent pathologies: depression, hypertension, breast cancer]. *Consiglio Nazionale delle Ricerche [Italian National Research Council].* Naples. Available from http://www.salutementaledonna.it/stress_engl_.htm (accessed February 21st, 2007)

Schmitt NM, Kirch W (2006) Council of the European Union: Conclusions on Women's Health – A Report. *Journal of Public Health,* 14(6), 391–393

World Health Organization, Department of Mental Health and Substance Dependency (WHO) (2000a) Women's mental health: An evidence based review, *World Health Organization.* Geneva. Available from http://whqlibdoc.who.int/hq/2000/WHO_MSD_MDP_00.1.pdf (accessed February 21st, 2007)

World Health Organization (WHO) (2000b) Factsheet N°248: Women and mental health. *World Health Organization.* Geneva. Available from http://www.who.int/mediacentre/ factsheets/fs248/en/ (accessed February 21st, 2007)

Further Publications and Links
Relevant to Mental Health and Work-Life Balance

Aparicio JC (2002) Workplace stress – a growing problem. In: European Agency for Safety and Health at Work (OSHA) Magazine. Issue 5: Working on stress. *European Agency for Safety and Health at Work.* Bilbao. Available from http://www.europe.osha.eu.int/ publications/magazine/5/index_6.htm

Chair in Occupational Health and Safety Management (COHSM) (2005) A Series: Mental Health at Work. From Defining to Solving the Problem. Québec: Université Laval. Stress assessment questionnaire (QUEST) Available from http://cgsst.fsa.ulaval.ca/ sante/eng/sources_du_stress.asp

Cleary M, Walter G (2005) Towards a healthier lifestyle for staff of a psychiatric hospital: Description of a pilot programme. *International Journal of Mental Health Nursing,* 14, 32–36

Cook R, Schlenger W (2002) Prevention of Substance Abuse in the Workplace: Review of Research on the Delivery of Services. *The Journal of Primary Prevention,* 23(1), 115–142

Directorate General for Health and Consumer Protection (DGHCP) (2004) The State of Mental Health in the European Union. *European Commission.* Luxembourg. Available from http://ec.europa.eu/health/ph_projects/2001/monitoring/fp_monitoring_2001_frep_06_en.pdf

Emdad R, Belkica K, Theorella T, Cizinskyb S (1998) What Prevents Professional Drivers from Following Physicians' Cardiologic Advice? *Psychother Psychosom,* 67, 226–240

European Foundation for the Improvement of Living and Working Conditions (2007) Dublin (January 11th, 2007); http://www.eurofound.eu.int/help/contact.htm The Foundation is a European Union body, one of the first to be established to work in specialized areas of EU policy. Specifically, it was set up by the European Council (Council Regulation (EEC) No. 1365/75 of 26 May 1975), to contribute to the planning and design of better living and working conditions in Europe

European Agency for Safety and Health at Work (OSHA) (2000) Research on work-related stress. *Office for Official Publications of the European Communities.* Luxembourg. Available from http://agency.osha.eu.int/publications/reports/203/stress_en.pdf

European Agency for Safety and Health at Work (OSHA) (2003c) Comment mâtriser les problèmes psychosociaux et réduire le stress d'origine professionnelle. *Office for Official Publications of the European Communities,* Luxembourg. Available from http://agency.osha.eu.int/publications/reports/309/fr/index.htm

European Network Education and Training in Occupational Safety and Health (ENETOSH) (2006) Dresden (February, 2007); Available from http://www.enetosh.net/webcom/ show_article.php/_c-29/i.html

European Women's Health Network (EWHNET) (2001) Transnationale Verständigung. Die Rolle von Leitlinien als Arbeitsgrundlage in Frauengesundheitsprojekten. *European Women's Health Network,* Hannover. Available from http://www.ghi.org.uk/EWHN/ Documentations/Leitlinienpapier.pdf

Landesvereinigung für Gesundheit Niedersachsen e.V., European Women's Health Network (2007) Hannover (revision date not specified); http://www.gesundheit-nds.de/ewhnet/start.htm

Hope A, Kelleher CC, O'Connor M (1998) Lifestyle practices and the health promoting environment of hospital nurses. *Journal of advanced nursing,* 28(2), 438–447

Kishi R, Kitahara T, Masuchi A, Kasai S (2002) Work-related Reproductive, Musculoskeletal and Mental Disorders among Working Women – History, Current Issues and Future Research Directions. *Industrial Health,* 40, 101–112

Kivimäki M, Sutinen R, Elovainio M, Vahtera J, Räsänen K, Töyry S, Ferrie JE, Firth-Cozens J (2001) Sickness absence in hospital physicians: 2 year follow up study on determinants. *Occup Environ Med*, 58, 361–366

Kompier MAJ, Geurts SAE, Gründemann RWM, Vink P, Smulders PGW (1998) Cases in stress prevention: the success of a participative and stepwise approach. *Stress medicine*, 14, 155–168

Lindquist TL, Beilin LJ, Knuiman MW (1997) Influence of Lifestyle, Coping, and Job Stress on Blood Pressure in Men and Women. *Hypertension*, 29, 1–7

Magyary D (2002) Positive mental health: A turn of the century perspective. *Issues in Mental Health Nursing*, 23, 331–349

Mangili A (2004) Alcol e lavoro. *G Ital Med Lav Erg*, 26(3), 1–27

McMahon SD, King C, Mautz B, Jason LA, Rossi JS, Redding CA (2001) Worksite Interventions: A Methodological Exploration and Pilot Study Promoting Behavior Change. *The Journal of Primary Prevention,* 22(2), 103–119

U.S. National Library of Medicine. Medline Plus Health Information. Mental Health (2007) Bethesda (February 19th, 2007), http://www.nlm.nih.gov/medlineplus/mentalhealth.html

O'Campo P, Eaton WW, Muntaner C (2004) Labor market experience, work organization, gender inequalities and health status: results from a prospective analysis of US employed women. *Social Science & Medicine,* 58, 585–594

Patterson CR, Bennett JB, Wiitala WL (2005) Healthy and unhealthy stress unwinding: promoting health in small businesses. *Journal of Business and Psychology*, 20(2), 221–247

Riemsma RP, Pattenden J, Bridle C, Sowden AJ, Mather L, Watt IS, Walker A (2002) A systematic review of the effectiveness of interventions based on a stages-of-change approach to promote individual behaviour change. *Health Technology Assessment*, 6(24), 1–231

Sauter SL, Murphy LR, Hurrell JJ Jr (1990) Prevention of work-related psychological disorders. A national strategy proposed by the National Institute for Occupational Safety and Health (NIOSH). *American Psychologist*, 45(10), 1146–1158

Talvi AI, Jarvisalo JO, Knutsf LR (1999) A health promotion programme for oil refinery employees: changes of health promotion needs observed at three years. *Occup Med*, 49(2), 93–101

Taveras EM, Capra AM, Braveman PA, Jensvold NG, Escobar GJ, Lieu TA (2003) Clinician Support and Psychosocial Risk Factors Associated With Breastfeeding Discontinuation. *Pediatrics*, 112, 108–115

Trenberth L, Dewe P, Walkey F (1999) Leisure and Its Role as a Strategy for Coping with Work Stress. *International Journal of Stress Management*, 6(2), 89–103

Ware N, Del Vecchio Good MJ (1995) Women. In R. Desjarlaid, L. Eisenberg, B. Good, & A. Kleinman (Eds.), World Mental Health: Problems, priorities, and responses in low-income countries. Oxford University Press, pp 179–206. Adapted version available from http://www.un.org/womenwatch/daw/csw/mental.htm (accessed February 21st, 2007)

Waters LE (2000) Coping with unemployment: A literature review and presentation of a new model. *International Journal of Management Reviews,* 2(2), 169–182

World Health Organization (WHO) (2007) Mental Health. *World Health Organization.* Geneva. Available from http://www.who.int/topics/mental_health/en/

Chapter 5
Musculoskeletal Disorders

Verka Koytcheva, Alexander Zhekov, George Lazarou and Elena Riza

Introduction

Musculoskeletal conditions (MSDs) are extremely common and have important consequences for the individual and the society. Around 50 percent of the population report musculoskeletal pain in one or more areas for at least one week in the last month (European Union (EU)-Public Health 2007).

MSDs are also one of the most common work-related health problems affecting millions of European workers across all occupational sectors, bearing a substantial cost on the employers. In the EU-27, 25 percent of European workers complained of backache and 23 percent complained of muscular pains (European Agency for Safety and Health at Work 2007).

Definitions

MSDs are conditions of the musculoskeletal system that are usually progressive and associated with pain. They can be categorized in diseases of the joints, spinal disorders, physical disability, and conditions resulting from trauma. MSDs carry a great impact on society, especially conditions such as rheumatoid arthritis, osteoarthritis, osteoporosis, lower-back pain and limb trauma (EU-Public Health 2007). Apart from pain, the main characteristics of MSDs are loss of physical function, limitation of activities, restriction of social life, low quality of life, and temporary or permanent work disability.

Work-related musculoskeletal disorders (WMSDs) are disorders and diseases of the musculoskeletal system with a multi-factorial etiology where work performance and workplace environment are, among others, two significant risk factors for those involved in the onset of the disease. Multiple other risk factors, such as lifestyle habits and individual predisposition, may act as trigger factors for their onset (European Agency for Safety and Health at Work 2007; Maier & Ross-Mota 2001).

Disease Burden of MSDs

According to the Bone and Joint Decade Report (2005), MSDs are the eighth leading cause of disease burden on Europe. About 25 percent of adults in Europe suffer from

A. Linos, W. Kirch (eds), *Promoting Health for Working Women.*
© Springer 2008

a longstanding MSD that limits their daily activities. A quarter of the European population has some form of rheumatism or arthritis. The prevalence of physical disabilities due to MSDs is 4-5 percent in the adult European population, higher in women than in men, and significantly increases with age.

The Fourth European Working Conditions Survey (2005) shows that 62 percent of workers in the EU-27 are exposed a quarter of the time or more to repetitive hand and arm movements, 46 percent of European workers report working in painful or tiring positions, and 35 percent carry or move heavy loads. European workers commonly report MSDs as a work-related health problem: 30 percent (about 44 million) complain of backache and 17 percent complain of muscular pains in their arms and legs. Health problems range from discomfort (minor aches and pains) to more serious medical conditions requiring time off from work, medical care, and hospital treatment. In more chronic cases, treatment and recovery are often unsatisfactory, and the result can be permanent disability leading to the loss of job.

Back pain is the second leading cause of sick leave, following respiratory conditions, but MSDs rank first in long-term work absence. The lifetime prevalence of back pain in Europe is 60 to 85 percent, while 12 to 30 percent of adults have lower-back pain at any time. Although lower-back pain may be due to a series of risk factors such as degenerative, inflammatory, and infective causes, congenital defects, or metabolic bone disease, workplace exposures constitute a major risk factor. Back pain can become a chronic condition when workplace factors are not overlooked, or when the person is obese and leads a sedentary lifestyle (Bone and Joint Decade Report 2005).

The cost of Treating WMSDs, together with the costs of absenteeism, has been estimated between 0.5 to 2 percent of the gross national product (GNP) in the Nordic countries (European Agency for Safety and Health at work 2000a).

Occupational Injuries

Occupational injuries form a subcategory of MSDs (Trauma and Injuries), together with major limb trauma and sports injuries where an injury occurs as a consequence of an activity at the workplace. They may affect muscles, tendons, joints, nerves, and related soft tissues anywhere in the body.

Occupational injuries are categorized in cumulative trauma disorders (CTDs), repetitive strain injuries (RSIs), overuse symptoms, and cervical-brachial disorders (Bone and Joint Decade Report 2005). The main symptoms of occupational injuries are pain, stiffness, tingling, clumsiness, loss of coordination, loss of strength, skin discoloration, and temperature differences. The lower back and upper extremities, including the neck and shoulders, are the most frequent sites.

CTDs are injuries developed gradually over a period of time—weeks, months, or years—and as a result of repeated pressure on a particular part of the body. The concept is based on the theory that each repetition of an activity produces some trauma or wear and tear of the tissues and joints of the body (Erdil et al. 1994; Frederick 1992).

RSIs are upper-limb disorders caused by awkward postures and repetitive or fast-paced movements as a consequence of repetitive work (working tasks may be repeated as often as every ten seconds, especially in factories). Lower limbs can also be affected. (European Agency for Safety and Health at Work 2007). Overuse syndromes are caused by repeated exposure of the same muscle, tendon, or region, to the same risk factor, and may result in injury and inflammation of the affected area. Cervical-brachial disorders involve the presence of symptoms affecting the neck and arms as a result of constant overhead motions and activities that pull the shoulders back and down.

Risk Factors for the Development of MSDs

Many factors contribute to the onset of MSDs, as well as WMSDs (including occupational injuries)—a) physical factors, b) organizational and psychosocial factors, and c) individual factors.

Physical Factors

The primary physical risk factors for occupational injuries are repetition of movement, high force, awkward joint posture, direct pressure, vibration, cold environments, and prolonged constrained posture. Exposure to these risk factors during work can be, to a large degree, eliminated by taking simple preventative measures.

Organizational and Psychosocial Factors

The main organizational factors that can lead to WMSDs include daily exposure to physical factors, repetitive work, and insufficient rest or recovery time. Mental strain can also cause muscular tension and increase existing physical strain. Work conditions that may increase mental strain are psychologically demanding activities that put the worker under stress, mental demands as a consequence of tight deadlines, and decreased levels of autonomy, low job satisfaction, high pace of work, and lack of support from colleagues, supervisors, and managers (European Agency for Safety and Health at Work 2007).

Individual Factors

Individual factors include prior medical history, physical capacity, age, smoking history, and obesity.

The Socioeconomic Impact of WMSDs

Work-related musculoskeletal disorders constitute a major concern regarding occupational safety and health in European countries (EWCO 2005), because:

- WMSDs have the highest impact on sickness absenteeism in Europe. A total of 39 percent of sickness absence of two or more weeks is related to MSD symptoms, compared to 19 percent of total sickness absence due to stress, depression, and anxiety
- Blue collar employees experience almost 20 times as many MSDs as white collar workers (e.g., clerks, managers). The relative number of WMSD complaints is highest among service workers and shop and market sales workers (3,700/100,000 workers)
- WMSDs are the most prevalent lost-time injuries and illnesses in almost every industry in Europe

Legislation

The significance of the problem is reflected in the European Union's Health and Safety policy. There are a number of regulations within the European Union that require employers to protect the health and safety of employees:

- On the terms, procedures, and the recurrence of conducting risk assessments
- On the implementation of physiologically sound work and rest schedules
- On the physiologically consistent standards and rules for manual handling of heavy loads
- On the minimum requirements for ensuring healthy and safe working conditions at workplaces where equipment is used
- On providing healthy and safe working conditions during handling and moving heavy loads.

The requirements, set forth by these regulations, apply to all companies where such work is carried out.

European Directives

The main European directives relevant to preventing musculoskeletal disorders are:

- Directive 89/391 provides a general framework for risk identification and prevention. It imposes upon the employers the duty to provide health and safety for the employees, assessing the risk at the workplace
- Directive 90/269 covers the identification and prevention of manual handling risks and states the minimal requirements for health and safety in manual han-

dling of heavy loads. The directive targets the risk of back injuries and promotes the implementation of special machinery/equipment for load handling

- Directive 90/270 covers the identification and prevention of risks from work with display screen equipment, including minimum requirements for equipment, work environment, and computer interface
- Directive 89/654 covers minimum standards for workplaces, including seating, lighting, temperature, and work station layout
- Directive 90/326/EEC requests the inclusion of a list of occupational disorders in the national legislation of the members of the EU. Eight (8) of these occupational disorders are musculoskeletal
- Directive 89/655 covers the suitability of work equipment.
- Directive 89/656 covers the suitability of personal protective equipment (PPE).
- Directive 98/37 covers machinery (replaced Directive 89/392).
- Directive 93/104 covers the organization of working time.
- Common standards for the design of work equipment are set at European level. These are known as CEN standards. The series of CEN standards entitled "Safety of Machinery-Human Physical Performance" is relevant to MSD risks

Work-Related Musculoskeletal Disorders in Women

It is well-documented that gender segregation exists in the workforce and that there is strong horizontal and vertical segregation. Horizontal segregation refers to the fact that men tend to occupy manual, technical, and transportation posts, while women mostly occupy service and sales posts. Vertical segregation refers to the fact that men tend to hold more senior, managerial posts than women, who tend to occupy non-specialized, blue-collar jobs (WHO 2004). The World Health Organization (WHO) also reports that women are more likely to work under fixed-term employments, and are, therefore under-represented in permanent job contracts.

This job segregation has a direct impact on female health and on WMSDs, in particular. Women tend to suffer more from pain in the upper back and upper limbs as a result of repetitive work in factories and in offices, while men tend to suffer more from lower-back pain from exerting high force at work. WMSDs can occur in every work setting and structure. Particularly affected are manual workers (skilled and unskilled) and older workers who tend to report more musculoskeletal problems.

Women are more exposed to repetitive work and work in painful and tiring conditions as a consequence of fixed-term contracts. Therefore, women suffer more from RSIs such as tendonitis, carpal tunnel syndrome (Messing 1998). These disorders can affect both upper and lower limbs, including the shoulders and neck, the wrists, the elbows and the knees. While men have more muscular conditions while they are young, women's WMSDs appear with age (Andersson et al. 1990).

Blue-collar employees experience many more MSDs than white-collar ones. Those particularly affected are shop, market, and service sales workers (women are primarily employed in these jobs), and laborers in mining, construction, manufacturing, and transport.

Complaints regarding MSDs are more frequent in men than women, mostly because of the immediate link of the condition to the work (e.g., lifting heavy loads hurts a person's back) whereas women's musculoskeletal conditions develop over a number of years (e.g., carpal tunnel syndrome in computer operators or secretaries).

WMSDs affect women workers more than men largely because of the different types of work in which they are employed. Men and women work in different sectors and perform different tasks. The common belief is that men do physically demanding work such as manual handling and heavy lifting, which makes them more susceptible to back problems, while women do the fine, repetitive work with high demands for accuracy and high pace ,demanding high static loading of the neck and shoulders that can lead to upper extremity problems.

The main causes for these differences between men and women are:

- Men and women differ in many aspects of physical body size and functional capacity, such as stature, body segment lengths, and muscle strength
- Work stations, tools, and Personal Protective Equipment (PPE) for women workers have been designed on the basis of anthropometric data for men, and therefore are ergonomically inappropriate for women
- Gender-related biological differences may result in differential vulnerability of women to physical risk workplace factors
- The two-fold work strain of women—both at their place of employment and at home caring for children and performing household work (which, for the most part, is still the responsibility of women)—results in greater overall exposure to physically demanding activities and psychosocial strain, as well as reducing the opportunities to recover after a day at work (European Agency for Safety and Health at work 2000a; Lundberg et al. 1994).
- Women are more likely than men to be working low-paid jobs requiring repetitive, monotonous, forceful, or prolonged exertion of the hands, prolonged awkward postures both at their place of employment and at home, and caring for children.

Women's Workplace Risk Factors

Female employees/workers are exposed to a combination of workplace risk factors. There is strong evidence confirming the relationship between exposure to a combination of risk factors (e.g., force and repetition, force and posture) and musculoskeletal disorders and a dose-response relationship for the number of hours of work per week (European Agency for Safety and Health at Work 2004) .

The main professional risk factors for the onset and aggravation of musculoskeletal disorders for women at the workplace are:

- Significant physical overload—manual lifting, handling, and moving of loads
- Repetitive motions—long periods of executing simple repetitive movements, or monotonous motor activity. Multiple (more than 1,500 to 2,000 times daily)

repetitions of the same movement at time intervals between repetitive cycles of less than 30 sec.

- Static effort for maintaining a certain posture of the body and during activities involving a marked component of the supporting equipment, or loads, and so on
- Vibration exposure in cases of frequent use of vibrating instruments, particularly while working at low ambient temperatures or driving for prolonged periods— whole body vibration
- Working in cold environments
- Working with arms raised above shoulder level, or in a highly back-bent posture
- Ergonomic inconsistencies of workplace, control panel, machinery and equipment designs, and work seat
- Prolonged squatting or kneeling

A high number of upper extremity disorders has been lined to the work intensity, as well as work characteristics such as perceived time pressure, high work pace, work variability, work load, monotonous work, low quality work, limited job control, and uncertainty about job expectations. The number of risk factors present and the duration of exposure to these factors contribute to the higher level of occupational risk associated with a given profession.

The presence of risk factors in a job does not necessarily mean that employees will develop WMSDs. Whether or not certain work activities put an employee at risk of injury depends on the duration (how long), frequency (how often), and magnitude (how intense) of the women's exposure to the risk factors. Jobs or working conditions that present multiple risk factors will have a higher probability of causing a problem. A number of determinants can influence a female's response to risk factors linked to WMSDs at the workplace. Among these are the:

- Personal characteristics of the female worker—inadequate fitness-for-work, physical features, health, skilfulness
- Organization of work—duration of work periods, the presence of approved rest break schedules
- Advanced age and increasing years on the same job—musculoskeletal impairments are among the most prevalent and symptomatic health problems of middle and old age (30–34 age group for women)
- Poor job design
- Poor female worker habits and behaviours—posture habits and body mechanics
- Stress

Adverse Organizational Factors

- Insufficient budget allocated to the prevention of WMSDs
- Quantity and quality production targets are higher priority
- No technological options available—technology is already established with no budget for improvements

- Limited choice of machinery and equipment. Poor choice because of limited funds and failure to take into account the standing and the role of female workers
- Belief that the human factor is the one to adapt to the technological economical and organizational characteristics of manufacture

The majority of negative consequences for the musculoskeletal system result from the lack of awareness of the nature of the occupational activities performed especially by female workers, and more particularly, the elements of activities performed by women. Extra attention should be placed on the following:

- The movements performed, the physical efforts exerted, the postures to be maintained
- The workplace furniture, the worker's seat
- The equipment, instruments and tools
- Age, and gender differences of the female body
- The fact that the work pace is a permanent value, and that the adaptive potential of the employee is limited
- The fact that health risks associated with their work are minimized by complying with instructions and standard operating procedures

These workplace risk factors, along with personal characteristics and societal factors, are thought to contribute to the development of WMSDs in women. The causative relationship between these factors and WMSDs is not fully established. It is accepted that the causal relationship is stronger between the psychosocial factors and the specific WMSDs symptomatic with shoulder and neck pain. Other studies show a possible connection between low work satisfaction and complaints of neck and back pain (Punett & Herbert 2000).

Although some systemic disorders, such as rheumatoid arthritis, diabetes, hormonal imbalances, or pregnancy, are related to the development of musculoskeletal disorders, they are not linked with occupational activities and cannot be considered work-related.

Consequences of Work-related Musculoskeletal Disorders

There is a distinct impact of WMSDs on the employee, the employer and the state.

Employee

- Damaged health and functional capacity of the worker—in certain cases full disability
- Lower income
- Limited ability to find a job
- Limited ability to improve skills
- Family and social problems.

Employer

- Reduced quantity and quality of production
- Costs incurred for sick leave compensations, the need of training of, and paying salaries to, replacement workers
- Costs associated with the workforce drift
- Insurance costs for new workers
- Litigation costs and payment of compensations for illegally inflicted occupational disorders

State

- Financial losses due to costs for supporting disabled individuals and for treatment of the ill

Most Common Occupational Musculoskeletal Disorders

The most common sites affected by WMSDs (Maier & Ross-Mota 2001) include:

- Wrists (14%)
  - Inflammation of the tendons—tendonitis
  - Inflammation of the tendon's capsule—tendosinovitis, tendovaginitis
  - Reynaud's disease—vasoconstriction in response to exposure to vibrations or cold
  - Carpal tunnel syndrome
  - De Kerven's disease

- Upper extremities (9%)
  - Epicondilitis, radiculitis, insertionitis
  - Inflammation of the muscle transition site—tendomyositis

- Shoulder (10%)
  - Periarthritis, insertionitis
  - Neuritis of the brachial plexus
  - Myotendonitis

- Lower extremities (5%)
- Back (44%)
- Trunk, other (12%)

The most prevalent types of work-related MSDs are (Healthline 2007):

- **Low-back pain**—a complex syndrome of multifactorial aetiology, highly prevalent in all age groups and among all professions. Much more frequently found among female complaints compared to male complaints. In modern society, back pain is the most widely spread disorder and the most costly one. About 70 percent of people suffer from back pain, with a greater relative proportion of affected females—particularly those of advanced age. The major reason is largely considered to be the poor ergonomic design of the workplace, the nonergonomic work seat, and working posture (Armstrong 1986, Bureau of Labour Statistics 1995; Webster & Snook 1994).

- **Shoulder and neck disorders**—shoulder pain appears as a symptom in different syndromes. The major causes are considered to be the poor ergonomic workplace layout, the height of the work surface, incompliance with the workers' posture, and the anthropometric peculiarities of female workers (NIOSH 1997a).
- **Osteoarthritis**—frequent handling and moving of heavy materials, badly coordinated workers' posture, vibrations, and repetitive movements are considered to be professional workplace-associated causes of osteoarthritis.

Occupations Most Affected by MSDs

The most commonly affected professions are those involving repetitive and intense overload of the muscles, joints, ligaments, nerves, and vascular structures of the musculoskeletal system. The highest incidence rates of WMSDs occur from overexertion among workers exposed to repetitive movements—repetitive use of tools, repetitive placing, and grasping or moving of objects. Younger workers (less than 30 years of age) are more frequently exposed to repetitive tasks, especially young female employees.

MSDs occur in all occupation and work settings but particularly high rates are found among (European Agency for Safety and Health at Work 2007):

- Agricultural, forestry, and fishing workers
- Construction workers
- Carpenters
- Drivers
- Nurses
- Cleaners
- Miners
- Machine operators
- Craft workers
- Tailors
- Retail workers
- Hotel, restaurant and catering workers
- Secretaries and typists
- Loaders and unloaders

Agriculture and construction are the most-affected sectors regarding exposure to physical risks, and MSDs complaints.

In general, women are less exposed to physical risk factors than men, but are more exposed to organizational and psychosocial factors with frequent hand or arm movements and work involving painful or tiring positions. For certain risks—jobs involving moving people such as nursing—women are significantly more exposed than men (11 percent and 6 percent, respectfully) a quarter of the time or more. Moreover, workers in nursing and personal care facilities regularly suffer from overexertion.

Video display terminal work involves data entry tasks that frequently include constrained postures, highly repetitive movements of the fingers, hands, and wrists, and static muscle loading resulting in increased prevalence of WMSDs by creating musculoskeletal strain and discomfort (Sauter & Swanson 1992).

Women's Workplace Risk Assessment

Risk assessment should be based upon the application of ergonomics principles, and this approach is implicit in many of the existing European Union health and safety directives. There is a variety of risk assessment methods used to measure the exposure to physical risk factors, and even more refined research methods are performed in laboratories. Some of the methods have been developed for use by practitioners at the workplace, such as Quick Exposure Check (Li & Buckle 1998).

Assessing the Risks of Musculoskeletal Disorders to Workers

Risk assessment refers to the identification of workplace risk factors and the application of practical measures in preventing or reducing risk exposure. To find an effective solution to a musculoskeletal problem, it is very important to carefully observe the real situation in the workplace, because many factors vary between jobs and every working environment is different. Attention should be paid on all the possible risk factors, because a combination of factors may be creating a risk. The workers should also be consulted.

Factors potentially linked to an increased risk of MSDs include a) the load, b) the workplace, c) the worker, and d) the task (European Agency for Safety and Health at work 2000b), therefore the risk assessment process should include a list of queries including:

The load
Is the load heavy?
Is the load awkward to lift or move, restricting vision, or difficult to hold?
Is it a live load (e.g., an animal or a liquid moving in a container)?

The workplace
Is the workplace untidy, with things to trip over?
Is there sufficient space to carry out the work?

Is the ground or floor uneven?

Is the floor slippery or the surface unstable?

Are the lighting conditions poor?

Is the work environment (e.g., temperature, humidity, or wind going to affect the work)?

If the task is carried out in a sitting position, is suitable seating provided?

The worker

Is the worker physically able to carry out the task? Do not assume.

Is the worker pregnant or has a particular health problem that may put him/her at risk?

Does the worker know what has to be done and how to do it safely?

Does the worker have any PPE or clothing that may impede them in the task?

Is the worker exposed to vibration, pressure, or stress that may increase his risk of ill-health?

Does the worker have sufficient recovery time between tasks?

Is the worker fatigued when carrying out the task?

Is the worker in control of the pace of work?

The task

Does the task require repetitive movements?

Does it require awkward, forceful, or twisting movements, including squeezing, hammering, or pounding?

Does the task require handling loads at a distance from the trunk?

Does the job require an awkward posture such as stooping or reaching upwards?

Does the task require loads to be lifted or carried excessive distances?

Staff complaints or days off sick with back pain or aches and pains indicate a problem. Consider if the work could be automated or reorganized to avoid the need for any manual lifting. To identify all the risks, the task, the working environment, and capabilities of the worker, all need to be looked at—including handling, carrying, pushing, and pulling of loads, as well as lifting. If the task can not be eliminated, and is able to be carried out manually (i.e., with risks reduced), training and information are an important part of the prevention plan.

Acting to Prevent MSD Risks

If the general assessment identifies risks from manually handling loads, the employer should:

- Eliminate the job if it is reasonably practical to do so
- Assess the operations that cannot be avoided
- Take steps to reduce the risk of injury

A combination of actions needs to be taken to solve MSD problems, such as:

- Physical measures—changing the workplace or load
- Changing work methods
- Information and training for the worker

Often the costs of these solutions are small, and they are always tiny in comparison to the costs of disabling and painful injuries. Reducing risks from manual handling will usually improve the efficiency of the task, reduce labor costs, and improve staff motivation.

Simple Solutions

Physical solutions to manual handling problems are often low cost and easy to apply.

Levers

Simple leverage can be a very cheap and effective solution. Examples of situations where you could use leverage include:

- Helping to make minor adjustments when hitching linkage-mounted machines or hanging gates
- Inching a heavy item—such as a water tank—horizontally
- Using a spare post or crowbar when fencing for removing posts, tensioning wire, and others
- Purpose-made tools for lifting manhole covers
- Long-handled wrenches or extension handles on some tools (taking care not to damage or over-tighten bolts, etc.)

Platforms

Tables and platforms, including temporary ones, can help ensure you are working at the best height. Consider:

- A swing-out *bench* over the tractor's front weight frame for maintenance work at a remote site
- A trolley or swing-out mounting on a tractor to present a heavy toolbox at a convenient height and avoid lifting
- A makeshift bench (e.g., of straw bales) to make livestock husbandry tasks easier
- Storing tractor weights at the same height as the mounting frame, (e.g., on pallets) if you cannot handle them mechanically

Counterbalances and Stored Energy

Using a counterbalance or stored energy helping the following situations:

- Consider applying a counterbalance weight to help when lifting loads such as heavy manhole lids. Remember not to compromise child safety where a lid or cover is secured shut by weight alone
- Fit and maintain effective tailgate assistors (counterbalances, springs, etc.) on livestock transporters
- To improve the task of linking equipment to tractors
- To position equipment accurately, using any slope to your advantage
- Maintain and use the three-point linkage leveling box and the adjustment in a top link
- Use quick attach/detach systems, e.g., with an *A* frame.
- Consider auto-attach and demount weight blocks in place of individual front weights

Prevention of Musculoskeletal Disorders at the Workplace that focus on Women

Undeniably, MSDs are an important public health problem that may be prevented or reduced by complying with existing health and safety laws and following guidance on good practice.

The European prevention approach (based on Directive 89/391, Article 6.2) for musculoskeletal disorders is as follows (European Agency for Safety and Health at work, 2000b):

- Eliminate MSD risks (e.g., by automating or mechanizing the task)
- Assess the MSD risks that can not be eliminated
- Combat the MSD risks at the source
- Adapt the work to the individual, especially the design of workplace, the choice of work equipment, and the choice of working and production methods
- Adapt to technical progress
- Replace the risk by replacing high-risk tasks with lower-risk, or risk-free tasks.
- Develop a coherent overall prevention policy that covers technology, the organization of work, working conditions, social relationships, and the influence of factors related to the working environment
- Give collective protective measures priority over individual protective measures
- Give appropriate instructions to workers.

Women employed in many workplaces are not aware of the requisite measures for the improvement of working conditions and fatigue reduction. This includes the use of specially designed furniture to ensure ergonomic layout of the workplace, which leads to the effective neglect of the special measures designed to reduce the adverse impact of the risk factors. There is a lack of educational programs and training courses specifically targeting women focusing on the risk factors in women's workplaces.

Policy

The high incidence of musculoskeletal disorders among working women requires a serious approach to the problem, and the implementation of competent measures to reduce, or eliminate, the risk factors for the onset or development of such disorders.

Activities aimed at preventing musculoskeletal disorders in women should become an integral part of management practice and of the working routine at all levels in any company (Leamon 1994; NIOSH 1992).

Company policy should:

- Develop a rigid program of regular assessments of workplace risk factors
- Develop clear targets
- Introduce, as a company policy, the commitment to reach these targets
- Provide appropriate resources
- Clearly formulate the responsibilities of the company with respect to the health problems of working women, in compliance with current legislation
- Assign responsibilities (training, job analysis, workplace layout, health checks, etc.) to designated staff members
- Integrate the issue of female health into the process of management decision-making with the active participation of workers
- Involve female workers in the planning, implementation, and evaluation of activities, in measures to ensure healthy workplaces, and in taking responsibility for their own health and the health of their peers
- Undertake risk assessment based upon the requirements of the relevant national and European legislation
- Identify appropriate measures to eliminate or reduce the risk by making changes in the women's workplaces and work organization with the cooperation of the workers
- Establish health care surveillance to ensure early detection and treatment of musculoskeletal disorders
- Assist in health education, disorder prevention, and protection of the health of women at work
- Establish health care management programs to encourage the return of the affected women back to work
- Ensure that assigned responsibilities are fulfilled

Activities Towards Preventing Musculoskeletal Disorders Among Women

Prevention of musculoskeletal disorders must start at the top and run through every level in the organization. Employers should consult with employees and their representatives to determine the approach and opinions on how to improve the working conditions. The measures for active prevention are important not only for identifying such disorders, but also for quantitative assessment of the risk factors, which could trigger the onset and accelerate the development of the disorders.

The commitment to the prevention policy should include:

- Assigning program responsibilities and authority to those running the program
- Providing adequate financial, personnel, and material resources
- Analysis of worksite activities and infrastructure to identify risk factors and hazards
- Information dissemination, training, and medical management

Activities to prevent occupational disorders may be successful if better working conditions are implemented and through improving the work characteristic.

Efforts should be directed towards improving the quality of labor, the workplace conditions, and the work habits of female workers. The primary effort to protect female workers should focus on avoiding repetitive patterns of work through job design and possible mechanization, job rotation, job enlargement, and enrichment or teamwork, workplace layout, tools and equipment design, and work practices to avoid unnecessary motion of the neck, shoulders, and upper limbs (Hendrick 2003; NIOSH 1997b; Owen 2000). The reduction of physically demanding work is often the first preventive step to be taken in the workplace.

Studies have been undertaken to establish the effect of rest breaks on the development of MSD in workers of Video Display Terminals (VDT). The results showed that conventional rest break schedules (mid-morning and mid-afternoon breaks of 10–15 min.) may not be optimal for highly repetitive VDT work. There was significant performance up to 15 percent, and comfort gains with more frequent, shorter breaks. The benefits were modest, if any, from including exercises in the break regimen (Sauter & Swanson 1992).

Actions to Prevent Musculoskeletal Disorders among Female Workers

Actions to prevent musculoskeletal disorders among female workers should include:

- Regular health checks
- Identification of the risk factors and analysis of the associated risk in women's workplaces. Identification of the hazards, risk evaluation, and risk management are the essence of a good prevention system for musculoskeletal disorders, together with the implementation of appropriate changes in the job design, the working environment, ergonomic workplace design, layout and proper work, and rest break schedules

- Ergonomic analysis of the work processes—number, time dispersion, duration, and demands for efforts—necessary for performing these actions, including analysis of posture during work and the static efforts.
- Ergonomic analysis of the workplace and its correlation with the anthropometric parameters of female workers.
- Analysis of the congruence between qualifications required for a certain activity and the actual skills and qualification of the workers.
- Studies on the opinion of female workers regarding workplace design, job design, work load, health problems, professional risk factors, and impact of exposure
- Development and implementation of specific programs for women's health and safety in the workplace, work and rest schedules based on risk assessment, and risk factor identification at each individual workplace, to include:

  - Adequate work and rest schedules
  - Optimal physical loading to the body
  - Optimizing the work posture and work movements
  - Optimizing the workplace and equipment in accordance with ergonomic requirements

- Provision for the necessary funding for health and safety program implementation
- Effective control on the implementation of the programs, which should include:

  - Control of compliance with the approved work and rest schedule, and proper utilization of rest breaks
  - Control of compliance with admissible musculoskeletal loads
  - Control of compliance with the basic ergonomic requirements for an adequate workplace and, if necessary, special furnishings compliant with the physiological health and safety requirements for the job

- Increase health awareness of the female workers through education—e.g., maintaining a healthy lifestyle, work and recreation, healthy diets, risk management, and so on
- Enhance female worker's motivation and job satisfaction.

Who Should Participate?

The prevention of WMSDs at workplaces with female employees must be based on a multidisciplinary approach, involving technical disciplines—ergonomics, work organization, industrial health and safety, the design and layout of the workstation—as well as medical disciplines such as taking medical factors into account, training, information, intervention as soon as symptoms emerge, and medical treatment of established disorders (NIOSH 1997c).

Risk assessment, development, and implementation of programs to prevent WMSDs require the participation of:

- Health care providers
- Health and safety personnel

- Human resource personnel
- Engineering personnel
- Maintenance personnel
- Ergonomic specialists
- Staff and management representatives

Workers' Involvement

The most effective solution for improved safety and reduced health hazards in the worksite is a combination of management and female workers' involvement. Employers should consult with employees and their representatives to determine the general opinion on how the policy for workplace improvement should be applied.

Involved employees should report the presence of risk factors in the workplace, understand the symptoms and injuries, have input into the design solutions, and provide the central resource for maintaining a risk-free workplace.

Female workers should take actions to identify general MSD hazards that result in discomfort and pain, and report to the supervisors without fear of reprisal or discrimination. If there is a health and safety committee/department, control, the prevention of musculoskeletal disorders should be one of its main areas of concern.

Employers should involve female workers in health and safety management and encourage them to:

- Submit suggestion and concerns
- Identify and report tasks that are difficult to perform
- Discus work methods
- Provide input in the design, layout of the workstations, equipment, procedures, and training
- Define the perceived real or suspected job hazards
- Suggest ways to control suspected hazards
- Help in the evaluation of the equipment
- Respond to surveys
- Report injuries as soon as they occur
- Participate fully in the investigations of MSD cases
- Participate in task groups assessing the ergonomics

Programs, Primers, Guidelines, and Checklists

A variety of primers, guidelines, manuals, and checklists have been developed. They can be used by industrial health and safety personnel, as well as management, for initial ergonomic evaluation of jobs/tasks and designing effective programs to prevent WMSDs. (Li & Buckle 1998 ; Vikari-Juntura 1997). According to National Institute for Occupational Safety and Health-USA (NIOSH 1997d), the seven actions to be included in an effective program are:

1. Look out for signs of a potential musculoskeletal problem in the workplace, such as frequent worker reports of aches and pains, or job tasks that require repetitive, forceful exertions.
2. Show management commitment in addressing possible problems and encouraging worker involvement in problem-solving activities.
3. Offer and organize training to expand management and workers' ability to evaluate potential musculoskeletal problems.
4. Gather data to identify jobs or work conditions that are most problematic, using sources such as injury and illness logs, medical records, and job analysis.
5. Identify effective controls over tasks that pose a risk of musculoskeletal injury and evaluate the approach taken to reduce the risk. Assess whether the approach has helped to reduce or eliminate the problems.
6. Establish health care management with an emphasis on the importance of early detection and treatment of musculoskeletal disorders to prevent impairment and disability.
7. Minimize the risk factors for musculoskeletal disorders when planning new work processes and operations. It is less costly to build good design into the workplace from start than to redesign later.

Guidelines

The large number of affected people and the significant prevalence of musculoskeletal disorders determine the interest in implementing guidelines and set forth requirements for healthy and safe conditions of labor in the workplace.

The information in the guidelines provides employers with effective approaches, as well as useful references to be used when determining the need of ergonomic solutions. The guidelines present recommendations for changing equipment, workstations, and work methods with the aim of preventing and reducing WMSDs. The guidelines should be adapted to each individual woman's workplace, taking into account its characteristics.

Checklists are useful tools for determining the presence of symptoms, hazards, and the risk factors of musculoskeletal disorders at the worksite. Checklists are also a way of collecting the same kind of information repeatedly. They serve as reminders to regularly examine the most important activities related to musculoskeletal disorders.

Program Evaluation

The development and delivery of prevention technologies are only the first steps in an effective prevention program. Of equal importance is the need to evaluate and demonstrate the effectiveness of the prevention strategies. Evaluating the effectiveness of a program is just as important as implementing the program itself.

The assessment should answer to the following questions:

- Is the program reducing musculoskeletal disorders, hazards, and risks?
- Does an initial upsurge in reporting of musculoskeletal disorders mean the project has became less safe because of the program?
- Does this upsurge mean that a hidden number of injured female workers has gotten treatment and will return to a healthier level of life and productivity?
- Have musculoskeletal hazards been successfully identified and targeted?

Program evaluation will answer all these questions and more.

Good Practice

The examples of good practice provide information for determining methods and different solutions that can be used for risk assessment and WMSD prevention at different workplaces. The European Agency for Safety and Health at work (2000c) presents an overview of practical solutions that are effective in a variety of workplaces.

These practical solutions in programs for prevention, however, have often been drawn for particular workplaces only. They will not be effective when applied at a workplace with different risk factors associated with different types of work, workplace conditions, equipment, and women's workforce specifics.

Training

Training is an additional important strategy to reduce the tension imposed on women's musculoskeletal systems (NIOSH 1997e). Knowledge of how to prevent WMSDs can significantly reduce the risk. Training efforts generally fall into three areas: training in specific techniques, teaching biomechanics, and training the body via physical fitness so that it is less susceptible to injury.

Training can also improve women's workplace culture and provide the basis for consistent awareness, identification, analysis, targeting, and control of musculoskeletal disorders hazards, as well as awareness of women's rights and responsibilities. Training should provide knowledge of the work tasks that may lead to pain or injury, understanding of the proper tools and work practices for performed tasks, the ability to recognize WMSDs and their early indications, the advantages of addressing early the MSDs before serious injury develops.

The training should reach female workers, foremen, and supervisors, as well as others participating in the musculoskeletal disorders control program. Training the medical community should improve the early identification of musculoskeletal disorders. Early recognition of these disorders is very important because medical treatment is not very effective once these injuries become longstanding. Training should be provided in a manner and language that all employees can understand. One of the main problems that a training program might face is the low participation rates of female workers.

Standards

The introduction of standards is another approach to WMSD prevention. The standards regulate the ergonomic requirements for the equipment, furnishings, and organization of the workplace because they play a part in the onset and development of WMSDs. Currently existing regulations and standards are highly inadequate for the prevention of WMSDs. Although WMSDs are a growing problem, they are not covered sufficiently in the existing European legislation, especially in the case of female workers, where additional emphasis should be placed.

The need for such legislation is confirmed by the fact that, despite all the regulations effective since 1989, no reduction in cases of WMSDs has been noted. Much remains to be done towards reducing the workplace-associated risk for musculoskeletal disorders—rigid implementation of ergonomic standards, training at all levels in identifying the early signs of disorders, implementation of technological processes to reduce manual work and, providing funds for ergonomic improvement at workplaces.

Practical Advice for Employers

- Provide education to female employees on the risk and prevention of musculoskeletal disorders at regular intervals (e.g. annually)
- Perform risk assessment in consultation with the employees on a regular basis to identify musculoskeletal disorders and formulate and implement controls for the prevention and reduction of these disorders
- Pay special attention on the workplace layout for female workers, and make the workplace adjustable—enabling different persons to fit comfortably and reach easily
- Pay special attention to female workers highly exposed to workplace risk factors
- Provide adjustable chairs, including lumbar (lower-back) support
- Provide a system of reporting and documenting acute or chronic musculoskeletal disorders among women with applicable regulations
- Conduct women's workplace risk assessment prior to the purchase of new equipment to ensure that it meets the needs of all female users
- Maintain all equipment in good working order
- Provide adequate rest breaks
- Encourage task rotation in the workplace as much as possible
- Research and apply good practices for prevention of WMSDs

Practical Advice for Female Workers

- Minimize sustained bending, twisting, reaching, *pressure*, and awkward postures; alternate sitting and standing; and avoid standing for prolonged periods in the same position, as this may lead to postural strain.
- Adjust all equipment to suit your height and weight
- Vary tasks as much as possible
- Relax muscles periodically throughout the day—stretch the hands, the wrists, the shoulders, and the back
- Take part in education and training to reduce the risk of developing WMSDs
- Report injuries as soon as they occur
- Speak to your employer, your union representative, or a health and safety representative who can relay your issues to your employer about WMSD hazards without fear of reprisal or discrimination

Medical Management and Alternate Duty

The key to successful and rapid return to health, duty, and productivity is the prompt access to health care for assessment, treatment, and follow-up care. The longer a woman is away from work, the less likely the woman will return. Replacement of skilled workers is expensive and, at times, difficult or impossible. It is of benefit to both workers and employers to bring an injured worker back to alternate or redesigned duties as soon as medically appropriate.

The treatment of MSDs can be complicated and depends on the individuals themselves as well as on the nature of their injury. There are a wide range of professional services and advice that could be used to assist an employee affected by WMSDs. These could include occupational health professionals, a general practitioner (GP), physiotherapists, ergonomists, and providers of a variety of complementary therapies.

Conclusion

Analysis of the health status of women, and the evaluation of the working conditions and work peculiarities at the women's workplaces, has shown the following:

- Women are more likely than men to be working in low-paid jobs requiring repetitive, monotonous, forceful, or prolonged exertion of the hands, prolonged awkward postures (both at their place of employment and at home), and caring for children.
- The number of female workers affected by musculoskeletal disorders is extremely high, which is reflected in the high relative rate of disability among that population

- Women employed in many workplaces are not acquainted with the requisite measures for the improvement of working conditions and fatigue reduction
- There is a lack of educational programs and training courses specifically targeting women and related to risk factors at women's workplaces.
- Prevention of musculoskeletal disorders among women must start at the top and run through every level in the organization
- Much remains to be done to reduce the workplace-associated risks of musculoskeletal disorders—rigid implementation of ergonomic standards, training at all levels in identifying the early signs of disorders, implementation of technological processes to reduce manual work and providing funds for ergonomic improvement at workplaces.

References

Andersson R, Kemmlert K, Kilborn A (1990) Etiological differences between accidental and non-accidental occupational over exertion injuries. J Occup Accidents 12, 177–186

Armstrong TJ(1986) Ergonomics and cumulative trauma disorders. Hand Clinics 2(3):553–565

Bernard BP (ed) (1997) Musculoskeletal Disorders and Workplace Factors: A Critical Review of Epidemiologic Evidence for Work Related Musculoskeletal Disorders of the Neck, Upper Extremity, and Low Back. U.S. Department of Health and Human Services, Cincinati, Ohio

Bureau of Labour Statistics (1995) Workplace injuries and illnesses by selected characteristics,1993. U.S. Department of Labour, Bureau of Labour Statistics, Washington, DC USDL 95–142

Bone and Joint Decade Report (2005) European Action Towards better Musculoskeletal Health. Published in BJDonline 5/10/2005. http://www.boneandjointdecade.org

Bongres PM, de Winter CR, Kompier MAJ Hildebrandt VH (1993) Psychosocial factors at work and musculoskeletal disease. Scandinavian journal of work and environmental Health, 19:297–312

Canadian Centre for Occupational Health and Safety (2005) How can we prevent WMSDs? http://www.ccohs.ca/oshanswers/diseases/rmirsi.html

European Agency for Safety and Health at work (2000) Issue 101 Preventing musculoskeletal disorders in practice. http://agency.eu.int/publications/reports/101/en/index.htm.

European Agency for Safety and Health at work (2000a) " The State of Occupational Safety and Health in the Member States" Agency report

European Agency for Safety and Health at work (2000b) Fact Sheet 4- Preventing Work-Related Musculoskeletal Disorders http://osha.europa.eu/publications/factsheets/4/facts4_en.pdf.

European Agency for Health and Safety at Work (2004) E-Facts 9 -Work-related musculoskeletal disorders (MSDs): an introduction http://osha.europa.eu/publications/e-facts/efact09/9_msds_introduction.pdf.

European Agency for Health and Safety at Work (2007) Musculoskeletal disorders: a painful condition. http://osha.europa.eu/topics/msds/facts_html

European Working Conditions Observatory (2005) Fourth European Working Conditions Survey. http://eurofound.europa.eu/ewco

Erdil M, Dickeson OB, Glackin E (1994) Cumulative trauma disorders of the upper extremity. In Occupational Medicine, 3 ed. C. Zenz, F.B. Dickerson, and E. Horvath (eds), Mosby, St. Luis

European Union Labour Force Survey. Principal results (2005) Statistics in focus. 13/2006. Catalogue number: KS-NK-06-013-EN-N

European Union Public Health (2007) Brussels (February 27, 2007). http://ec.europa.eu/health/ph_information/dissemination/diseases/muculo_en.htm

Frederick LJ (1992) Cumulative trauma disorders—an overview. AAOHNJ. 40(3):113–116

Haartz JC, Sweeney MH (1995) Proceedings of the Sixth FIOH-NIOSH Joint Symposium on Occupational Health and Safety.8–10 August 1995, Espoo, Finland

Healthline Encyclopedia of Public Health (accessed 26/3/2007) Signs, symptoms and treatments for musculoskeletal disorders. http://www.Healthline.com

Hendrick HW (2003) Determining the costs-benefits of ergonomics projects and factors that lead to their success. Applied Ergonomics, 34, 419–427

Lundberg U, Mardberg B, Frankenhauser M (1994) The total workload of male and female white collars workers as related to age, occupational level and number of children. Scandinavian Journal of Psychology, 35:315–327

Li G, Buckle P (1998) A practical method for the assessment of work related musculoskeletal risks—Quick Exposure Check (QEC). Proceedings of the Human factors and Ergonomics Society 42nd Annual Meeting, 5-9 October, Chicago, Illinois, V 2, 1351–1355

Leamon T (1994) Research to reality: A critical review of the validity of various criteria for the prevention of occupational induced low back pain disability. Ergonomics, 37(12): 1959–1974

Maier M, Ross-Mota J (2001) Work Related Musculoskeletal Disorders, Oregon, 1990-2000. Available at http://www.cbs.or.us

Messing K (1998) One-eyed science. Occupational health and women workers. Temple University Press, Philadelphia

NIOSH (1992) A national strategy for occupational musculoskeletal injuries: implementation issues and research needs. U.S. Department of Health and Human Services, Public Health Service, Centre for Disease Control and Prevention, Cincinati , Ohio Publication 93–101

NIOSH (1997a) Musculoskeletal Disorders and Workplace Factors. Work related Muskuloskeletal Disorders and Psychosocial Factors. Available at http://www.cdc.gov/niosh/ergtxt7.html

NIOSH (1997b) Elements of Ergonomics Programs. Proactive Ergonomics. Available at http://www.cdc.gov/niosh/eptbtr9.html

NIOSH (1997c) Elements of Ergonomics Programs. Available at http://www.cdc.gov/niosh/epintro.html

NIOSH (1997d) Elements of Ergonomics Programs. A Primer Based on Workplace Evaluation of Musculoskeletal Disorders. Available at http://www.cdc.gov/niosh/ephome2.html

NIOSH (1997e) Elements of Ergonomics Programs. Training. Available at http://www.cdcgov/niosh/epstep3html

Owen BD (2000) Preventing injuries using an ergonomics approach. Association of Operating Room Nurses Journal, 72(6),1031–1036

Punett L, Herbert R (2000) Work related Musculoskeletal Disorders: There is a Gender Differential, and if So, What Does It Mean? In Women and Health. (M. Goldman and M. Hatch (eds), pp. 474–492

Sauter SL, Swanson NG (1992. The effect of increased rest breaks on the health and performance of data entry operators. Presented at the Work with Display Units'92, Berlin, Germany, September 1992

Vikari-Juntura ERA (1997) The scientific basis for making guidelines and standards for prevent work-related musculoskeletal disorders. Ergonomics. (1997). 40(10):1097–1117

Webster BS, Snook SH (1994) The cost of 1989 workers' compensation low back pain claims. Spine, 10:1111–1115

World Health Organization (2004) Gender, Health and Work. Geneva: Department of Gender, Women and Health (GWH), http://www.who.int/gender/documents/en/

Workplace Health and Safety (2000) Manual tasks. Code of Practice. Available at http://www.dir.qld.gov.au/workplace/law/codes/manualtasks/intro/disorder/index.htm

Chapter 6
Work-Related Violence, Bullying, and Sexual Harassment

Kaisa Kauppinen and Tarita Tuomola

Introduction

Work plays a significant part in the lives of most Europeans. In the EU, women's participation in the workforce has steadily increased. Today, women make up 44 percent of the workforce in the enlarged EU. Many sectors are still largely dominated by one sex. Women account for the majority of workers in health (79%), education (72%), other service industries (61%), the wholesale and retail trade (55%), and hotels and restaurants (48%). These sectors employ more than half of all women in employment throughout the EU. Any changes in the working conditions in these sectors have a considerable impact on the quality of work and employment for women.

Men constitute the majority (89%) of those employed in the construction sector, public utilities (80%), and transport and communication (74%). Only 23 percent of the workforce is employed in gender-integrated occupations (i.e., where between 40 and 60 percent of the workers are women). Even in the same jobs within the same organizations, women and men often carry out different tasks.

The labor market is also strongly vertically segregated, with more men in managerial and senior positions. Women are far more likely to work part-time than men, and they are under-represented in permanent job contracts.

These figures are from the Fourth European Working Conditions Survey that was carried out in late 2005. The survey monitors developments in quality of work and employment in the EU member states and at the EU level. Its key areas of focus include: employment security, health and well-being, competence and skills development, and work-life balance (www.eurofound.europa.eu/ewco/surveys).

The experience of women in the labor market has brought a new focus on psychosocial issues into the occupational health and safety debate. With the majority of employed women working in services and related sectors, their rates of actual accidents are lower than that of men. Men—particularly young men—report higher exposures to traditional physical risks than women. Around 15 percent of men report exposure to vibration, and 14 percent to noise (all or almost all the time), compared to between 5 and 7 percent, respectively, of women. Ergonomic risks tend to be more gender-neutral. Women, on the other hand, report higher incidences of other types of problems: allergies, infectious illnesses, hepatitis, and dermatological conditions, as well as mental health problems (Gender Issues in Safety and Health at Work 2003).

In 2000, 10.2 percent of female workers claimed to have been subjected to intimidation, compared to 7.3 percent of men, while 3.1 percent said they had experienced gender discrimination, compared to just 0.8 percent of men (Social Agenda 2006).

Young people appear to be more susceptible than older people if exposed to health risks at work. They are also more subject to harassment and bullying at work. This may be due to job segregation, with younger people having more direct contact with members of the public—possibly coupled with less experience, as well as lack of authority in the job, for example, to solve a client's problem (http://ew2006.osha.eu.int/).

Bullying or harassment, violence or the threat of violence, and various forms of discrimination, all contribute to psychological ill-health and stress. According to the Fourth Working Conditions Survey, around 5 percent of workers reported having experienced some form of violence, bullying, or harassment in the workplace in the previous 12-month period.

This chapter focuses on workplace violence in its various forms—physical violence, verbal violence, bullying, and sexual harassment. It introduces the basic concepts and definitions, the various forms and tactics of negative behavior at work, the prevalence of the phenomena in the EU context, the risky factors and sectors, and the various consequences of workplace violence on health and safety at work. The main focus is on how to prevent workplace violence at an early stage.

Work-Related Violence

Definition—What is Workplace Violence

Workplace violence is defined as violence or the threat of violence against workers that endangers their health, safety, or well-being at work. It can occur at or outside the workplace, and can range from threats and verbal abuse to physical assaults and even homicide. However it manifests itself, workplace violence is a growing concern for employers and employees in workplaces across the EU (Fact Sheet 2002).

The European Commission defines violence arising out of work as "incidents where persons are abused, threatened or assaulted in circumstances related to their work, involving an explicit or implicit challenge to their safety, wellbeing or health." This definition covers both verbal and physical abuse, such as physical attacks, robbery, threats, shouting, and verbal abuse. There may also be a racial or sexual dimension to the violence. In real situations, physical and psychological violence often occurs simultaneously or consecutively (Di Martino, Hoel & Cooper 2003).

The concept of external workplace violence covers insults, threats, or physical or psychological aggressions exerted by people from outside the organization—including customers and clients—against a person at work. Aggressive or violent acts can take various forms, such as:

Uncivil behavior—a lack of respect for others
Physical or verbal aggression—intention to injure
Assault—intention to harm other person

Who is Vulnerable? Who is Affected?

Results from the Third European Survey on Working Conditions show that 4 percent of the working population report that they have been victims of physical violence outside the workplace, with women reporting higher levels. Many more have suffered from threats and insults or other forms of external workplace violence (http://www.eurofound.europa.eu/publications/htmlfiles/ef0121.htm).

The Fourth European Survey on Working Conditions indicated a slight increase in the level of physical violence reported—4 percent between 1995 and 2005 (for the EU15), compared to 6 percent in 2005. Exposure to violence and threats of violence is greater in Northern Europe, with higher than average levels reported in the Netherlands (10%), France and the UK (9%), and Ireland (http://www.eurofound.europa.eu/ewco/surveys).

In the United States, some two million American workers are victims of workplace violence each year (www.osha.gov). Homicide is the leading cause of injury death for women in the workplace in the United States. Workplace homicides are primarily robbery-related, and often occur in grocery or convenience stores, eating and drinking establishments, and gasoline service stations. Over 25 percent of female victims of workplace homicide are assaulted by people they know (co-workers, customers, spouses, or friends). Domestic violence incidents that spill into the workplace account for 16 percent of female victims in jobsite-related homicides (Fact Sheet: Women's Safety and Health Issues at Work NIOSH).

Workplace violence can strike anywhere, and no one is immune, however some workers are at increased risk. Contact with customers or clients increases the risk of facing violence. Among them are workers who exchange money with the public; deliver passengers, goods, or services; or who work alone or in small groups during late night or early morning hours.

The following occupations are examples of those especially at risk of violence (http://osha.eu.int/ew2002/):

- nurses and other healthcare workers
- taxi and bus drivers
- employees performing repairs in the customer homes
- service station staff
- cashiers
- security guards, police officers, parking inspectors, and prison guards
- social workers and social housing managers

Risky environments are largely concentrated in the service sector—in particular, organizations in the health, transport, retail, catering, financial, and education sectors. The health care sector is identified in EU countries as one of the most affected.

According to the Fourth European Working Conditions Survey, workers in the education and health sectors are six times more likely to encounter the threat of physical violence than their counterparts in the manufacturing sector (www.eurofound.europa.eu/ewco/surveys). Violence in the health care sector is a major problem worldwide, affecting over 50 percent of health care workers. Ambulance and emergency staff nurses, for instance, are at great risk of violence (ILO 2002).

Women's increased risk of violence from members of the public is closely related to job segregation. Women are often concentrated in high-risk jobs and occupations such as nursing, social work, and teaching. The problem of increasing physical violence concerns mostly occupations where *difficult* customers and clients have to be dealt with.

People who suffer violence or harassment in the workplace tend to report higher levels of work-related illness than those who do not—nearly four times the level of symptoms of psychological disturbances such as sleeping problems, anxiety and irritability, and physical ailments such as stomachaches (www.eurofound.europa.eu/ewco/surveys).

How to Prevent Violence at Work?

Prevention of harm takes place at two levels. On the *first* level, the aim is to prevent acts of violence from occurring, or at least to reduce them. On the *second* level, if the act of violence has occurred, support is required for the person who has experienced the incident. The support should try to minimize the harmful effects of the incident and prevent any guilty feelings that may appear after an act of aggression. It is important to offer stress debriefing sessions and post-traumatic counseling services to help workers recover from a violent event (http://osha.eu.int/ew2002/).

The best protection employers can offer is to establish a zero-tolerance policy toward workplace violence against or by their employees. The employer should establish a workplace prevention program, or incorporate the information into an existing accident prevention program, employee handbook, or manual. It is critical that all employees know the policy and understand it. In addition, employers can provide additional protections, such as the following:

- Provide safety education for employees so that they know what conduct is not acceptable, what to do if they witness or are subjected to workplace violence, and how to protect themselves
- Secure the workplace. Where appropriate in the workplace, install video surveillance, extra lightning, and alarm systems, and minimize access by outsiders through identification badges, electronic keys, and guards
- Provide drop safes to limit the amount of cash on hand. Keep a minimal amount of money in registers during evenings and late-night hours
- Equip field staff with mobile phones, hand-held alarms, and panic buttons or noise devices

- Instruct employees not to enter any location where they feel unsafe. Provide an escort service or police assistance in potentially dangerous situations or at night
- Discuss the circumstances of any incident with staff members. Encourage employees to share information about ways to avoid similar situations in the future
- Investigate all violent incidents and threats, monitor trends in violent incidents by type or circumstance, and institute corrective actions (www.osha.gov)

Nothing can fully guarantee that an employee will not become a victim of workplace violence. These steps can help reduce the difficulties:

- Learn how to recognize, avoid, or diffuse potentially violent situations by attending personal safety training courses
- Alert supervisors to any concerns about safety or security and report all incidents in writing immediately
- Avoid traveling alone into unfamiliar locations or situations whenever possible
- Carry minimal money and required identification during home visits

Legislation

The European Commission has introduced measures to ensure the safety and health of workers. The 1989 Council Directive (89/391) contains the basic provisions for health and safety at work and makes employers responsible for ensuring that employees do not suffer any harm through work—including violence at work.

All member states have implemented this Directive through national legislation, and some countries have developed special guidance on preventing violence at work. Following the approach in the Directive, employers in consultation with employees and their representatives should:

- Aim to prevent violence at work
- Assess the risks of violence at work
- Take adequate action to prevent any harm (http://agency.osha.eu.int)

The steps to successful prevention of work-related violence are well documented. Further research and development of good practice in specific sectors, occupations, and types of violence, however, is strongly recommended with a well-grounded gender perspective. Gender mainstreaming is needed when implementing the Safety and Health at Work legislation within the national contexts—workplace violence in its various manifestations is not a gender-neutral issue.

Bullying at Work

Definition and Concepts: What is Workplace Bullying?

According to the European Agency for Safety and Health at Work, bullying at work constitutes a significant problem in the European workforce. The costs are considerable for both the worker and the organization. Bullying is regarded as unethical, oppressive behavior, and therefore unacceptable in the work environment (Fact Sheets 2002).

There is no single, agreed-upon definition of *bullying* and several terms have been used interchangeably with it (Vartia 2003). One of them is *mobbing*, which is widely used in German-speaking countries. Other terms close in meaning to workplace bullying include *nonsexual harassment, victimization, psychological terror, scapegoating*, and *petty tyranny*. *Psychological* or *moral harassment* are also terms used to describe intimidating behavior between colleagues in the workplace. In the United States, concepts like *abusive behavior* or *negative behavior, intimidation*, and *workplace trauma* have been used to describe hostile behaviors relevant to workplace bullying.

An example of a definition is:

> "Workplace bullying is repeated, unreasonable behaviour directed towards an employee, or a group of employees, that creates a risk to health and safety. Bullying often involves a misuse of power, where the targets can experience difficulties in defending themselves" (http://agency.osha.eu.int).

The Swedish researcher, Heinz Leymann, is one of the well-known researchers in this field—his work has inspired further research. He has defined psychological terror or mobbing in the following way (1990; 1996):

> "Psychological terror or mobbing in working life involves hostile and unethical communication, which is directed in a systematic way by one or a few individuals mainly towards one individual who, due to mobbing is pushed into a helpless and defenseless position, being held there by means of continuing mobbing activities. These actions occur on a very frequent basis (statistical definition; at least once a week) and over a long period of time (statistical definition; at least six months)".

Different forms of bullying can be identified according to Vartia (1993): slander, gossip, and rumors; social isolation and keeping people uninformed; giving people too few or overly simple work tasks; continuous criticism of people's work and its results; threats or acts of physical violence; and insinuations about a person's mental state. These examples indicate that bullying can involve both verbal and physical attacks, as well as more subtle acts like devaluation of colleague's work or social isolation. Bullying often involves a misuse of power, where the targets can experience difficulties in defending themselves.

All definitions of workplace bullying have the following characteristics in common:

- Bullying involves negative or hostile behaviors occurring regularly, repeatedly, and over time

- The victim has difficulty defending her/himself
- Although bullying is usually regarded as a conflict between co-workers or supervisors and subordinates, people outside the workplace (e.g., customers, clients, and patients) can also be identified as bullies (Vartia 2003).

Who is Vulnerable? Who is Affected?

Anyone in any organization can be the victim of bullying. Results from The Third European Survey on Working Conditions show that 9 percent of workers in Europe—or about 12 million people—reported being subjected to bullying over a 12-month period in 2000. Women are more likely to experience intimidation and bullying at work than men (10%, as opposed to 7% of men) (www.eurofound.europa.eu/publications/htmlfiles/ef0121.htm).

There is a wide variation in the reported prevalence of bullying or harassment in different EU member states—ranging from 15 percent of workers being subjected to intimidation in Finland and 12 percent in the Netherlands, to 4 percent in Portugal and 2 percent in Italy. It should be noted that country-to-country differences may reflect awareness of the issue and willingness to report, as well as actual variations in the prevalence (www.eurofound.europa.eu/ewco/surveys). According to other surveys, approximately 5 to 10 percent of the population perceive themselves as being bullied at any one time, while a higher number are exposed to behavior that may be described as bullying without necessarily feeling victimized (Di Martino et al. 2003).

There are also gender differences in bullying. Women are more likely to be bullied by women than by men, while men are more likely to be bullied by other men. Although both genders can be bullies as well as targets of bullying, the forms of negative behavior between genders vary (The Workplace Bullying and Trauma Institute 2005; www.bullyinginstitute.org).

Job segregation is one of the reasons for women being more exposed to bullying. Surveys suggest that there is a high incidence of bullying in the female-dominated sectors of public administration, education, healthcare, and social work as well as the financial services sectors. Bullying has also been found to be typical of large, poorly run hierarchical organizations with high workplace pressure (Gender Issues in Safety and Health at Work 2003).

The Forth European Survey on Working Conditions shows that a greater level of bullying or harassment is reported in large establishments (over 250 workers) and in the education, health, and hostels and restaurants sectors. Those exposed to bullying or harassment at work are also significantly more likely than average to report absence due to work-related illness (23% compared to 7%). They also tend to be absent from work for longer periods (www.eurofound.europa.eu/ewco/surveys).

Other research indicates that exposure to bullying is associated with high levels of stress. Bullying affects both physical and psychosocial well-being and increases sickness absenteeism. The sickness absence is more common among victims of bullying than other workers (Kivimäki et al. 2000).

Workplace violence, including bullying, affects even those who are not directly involved—so-called observers or by-standers. It implies that bullying or other forms of workplace violence are not purely individual issues. Observers may also feel stress—symptoms of mental distress and job dissatisfaction (Vartia 2003). Workplace violence in its various forms can demoralize the organizational climate with negative effects on productivity and employee output.

How to Prevent Bullying in the Workplace?

The prevention of bullying is a key element in the improvement of working life. It is important to take early action against a destructive behavior. Workplaces need to have a clear statement outlining that bullying and harassment are not tolerated.

It sometimes may be difficult to distinguish between bullying and *normal* interpersonal conflicts between colleagues at work. There is, however, general agreement that factors giving rise to workplace bullying relate to workplace culture and work organizational issues.

The elements of effective workplace policies that can prevent negative interactions include:

- Ethical commitment from the employer and the employees to foster an environment free from bullying
- Outlining which kinds of actions are acceptable and which are not
- Stating the consequences of breaking the organizsational values and standards
- Clarifying the role of the manager, the supervisor, the colleague(s), and the trade union representative
- Indicating where and how victims can get help. Details of counseling and support services available
- Maintaining confidentiality (European Agency for Safety and Health at Work 2002; http://agency.osha.eu.int)

Legislation

The European Commission has introduced measures to ensure the safety and health of workers. The 1989 Council Directive (89/391) contains the basic provisions for health and safety at work and it makes employers responsible for making sure employees do not suffer any harm through work—including workplace bullying. All member states have implemented this Directive through national legislation, and some countries have developed special guidance on preventing bullying at work.

Following the approach in the Directive, employers in consultation with employees and their representatives should (http://agency.osha.eu.int):

- Aim to prevent bullying at work
- Assess the risks of bullying at work
- Take adequate action to prevent any harm as a consequence of bullying

In addition, bullying is mentioned in the European Commission's guidance on work-related stress: "Spice of Life or Kiss of Death?" (http://ec.europa.eu/employment_social/publications/2002/ke4502361_en.pdf).

The European Parliament has called upon the member states to review and, if appropriate, to supplement their national legislation on the prevention of bullying in the workplace. In addition, it is important to review and standardize the definition of bullying, with a view to counteracting bullying and sexual harassment at work. Effective European action in this area will reduce a source of work-related stress that affects women more often than men in the workplaces across the EU.

Sexual Harassment at Work

Definition and Concepts: What is Sexual Harassment at Work?

The European Commission's code of practice defines sexual harassment as "unwanted conduct of sexual nature, or other conduct based on sex affecting the dignity of women and men at work" (European Commission 1991; www.europa.eu.int/comm/employment_social/equ_opp/rights_en.html).

The 2002 Amendment to the Equal Treatments Directive (Directive 2002/73/EC) introduces two forms of harassment—harassment related to sex, and harassment of a sexual nature. The Directive defines harassment as "unwanted conduct related to the sex of a person occurring with the purpose or effect of violating the dignity of a person, and of creating an intimidating, hostile, degrading, humiliating or offensive environment."

This concept of harassment is similar to the concept of harassment based on sex under the U.S. law, which encompasses harassing behavior related to pregnancy, jokes about the competency of the female sex, or comments reflecting pejorative stereotypes about the female sex.

The definition includes unwanted, improper, or offensive behavior; Or behavior that creates a working environment that is intimidating, hostile, or humiliating. Forms of sexual harassment include verbal (e.g., sexual jokes), nonverbal (e.g., staring), and physical, (e.g., unwanted touching) (www.who.int/occupational_health/publications/womandoh/en/index.html). Examples of sexual harassment include:

- unwanted sexual advances or requests for sexual favors
- repeated sexually oriented comments or gestures about the body, appearance, or lifestyle of a person
- pressure for a date or a personal relationship
- persistent invitations to social activities after the person has made it clear they are not welcome
- unwanted touching or unnecessary close physical proximity
- angry, intimidating, and/or threatening behavior based on a person's sex

- questions or insinuations about a person's private life
- offensive phone calls, letters, or e-mail messages
- sexual jokes, comments, or innuendoes
- sex-based cartoons or visuals that ridicule or denigrate a person (www2.ucsc.edu/).

It is the recipient's subjective feelings and responses that are crucial in determining whether or not that conduct constitutes sexual harassment. Because personal experiences differ, what one may consider positive or friendly, another may experience as threatening, undermining, and offensive. It is therefore everyone's task to understand the boundaries of acceptable behavior and be sensitive about it.

Sexual harassment often refers to unbalanced power relations at work. The harassed person feels powerless for various reasons—a lower position in the hierarchy, personal circumstances, the need to keep the job, and the sense of being less important to the organization than the harasser (Herbert 1999).

Attitudes and values in the workplace have changed. What may have been acceptable in some workplaces and establishments ten years ago may today be seen as bad practice, weak management, or sexist and inappropriate behavior.

Work environments and work cultures also differ in terms of what is meant by a *hostile environment*. There is a distinction between a *blue-collar* and *white-collar* work environment in this regard. Research has found that foul language, sexual banter, and the like, are common in certain blue-collar work environments. Country-to-country differences in the prevalence of sexual harassment may also reflect both cultural attitudes and awareness of the issue (Rubinstein 1987, Kauppinen 1999).

Who is Vulnerable? Who is Affected?

Sexual harassment is a workplace stressor experienced much more frequently by women than by men. European studies estimate that between 30 to 50 percent of women (and 10 percent of men) have experienced sexual harassment at some point in their working lives. Men tend to perceive harassment as less offensive, and they experience less negative consequences of harassment than women do (Social Agenda 2002.)

According to the Third European Survey on Working Conditions, sexual harassment was experienced by two percent of respondents in the previous 12 months. Women are subjected to these issues to a greater extent than men (4% of women compared to 2% of men), and the rate is higher for temporary agency workers than for employed workers (http://www.eurofound.ie/publications/EF0121.htm).

The Fourth Working Conditions Survey confirms these results and further shows that women—particularly younger women—suffer more from bullying and harassment than men. For example, three times as many women as men suffer from unwanted sexual attention.

The Finnish Gender Barometer has shown that 18 percent of the surveyed female respondents experienced sexual harassment at work in 2004 (Melkas 2005). The reported forms of sexual harassment were mainly inappropriate verbal remarks about one's appearance and sexual jokes from customers or colleagues. The incidences of sexual harassment were primarily reported by women under the age of 35. This is a typical result from various studies—younger women are more subject to sexual harassment at work than older women.

Despite being quite commonplace, sexual offences and other forms of sexual harassment often go unreported due to factors such as fear of losing one's job, being considered the guilty party, or being socially ostracized among work colleagues (Di Martino, Hoel & Cooper 2003).

There is no typical profile of a harasser or a harassed person. In most cases, the harassers are identified as colleagues or supervisors. Clients and customers have also increasinly been found to be harassers. Some specific groups are particularly vulnerable, such as divorced or separated women, new entrants to the labor market, those with irregular or precarious employment contracts, women with disabilities, women who are racial minorities, homosexuals, and young men (http://europa.eu/scadplus/leg/en/cha/c10917c.htm).

Young women and women under the age of 35 are more likely to be harassed than older women. Women working in male-dominated jobs also experience more sexual harassment than in female-dominated, or mixed, jobs. Harassment-prone jobs for women include police officer, bus or taxi driver, waitress, nurse, saleswoman/cashier (Rubinstein 1987; Herbert 1999).

Power differences are likely to affect all types of psychological harassment, as stated before, but are particularly connected to sexual harassment (Di Martino, Hoel & Cooper 2003). Incidents of sexual harassment are more common for those who work in jobs with a very unbalanced gender ratio. This situation is often referred to as a *token position*. When a person has a token position, she or he is in an environment where their colleagues are mostly of the opposite sex.

An example of a male-dominated job for women is a police officer's job. According to a Finnish study, female police officers experience high levels of sexual harassment—such as sexist jokes and offensive comments—from clients as well as from colleagues. The research results suggest that sexual harassment can be linked to job stress and burnout (Kauppinen & Patoluoto 2005).

Sexual harassment also appears to be experienced widely in the hotel, catering, and tourism industry. In Denmark, 6 percent of workers in the sector report experiences of sexual harassment compared to a national average of 2 percent. In the UK, 24 percent of respondents report having experienced unwanted sexual harassment at work. A Finnish study of all occupations in the economy found that waitresses were the occupational group most prone to sexual harassment, with almost half of all respondents reporting such experiences. (Hoel & Einarsen 2003).

Sexual harassment is a well-recognized workplace stressor, and affected employees report negative effects on their health and well-being as well as in job motivation. Studies show that employees experience less harassment and better job satisfaction in organizations that are characterized by a positive and open social atmosphere (Herbert 1999).

How to Prevent Sexual Harassment at Work?

The best protection that employers can offer is to establish a zero-tolerance policy toward sexual harassment. In the workplaces, there should be a clear message that sexual harassment is not accepted, and organizations should adopt preventive policies and procedures to deal with sexual harassment. Key elements that policies should cover include the following:

- A clear contextual definition of sexual harassment, and examples of behaviors that constitute it
- Clear messages that sexual harassment is not tolerated
- Supportive initiatives such as special training programs designed to raise awareness of the issue and to equip those with responsibility to carry out the procedures
- Detailed provisions for preventive measures, and a complaint procedure
- Skills and awareness training in support of the antiharassment policy
- Protection and support for harassed employees
- Applicable disciplinary measures
- External assistance (Gender Issues in Safety and Health at Work 2003).

Young people, and particularly young women, should be a special target of preventive actions, because studies systematically show young women to be the most vulnerable to sexual harassment at work. Employers, supervisors, and safety officials should be aware of the risks of sexual and/or moral harassment to young people, and take the steps needed to protect them. Employees can be informed of the company's policy towards harassment during job reviews and training sessions, and in the company's equality plan.

Because many cases of sexual harassment take place between persons at the same level in the hierarchy—not always between employees and their supervisors—the employees have a special responsibility to take steps to prevent sexual harassment at work:

- By creating a climate at work in which sexual harassment is not tolerated nor accepted
- By discouraging any form of negative behavior toward fellow workers at the same level
- By ensuring that their colleague's behavior does not cause offense to other workers
- By supporting the victims of harassment, and by informing management and/or staff representative through appropriate channels

The majority of preventive actions are focused on the employers and their representatives, becaus they have the main obligation to ensure the protection of the dignity of women and men at work. The trade unions and their representatives, however, also have responsibilities to their members, and they play an increasingly important role in the prevention of sexual harassment in the workplace (European Social Dialogue; Framework Agreement on Harassment and Violence at Work, 2007).

Legislation

The 2002 Amendment to the Equal Treatment Directive (2002/73/EC) introduces the concepts of harassment related to sex and sexual harassment and states that they are forms of discrimination in violation of the equal treatment principle. European Union directives are legally binding on member states, but they require the adoption of implementing legislation on the member state level.

The new Directive came into force in 2005. With the approval of the Directive, the European Union has taken a major step toward harmonization of public policy aimed at reducing sexual harassment in the workplace.

The directive requires all member states to establish agencies to promote equality and enforce antidiscriminatory laws. Member states must also encourage employers and those responsible for vocational and professional training to institute preventive measures to protect against sexual harassment in the workplace.

As the member states implement their national legislation and machinery, employers throughout Europe will enjoy new opportunities for advancing the principle of equality between women and men. There are various examples of legislative approaches, national initiatives, and good practices aimed at prevention of sexual harassment at work.

For example, Kauppinen (2005) describes how the prevention of sexual harassment has been included in workplace equality plans in Finland. As a result of the Finnish Act on Equality between Women and Men, Finnish employers have to take steps to protect employees against sexual harassment in the workplace. The Equality Act also stipulates that employers with 30 or more regular workers must draft an equality plan that includes specific measures on how to promote equality and well-being at work.

All universities in Finland have drafted an equality plan, including the Academy of Finland (www.aka.fi). Another good example is the Finnish Sports Federation's recommendation for preventing sexual harassment in sports and physical activities (www.slu.fi). It is an attempt to encourage the education community—colleges, universities and youth organizations—to better prepare young people for work.

A Case: Good Behavior Encouraged—Sexual Harassment Forbidden

The Finnish Confederation of Salaried Employees (STTK) has made a guideline for preventing sexual harassment in the workplace, in cooperation with other trade unions and governmental officials.
Source: (http://www.sttk.fi/en/socialissues/2039/)

STTK represents approximately 650,000 professional employees (68% women) working in a wide range of occupations, such as nurses, police officers, secretaries, technical engineers, and salespeople.

Guidelines Preventing Sexual Harassment in the Workplace Sexual harassment is not acceptable. Sexual harassment impairs working atmosphere by causing health problems and economic loss. Harassment can be used as an instrument of negative power. Sexual harassment is both an individual problem as well an issue concerning the whole workplace. Even though the employer has the main responsibility to handle the matter, it is important that fellow workers show disapproval of harassment. An open workplace culture can prevent interpersonal misunderstandings, which prevents harassment in advance.

What is Sexual Harassment? Sexual harassment is unwanted and one-sided. Behavior is defined as harassing when the subject has stated that he/she finds it offending or unwelcomed. The basis is a person's own subjective experience.

The offender can be a man or a woman, and he or she can be a colleague, a supervisor, or a customer. The following are examples of harassment:

> Sexually offensive gestures or expressions
> Dubious jokes and irrelevant remarks about your body, clothing, or private life
> Displayed pornographic material, sexually worded letters, phone messages, or e-mails
> Unwelcome touching and other undesired physical approaches
> Unwanted proposals or pressure for an intimate relationship

What can a Person Subjected to Harassment do? No one should tolerate sexual harassment in his/her workplace. If an employee is subjected to harassment, he/she should bring the matter up. The employer must act immediately and prevent the situation from escalating.

The affected person should inform the harasser that he/she finds this behavior annoying and it should be stopped. If it is awkward or impossible to talk face-to-face, one way is to write a letter or send a message to the offender.

It is good to write down where and when the incident took place and what happened. A written record may be of importance at a later stage when the matter is further analyzed.

If the harassment continues despite the above protests, the next step is to inform one of the following persons:

The immediate supervisor or his/her representative
The industrial safety officer, industrial safety delegate or other employee representative
Occupational health care personnel

Advice and help is also available from the industrial safety representatives, the trade union, or the office of the Ombudsman for Equality.

What is the Position of the Offender? The harasser is responsible for the consequences of the harassment. The harasser carries the consequences, not the victim. The harasser may receive a warning or, in severe cases, he/she may even be dismissed. The person who is suspected of harassment is to be judged without prejudice.

What is the Responsibility of the Employer? According to the Equality Act, the employer has to take steps to protect employees against sexual harassment in the workplace.

The employer's responsibility is to act immediately after the matter has been reported to him/her, by the victim, or by another person. In more obvious cases, the employer has to take action on his own initiative.

If the employer does not act after being informed, the company could be liable for compensation according to the Equality Act.

When settling harassment claims, both parties should have a chance to be heard separately. If possible, the matter could also be discussed in the presence of both parties. Both parties should be heard in a neutral and confidential atmosphere.

The employer should establish the facts according to the information given. The employer decides the procedures after having heard all parties involved.

The employer or the representative should keep a record of the discussions and of the actions taken.

Additional Actions If the matter cannot be solved by discussions, or if the harassment continues, the employer must take further actions to stop the harassment. The offender could be given a file note or a warning, or the offender could even be dismissed.

References

European Agency for Safety and Health at Work (2002) *Bullying at Work*. Fact Sheet 23. Retrieved February 20, 2007 from http://ew2002.osha.eu.int/resources/104_html

European Agency for Safety and Health at Work (2002) *Violence at Work*. Fact Sheet 24. Retrieved February 20, 2007 from http://osha.europa.eu/publications/factsheets/24/index.htm?language=en

European Agency for Safety and Health at Work (2006) *European Week (Young Workers)— European Network*. Retrieved February 20, 2007 from http://ew2006.osha.europa.eu/

European Agency for Safety and Health at Work (2003) *Gender Issues in Safety and Health at Work - A Review*. Luxembourg: Office for Official Publications of the European Communities. Retrieved February 20, 2007 from http://osha.europa.eu/publications/reports/209/en/index.htm

European Commission (1989) *Council Directive 89/391/EEC of 12 June 1989 on the introduction of measures to encourage improvements in the safety and health of workers at work*. Retrieved February 20, 2007 from http://europa.eu.int/smartapi/cgi/sga_doc?smartapi!celexapi!prod!CELEXnumdoc&lg=EN&numdoc=389L0391&model=guichett

European Commission (1991) *Commission Recommendation of 27 November 1991 on the protection of the dignity of women and men at work, (92/131/EEC)*. Retrieved February 20, 2007 from http://ec.europa.eu/employment_social/equ_opp/rights_en.html

European Commission, Employment and Social Affairs (2002) Sexual harassment outlawed. *Social Agenda, July*. Brussels: European Commission's Directorate General for Employment and Social Affairs

European Commission (2002) *Spice of Life or Kiss of Death*. European Commission: Employment and Social Affairs. Retrieved February 20, 2007 from http://ec.europa.eu/employment_social/publications/2002/ke4502361_en.pdf

European Commission, Employment and Social Affairs (2006) Adapting health and safety at work to a changing world. *Social Agenda, July*. Brussels: European Commission's Directorate General for Employment and Social Affairs

European Foundation for the Improvement of Living and Working Conditions (2001) *Third European survey on working conditions 2000*. Dublin: European Foundation for the Improvement of Living and Working Conditions. Retrieved February, 20 from http://eurofound.europa.eu/pubdocs/2001/21/en/1/ef0121en.pdf

European Foundation for the Improvement of Living and Working Conditions (2004) *Seminar on violence and harassment in the workplace. Summary*. Dublin: European Foundation for the Improvement of Living and Working Conditions. Retrieved February 20, 2007 from http://www.eurofound.eu.int/pubdocs/2004/64/en/1/ef0464en.pdf

European Foundation for the Improvement of Living and Working Conditions (2007) *Fourth European Working Conditions Survey: résumé*. Dublin: European Foundation for the Improvement of Living and Working Conditions. Retrieved February 20, 2007 from http://www.eurofound.europa.eu/ewco/surveys/

European Network of Adult Education Organizations working on Women's Employment Issues (2003) *Women's Human Rights - A Handbook*. Kaunas: Social Innovation Fund

European Parliament (2002) *Amendment to Equal Treatments Directive (Directive 2002/73/EC)*. Retrieved February 20, 2007 from http://europa.eu/scadplus/leg/en/cha/c10906.htm

Di Martino V, Hoel H, Cooper CL (2003) *Preventing violence and harassment in the workplace*. Luxembourg: European Foundation for the Improvement of Living and Working Conditions, Office for the Official Publications of the European Communities. Retrieved February 20, 2007 from http://www.eurofound.eu.int/publications/files/EF02109EN.pdf

The Finnish Confederation of Salaried Employees, STTK (2006) *Good behavior encouraged—Harassment forbidden*. Social Issues. Retrieved February 20, 2007 from http://www.sttk.fi/en/print/socialissues/2039

Herbert C (1999) *Preventing sexual harassment at work.* Geneva: International Labour Office

Hoel H, Einarsen S (2003) *Violence at work in hotels, catering and tourism.* Geneva: International Labour Office. Retrieved February 20, 2007 fromhttp://www.ilo.org/public/english/dialogue/sector/papers/tourism/wp211.pdf

International Labour Office, ILO (1999) *Sexual Harassment – An ILO survey on company practices.* Geneva: International Labour Office

International Labor Office, ILO (2002) *Framework Guidelines for Addressing Workplace violence in the Health Sector.* Geneva: International Labor Office. Retrieved February 20, 2007 from http://whqlibdoc.who.int/publications/9221134466.pdf

Kauppinen K (1999) *Sexual Harassment in the Workplace.* In: Women and Occupational Health: Issues and policy paper prepared for the Global Commission on Women's Health (ed.) Penny Kane. World Health Organisation, 83–90 (http://www.who.int/occupational_health/publications/womandoh/en/index.html.

Kauppinen K, Patoluoto S (2005) *Sexual Harassment and Violence toward Policewomen in Finland.* In: Gruber JE, Morgan P (eds) In the Company of Men. Male Dominance and Sexual Harassment.

Kauppinen K (2005) *OSH in workplace equality plans.* In 'Mainstreaming gender into occupational safety and health'. European Agency for Safety and Health at Work. Working Environment Information, Working Paper 1. Luxembourg: Office for Official Publications of the European Communities. Retrieved February 20, 2007. http://osha.europa.eu/publications/reports/6805688/full_publication_en.pdf

Kivimäki M, Elovainio M, Vahtera J (2000) Workplace bullying and sickness absence in hospital staff. *Occupational and Environmental Medicine 57,* 656–660

Leymann H (1990) Mobbing and psychological terror at workplaces. *Violence and victims 5 (2),* 119–126

Leymann H (1996) The content and development of the mobbing at work. *European Journal of Work and Organizational Psychology 5 (2),* 165–184

Melkas T (2005) *Gender Equality. Barometer 2004.* Ministry of Social Affairs and Health Publications 2005:11. Helsinki: Ministry of Social Affairs and Health

National Institute for Occupational Safety and Health, NIOSH (2007) *Women's Safety and Health Issues at Work.* Fact Sheet. Retrieved February 20, 2007 from http://www.cdc.gov/niosh/topics/women/

Paoli P, Merllié D (2001) *Third European survey on working conditions 2000.* Dublin: European Foundation for the Improvement of Living and Working Conditions. Retrieved February 20, 2007 from http://eurofound.europa.eu/pubdocs/2001/21/en/1/ef0121en.pdf

Rubinstein M (1987) *The Dignity of Women at Work. Part I and II.* COM, V/412/87. Brussels: European Commission

University of California (2004) *No Harassment.* http://www2.ucsc.edu/

U.S. Department of Labor (2002) *Workplace Violence.* OSHA Fact Sheet. Occupational Safety and Health Administration. Retrieved February 20, 2007 from http://www.osha.gov/OshDoc/data_General_Facts/factsheet-workplace-violence.pdf

Vartia M (1993) *Psychological harassment (bullying and mobbing) at work.* In: Kauppinen K- Toropainen (eds) OECD panel group on women, work and health. National report, Finland. Helsinki: Ministry of Social Affairs and Health, Publication 6/1993

Vartia M (2003) *Workplace bullying - A study on the work environment, well-being and health.* Academic dissertation, University of Helsinki, Department of Psychology. Retrieved February 20, 2007 from http://ethesis.helsinki.fi/julkaisut/hum/psyko/vk/vartia-vaananen/

World Health Organization, WHO (2004) *Gender, Health and Work.* Geneva: Department of Gender, Women and Health (GWH). Retrieved February 20, 2007 from http://www.who.int/ gender/documents/en/

The Workplace Bullying and Trauma Institute, WBTI (2005) *Online Newsletter, July.* Retrieved February 20, 2007 from http://www.bullyinginstitute.org

Appendix 1

Selected Internet Resources of Work-related Violence, Bullying, and Sexual Harassment

Work–Related Violence

European Agency for Safety and Health at Work

Factsheet 24: Violence at work
http://osha.europa.eu/publications/factsheets/24/en/index.htm
Report: How to Tackle Psychosocial Issues and Reduce Work-related Stress
http://osha.europa.eu/publications/reports/309/en/index.htm
Report: Prevention of psychosocial risks and stress at work in practice (Results of the Good Practice Awards)
http://osha.europa.eu/publications/reports/104/en/index.htm#en
Report: Gender issues in safety and health at work
http://osha.europa.eu/publications/reports/209/en/index.htm
Report: Research on work-related stress
http://osha.europa.eu/publications/reports/203/en/index.htm
Report: State of Occupational Safety and Health in the European Union
http://osha.europa.eu/publications/reports/401/en/index.htm
Factsheet 31: Practical advice for workers on tackling work-related stress and its causes
http://osha.europa.eu/publications/factsheets/31/en/index.htm
Work Guide sheet for Good Practice Data Collection, Evaluation and Dissemination, Version 07.
http://osha.europa.eu/good_practice/gp_guidelines.pdf
Violence at work from members of the public (external violence)
http://osha.europa.eu/good_practice/risks/stress/violence.stm

European Foundation for the Improvement of Living and Working Conditions

http://www.eurofound.eu.int/
http://osha.europa.eu/search?SearchableText=physical+violence

WHO – World Health Organization

Workplace violence in the health sector
http://www.who.int/violence_injury_prevention/violence/activities/workplace/en/

GOHNET (Global Occupational Health Network) newsletter
http://www.who.int/occupational_health/publications/newsletter/en/index.html
GOHNET (2006) Psychosocial Factors and Mental Health at Work. The Global
Occupational Health Network, Issue No. 10 - 2006.
http://www.who.int/occupational_health/publications/newsletter/
gohnet10e310806.pdf

NIOSH – The National Institute for Occupational Safety and Health (U.S.)

Traumatic occupational injuries: occupational violence
http://www.cdc.gov/niosh/injury/traumaviolence.html

U.S. Department of Labor, Occupational Safety & Health Administration

Workplace violence
http://www.osha.gov/SLTC/workplaceviolence/index.html

ILO – International Labour Organization

Violence and stress at work in service sectors
http://www.ilo.org/public/english/dialogue/sector/themes/violence.htm

Hazards Magazine

Workers Health International News.
http://www.hazards.org/

Bullying

European Agency for Safety and Health at Work

http://osha.europa.eu/OSHA
Factsheet 23: Bullying at work
http://osha.europa.eu/publications/factsheets/23/en/index.htm

Report: How to Tackle Psychosocial Issues and Reduce Work-related Stress
http://osha.europa.eu/publications/reports/309/en/index.htm

Report: Prevention of psychosocial risks and stress at work in practice
http://osha.europa.eu/publications/reports/104/en/index.htm#en

Report: Gender issues in safety and health at work
http://osha.europa.eu/publications/reports/209/en/index.htm

Report: Research on work-related stress
http://osha.europa.eu/publications/reports/203/en/index.htm

Agency Factsheet 8
http://osha.europa.eu/publications/factsheets/8/en/index.htm

Report: State of Occupational Safety and Health in the European
Union http://osha.europa.eu/publications/reports/401/en/index.htm

Factsheet 31: Practical advice for workers on tackling work-related stress and its
causes
http://osha.europa.eu/publications/factsheets/31/en/index.htm

Advice for bullied workers and some organizations offering help
http://osha.europa.eu/good_practice/risks/stress/bullying.stm/view?searchterm=
advice%20for%20bullied

European Foundation for the Improvement of Living and Working Conditions

Lehto, A.-M & Pärnänen, A (2006). Violence, bullying and harassment in the
workplace. Dublin: European Foundation for the Improvement of Living and
Working Conditions. http://www.eurofound.eu.int/ewco/reports/TN0406TR01/
TN0406TR01.htm

Di Martino, Vittorio & Hoel, Helge & Cooper, Cary L (2003). Preventing violence and harassment in the workplace. Dublin: European Foundation for the
Improvement of Living and Working Conditions http://www.eurofound.eu.int/
publications/files/EF02109EN.pdf

European Parliament

http://www.europarl.europa.eu/

European Commission Guidelines on Work-related Stress

http://osha.europa.eu/legislation/guidelines/ec

TUTB: Health and Safety at Work - European Trade Union Institute

http://hesa.etui-rehs.org/uk/default.asp

WHO – World Health Organization

Psychosocial risk factors and hazards
http://www.who.int/occupational_health/topics/risks_psychosocial/en/

World Health Organization (2003). Raising Awareness of Psychological Harassment at Work. Protecting Workers' Health Series No 4. Edited by Gilioli, R.; Fingerhut M. A.; Kortum-Margot, E. Geneva: World Health Organization. http://www.who.int/occupational_health/publications/harassment/en/index.html

Workplace Bullying Institute, U.S. and Canada

Education and research to stop bullying at work.
http://www.bullyinginstitute.org/

Worktrauma.org

About workplace bullying, violence and people problems. A resource, educational and self-help site for managers, academics and victims
http://www.worktrauma.org/index.html

Sexual Harassment

European Foundation for the Improvement of Living and Working Conditions

Sexual harassment of women in the workplace
http://eurofound.europa.eu/ewco/2006/07/ES0607019I.htm

Quality of work, equal opportunities
http://www.eurofound.eu.int/areas/gender/equal.htm

European Agency for Safety and Health at Work

Gender issues in safety and health at work.
http://osha.europa.eu/publications/reports/209/en/index.htm

The European Commission

Sexual harassment outlawed.
http://www.europa.eu.int/comm/employment_social/publications/2002/
keaf02002_en.html
http://www.stopvaw.org/EU_Commission_Code_of_Practice_on_Measures_
to_Combat_Sexual_Harassment.html
http://europa.eu/scadplus/leg/en/cha/c10917c.htm

The Finnish Confederation of Salaried Employees

Guidelines for preventing sexual harassment at work
http://www.sttk.fi/en/socialissues/2039/

Finnish Sports Federation

A guidebook offering a set of guidelines to prevent sexual harassment in sports
http://www.slu.fi/mp/db/file_library/x/IMG/13153/file/allowedtocare.pdf

Ethical principles for Finnish sports and physical activities
http://www.slu.fi/mp/db/file_library/x/IMG/31381/file/fairplay.pdf

European Social Dialogue

Framework Agreement on Harassment and Violence at Work, 2007. 26 April, 2007.
This agreement deals with those forms of harassment and violence at which are
within the competence of social partners. http://ec.europa.eu/employment_social/
news/2007/apr/harassment_violence_at_work_en.pdf

Chapter 7
Promoting Health for Working Women—Communicable Diseases

Sotirios Tsiodras

Concepts and Introduction

Any person is exposed to communicable diseases on the job site. Employees in certain professions, such as health care workers, may be at a higher risk for exposure to such diseases. The identification of communicable diseases in the area of work has led to the establishment of specific procedures concerning appropriate prevention and intervention measures (Al-Saden & Wachs 2004; Baussano et al. 2006; Chen et al. 2004; Dettenkofer & Block 2005; El-Masri Williamson & Fox-Wasylyshyn 2004; Keller, Daley, Hyde, Greif & Church 2005; Koh, Lim, Ong & Chia 2005; Lateef, Lim & Tan 2004; P. W. Stone, Clarke, Cimiotti & Correa-de-Araujo 2004). During recent years, increasing attention has been paid to emerging infectious diseases that may affect the workplace, such as avian influenza and SARS (Halpin 2005; Koh et al. 2005; Swayne 2006). Global traveling has affected the epidemiology of communicable diseases (Singer 2005) and a veterinarian in the United States may now be exposed to an infectious disease identified in an exotic pet coming from abroad (Johnson-Delaney 2005).

Occupational communicable diseases affecting women should not differ from those affecting men, although by means of tradition certain occupations are primarily occupied by men (e.g., slaughterers/butchers) whereas others by women (Su, Wang, Lu & Guo 2006; Ward & Day 2006). By virtue of her profession, a woman that practices veterinary medicine may be exposed to zoonoses because all vets and their staff do (Nienhaus, Skudlik & Seidler 2005). There have been reports of a greater percentage of women being affected by occupational infectious diseases (Brhel & Bartnicka 2003). There maybe a pattern of communicable diseases affecting female workers that relates to specific professions (Gyorkos et al. 2005), the status of the worker (e.g., immigrants) (Fitzgerald, Chakraborty, Shah, Khuder & Duggan 2003; Krejci-Manwaring et al. 2006), and geographical locations, because not only the epidemiology of some of the infectious diseases differs from country to country but also the professional activities where women are engaged (Brhel & Bartnicka 2003; Cinco et al. 2004; Golshan, Faghihi & Marandi 2002; Krejci-Manwaring et al. 2006; Reimer et al. 2002; Vilaichone, Vilaichone, Nunthapisud & Wilde 2002; Werner, Nordin, Arnholm, Elgefors & Krantz 2001). Moreover,

A. Linos, W. Kirch (eds), *Promoting Health for Working Women*.
© Springer 2008

women maybe exposed to infectious hazards in their occupation during the prenatal and the maternity period. Some exposures may harm the embryo (Crane 2002;
Gilbert 2000), whereas others may actually reduce the risk of certain childhood
diseases such as diabetes (Fear, McKinney, Patterson, Parslow & Bodansky 1999).
Certain exposures may be more important than infectious diseases in affecting the
well-being of female workers (Krejci-Manwaring et al. 2006; Selvaratnam, de Silva,
Pathmeswaran & de Silva 2003; Ward & Day 2006).

The current chapter discusses the available knowledge of communicable diseases
in the workplace, and attempts to elucidate certain features of these entities that are
more relevant to the female population.

Definitions

Infectious diseases arising from the workplace define the term *occupational communicable diseases*. A subtle difference that is not well-specified may exist between
infectious diseases (any disease that can be caused by an infectious agent—e.g.,
tetanus) and communicable diseases (any infectious disease that can be transmitted
directly or indirectly by an infected person). The dynamics of infection may be different from the dynamics of the clinical disease itself. Thus, the incubation period
for a clinically visible infectious disease may overlap with the infectious period
(period of transmissibility). Moreover, infections may frequently be subclinical but
may be transmitted from an infected person. An infectious disease is the result of
interactions within a dynamic system consisting of the pathogen, the environment,
and the characteristics of the host. Several factors may influence the transmission
dynamics related to the pathogen (e.g., antigenic stability, virulence, reservoir), the
environment (e.g., occupational setting, climatic conditions) and finally the host
(e.g., age, gender, genetic predisposition, immunity, behavior).

The list of occupational communicable infectious diseases is huge. In a formal recommendation (Commission Recommendations 19-09-2003 concerning the
European schedule of occupational diseases) the European Commission defined
occupational infectious diseases as any infectious or parasitic (sic) disease that can
be transmitted to man by animals or remains of animals, as well as other infectious
diseases caused by work in disease prevention, healthcare, domiciliary assistance,
and other comparable activities for which an infection risk has been proven. These
definitions are added in a short list of five agents, including tetanus, tuberculosis, brucellosis, amoebiasis, and viral hepatitis. A classification of communicable
occupational diseases can be made according to the pathogen involved—i.e., bacterial, viral, fungal, parasitic (see Table 7.1). Other classification schemes relative
to the mode of transmission may be used, such as contact- (direct or indirect, inter-
human vs. zoonotic), vector- (mechanical or biological), or vehicle- (air, food, or
water) borne. In this regard, the difference between a reservoir (the agent multiplies
within the host) and a vector (just carrier of the pathogen) of an infectious agent
may be important. Biological terrorism agents may form a specific subcategory
themselves.

Table 7.1 Significant representative pathogens/diseases causing communicable diseases that may be occupationally acquired

Bacteria

Anaplasma phagocytophilum	Ehrlichiosis
Anthrax spp.	Cutaneous and inhalational anthrax
Bordetella pertussis	Pertussis
Borrelia burgdorferii	Lyme's disease
Brucella spp	Brucellosis
Burkholderia mallei	Glanders
Burkholderia pseudomallei	Melioidosis, pseudo-glanders
Campylobacter spp.	Gastroenteritis
Capnocytophaga spp	Dog bite infection
Chlamydia spp	Psittacosis
Clostridium tetani	Tetanus
Corynebacterium diphtheriae	Diphtheria
Eryspelothrix rhusiopathiae	Erysipeloid
Francinsella tularensis	Tularemia
Legionella spp	Legionellosis
Leptospira interrogans	Leptospirosis
Mycobacterium marinum	Fish-tank granuloma
Mycobacterium tuberculosis	Tuberculosis
Neiserria meningitides	Meningococcal meningitis
Pasteurella multocida	Cat or dog bite infection
Ricketssiae spp, *Coxiella burnettii*	RMSF, Q fever, murine typhus, scrub typhus
Streptobaccilus moniliformis	Rat bite fever
Steptococcus suis	Severe infection, meningitis, sepsis in pig owners
Vibrio vulnificus	Skin lesion after exposure to marine waters
Yershinia pestis	Plague

Viruses

Adenovirus spp	Adenoviral infections
Hantaviruses	Hantavirus pulmonary syndrome
Hemorrhagic fever group viruses (e.g., Ebola, Marburg, Lassa)	Hemorrhagic fever, Lassa fever, Omsk fever, Crimean Congo fever, Rift Valley fever
Henipavirus spp	encephalitis
Hepatitis A, B, C, B	Hepatitis
Herpes simplex viruses type 1 and 2	Herpetic infections, herpetic whitlow
Human immunodeficiency virus	HIV-AIDS
Influenza viruses types A and B	Influenza – avian influenza
Lymphocytic choriomeningitis virus	Meningitis
Lyssaviruses	Rabies
Measles virus	Measles
Monkey B Virus	B virus infection
Monkeypox virus	Monkeypox
Mumps virus	Mumps
Newcastle disease virus	Newcastle disease
Parapox virus	Orf -contagious pustular dermatitis
Parvovirus	*Parvovirus* infection
SARS coronavirus	SARS
Varicella zoster virus	Chickenpox - shingles
West Nile virus	West Nile virus encephalitis

(continued)

Table 7.1 (continued)

Fungi

Aspergillus spp	Mold infections
Candida spp	Candidal infections - paronychia
Coccidioides immitis	Coccidioidomycosis
Dematiaceous fungi *Fonsecaea* spp, *Phialophora* spp, *Cladosporium carrionii*, *exophiala* spp)	Chromomycosis
Histoplasma spp	Histoplasmosis
Paracoccidioides spp	Paracoccidioidomcosis (S. American blastomycosis)
Sporothrix spp	Sporotrichosis
Trichophyton spp, *microspum* spp	Tinea – ringworm infections

Parasites

Amoeba spp	Amebiasis
Avian schistosomes	Avian schistosomiasis – swimmer's itch
Ancylostoma spp	Cutaneous larvae migrans
Babesia spp	Babesiosis
Cryptosporidium parvum	Cryptosporidiosis
Echinococcus granulosus	Echinococcosis – hydatid cyst
Echinococcus multilocularis	Alveolar echinococcosis
Giardia lamblia	Giardiasis
Leishmania spp	Cutaneous leishmaniasis
Naegleria fowleri	Primary amoebic meningoencephalitis
Sarcoptes scabei	Scabies

Basic epidemiologic characteristics

The prevalence of communicable diseases affecting the workplace depends on the specific occupation examined. In work presented by the International Labor Organization, it is estimated that between 1.9–2.3 million work-related deaths occurred worldwide in 2000 (data available at www.ilo.org/safework). In the same work, the lower limit of work-related diseases was 1.6 million and approximately 320,000 (20%) were attributed to communicable diseases (data available at www.ilo.org/safework). The epidemiology appears to differ per country and depends on gross domestic product (GDP) per sector. The type of profession is also very important. The healthcare professions are characteristically associated with an occupational risk from blood-borne pathogens that has led to the implementation of specific protection measures (Beekmann & Henderson 2005; Brunetti et al. 2006; Puro et al. 2005; Sadoh, Fawole, Sadoh, Oladimeji & Sotiloye 2006). A large study from the Netherlands examining data from a region with a half-million people (and two major hospitals) discovered an incidence of exposure to blood-borne pathogens of 1.2 cases per day—both in the hospital and the community setting (van Wijk et al. 2006). Athough the incidents were split between the hospital and the community setting, they were related to occupational activities 95 percent of the time and, more specifically, healthcare activities in 84 percent of the cases (van Wijk et al. 2006). High-risk incidents predominantly involved hospital personnel (van Wijk et al. 2006). In another large study from the United Kingdom, known hepatitis C virus or human immunodeficiency virus (HIV) transmissions to health care workers was reported to be at the rate of 1.43 per year. In the same study, HIV and hepatitis C transmissions were occurring at an approximate rate of 0.009 per 1,000 hospital beds per year. The risk of infection when exposure involved sources with no risk factors was significantly lower (less than one in one million for HIV transmission).

More work is necessary to correctly identify prevalence and incidence of specific disease entities according to profession, and recent studies have shown unexpected observations (Olsen, Axelsson-Olsson, Thelin & Weiland 2006). In particular, health care workers have an increased risk from occupational infectious diseases that may occasionally lead to death. The annual death rate for occupational events, including communicable diseases has been calculated around 17-57 deaths per 1 million workers, however more accurate estimations are necessary (Sepkowitz & Eisenberg 2005).

There is no clear gender-specific predisposition to certain infectious diseases in relation to the frequency of their appearance in women in comparison with the general population. Harmonized case definitions should be used for surveillance purposes and may help in clarifying issues such as an increased prevalence of confirmed cases in the male vs. female population (Stefanoff, Eidson, Morse, & Zielinski 2005). Occupational communicable disease statistics relevant to women are urgently needed.

The epidemiology of a specific infectious disease in different countries varies and affects its prevalence if it is occupationally acquired, such as is the case with HIV infections (Ghys, Kufa, & George 2006). Several other examples exist depending on infectious entity, professional activity, and country (Brhel & Bartnicka 2003; Cinco et al. 2004; Golshan et al. 2002; Krejci-Manwaring et al. 2006; Reimer et al. 2002; Vilaichone et al. 2002; Werner et al. 2001). For example, serological evaluation disclosed antibodies *Borrelia burgdorferi sensu lato* in 41 percent of the tested forestry workers in Poland, compared to only 7 percent of the control blood donor population. The corresponding figures for the also tick-borne *Anaplasma phagocytophilum* were 17 percent vs. 5 percent, respectively (Cisak et al. 2005). A high proportion of asymptomatic cases was noted in the same study. Much lower rates of seropositivity have been described in similar studies examining forestry rangers from Italian regions (Santino et al. 2004), although regional variations for some of the pathogens may exist within the same country (Cinco et al. 2004).

Occupational communicable diseases may have a pronounced economical effect. Costs burden not only the affected population but also the respective industry. They include costs for leave of absence and lost work hours, costs for diagnosis and treatment, and indirect costs (e.g., via family transmission). Countries with poor economical resources experience a more significant financial burden.

Other factors may contribute to the epidemiological characteristics of certain communicable diseases. Climate and climatic changes, for example, may play an important role in the geographical distribution of pathogens. For example, colder than usual temperatures were blamed for the recent H5N1 avian influenza epidemic in Turkey (Giesecke 2006). Other infections whose epidemiology is especially affected by climatic changes are those that are vector-borne (e.g., malaria, dengue, leishmaniasis), and tick-borne diseases (Kovats, Campbell-Lendrum, McMichael, Woodward & Cox 2001; Lindgren & Gustafson 2001; Lindgren, Talleklint & Polfeldt 2000; Lindsay & Birley 1996). This is not due to effects of the climate on the microorganism itself, but rather to the vectors of the microorganism. Disease incidence for tick-borne encephalitis significantly increased in a Northern European country, and was highly related to factors such as consecutive mild winters and higher temperatures that favored tick activity (Lindgren & Gustafson 2001). Climatic changes may have more pronounced effects in vulnerable populations that are protected by low-quality health services (Lindsay & Birley 1996; Lindsay & Martens 1998). The detection and attribution of changes in the epidemiology of certain communicable diseases to climate change is a difficult emerging task for epidemiologists around the world.

A specific legislative framework has been established to address the issue of occupationally acquired communicable diseases, but several gaps still exist. The European Commission has established a framework for communicable diseases (Commission Decision 2002/253/EC), which lays down case definitions for reporting communicable diseases to the community network. This decision should be further harmonized with decisions or recommendations relevant to occupational diseases (Commission Recommendations 19-09-2003 concerning the European schedule of occupational diseases). The difficulties in comparing the data collected for statutory and nonstatutory surveillance networks should be further addressed. The newly established European Center for Disease Control and its activities (founding regulation 851/2004/EC) may be of paramount importance in this regard.

Activities that include surveillance of health, choice and correct use of personal protective equipment (PPE), environmental monitoring, and adequate education and training of workers potentially exposed to communicable diseases should be among the first priorities set during the establishment of an institutional or legislative framework. According to the framework, the occupational physician will establish priorities in his/her environment. Of great importance in controlling communicable diseases in the working environment are institutional guidelines and standard operating procedures regarding exposure to certain pathogens. Such guidelines have been established, especially for the health care environment, and especially with regard to blood-borne pathogens and agents of biological terrorism. Competent occupational physicians, together with other available specially trained personnel (e.g., infectious disease specialists or infection control nurses for the healthcare environments), implement guidelines and intervention measures when required. Although harmonization of procedures at a global level has not been established yet, guidelines for specific exposures from organizations with an established expertise—e.g., Occupational Safety and Health Administration (OSHA) or other similar organizations and committees (Puro et al. 2005)—are universally accepted and incorporated into infection control manuals in hospitals and other institutions around the globe.

Specific legislation is required to protect workers from exposure to communicable diseases. Several key actions should be incorporated into relevant legislation, including

- There must be adequate health care staffing at all levels of work to provide assistance to the worker
- Regulations covering biohazards and communicable diseases in the workplace are necessary for all countries and a harmonization procedure should be discussed at a political level
- Settlement of claims related to communicable diseases acquired in the workplace
- Establishment of minimum standards to protect air crew members from outbreaks of communicable diseases either of domestic or international origin—e.g., SARS (Breugelmans et al. 2004; Lee, Tsai, Wong & Lau 2006; Vogt et al. 2006)

Risk Factors

Risk factors for communicable diseases in working women appear not to be gender-related. Rather, there is an association with certain occupations where female workers are traditionally employed (Su et al. 2006; Ward & Day 2006).

All women occupied in professions where there is chance for high-risk exposure are considered *at-risk*. These include, but are not limited to, health care personnel, workers in research laboratories, workers in the food industry, animal husbandry workers, forest and field workers, construction workers, workers who handle human waste, sex workers, and even funeral service practitioners (Gershon, Vlahov, Farzadegan & Alter 1995). Other at-risk populations emerge according to epidemiological characteristics specific to certain geographical locations, as is the case with the HIV-1 infection in subSaharan Africa (Zelnick & O'Donnell 2005). Causal factors include, among others, inadvertent accidents and failure to institute appropriate preventive measures.

Conditions such as overworking and poor socioeconomic status may promote exposure to communicable diseases. Social conditions may affect the risk of occupational infections. Infection with HIV and AIDS has been associated with social class differences in highly affected areas (Ugwu et al. 2006). The working conditions of vulnerable populations (e.g., migrant workers, sex workers) may promote the acquisition of sexually transmitted infections (Yang et al. 2005).

Certain risk factors, such as failure to institute appropriate preventive measures may reflect a lack of education and training. Frequent exercises using real life scenarios are important in eliminating such factors, especially in the healthcare environment (Ganczak, Milona & Szych 2006; van Gemert-Pijnen, Hendrix, Van der Palen & Schellens 2006). The implementation of specific standard operating procedures according to guidelines is a prerequisite in such efforts. Recent research shows that compliance may be influenced by risk perception of the worker (Ganczak et al. 2006; van Gemert-Pijnen et al. 2006). Primary prevention is of paramount importance in instances of vulnerable populations where low rates of use of such measures have been reported (Yang et al. 2005); however, one should not underscore the importance of education and training in such populations. In a cohort study of 600 female bar workers, a simple intervention consisting of regular screening for sexually transmitted infections, together with syndromic management and relevant information and counseling was offered—it was not only well-received, but also resulted in significant reductions in the prevalence of gonorrhea, HIV, and other sexually transmitted infections (Riedner et al. 2006).

Communicable Diseases and Working Women

Several worksite factors may contribute to occupationally acquired infections. Women working in direct exposure to communicable diseases, or vectors of certain pathogens, have a significantly higher risk for acquiring the disease (e.g., working with animals creates exposure to certain zoonoses like avian influenza and brucellosis). On the other hand, women who work indoors maybe more exposed to airborne communicable diseases such as tuberculosis. Women working under conditions of extreme stress, and in areas where communicable diseases such as HIV-1 are endemic, may experience lapses in appropriate preventive measures and may fail to receive adequate post-exposure prophylaxis (Zelnick & O'Donnell 2005). Addressing the dramatic shortage of nurses in such environments, as well as involving them in the policy processes, could contribute to a better occupational health and improved quality of patient care (Zelnick & O'Donnell 2005).

Communicable diseases and even exposure to communicable diseases may have a profound effect on the professional life of affected women. Psychological stress, health impairment with its consequences, and the resulting absence from the work environment, are among the important adverse effects of an occupational communicable disease. In the worst case scenario, such a disease may lead to a permanent event such as chronic illness, loss of employment (Dray-Spira et al. 2006), or even death (Sepkowitz & Eisenberg 2005). Female gender (adjusted odds ratio 3.1; 95 percent confidence interval 1.1–8.5), together with a nonpermanent job and poor accommodation, were independent risk factors for employment loss in a study of patients with HIV infection in the highly aggressive antiretroviral therapy era (Dray-Spira et al. 2006). In the same study, patients with hierarchically higher positions had a lower chance of losing their job (Dray-Spira et al. 2006), while recent hospitalization and the presence of a chronic comorbidity conferred a higher risk (Dray-Spira et al. 2006).

Furthermore, in countries with poor recourses, extended unpaid leave from work or job loss may have significant implications on household income. This is particularly true for HIV infections observed in African countries, where failure of the patients to meet basic needs such as food, education, and access to healthcare both in the short and long-term is an undesirable consequence.

Examples of Occupational Communicable Diseases Affecting Women

A few examples, together with a short description of communicable diseases that could affect women in their work environment, are listed below with representative bacterial, viral, fungal, and parasitic pathogens. The list is not inclusive, as evidenced from the data depicted in Table 7.1.

Bacterial Infections

Anthrax

Anthrax is caused by *Bacillus anthracis*, and is one of the most important biological terrorism agents (Bossi et al. 2004a). *Bacillus anthracis* produces spores that can be inhaled or ingested, leading to the pulmonary and gastrointestinal forms of the disease, respectively (Bossi et al. 2004a). Inhalational anthrax is of particular interest for possible deliberate release (Bossi et al. 2004a), and it was observed during the most recent outbreak in the United States relating to a bioterrorist attack. It affected workers in processing and distribution centers of the United States postal service who handled envelopes contaminated with anthrax spores (Greene et al. 2002; Holtz et al. 2003; Jernigan et al. 2001). The most commonly seen occupationally acquired form of anthrax is the cutaneous form that occurs through direct skin exposure of people working with sick animals (Oncu & Sakarya 2003). It presents with the characteristic black eschar. This form of the disease was observed in wool-sorters in the past (Carter 2004), and occupations at risk include agricultural workers, herdsmen, and those handling sick animals or their products—e.g., hair, meat, bone and bone products, and wool (Oncu & Sakarya 2003; Smego, Gebrian & Desmangels 1998). In nonendemic areas, imported goat hair, hides (Need author names here, not article name 2006) and wool may be implicated in human cases. If left untreated, all forms may lead to sepsis and death. Treatment consists of supportive care and appropriate antimicrobials that can also be used for prophylaxis over an extended duration (Bossi et al. 2004a). Vaccines focusing on the protective antigen of the microorganism are available and are used especially in military vaccination programs (Grabenstein, Pittman, Greenwood & Engler 2006). A lot of research in newer vaccines is ongoing (Baillie 2006; Scorpio, Blank, Day & Chabot 2006).

Brucellosis

Brucellosis is probably the most common zoonosis worldwide (Pappas, Akritidis, Bosilkovski & Tsianos 2005), and the causative microorganism is *Brucella* spp (Pappas, Papadimitriou, Christou & Akritidis 2006). Occupations at risk include those involving direct exposure to contaminated animals (Pappas et al. 2005; Reid 2005), or dairy products (Pappas et al., 2005), such as livestock producers, slaughterers, (Karimi, Alborzi, Rasooli, Kadivar & Nateghian 2003), butchers (Karimi et al. 2003), meat packers, inspectors, veterinarians, and researchers and microbiology personnel working with the organism (Fiori, Mastrandrea, Rappelli & Cappuccinelli 2000; Memish & Mah 2001; Yagupsky & Baron 2005). In a recent epidemiological study from Ireland, veterinarians, laboratory staff, and workers based in meat plants were at increased risk of exposure to the bacteria (Reid 2005). Clinically, it can be a multisystemic disease manifesting with fever, hepatic and skeletal involvement, and other systemic signs and symptoms (Pappas et al. 2005). Clinicians should make clinical laboratory workers aware when brucellosis is suspected to avoid exposure (Gruner et al. 1994), especially in endemic areas (Yagupsky, Peled, Riesenberg & Banai 2000).

Plague

Plague is caused by *Yershinia pestis* (Bossi et al. 2004b). The bacterium is transmitted from infected animals (most frequently rodents or other wild animals—such as infected rabbits (von Reyn, Barnes, Weber & Hodgin 1976)—to humans by its critical vector the flea bite (Bossi et al. 2004b). After the bite, the microorganism spreads to the regional lymph nodes and causes acute inflammation and pain (buboes). Close contact between humans, rats, and shrews has been described in areas with frequent epidemics (Boisier et al. 2002). It also belongs to Class A of bioterrorism agents (Bossi et al. 2004b) because infection with the bacterium may lead to a very serious pulmonary infection and sepsis (Bossi et al. 2004b). At-risk occupations include farmers, people herding sheep, rabbit hunters, geologists, and other professionals working in the field in endemic areas.

Rickettsial Infections

Diseases caused by *rickettsia* spp are well-known occupational pathogens (Fox 1964) and have been associated with certain field exposures to the tick vectors carrying the pathogen, or research laboratories handling the pathogen (Johnson & Kadull 1967). More specifically, foresters, rangers, farmers, ranchers, trappers (Heidt, Harger, Harger & McChesney 1985), and hunters are at risk for contracting Rocky Mountain Spotted Fever—a disease characterized by fever, headache, and a maculopapular rash after a tick bite (Lacz, Schwartz & Kapila 2006; Sexton & Kaye 2002). Possible disease transmission through needle stick exposure has been described (Sexton, Gallis, McRae & Cate 1975).

Other ricckettsiae such as *Coxiella burnettii*—the etiologic agent of Q fever—can be occupationally transmitted. Humans are infected either through direct contact or inhalation of contaminated dust (Carrieri et al. 2002) and develop Q fever an influenza-like illness with pneumonia and hepatic involvement (Parker, Barralet & Bell 2006), whereas chronic infection is characterized by endocarditis (Parker et al. 2006). The microorganisms are shed by the genital material of infected animals (e.g., placental tissue) and may exist in the environment for months (Parker et al. 2006). Professionals at risk include veterinarians (Abe et al. 2001), meat processing plant workers, sheep and dairy workers, cattle and livestock handlers (Sadecky 1981), and staff working in research laboratories using sheep (Simor et al. 1984). Zoo workers also may be at risk (Ohguchi et al. 2006). In a recent epidemiological study, two high-risk village areas for positive Q fever serology were identified (Psaroulaki et al. 2006). Use of manure in the garden, ownership of animals (especially goats), and the presence of tick-infested or aborting animals were identified as important risk factors for Q fever seropositivity (Psaroulaki et al. 2006). Outbreaks in slaughter houses have been described (Carrieri et al. 2002;

Gilroy et al. 2001). An effective whole-cell vaccine is licensed in Australia (Parker et al. 2006).

Tuberculosis

Tuberculosis is caused by the microorganism *Mycobacterium tuberculosis*. It is one of the most frequent infectious diseases worldwide, and its transmission is air-borne. The disease can be extremely contagious. During an occupational outbreak, a single patient working in a shipyard (with an eight-month delay in diagnosis) was the source of a huge outbreak in a small town in Maine (Allos et al. 1996). Those at highest risk were the ones working closest to the infected person (Allos et al. 1996). Unfortunately, tuberculosis infections may not be recognized early (de Vries, Sebek & Lambregts-van Weezenbeek 2006). The infection usually involves the lung parenchyma, but can also present in extra-pulmonary forms such as lymphadenopathy, bone and joint infections, and serious meningoencephalitis. Occupations at risk include health care workers and correctional workers. Nurses are among the professions at highest risk (Tzeng 2005). Rates of latent infection in health care workers may be extremely high, especially in endemic areas with poor quality of protection (Kayanja, Debanne, King & Whalen 2005). Transmission, however, has been found to be strongly associated with health care work, even in settings with low incidence of tuberculosis (Diel, Seidler, Nienhaus, Rusch-Gerdes & Niemann 2005). From 2510 reported cases of tuberculosis during a 10-year study in San Fransisco (1993–2003), 31 (1.2%) occurred in healthcare workers (Ong et al. 2006). Work-related transmission was documented in about one in three of these healthcare workers, but rates of such acquisition gradually decreased over the study period (Ong et al. 2006). Delayed diagnosis of tuberculosis (especially if the index case is an older patient) may be one of the main causes of transmission from patient to health care worker (de Vries et al. 2006). Although several outbreaks have been described in prisons (Bergmire-Sweat et al. 1996; Drobniewski 1995; Jones, Craig, Valway, Woodley & Schaffner 1999; Laniado-Laborin 2001; McLaughlin et al. 2003; Ruddy et al. 2004; Skolnick 1992; Valway, Greifinger et al. 1994), a recent study identified mainly demographic (rather than occupational) factors associated with the disease in correctional health care workers (Mitchell et al. 2005). Nevertheless, continued vigilance to control occupational exposure is warranted (Mitchell et al. 2005).

Unfortunately, conventional contact tracing alone may not suffice to discover recent transmission chains for health care-associated tuberculosis (Diel et al. 2005). Thus, improved control strategies in the health care environment are necessary (Diel et al. 2005). The transmission of multidrug-resistant strains in recent years (Portugal et al. 1999; Ruddy et al. 2004; Valway et al. 1994), and the emergence of HIV infection as an important epidemiological comorbidity emphasizes such a need (Masur, Kaplan & Holmes 2002; Mohle-Boetani et al. 2002; Moro et al. 1998; Sonnenberg et al. 2005; "Tuberculosis outbreaks in prison housing units for HIV–infected inmates–California, 1995-1996" 1999). New guidelines have been developed to this effect (Jensen, Lambert, Iademarco & Ridzon 2005).

Tularemia

Tularemia is caused by *Francinsella tularensis*. The pathogen can be directly transmitted though animal handling, insect bites, or inhalation. The disease is characterized by a febrile syndrome, characteristic skin ulcers, and possibly a serious pulmonary infection with high fatality rates. It is also considered a Class A biological agent. At-risk occupations include farmers and agricultural workers (especially in endemic areas), butchers, cooks, and professional hunters.

Viral Infections

Human Immunodeficiency Virus Type 1 Infections

The Human Immunodeficiency Virus Type 1 (HIV-1) has been one of the most important pathogens recognized during the twentieth century. The progression of the infection from HIV to the acquired immunodeficiency syndrome (AIDS), and the high mortality associated with AIDS, has dramatically changed our approach to infectious diseases during the last two decades. Professions with a higher risk of exposure to the virus include healthcare workers, emergency response personnel, police, waste handlers, and (last but not least) professional sex workers. The risk depends on the prevalence and other epidemiological characteristics of the disease (e.g., social class) in specific countries, and may be less than that of Hepatitis B (Ugwu et al. 2006).

Occupationally acquired HIV-1 infection continues to be a rare event independent of the source of the data examined (Rapparini 2006). Iatrogenic infection has been estimated to occur once in every 8-52 procedures involving HIV-infected individuals. It has been estimated that the rate of seroconversion after percutaneous injury with a sharp device is only around 0.3 percent (Bell 1997; Case-control Study of HIV Seroconversion in Health-care Workers after Percutaneous Exposure to HIV-infected blood 1995; Gisselquist, Upham & Potterat 2006; McCray 1986). From the largest report so far, 56 health care workers were reported to have occupationally acquired HIV-1 infection, of whom 25 developed AIDS through exposure to blood or blood products (CDC HIV/AIDS Surveillance Report 2000).

The probability of HIV seroconversion after exposure to an infected patient depends on the type of exposure and the HIV status of the source patient. Deep injuries, a high volume of visible blood, and an uncontrolled HIV infection increase the risk of seroconversion (Cardo et al. 1997). Thoracotomy in the emergency department in a population with a prevalence of 7 percent has been estimated to carry a probability of 0.00004 for HIV seroconversion (Sikka, Millham & Feldman 2004).

Occupations traditionally occupied by women, such as nurses, have a high risk of exposure to blood-borne pathogens, including HIV. In one study examining 601 nurses from surgical wards, operating rooms, and emergency departments, almost half reported a percutaneous exposure during the year prior to the study (Ganczak et al. 2006). Employment conditions may be associated with HIV-1 acquisition, especially in vulnerable populations, such as immigrants. In a study from China examining 1,543 female migrant workers, those that were sexually experienced (43.2 percent), and either worked in entertainment establishments (e.g., nightclubs, dancing halls) or provided personal service (e.g., beauty salons, massage parlors), were two times more likely to have engaged in risky sexual practices compared to those employed in non-entertainment establishments like restaurants or factories (Yang et al. 2005). Unfortunately the rate of consistent condom use in the same study was less than 15 percent (Yang et al. 2005).

Molecular diagnosis has greatly enhanced our preventive and therapeutic efforts for HIV-1 infection, and may shorten the window period for accurate diagnosis. The introduction and increasing use of rapid-HIV testing will assist in future preventive efforts (Franco-Paredes, Tellez & del Rio 2006). Limitations, however, still exist. A cluster of infections in workers within the legal multibillion adult film industry is the most recent best example. Infection with HIV-1 appeared in 3 out of 13 female partners (attack rate of 23%) of a previously uninfected HIV positive male partner who was undergoing frequent testing for the virus (Taylor et al. 2007). This observation underscores the significance of primary prevention for HIV-1 infection (Taylor et al. 2007).

Suspicion of an occupational exposure to HIV should lead to the immediate application of protocols investigating the incident and providing prophylactic antivirals to those involved in high-risk scenarios, as well as psychological support. Guidelines for management have been published and are widely available (Updated U.S. Public Health Service Guidelines for the Management of Occupational Exposures to HBV, HCV, and HIV and Recommendations for Postexposure Prophylaxis 2001). Careful discussion of adverse effects associated with prophylactic antiviral regimens is necessary (Kiertiburanakul et al. 2006). These actions reduce the likelihood of HIV disease, as well as concomitant stress and anxiety from the exposure.

Hepatitis B

Occupational exposure to blood or other potentially infectious material is considered the main risk factor for HBV acquisition in the workplace. Thus, professions with such exposure (and especially healthcare workers) comprise the main risk groups. Hepatitis B has been associated with a higher risk for transmission to health care workers in comparison with HIV or Hepatitis C. The risk of transmission relates to the degree of contact, the Hepatitis B e antigen (HBeAg) status of the source patient, and the serological conversion, which is estimated around 30 percent (Werner & Grady 1982). The risk appears to be higher during the first five years of employment (Snydman et al. 1984). Prevaccination with HBV vaccine, and the application of universal precautions in dealing with blood or other potentially infectious material, is paramount in preventive efforts against HBV. Recommendations for postexposure measures have been published, and HBV vaccine (if unvaccinated or with low serological titers), Hepatitis B immunoglobulin, or both, must be started as soon as possible (within 1-7 days) (Puro et al. 2005; Updated U.S. Public Health Service

Guidelines for the Management of Occupational Exposures to HBV, HCV, and HIV
and Recommendations for Postexposure Prophylaxis 2001).

Hepatitis C

Hepatitis C is also acquired through exposure to blood or other potentially infectious
material. Health care workers are again the primary risk group for exposure. The
risk of transmission after a percutaneous exposure is in between that of Hepatitis B
and HIV, and estimated around 1.8 percent (Range: 0%–7%)(Updated U.S. Public
Health Service Guidelines for the Management of Occupational Exposures to HBV,
HCV, and HIV and Recommendations for Postexposure Prophylaxis 2001). The risk
depends on the type of procedure and the prevalence of the disease in the general
population. For emergent thoracotomy and a prevalence in the population of 17
percent, a probability of 0.0027 for chronic Hepatitis C seroconversion has been
calculated (Sikka et al. 2004). Following exposure, close follow-up and treatment of
acute seroconversion is indicated because there is no immediate prophylactic action
(Puro et al. 2005; Updated U.S. Public Health Service Guidelines for the Management of Occupational Exposures to HBV, HCV, and HIV and Recommendations for
Postexposure Prophylaxis 2001).

Avian Influenza H5N1

Direct exposure to poultry infected with the H5N1 subtype of Influenza A has
been identified as the main risk factor associated with infection in humans. Professions with increased risk for exposure include veterinarians, cullers and poultry workers, farmers or those exposed to commercial poultry, people involved in
litter management and carcass disposal in affected areas, zoo and nature reserve
workers, gamekeepers, biologists, laboratory technicians, and health workers caring for possible human cases. Poultry workers, especially those involved in activities such as butchering and contact with ill birds in the affected areas, seem to
carry the highest risk (Bridges et al. 2002). The role of occupational exposure
for health care workers has not been well established. Serological data from the
1997 Hong Kong epidemic indicate that subclinical H5N1 infections may occur
(Swayne 2006), however others have failed to prove such an association during
the recent phases of the outbreak in Southeast Asia (Apisarnthanarak et al. 2005).
Person-to-person transmission is probable and requires close and extensive contact (Ungchusak et al. 2005). The disease has milder forms that present with
influenza-like illnesses and/or symptoms from other systems (e.g., conjunctivitis)
(Swayne 2006) and severe forms associated with respiratory distress and death
(Beigel et al. 2005; de Jong et al. 2005; Shu, Yu & Li 2006; Tran et al. 2004;
Yu et al. 2006). Occupational medicine has its own role and can significantly
contribute in reducing the risk of transmission of avian flu to workers at risk
via prevention and prophylactic measures (Halpin 2005; Stone 2006; Whitley &
Monto 2006). Such efforts are of paramount importance because humanity is prepar-

ing to face a pandemic caused by a novel influenza strain and the first target group with the highest risk is poultry workers (Stone 2006; Swayne 2006; Whitley & Monto 2006).

Hantavirus Pulmonary Syndrome

People exposed to infected rodents or their droppings are at risk for contracting the new and old world viral agents of hantavirus pulmonary syndrome (Sin Nombre virus) (Mills et al. 2002). Exposure in closed spaces to active infestations of infected rodents seems to be the most important factor for infection (Mills et al. 2002). This probably explains the observations of no serological evidence of infection in workers widely exposed to rodents (Fritz et al. 2002). The virus was first recognized in the United States during 1993 (Duchin et al. 1994). Farmers appear to be at an increased risk through exposure to rodents or their excreta (Mills et al. 2002; Vapalahti, Paunio, Brummer-Korvenkontio, Vaheri & Vapalahti 1999), and farm and timber workers were most frequently affected in an epidemic in Chile (Castillo, Naranjo, Sepulveda, Ossa & Levy 2001). People occupied in hand plowing or planting (Mills et al. 2002), harvesting field crops (Mills et al. 2002), or involved in cleaning or other activities of rodent-infested buildings (e.g., barns, vacant dwellings) (Mills et al. 2002) are considered at risk. The disease is a laboratory hazard for personnel working with the virus (Mills et al. 2002; Shi, McCaughey & Elliott 2003).

The disease may progress to fatal pulmonary infection with or without renal involvement and hemorrhagic manifestations. Person-to-person transmission in the healthcare setting during outbreaks has not been confirmed (Chaparro et al. 1998). Risk reduction through the use of appropriate PPE and hygiene practices that deter rodents from colonizing the home and work environment is an appropriate control measure(Mills et al. 2002).

Rabies

This disease may affect workers exposed to infected animals harboring the virus in their nervous system and their salivary glands (Brookes & Fooks 2006; Warrell & Warrell 2004). It takes the form of an acute encephalitis, usually with a fatal outcome (Warrell & Warrell 2004). Occupations at risk include those exposed in infected rodents (Mendes et al. 2004; Warrell & Warrell 2004), veterinarians (Warrell & Warrell 2004; Weese, Peregrine & Armstrong 2002), animal handlers such as farmers (Brookes & Fooks 2006; Tariq, Shafi, Jamal & Ahmad 1991; Warrell & Warrell 2004), and people exposed to bats (Brookes & Fooks 2006; Warrell & Warrell 2004). Although a vaccine is available, animal rabies control and the provision of accessible and appropriate human prophylaxis worldwide remains a challenge (Warrell & Warrell 2004).

Fungal Infections

Coccidioidomycoses

Coccidioidomycoses belongs to the endemic mycoses. It is caused by the fungus *Coccidioides immitis* (Anstead & Graybill 2006), and is endemic in the southwestern United States (Anstead & Graybill 2006; Pappagianis 1988). The disease is transmitted through inhalation and has myriad manifestations (Anstead & Graybill 2006). It may begin as a flu-like illness that may progress to pneumonia and shock especially in immunocompromised subjects (Anstead & Graybill 2006). At-risk occupations include farmers and migrant farm workers, construction and excavation workers, as well as workers in archeological sites (Coccidioidomycosis in Workers at an Archeologic Site 2001; Werner, Pappagianis, Heindl & Mickel 1972) because the organism is found in the soil in endemic areas (Schmelzer & Tabershaw 1968). Physicians should keep this entity in the differential diagnosis in people who developed a respiratory infection after traveling to affected endemic areas (Desai et al. 2001).

Histoplasmosis

Histoplasmosis is caused by the fungus *Histoplasma capsulatum* found in the Americas, Asia, and Africa (Kauffman, 2006; Wheat 2006). The organism grows in soils enriched by bird and chicken droppings, as well as the guano of bats (Sorley, Levin, Warren, Flynn & Gersenblith 1979; Stobierski et al. 1996). People exposed to bats during spelunking activities are also considered at-risk (Lottenberg et al. 1979). During an outbreak at a bridge construction site, seeing or having contact with a bat and disposal of bat waste were the main risk factors for acquiring the disease (Huhn et al. 2005). Infection ranges from a mild self-limiting infection to a more systemic disease characterized by pulmonary involvement that reminds tuberculosis (Kauffman 2006; Wheat 2006). Occupational risk is observed in laborers at landfills or building construction (Huhn et al. 2005; Jones, Swinger et al. 1999), as well as people working in the agricultural industry (Outbreak of Histoplasmosis among Industrial Plant Workers 2004).

Dermatophytose—Tinea infections

Professions that require extensive manual work or activities with exposed skin surfaces, such as farming and other field work, have been associated with fungal infections of the skin. Fungal skin disease was the most prevalent infection in a study of migrant Latino farmworkers in the United States (Krejci-Manwaring et al. 2006). In a study of 467 forestry workers and farmers in Turkey, anywhere from 8-20 percent of the study population was affected by *tinea pedis et manus* infections and/or *onychomycosis* (Sahin, Kaya, Parlak, Oksuz & Behcet 2005). *Tinea corporis* and *tinea inguinalis* were also observed (Sahin et al. 2005). *Trichphyton rubrum* was the most frequently isolated fungus, and farmers had higher frequencies of superficial mycoses that was likely attributed to the wearing of rubber shoes and nylon socks, and the practice of animal husbandry (Sahin et al. 2005). Nevertheless, dermatophytoses have a worldwide prevalence and have been described in association with other occupations, including healthcare workers—such as those working in nursing homes (Smith et al. 2002)—or professional ice hockey players (Mohrenschlager, Seidl, Schnopp, Ring & Abeck 2001).

Parasitic infections

Echinococcosis

Humans serve as the intermediate host of the tapeworm (*Echinococcus granulosus*) of dogs and other carnivores. Evidence of infection is occasionally found among sheep workers, especially in endemic areas (Moro et al., 1994; Sotiraki, Himonas & Korkoliakou 2003) or veterinary workers (Biffin, Jones & Palmer 1993). It is the cause of the hydatid disease characterized by formation of cysts in the liver and other body sites. Alveolar echinococcosis is another zoonosis caused by *Echinococcus multilocularis* (McManus, Zhang, Li & Bartley 2003)that can be transmitted to farmers in endemic areas (Craig et al. 2000).

Giardiasis

Caused by the parasite *Giardia lamblia*, giardiasis is a parasitic disease (Huang & White 2006) that can infect farmers using untreated wastewater in agriculture (Ensink, van der Hoek & Amerasinghe 2006; Srikanth & Naik 2004) as well as other occupational groups exposed to human waste (Hoque, Hope, Kjellstrom, Scragg & Lay-Yee 2002; Sehgal & Mahajan 1991). Field workers that drink water from contaminated sources (e.g., wells, streams, or lakes) are also at-risk, and prevention efforts focusing on water hygiene should be effective (Rose, Haas & Regli 1991).

The Two-Fold Role of Working Women

Women should participate at all levels of decision-making in local, national, and international institutions and mechanisms for the prevention and management of infectious diseases in the workplace. The integration of a gender perspective is of essential importance in all activities aimed at communicable diseases in the working environment for successful outcomes, especially with regard to prevention. Occupationally acquired communicable diseases are not limited by the borders of the working environment. Working mothers will be role models for their young, not only during private discussions in the household environment, but also by their participation in community campaigns and efforts against communicable diseases aimed at more widely implemented measures for such diseases, such as during a pandemic. Well-informed and trained women may convey healthier lifestyles to their families regarding ways of handling exposure to communicable diseases and appropriate preventive and protective measures. They will also focus on maintaining a high level of health in their offspring by maintaining a complete vaccination schedule and scheduling regular health check-ups. Furthermore, instituting healthier nutritional habits, together with other activities targeting communicable diseases, may lead to an overall healthier lifestyle at home and will be of paramount importance in this regard.

Prevention

Examples of Best Practice, Case Studies

The control of communicable diseases resulting from health care worker exposure to blood-borne pathogens and other potentially infectious material remains the best example. Preventive measures against Hepatitis B acquisition involve vaccination and other prophylactic measures— e.g., administration of the specific immunoglobulin—and have been proven safe and effective in large trials (Grady et al. 1978; Prince et al. 1978; Prince et al. 1975; Szmuness, Stevens, Zang, Harley & Kellner 1981).

Reduction in HIV transmissions after percutaneous exposure has been shown in small studies as a result of post-exposure prophylaxis with antivirals (Cardo et al. 1997). Failures, however, have been described (Ippolito et al. 1998; Jochimsen 1997; Jochimsen et al. 1999; Pratt, Shapiro, McKinney, Kwok & Spector 1995) and the administration of prophylaxis and follow-up should be instituted by experienced staff according to national guidelines (Ippolito, Puro, Petrosillo & De Carli 1999) and recommendations from internationally acknowledged organizations (Puro et al. 2005; Updated U.S. Public Health Service Guidelines for the Management of Occupational Exposures to HBV, HCV, and HIV and Recommendations for Postexposure Prophylaxis 2001).

Administration, together with the occupational health department, should ensure the availability of policies and procedures relevant to occupational infections affecting specific job environments. These policies and procedures should adhere to legislative requirements and published literature and guidelines. Surveillance of exposures (even if only potential exposures) and analysis of collected data, together with the communication of the results, should be established in high-risk professions. Confidentiality and maintenance of a secure medical record in affected female workers is essential in following such infections. A referral process for exposed female workers and for further diagnostic and clinical evaluation and management is necessary in all environments.

Ongoing evaluation of strategies to minimize exposure to occupational infections is a continuous challenge in the workplace. The occupational health department should develop indicators that can assist in the evaluation of any preventive strategy instituted in the work environment. These could include, for example: a) rates of immunization for vaccine-preventable diseases, b) availability of engineering controls for sharp-related injuries, c) rates of percutaneous injuries for blood-borne pathogens, d) impact of training programs for use of newer preventive technologies for any relevant communicable diseases, e) product evaluation before and after implementation, and f) periodic screening of female workers for acquisition of infection, and so forth. To ensure consistency, collaboration with a more central authority such as the local public health authority may be preferable when assessing these indicators. The collection, analysis, interpretation, and finally the dissemination of such epidemiological information on occupational infections will enhance infection prevention and control at work.

Avoidance of Exposure to Risk Factors

Working women should be educated via training and information sessions provided by experts in occupational diseases and infectious diseases specialists to avoid exposure to risk factors associated with communicable diseases in the working environment. It is the primary responsibility of the health care department and occupational physician, however, to organize risk-reduction strategies to this effect and implement appropriate control measures, as well as institute appropriate educational activities. For example, a working woman could not have prevented transmission of legionellosis to herself from an infected water source in her work environment (Muraca, Stout, Yu & Yee 1988) ,and b) if engineering controls are not instituted, a female health care worker is at a much higher risk for a sharp-related injury.

Furthermore, the appropriate analysis of surveillance data collected at work will help in establishing safer work practices or identify groups at highest risk for contraction of an occupational infection.

Developing and Preserving Healthy Lifestyles

Prevention of exposure and acquisition of an infectious disease contributes to the well-being of a woman and assists in developing and preserving an overall healthier lifestyle. Through such prevention efforts, healthier habits are also acquired and become a part of the woman's life and are sometimes passed along to her immediate environment (e.g., preventive measures for transmission of a sexually transmitted infection, Hepatitis B vaccinations, and others).

General Guidelines on the Subject for Working Women

Women, and especially working women, should be aware of a large list of communicable pathogens that can be transmitted in the workplace (see Table 7.1). They should also participate in preventive efforts concerning these entities in their environment under the close collaboration and expert guidance of an occupational physician supervising their health. Diseases they encounter may differ according to the type of occupation and the overall prevalence of the disease in the general population, thus preventive measures will vary from one working environment to the other and between different countries. Guidelines have been established for specific infection control measures for occupational infections in the health care setting. According to the working environment and relevant infections, similar guidelines should be established for other professions. For global threats such as an influenza pandemic, the world should stand united in its preventive efforts (Whitley & Monto 2006), and special measures for the workplace should be incorporated in national pandemic plans. More education and training together with real-life exercises will be necessary for the successful implementation of preventive policies.

Resources on the Health Issue

Useful Links and Websites with Educational Materials

Useful web links about communicable diseases affecting women in their workplace include the following:

- http://www.osha.gov
- http://osha.europa.eu/OSHA
- http://www.ecdc.eu.int/
- http://www.efsa.eu.int
- http://www.cdc.gov
- www.haz-map.com
- www.occupationaldiseases.nl/ondex.php
- http://www.phac-aspc.gc.ca/noise-sinp/index.html
- www.ilo.org/safework
- www.ttl.fi (Finnish Institute of Occupational Health)

Related Published Material

Published and educational material can be found readily on the Web. Examples include the following:

- OSHA Guidance update on protecting employees from avian flu (avian influenza) viruses. Available at: http://www.osha.gov
- Hand hygiene quick card available at: http://www.osha.gov/pls/publications/pubindex.list
- Mold quick card available at: http://www.osha.gov/pls/publications/pubindex.list

Educational Material

Table 7.1 lists significant representative pathogens/diseases causing communicable diseases that may be occupationally acquired.

References

Abe T, Yamaki K, Hayakawa T, Fukuda H, Ito Y, Kume H, et al. (2001) A seroepidemiological study of the risks of Q fever infection in Japanese veterinarians. *Eur J Epidemiol, 17*(11), 1029–1032

Al-Saden PC, Wachs JE (2004) Hepatitis C: an update for occupational health nurses. *Aaohn J, 52*(5), 210-217; quiz 218–219

Allos BM, Genshelmer KF, Bloch AB, Parrotte D, Horan JM, Lewis V, et al. (1996) Management of an outbreak of tuberculosis in a small community. *Annals of internal medicine, 125*(2), 114–117

Anstead GM, Graybill JR (2006) Coccidioidomycosis. *Infectious disease clinics of North America, 20*(3), 621–643

Apisarnthanarak A, Erb S, Stephenson I, Katz JM, Chittaganpitch M, Sangkitporn S, et al. (2005) Seroprevalence of anti-H5 antibody among Thai health care workers after exposure to avian influenza (H5N1) in a tertiary care center. *Clin Infect Dis, 40*(2), e16–18

Baillie LW (2006) Past, imminent and future human medical countermeasures for anthrax. *Journal of applied microbiology, 101*(3), 594–606

Baussano I, Bugiani M, Carosso A, Mairano D, Barocelli AP, Tagna M, et al. (2006) Risk of tuberculin conversion among health care workers and the adoption of preventive measures. *Occup Environ Med*

Beekmann SE, Henderson DK (2005) Protection of healthcare workers from bloodborne pathogens. *Curr Opin Infect Dis, 18*(4), 331–336

Beigel JH, Farrar J, Han AM, Hayden FG, Hyer R, de Jong MD, et al. (2005) Avian influenza A (H5N1) infection in humans. *N Engl J Med, 353*(13), 1374–1385

Bell DM (1997) Occupational risk of human immunodeficiency virus infection in healthcare workers: an overview. *The American journal of medicine, 102*(5B), 9–15

Bergmire-Sweat D, Barnett BJ, Harris SL, Taylor JP, Mazurek GH, Reddy V (1996) Tuberculosis outbreak in a Texas prison, 1994. *Epidemiology and infection, 117*(3), 485–492

Biffin AH, Jones MA, Palmer SR (1993) Human hydatid disease: evaluation of an ELISA for diagnosis, population screening and monitoring of control programmes. *Journal of medical microbiology, 39*(1), 48–52

Boisier P, Rahalison L, Rasolomaharo M, Ratsitorahina M, Mahafaly M, Razafimahefa M, et al. (2002) Epidemiologic features of four successive annual outbreaks of bubonic plague in Mahajanga, Madagascar. *Emerging infectious diseases, 8*(3), 311–316

Bossi P, Tegnell A, Baka A, Van Loock F, Hendriks J, Werner A, et al. (2004a) Bichat guidelines for the clinical management of anthrax and bioterrorism-related anthrax. *Euro surveillance, 9*(12), E3-4

Bossi P, Tegnell A, Baka A, Van Loock F, Hendriks J, Werner A, et al. (2004b) Bichat guidelines for the clinical management of plague and bioterrorism-related plague. *Euro surveillance, 9*(12), E5-6

Breugelmans JG, Zucs P, Porten K, Broll S, Niedrig M, Ammon A, et al. (2004) SARS transmission and commercial aircraft. *Emerging infectious diseases, 10*(8), 1502–1503

Brhel P, Bartnicka M (2003) [Occupational infectious diseases in the Czech Republic]. *Med Pr, 54*(6), 529–533

Bridges CB, Lim W, Hu-Primmer J, Sims L, Fukuda K, Mak KH, et al. (2002) Risk of influenza A (H5N1) infection among poultry workers, Hong Kong, 1997-1998. *J Infect Dis, 185*(8), 1005–1010

Brookes SM, Fooks AR (2006) Occupational lyssavirus risks and post-vaccination monitoring. *Developments in biologicals, 125*, 165–173

Brunetti L, Santoro E, De Caro F, Cavallo P, Boccia G, Capunzo M, et al. (2006) Surveillance of nosocomial infections: a preliminary study on hand hygiene compliance of healthcare workers. *J Prev Med Hyg, 47*(2), 64–68

Cardo DM, Culver DH, Ciesielski CA, Srivastava,PU, Marcus R, Abiteboul D, et al. (1997) A case-control study of HIV seroconversion in health care workers after percutaneous exposure. Centers for Disease Control and Prevention Needlestick Surveillance Group. *The New England journal of medicine, 337*(21), 1485–1490

Carrieri MP, Tissot-Dupont H, Rey D, Brousse P, Renard H, Obadia Y, et al. (2002) Investigation of a slaughterhouse-related outbreak of Q fever in the French Alps. *European journal of clinical microbiology & infectious diseases, 21*(1), 17–21

Carter T (2004) The dissemination of anthrax from imported wool: Kidderminster 1900-14. *Occupational and environmental medicine, 61*(2), 103–107

Case-control study of HIV seroconversion in health-care workers after percutaneous exposure to HIV-infected blood–France, United Kingdom, and United States, January 1988-August 1994. (1995) *MMWR, 44*(50), 929–933

Castillo C, Naranjo J, Sepulveda A, Ossa G, Levy H (2001) Hantavirus pulmonary syndrome due to Andes virus in Temuco, Chile: clinical experience with 16 adults. *Chest, 120*(2), 548–554

CDC (2000) *HIV/AIDS Surveillance Report*. Department of Health and Human Services, Atlanta, GA 24 (vol 12, no. 1)

Chaparro J, Vega J, Terry W, Vera JL, Barra B, Meyer R, et al. (1998) Assessment of person-to-person transmission of hantavirus pulmonary syndrome in a Chilean hospital setting. *The Journal of hospital infection, 40*(4), 281–285

Chen YC, Chen PJ, Chang SC, Kao CL, Wang SH, Wang LH, et al. (2004) Infection control and SARS transmission among healthcare workers, Taiwan. *Emerg Infect Dis, 10*(5), 895–898

Cinco M, Barbone F, Grazia Ciufolini M, Mascioli M, Anguero Rosenfeld M, Stefanel P, et al. (2004) Seroprevalence of tick-borne infections in forestry rangers from northeastern Italy. *Clin Microbiol Infect, 10*(12), 1056–1061

Cisak E, Chmielewska-Badora J, Zwolinski J, Wojcik-Fatla A, Polak J, Dutkiewicz . (2005) Risk of tick-borne bacterial diseases among workers of Roztocze National Park (south-eastern Poland). *Ann Agric Environ Med, 12*(1), 127–132

Coccidioidomycosis in workers at an archeologic site–Dinosaur National Monument, Utah, June-July 2001. (2001) *MMWR, 50*(45), 1005–1008

Craig PS, Giraudoux P, Shi D, Bartholomot B, Barnish G, Delattre P, et al. (2000) An epidemiological and ecological study of human alveolar echinococcosis transmission in south Gansu, China. *Acta tropica, 77*(2), 167–177

Crane J (2002) Parvovirus B19 infection in pregnancy. *J Obstet Gynaecol Can, 24*(9), 727-743; quiz 744-726

de Jong MD, Bach VC, Phan TQ, Vo MH, Tran TT, Nguyen BH, et al. (2005) Fatal avian influenza A (H5N1) in a child presenting with diarrhea followed by coma. *N Engl J Med, 352*(7), 686–691

de Vries G, Sebek MM, Lambregts-van Weezenbeek CS (2006) Healthcare workers with tuberculosis infected during work. *Eur Respir J, 28*(6), 1216–1221

Desai SA, Minai OA, Gordon SM, O'Neil B, Wiedemann HP, Arroliga AC (2001) Coccidioidomycosis in non-endemic areas: a case series. *Respiratory medicine, 95*(4), 305–309

Dettenkofer M, Block C (2005) Hospital disinfection: efficacy and safety issues. *Curr Opin Infect Dis, 18*(4), 320–325

Diel R, Seidler A, Nienhaus A, Rusch-Gerdes S, Niemann S (2005) Occupational risk of tuberculosis transmission in a low incidence area. *Respir Res, 6*, 35

Dray-Spira R, Persoz A, Boufassa F, Gueguen A, Lert F, Allegre T, et al. (2006) Employment loss following HIV infection in the era of highly active antiretroviral therapies. *Eur J Public Health, 16*(1), 89–95

Drobniewski F (1995) Tuberculosis in prisons–forgotten plague. *Lancet, 346*(8980), 948–949

Duchin JS, Koster FT, Peters CJ, Simpson GL, Tempest B, Zaki SR, et al. (1994) Hantavirus pulmonary syndrome: a clinical description of 17 patients with a newly recognized disease. The Hantavirus Study Group. *The New England journal of medicine, 330*(14), 949–955

El-Masri MM, Williamson KM, Fox-Wasylyshyn SM (2004) Severe acute respiratory syndrome: another challenge for critical care nurses. *AACN Clin Issues, 15*(1), 150–159

Ensink JH, van der Hoek W, Amerasinghe FP (2006) Giardia duodenalis infection and wastewater irrigation in Pakistan. *Transactions of the Royal Society of Tropical Medicine and Hygiene, 100*(6), 538–542

Fear NT, McKinney PA, Patterson CC, Parslow RC, Bodansky HJ (1999) Childhood Type 1 diabetes mellitus and parental occupations involving social mixing and infectious contacts: two population-based case-control studies. *Diabet Med, 16*(12), 1025–1029

Fiori PL, Mastrandrea S, Rappelli P, Cappuccinelli P (2000) Brucella abortus infection acquired in microbiology laboratories. *Journal of clinical microbiology, 38*(5), 2005–2006

Fitzgerald K, Chakraborty J, Shah T. Khuder S, Duggan J (2003) HIV/AIDS knowledge among female migrant farm workers in the midwest. *J Immigr Health, 5*(1), 29–36

Fox JP (1964) Rickettsial Diseases Other Than Q Fever as Occupational Hazards. *Industrial medicine & surgery, 33*, 301–305

Franco-Paredes C, Tellez I, del Rio C (2006) Rapid HIV testing: a review of the literature and implications for the clinician. *Curr HIV/AIDS Rep, 3*(4), 169–175

Fritz CL, Fulhorst CF, Enge B, Winthrop KL, Glaser CA, Vugia DJ (2002) Exposure to rodents and rodent-borne viruses among persons with elevated occupational risk. *Journal of occupational and environmental medicine / American College of Occupational and Environmental Medicine, 44*(10), 962–967

Ganczak M, Milona M, Szych Z (2006) Nurses and occupational exposures to bloodborne viruses in Poland. *Infect Control Hosp Epidemiol, 27*(2), 175–180

Gershon RR, Vlahov D, Farzadegan H, Alter MJ (1995) Occupational risk of human immunodeficiency virus, hepatitis B virus, and hepatitis C virus infections among funeral service practitioners in Maryland. *Infect Control Hosp Epidemiol, 16*(4), 194–197

Ghys PD, Kufa E, George MV (2006) Measuring trends in prevalence and incidence of HIV infection in countries with generalised epidemics. *Sex Transm Infect, 82 Suppl 1*, i52-56

Giesecke J (2006) Human cases of avian influenza in eastern Turkey: the weather factor. Euro Surveill;11(1):E060119.2. Available from: http://www.eurosurveillance.org/ew/2006/060119.asp#2

Gilbert GL (2000) Parvovirus B19 infection and its significance in pregnancy. *Commun Dis Intell, 24 Suppl*, 69–71

Gilroy N, Formica N, Beers M, Egan A, Conaty S, Marmion B (2001) Abattoir-associated Q fever: a Q fever outbreak during a Q fever vaccination program. *Aust N Z J Public Health, 25*(4), 362–367

Gisselquist D, Upham G, Potterat JJ (2006) Efficiency of human immunodeficiency virus transmission through injections and other medical procedures: evidence, estimates, and unfinished business. *Infection control and hospital epidemiology, 27*(9), 944–952

Golshan M, Faghihi M, Marandi MM (2002) Indoor women jobs and pulmonary risks in rural areas of Isfahan, Iran, 2000. *Respir Med, 96*(6), 382–388

Grabenstein JD, Pittman PR, Greenwood JT, Engler RJ (2006) Immunization to protect the US Armed Forces: heritage, current practice, and prospects. *Epidemiologic reviews, 28*, 3–26

Grady GF, Lee VA, Prince AM, Gitnick GL, Fawaz KA, Vyas GN, et al. (1978) Hepatitis B immune globulin for accidental exposures among medical personnel: final report of a multicenter controlled trial. *The Journal of infectious diseases, 138*(5), 625–638

Greene CM, Reefhuis J. Tan C, Fiore AE, Goldstein S, Beach MJ, et al. (2002) Epidemiologic investigations of bioterrorism-related anthrax, New Jersey, 2001. *Emerg Infect Dis, 8*(10), 1048–1055

Gruner E, Bernasconi E, Galeazzi RL, Buhl D, Heinzle R, Nadal D (1994) Brucellosis: an occupational hazard for medical laboratory personnel. Report of five cases. *Infection, 22*(1), 33–36

Gyorkos TW, Beliveau C, Rahme E, Muecke C, Joseph S, Soto JC (2005) High rubella seronegativity in daycare educators. *Clin Invest Med, 28*(3), 105–111

Halpin J (2005) Avian flu from an occupational health perspective. *Arch Environ Occup Health, 60*(2), 62–69

Heidt GA, Harger C, Harger H, McChesney TC (1985) Serological study of selected disease antibodies in Arkansas–furbearer trappers, a high risk group. *The Journal of the Arkansas Medical Society, 82*(6), 265–269

Holtz TH, Ackelsberg J, Kool JL, Rosselli R, Marfin A, Matte T, et al. (2003) Isolated case of bioterrorism-related inhalational anthrax, New York City, 2001. *Emerging infectious diseases, 9*(6), 689–696

Hoque ME, Hope VT, Kjellstrom T, Scragg R, Lay-Yee R (2002) Risk of giardiasis in Aucklanders: a case-control study. *International journal of infectious diseases, 6*(3), 191–197

Huang DB, White AC (2006) An updated review on Cryptosporidium and Giardia. *Gastroenterology clinics of North America, 35*(2), 291–314, viii

Huhn GD, Austin C, Carr M, Heyer D, Boudreau P, Gilbert G, et al. (2005) Two outbreaks of occupationally acquired histoplasmosis: more than workers at risk. *Environmental health perspectives, 113*(5), 585–589

Inhalation anthrax associated with dried animal hides–Pennsylvania and New York City, 2006 (2006) *MMWR, 55*(10), 280–282

Ippolito G, Puro V, Petrosillo N, De Carli G (1999) Surveillance of occupational exposure to bloodborne pathogens in health care workers: the Italian national programme. *4*(3), 33–36

Ippolito G, Puro V, Petrosillo N, De Carli G, Micheloni G, Magliano E (1998) Simultaneous infection with HIV and hepatitis C virus following occupational conjunctival blood exposure. *JAMA, 280*(1), 28

Jensen PA, Lambert LA, Iademarco MF, Ridzon R (2005) Guidelines for preventing the transmission of Mycobacterium tuberculosis in health-care settings, 2005. *MMWR Recomm Rep, 54*(17), 1–141

Jernigan JA. Stephens DS, Ashford DA, Omenaca C, Topiel MS, Galbraith M, et al. (2001) Bioterrorism-related inhalational anthrax: the first 10 cases reported in the United States. *Emerging infectious diseases, 7*(6), 933–944

Jochimsen EM (1997) Failures of zidovudine postexposure prophylaxis. *The American journal of medicine, 102*(5B), 52–55; discussion 56–57

Jochimsen EM, Luo CC, Beltrami JF, Respess RA, Schable CA, Cardo DM (1999) Investigations of possible failures of postexposure prophylaxis following occupational exposures to human immunodeficiency virus. *Archives of internal medicine, 159*(19), 2361–2363

Johnson-Delaney CA (2005) Safety issues in the exotic pet practice. *Vet Clin North Am Exot Anim Pract, 8*(3), 515–524, vii

Johnson JE 3rd, Kadull PJ (1967) Rocky Mountain spotted fever acquired in a laboratory. *The New England journal of medicine, 277*(16), 842–847

Jones TF, Craig AS, Valway SE, Woodley CL, Schaffner W (1999) Transmission of tuberculosis in a jail. *Annals of internal medicine, 131*(8), 557–563

Jones TF, Swinger GL, Craig AS, McNeil MM, Kaufman L, Schaffner W (1999) Acute pulmonary histoplasmosis in bridge workers: a persistent problem. *The American journal of medicine, 106*(4), 480–482

Karimi A, Alborzi A, Rasooli M, Kadivar MR, Nateghian AR (2003) Prevalence of antibody to Brucella species in butchers, slaughterers and others. *Eastern Mediterranean health journal = La revue de sante de la Mediterranee orientale = al-Majallah al-sihhiyah li-sharq al-mutawassit, 9*(1–2), 178–184

Kauffman CA (2006) Endemic mycoses: blastomycosis, histoplasmosis, and sporotrichosis. *Infectious disease clinics of North America, 20*(3), 645-662, vii

Kayanja HK, Debanne S, King C, Whalen CC (2005) Tuberculosis infection among health care workers in Kampala, Uganda. *Int J Tuberc Lung Dis, 9*(6), 686–688

Keller S, Daley K, Hyde J, Greif RS, Church DR (2005) Hepatitis C prevention with nurses. *Nurs Health Sci, 7*(2), 99–106

Kiertiburanakul S, Wannaying, Tonsuttakul S, Kehachindawat P, Apivanich S, Somsakul S, et al. (2006) Use of HIV Postexposure Prophylaxis in healthcare workers after occupational exposure: a Thai university hospital setting. *J Med Assoc Thai, 89*(7), 974–978

Koh D, Lim MK, Ong CN, Chia SE (2005) Occupational health response to SARS. *Emerg Infect Dis, 11*(1), 167–168

Kovats RS, Campbell-Lendrum DH, McMichael AJ, Woodward A, Cox JS (2001) Early effects of climate change: do they include changes in vector-borne disease? *Philos Trans R Soc Lond B Biol Sci, 356*(1411), 1057–1068

Krejci-Manwaring J, Schulz MR, Feldman SR, Vallejos QM, Quandt SA, Rapp SR, et al. (2006) Skin disease among Latino farmworkers in North Carolina. *J Agric Saf Health, 12*(2), 155–163

Lacz NL, Schwartz RA, Kapila R (2006) Rocky Mountain spotted fever. *Journal of the European Academy of Dermatology and Venereology, 20*(4), 411–417

Laniado-Laborin R (2001) Tuberculosis in correctional facilities : a nightmare without end in sight. *Chest, 119*(3), 681–683

Lateef F, Lim SH, Tan EH (2004) New paradigm for protection: the emergency ambulance services in the time of severe acute respiratory syndrome. *Prehosp Emerg Care, 8*(3), 304–307

Lee CW, Tsai YS, Wong TW, Lau CC (2006) A loophole in international quarantine procedures disclosed during the SARS crisis. *Travel medicine and infectious disease, 4*(1), 22–28

Lindgren E, Gustafson R (2001) Tick-borne encephalitis in Sweden and climate change. *Lancet, 358*(9275), 16–18

Lindgren E, Talleklint L, Polfeldt T (2000) Impact of climatic change on the northern latitude limit and population density of the disease-transmitting European tick Ixodes ricinus. *Environ Health Perspect, 108*(2), 119–123

Lindsay SW, Birley MH (1996) Climate change and malaria transmission. *Ann Trop Med Parasitol, 90*(6), 573–588

Lindsay SW, Martens WJ (1998) Malaria in the African highlands: past, present and future. *Bull World Health Organ, 76*(1), 33–45

Lottenberg R, Waldman RH, Ajello L, Hoff GL, Bigler W, Zellner SR (1979) Pulmonary histoplasmosis associated with exploration of a bat cave. *American journal of epidemiology, 110*(2), 156–161

Masur H, Kaplan JE, Holmes KK (2002) Guidelines for preventing opportunistic infections among HIV-infected persons–2002. Recommendations of the U.S. Public Health Service and the Infectious Diseases Society of America. *Ann Intern Med, 137*(5 Pt 2), 435–478

McCray E (1986) Occupational risk of the acquired immunodeficiency syndrome among health care workers. *The New England journal of medicine, 314*(17), 1127–1132

McLaughlin SI, Spradling P, Drociuk D, Ridzon R, Pozsik CJ, Onorato I (2003) Extensive transmission of Mycobacterium tuberculosis among congregated, HIV-infected prison inmates in South Carolina, United States. *The international journal of tuberculosis and lung disease, 7*(7), 665–672

McManus DP, Zhang W, Li J, Bartley PB (2003) Echinococcosis. *Lancet, 362*(9392), 1295–1304

Memish ZA, Mah MW (2001) Brucellosis in laboratory workers at a Saudi Arabian hospital. *Am J Infect Control, 29*(1), 48–52

Mendes WS, da Silva AA, Aragao LF, Aragao NJ, Raposo Mde L, Elkhoury MR, et al. (2004) Hantavirus infection in Anajatuba, Maranhao, Brazil. *Emerg Infect Dis, 10*(8), 1496–1498

Mills JN, Corneli A, Young JC, Garrison LE, Khan AS, Ksiazek TG (2002) Hantavirus pulmonary syndrome–United States: updated recommendations for risk reduction. Centers for Disease Control and Prevention. *MMWR. Recommendations and reports, 51*(RR-9), 1–12

Mitchell CS, Gershon RR, Lears MK, Vlahov D, Felknor S, Lubelczyk RA, et al. (2005) Risk of tuberculosis in correctional healthcare workers. *J Occup Environ Med, 47*(6), 580–586

Mohle-Boetani JC, Miguelino V, Dewsnup DH, Desmond E, Horowitz E, Waterman SH, et al. (2002) Tuberculosis outbreak in a housing unit for human immunodeficiency virus-infected patients in a correctional facility: transmission risk factors and effective outbreak control. *Clinical infectious diseases, 34*(5), 668–676

Mohrenschlager M, Seidl HP, Schnopp C, Ring J, Abeck D (2001) Professional ice hockey players: a high-risk group for fungal infection of the foot? *Dermatology, 203*(3), 271

Moro ML, Gori A, Errante I, Infuso A, Franzetti F, Sodano L, et al. (1998) An outbreak of multidrug-resistant tuberculosis involving HIV-infected patients of two hospitals in Milan, Italy. Italian Multidrug-Resistant Tuberculosis Outbreak Study Group. *AIDS (London, England), 12*(9), 1095–1102

S. Tsiodras

Moro PL, Guevara A, Verastegui M, Gilman RH, Poma H, Tapia B, et al. (1994) Distribution of hydatidosis and cysticercosis in different Peruvian populations as demonstrated by an enzyme-linked immunoelectrotransfer blot (EITB) assay. The Cysticercosis Working Group in Peru (CWG). *The American journal of tropical medicine and hygiene, 51*(6), 851–855

Muraca PW, Stout JE, Yu VL, Yee YC (1988) Legionnaires' disease in the work environment: implications for environmental health. *American Industrial Hygiene Association journal, 49*(11), 584–590

Nienhaus A, Skudlik C, Seidler A (2005) Work-related accidents and occupational diseases in veterinarians and their staff. *International archives of occupational and environmental health, 78*(3), 230–238

Ohguchi H, Hirabayashi Y, Kodera T, Ishii T, Munakata Y, Sasaki T (2006) Q fever with clinical features resembling systemic lupus erythematosus. *Internal medicine (Tokyo, Japan), 45*(5), 323–326

Olsen B, Axelsson-Olsson D, Thelin A, Weiland O (2006) Unexpected high prevalence of IgG-antibodies to hepatitis E virus in Swedish pig farmers and controls. *Scand J Infect Dis, 38*(1), 55–58

Oncu S, Sakarya S (2003) Anthrax–an overview. *Medical science monitor, 9*(11), RA276-283

Ong A, Rudoy I, Gonzalez LC, Creasman J, Kawamura LM, Daley CL (2006) Tuberculosis in healthcare workers: a molecular epidemiologic study in San Francisco. *Infect Control Hosp Epidemiol, 27*(5), 453–458

Outbreak of histoplasmosis among industrial plant workers–Nebraska, 2004 (2004) *MMWR, 53*(43), 1020–1022

Pappagianis D (1988) Epidemiology of coccidioidomycosis. *Current topics in medical mycology, 2*, 199–238

Pappas G, Akritidis N, Bosilkovski M, Tsianos E (2005) Brucellosis. *The New England journal of medicine, 352*(22), 2325–2336

Pappas G, Papadimitriou P, Christou L, Akritidis N (2006) Future trends in human brucellosis treatment. *Expert opinion on investigational drugs, 15*(10), 1141–1149

Parker NR, Barralet JH, Bell AM (2006) Q fever. *Lancet, 367*(9511), 679–688

Portugal I, Covas MJ, Brum L, Viveiros M, Ferrinho P, Moniz-Pereira J, et al. (1999) Outbreak of multiple drug-resistant tuberculosis in Lisbon: detection by restriction fragment length polymorphism analysis. *The international journal of tuberculosis and lung disease, 3*(3), 207–213

Pratt RD, Shapiro JF, McKinney N, Kwok S, Spector SA (1995) Virologic characterization of primary human immunodeficiency virus type 1 infection in a health care worker following needlestick injury. *The Journal of infectious diseases, 172*(3), 851–854

Prince AM, Szmuness W, Mann MK, Vyas GN, Grady GF, Shapiro FL, et al. (1978) Hepatitis B immune globulin: final report of a controlled, multicenter trial of efficacy in prevention of dialysis-associated hepatitis. *The Journal of infectious diseases, 137*(2), 131–144

Prince AM, Szmuness W, Mann MK, Vyas GN, Grady GF, Shapiro FL, et al. (1975) Hepatitis B "immune" globulin: effectiveness in prevention of dialysis-associated hepatitis. *The New England journal of medicine, 293*(21), 1063–1067

Psaroulaki A, Hadjichristodoulou C, Loukaides F, Soteriades E, Konstantinidis A, Papastergiou P, et al. (2006) Epidemiological study of Q fever in humans, ruminant animals, and ticks in Cyprus using a geographical information system. *European journal of clinical microbiology & infectious diseases, 25*(9), 576–586

Puro V, De Carli G, Cicalini S, Soldani F, Balslev U, Begovac J, et al. (2005) European recommendations for the management of healthcare workers occupationally exposed to hepatitis B virus and hepatitis C virus. *Euro Surveill, 10*(10), 260–264

Rapparini C (2006) Occupational HIV infection among health care workers exposed to blood and body fluids in Brazil. *Am J Infect Control, 34*(4), 237–240

Reid AJ (2005) Brucellosis–a persistent occupational hazard in Ireland. *International journal of occupational and environmental health, 11*(3), 302–304

Reimer B, Erbas B, Lobbichler K, Truckenbrodt R, Gartner-Kothe U, Kapeller N, et al. (2002) Seroprevalence of Borrelia infection in occupational tick-exposed people in Bavaria (Germany). *Int J Med Microbiol, 291 Suppl 33*, 215

Riedner G, Hoffmann O, Rusizoka M, Mmbando D, Maboko L, Grosskurth H, et al. (2006) Decline in sexually transmitted infection prevalence and HIV incidence in female barworkers attending prevention and care services in Mbeya Region, Tanzania. *Aids, 20*(4), 609–615

Rose JB, Haas CN, Regli S (1991) Risk assessment and control of waterborne giardiasis. *American journal of public health, 81*(6), 709–713

Ruddy MC, Davies AP, Yates MD. Yates S, Balasegaram S, Drabu Y, et al. (2004) Outbreak of isoniazid resistant tuberculosis in north London. *Thorax, 59*(4), 279–285

Sadecky E (1981) Infection of cattle and livestock handlers with Coxiella burnetti and Chlamydiae in the farm of Bernolakovo (West Slovakia). *Journal of hygiene, epidemiology, microbiology, and immunology, 25*(1), 52–59

Sadoh WE, Fawole AO, Sadoh AE, Oladimeji AO, Sotiloye OS (2006) Practice of universal precautions among healthcare workers. *J Natl Med Assoc, 98*(5), 722–726

Sahin I, Kaya D, Parlak AH, Oksuz S, Behcet M (2005) Dermatophytoses in forestry workers and farmers. *Mycoses, 48*(4), 260–264

Santino I, Cammarata E, Franco S, Galdiero F, Oliva B, Sessa R, et al. (2004) Multicentric study of seroprevalence of Borrelia burgdorferi and Anaplasma phagocytophila in high-risk groups in regions of central and southern Italy. *Int J Immunopathol Pharmacol, 17*(2), 219–223

Schmelzer LL, Tabershaw IR (1968) Exposure factors in occupational coccidioidomycosis. *American journal of public health and the nation's health, 58*(1), 107–113

Scorpio A, Blank TE, Day WA, Chabot DJ (2006) Anthrax vaccines: Pasteur to the present. *Cellular and molecular life sciences, 63*(19-20), 2237–2248

Sehgal R, Mahajan RC (1991) Occupational risks in sewage work. *Lancet, 338*(8779), 1404–1405

Selvaratnam RR, de Silva LD, Pathmeswaran A, de Silva NR (2003) Nutritional status and productivity of Sri Lankan tea pluckers. *Ceylon Med J, 48*(4), 114–118

Sepkowitz KA, Eisenberg L (2005) Occupational deaths among healthcare workers. *Emerg Infect Dis, 11*(7), 1003–1008

Sexton DJ, Gallis HA, McRae JR, Cate TR (1975) Letter: Possible needle-associated Rocky Mountain spotted fever. *The New England journal of medicine, 292*(12), 645

Sexton DJ, Kaye KS (2002) Rocky mountain spotted fever. *The Medical clinics of North America, 86*(2), 351-360, vii-viii

Shi X, McCaughey C, Elliott RM (2003) Genetic characterisation of a Hantavirus isolated from a laboratory-acquired infection. *Journal of medical virology, 71*(1), 105–109

Shu Y, Yu H, Li D (2006) Lethal avian influenza A (H5N1) infection in a pregnant woman in Anhui Province, China. *N Engl J Med, 354*(13), 1421–1422

Sikka R, Millham FH, Feldman JA (2004) Analysis of occupational exposures associated with emergency department thoracotomy. *The Journal of trauma, 56*(4), 867–872

Simor AE, Brunton JL, Salit IE, Vellend H, Ford-Jones L, Spence LP (1984) Q fever: hazard from sheep used in research. *Canadian Medical Association journal, 130*(8), 1013–1016

Singer DA (2005) Transmission of infections during commercial air travel. *Lancet, 365*(9478), 2176–2177

Skolnick AA (1992) Correction facility TB rates soar; some jails bring back chest roentgenograms. *JAMA, 268*(22), 3175–3176

Smego RA Jr, Gebrian B, Desmangels G (1998) Cutaneous manifestations of anthrax in rural Haiti. *Clinical infectious diseases, 26*(1), 97–102

Smith DR, Choi JW, Yu DS, Ki M, Oh CH, Yamagata Z (2002) Skin disease among staff in a large Korean nursing home. *Tohoku J Exp Med, 198*(3), 175–180

Snydman DR, Munoz A, Werner BG, Polk BF, Craven DE, Platt R, et al. (1984) A multivariate analysis of risk factors for hepatitis B virus infection among hospital employees screened for vaccination. *American journal of epidemiology, 120*(5), 684–693

Sonnenberg P, Glynn JR, Fielding K, Murray J, Godfrey-Faussett P, Shearer S (2005) How soon after infection with HIV does the risk of tuberculosis start to increase? A retrospective cohort study in South African gold miners. *J Infect Dis, 191*(2), 150–158

Sorley DL, Levin ML, Warren JW, Flynn JP, Gersenblith (1979) Bat-associated histoplasmosis in Maryland bridge workers. *The American journal of medicine, 67*(4), 623–626

Sotiraki S, Himonas C, Korkoliakou P (2003) Hydatidosis-echinococcosis in Greece. *Acta tropica,* *85*(2), 197–201

Srikanth R, Naik D (2004) Health effects of wastewater reuse for agriculture in the suburbs of Asmara city, Eritrea. *International journal of occupational and environmental health, 10*(3), 284–288

Stefanoff P, Eidson M, Morse DL, Zielinski A (2005) Evaluation of tickborne encephalitis case classification in Poland. *Euro Surveill, 10*(1), 23–25

Stobierski MG, Hospedales CJ, Hall WN, Robinson-Dunn B, Hoch D, Sheill DA (1996) Outbreak of histoplasmosis among employees in a paper factory–Michigan, 1993. *Journal of clinical microbiology, 34*(5), 1220–1223

Stone PW, Clarke SP, Cimiotti J, Correa-de-Araujo R (2004) Nurses' working conditions: implications for infectious disease. *Emerg Infect Dis, 10*(11), 1984–1989

Stone R (2006) Avian influenza. Combating the bird flu menace, down on the farm. *Science, 311*(5763), 944–946

Su SB, Wang JN, Lu CW, Guo HR (2006) Reducing urinary tract infections among female clean room workers. *J Womens Health (Larchmt), 15*(7), 870–876

Swayne DE (2006) Occupational and consumer risks from avian influenza viruses. *Dev Biol (Basel), 124,* 85–90

Szmuness W, Stevens CE, Zang EA, Harley EJ, Kellner A (1981) A controlled clinical trial of the efficacy of the hepatitis B vaccine (Heptavax B): a final report. *Hepatology (Baltimore, Md, 1*(5), 377–385

Tariq WU, Shafi MS, Jamal S, Ahmad M (1991) Rabies in man handling infected calf. *Lancet, 337*(8751), 1224

Taylor MM, Rotblatt H, Brooks JT. Montoya J, Aynalem G, Smith L, et al. (2007) Epidemiologic Investigation of a Cluster of Workplace HIV Infections in the Adult Film Industry: Los Angeles, California, 2004. *Clin Infect Dis, 44*(2), 301–305

Tran TH, Nguyen TL, Nguyen TD, Luong TS, Pham PM, Nguyen VC, et al. (2004) Avian influenza A (H5N1) in 10 patients in Vietnam. *N Engl J Med, 350*(12), 1179–1188

Tuberculosis outbreaks in prison housing units for HIV-infected inmates–California, 1995-1996. (1999) *MMWR, 48*(4), 79–82

Tzeng HM (2005) Promoting a safer practice environment as related to occupational tuberculosis: a nursing care quality issue in Taiwan. *J Nurs Care Qual, 20*(4), 356–363

Ugwu BT, Thacher TD, Imade GE, Sagay AS, Isamade EI, Ford RW (2006) HIV and hepatitis B seroprevalence in trauma patients in North Central Nigeria. *West Afr J Med, 25*(1), 6–9

Ungchusak K, Auewarakul P, Dowell SF, Kitphati R, Auwanit W, Puthavathana P, et al. (2005) Probable person-to-person transmission of avian influenza A (H5N1). *N Engl J Med, 352*(4), 333–340

Updated U.S. Public Health Service Guidelines for the Management of Occupational Exposures to HBV, HCV, and HIV and Recommendations for Postexposure Prophylaxis. (2001) *MMWR Recomm Rep, 50*(RR-11), 1–52

Valway SE, Greifinger RB, Papania M, Kilburn JO, Woodley C, DiFerdinando GT, et al. (1994) Multidrug-resistant tuberculosis in the New York State prison system, 1990–1991. *The Journal of infectious diseases, 170*(1), 151–156

Valway SE, Richards SB, Kovacovich J, Greifinger RB, Crawford JT, Dooley SW (1994) Outbreak of multi-drug-resistant tuberculosis in a New York State prison, 1991. *American journal of epidemiology, 140*(2), 113–122

van Gemert-Pijnen J, Hendrix MG, Van der Palen J, Schellens PJ (2006) Effectiveness of protocols for preventing occupational exposure to blood and body fluids in Dutch hospitals. *J Hosp Infect, 62*(2), 166–173

van Wijk PT, Pelk-Jongen M, de Boer E, Voss A, Wijkmans C, Schneeberger PM (2006) Differences between hospital- and community-acquired blood exposure incidents revealed by a regional expert counseling center. *Infection, 34*(1), 17–21

Vapalahti K, Paunio M, Brummer-Korvenkontio M, Vaheri A, Vapalahti O (1999) Puumala virus infections in Finland: increased occupational risk for farmers. *American journal of epidemiology, 149*(12), 1142–1151

Vilaichone RK, Vilaichone W, Nunthapisud P, Wilde H (2002) Streptococcus suis infection in Thailand. *J Med Assoc Thai, 85 Suppl 1*, S109-117

Vogt TM, Guerra MA, Flagg EW, Ksiazek TG, Lowther SA, Arguin PM (2006) Risk of severe acute respiratory syndrome-associated coronavirus transmission aboard commercial aircraft. *Journal of travel medicine, 13*(5), 268–272

von Reyn CF, Barnes AM, Weber NS, Hodgin UG (1976) Bubonic plague from exposure to a rabbit: a documented case, and a review of rabbit-associated plague cases in the United States. *American journal of epidemiology, 104*(1), 81–87

Ward H, Day S (2006) What happens to women who sell sex? Report of a unique occupational cohort. *Sex Transm Infect, 82*(5), 413–417

Warrell MJ, Warrell DA (2004) Rabies and other lyssavirus diseases. *Lancet, 363*(9413), 959–969

Weese JS, Peregrine AS, Armstrong J (2002) Occupational health and safety in small animal veterinary practice: Part I–nonparasitic zoonotic diseases. *The Canadian veterinary journal, 43*(8), 631–636

Werner BG, Grady GF (1982) Accidental hepatitis-B-surface-antigen-positive inoculations. Use of e antigen to estimate infectivity. *Annals of internal medicine, 97*(3), 367–369

Werner M, Nordin P, Arnholm B, Elgefors B, Krantz I (2001) Borrelia burgdorferi antibodies in outdoor and indoor workers in south-west Sweden. *Scand J Infect Dis, 33*(2), 128–131

Werner SB, Pappagianis D, Heindl I, Mickel A (1972) An epidemic of coccidioidomycosis among archeology students in northern California. *The New England journal of medicine, 286*(10), 507–512

Wheat LJ (2006) Histoplasmosis: a review for clinicians from non-endemic areas. *Mycoses, 49*(4), 274–282

Whitley RJ, Monto AS (2006) Seasonal and pandemic influenza preparedness: a global threat. *The Journal of infectious diseases, 194 Suppl 2*, S65–69

Yagupsky P, Baron EJ (2005) Laboratory exposures to brucellae and implications for bioterrorism. *Emerg Infect Dis, 11*(8), 1180–1185

Yagupsky P, Peled N, Riesenberg K, Banai M (2000) Exposure of hospital personnel to Brucella melitensis and occurrence of laboratory-acquired disease in an endemic area. *Scandinavian journal of infectious diseases, 32*(1), 31–35

Yang H, Li X, Stanton B, Fang X, Lin D, Mao R, et al. (2005) Workplace and HIV-related sexual behaviours and perceptions among female migrant workers. *AIDS Care, 17*(7), 819–833

Yu H, Shu Y, Hu S, Zhang H, Gao Z, Chen H, et al. (2006) The first confirmed human case of avian influenza A (H5N1) in Mainland China. *Lancet, 367*(9504), 84

Zelnick J, O'Donnell M (2005) The impact of the HIV/AIDS epidemic on hospital nurses in KwaZulu Natal, South Africa: nurses' perspectives and implications for health policy. *J Public Health Policy, 26*(2), 163–185

Chapter 8
Screening at the Workplace and Female Employees

Elena Riza and Athena Linos

Introduction

Women constitute 51.2 percent (191 million) of the total population of the European Union (EU). Due to longer life expectancy, the number of women in older age groups exceeds that of men, with a substantial difference in the 80-year olds where there are 221 women for every 100 men (http://ec.europa.eu/health).

Women's lives have greatly changed over the past few decades, primarily because of their participation in the workforce. At present, over 42 percent of the labor force in the EU are women (WHO 2004). Despite the fact that there is variation across the EU Member States in the percentage of working women, there has been an increase in the unemployment rates of women higher than that of men.

Looking at a variety of health indicators, women in the EU have a good level of health, and 62 percent of women themselves report being healthy or very healthy. Life expectancy has increased over the past few decades and has now reached 80 years compared to an average 74 years for men in the EU (http://ec.europa.eu/health).

Looking at female mortality, the major causes of death are diseases of the circulatory system (43% of all female deaths), followed by cancer (26%). According to the International Agency for Research on Cancer (IARC) (Press Release No. 174, Feb 2007), 47 percent of all new cancer cases in Europe in 2006 occurred in women, and 44 percent of all cancer deaths were women. Moreover, most female cancer deaths in the 35-64 year age group are due to breast and cervical cancers combined—also referred to as *female cancers*.

Both major causes of female mortality are preventable to a certain extent, either through primary (e.g., healthier lifestyles) or secondary (e.g., early detection by means of screening) prevention. Based on the Eurobarometer survey, cancer screening rates in the EU are quite high, with 40 percent of women reporting having had a smear test and self-breast examination in the past year. About 18 percent of women report having had a mammogram.

A. Linos, W. Kirch (eds), *Promoting Health for Working Women.*
© Springer 2008

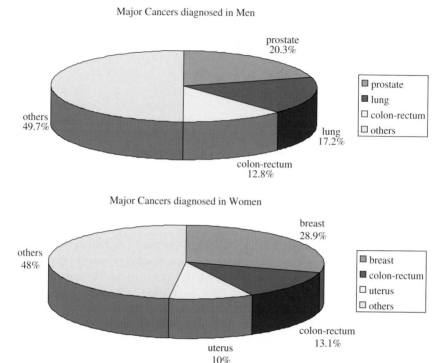

Fig. 8.1 Major cancers diagnosed in men and in women in 2006 (IARC Press Release No. 174, Feb 2007)

Screening Terms and Definitions

Screening for disease control is defined as the examination of asymptomatic people in an effort to classify them as likely or unlikely to have the disease that is the object of screening. People who are likely to have the disease in question are examined further to arrive at a final diagnosis. Those who are found to have the disease are treated. Screening aims at reducing morbidity and mortality from the disease among the people screened. The success of a screening program in reducing morbidity or mortality depends on the interrelations between the characteristics of the screening procedures and the effectiveness of the methods of early treatment (Riza & Linos 2001).

According to the U.K. National Screening Committee, "Screening is a public health service in which members of a defined population, who do not necessarily perceive they are at risk of, or are already affected by a disease or its complications, are asked a question or offered a test, to identify those individuals who are more likely to be helped than harmed by further tests or treatment to reduce the risk of a disease or its complications" (http://www.nsc.nhs.uk/whatscreening/ whatscreen_ind.htm).

One must always bear in mind that there are several limitations to screening because the screening tests may produce risks and people need to have clear information as to what screening programs can offer. From an ethical point of view, screening is quite different from clinical practice, because it targets healthy people in an effort to increase their health awareness and does not deal with patients (British Medical Association 2005).

Medical screening in the context of occupational medicine has been used as synonymous to *medical surveillance* (Halperin et al. 1986). These two terms have been used interchangeably with medical supervision and periodic examinations in the workplace (Yodaiken 1986). To avoid confusion, it is important to distinguish the different concepts underlying each term. *Medical screening* in the workplace is the examination of a specific group of workers that have been identified as high risk for the development of a certain disease or condition at a certain point in time, therefore it includes a cross-sectional element. To be effective, however, it is repeated at regular intervals. *Medical surveillance* focuses on detecting early pathophysiological changes occurring as a result of exposures in the workplace (Gochfeld 1992). Medical surveillance is synonym to medical supervision and includes periodic examinations in the workplace, therefore it has a longitudinal element. Moreover, medical surveillance usually addresses the general health status of the employee and not just one disease.

According to the Occupational Safety and Health Administration (OSHA), the distinction between medical screening and medical surveillance is that medical screening has a clinical focus because its fundamental purpose is to diagnose early and treat a worker, while medical surveillance has a prevention focus because it aims to detect and eliminate the exposures or hazards at the workplace that can initiate disease (http://www.osha.gov/SLTC/medicalsurveillance/index.html).

Screening at the workplace can be used to screen workers for occupational diseases but also for conditions not related to work. Quite often, the tests used for periodic examinations (i.e., medical surveillance) and for medical screening are the same, so it is sometimes difficult to distinguish between the two. Moreover, both are secondary prevention strategies that aim at the prevention, early detection of disease, and reduction of exposure in the workplace. Biological monitoring refers to testing workers for specific substances—their metabolites or their effects—and is often used as a component of either medical surveillance or medical screening in the workplace.

The concept of workplace screening in this chapter does *not* include preplacement screening—i.e., a series of tests to decide whether or not the individual may be placed in a specific setting within a workplace.

Screening Philosophy and Principles

The objective of screening is to use a simple, safe, quick, and inexpensive test on a large number of individuals to determine whether or not they have the disease in question. The ultimate goal of screening is to reduce the burden of disease through early detection of presymptomatic disease and to facilitate follow-up and proper treatment of disease-positive cases. The theory on which the concept of screening is based depends heavily on the assumption that the disease for which it is applied falls within the description of a natural history that follows:

1. *Biological onset*—exposure of an individual to risk factors. The onset of some diseases may start with conception
2. *Possibility of preclinical diagnosis*—following the onset of disease, and despite the fact that the affected person may be free of symptoms or signs, the disease mechanisms produce structural or functional changes at some point, so provided that the proper test is applied, the disease may be diagnosed at a pre-symptomatic stage
3. *Clinical diagnosis*—if no intervention is applied during the preclinical stage, the disease progresses so that now symptoms or signs are present and the affected individual may seek medical help
4. *Outcome*—the disease follows its course, which may depend on applied treatment and arrives at its *outcome*, which may range from cure to long-term adverse health effects, or death

This step-by-step presentation of the natural history of disease is rather simplistic, and the identification of positive cases is not enough to modify illness outcome either at the individual or population level. An important element of early diagnosis first described by Hutchinson (1960) is the critical point in the natural history of the disease, before which treatment is more effective or easier to apply than afterwards. It is fully understood that a disease may have several critical points (e.g., pulmonary tuberculosis) or none at all (such as in the case of many malignancies). Moreover, the location of the critical point in each disease is crucial for the effectiveness of early treatment. If the critical point of a disease lies between biological onset and possible early diagnosis, then the application of any screening test would be useless. Similarly, if the critical point of a disease lies between clinical diagnosis and outcome, then screening would equally be of no use to the affected person. Only when the critical point lies between possible early diagnosis and clinical diagnosis is it sensible to apply a screening test because of high probability that the disease outcome of the individuals who have the disease can be improved.

Diseases Targeted by Screening

Although several diseases or conditions can be targeted by screening, the most common ones are cancer and genetic determinants. The main difference between these two types is the fact that cancer screening requires repeated examinations over a set time interval, while genetic screening consists of a one-time examination—i.e., the individual tested either has the genetic determinant in question or not. It is generally accepted that for screening to be effective in terms of improving the health profile of a given population, it has to address the whole population presumed to be at risk of developing a certain disease based on scientific criteria. The participation rate of

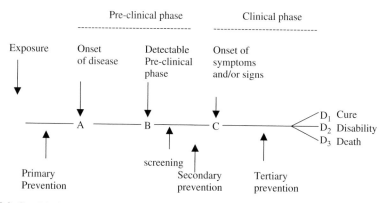

Fig. 8.2 Graphical representation of the natural history of a disease (such as cancer) and the levels of prevention
(Adapted from dos Santos Silva, 1999, pp. 355)

the population in the screening program is a critical element in the evaluation and effectiveness of the screening.

Cancer Screening

Cancer screening refers to the application of specific tests that detect cancer when there are no symptoms (NCI-NIH 2007), with the goal of detecting the disease at an early stage. The screening procedure aims at separating the participating individuals into those who may have the disease in question and in those who do not, so that those who tested positive can be further evaluated. The screening test is not meant to provide a definite diagnosis.

Current Challenges

Perhaps the biggest challenge secondary prevention is facing in the working environment is genetic screening. Genetic screening refers to the application of genetic tests on individuals to identify the presence or absence of specific genetic determinants—an important factor for individual health. The mapping and sequencing of the human genome has introduced a vast area of new information that needs to be explored further to identify susceptible people with a specific disease and to improve disease treatment. The identification of disease susceptibility genes can provide a substantial amount of new information that can be used to determine disease diagnosis and disease treatment (http://www.acoem.org).

Yet, genetic screening raises a number of ethical, social, and legal issues, mostly because of its immediate reference to life and health insurances and occupational safety standards, among others—all of which affect public health but could also affect susceptibility. Because genetic screening may be conducted in the workplace, it is imperative that all practitioners of occupational and environmental medicine are well-informed about all aspects of genetic screening so that proper advice can be provided to employers, employees, insurance companies, and other regulatory agencies (http://ec.europa/eu/health). Debate on the general ethical and legal considerations of genetic screening is taking place both at the European and international levels, and especially in the working environment.

The International Labour Organisation (ILO 1997) declares that "genetic screening in relation to work is a disproportionate infringement of individual rights. Current scientific knowledge is not sufficient to warrant its use for an occupational health purpose." In contrast to the ILO, the American College of Occupational and Environmental Medicine (ACOEM) states that "the underlying notion of genetic screening does not differ from the other types of medical screening, and should therefore abide to the same ethical standards, good scientific practices, and confidentiality issues safeguarding the individuals' rights, while allowing new information to be used to the benefit of the individual in all environments, including the workplace" (ACOEM 1994).

Genetic screening at the workplace has been limited so far, and its ethical implications have not been well-studied. However, ACOEM proposes that "genetic screening is conducted following the law, medical ethical standards and good scientific practices, that care should be given to the reliability of the screening tests and the interpretation of the results and that the results should be discussed with a trained health professional" (http://www.acoem.org). Moreover, it is suggested that "genetic screening at the workplace should be performed only upon indication that a specific genetic component affects a worker's health, in the sense that this genetic component predisposes the worker to an adverse health outcome resulting from work in an otherwise acceptable workplace exposure, or it consists an element of a confidential general medical examination offered to the employees. In any case, the employee should be informed of the results and have the right to choose whether they wish to make these results known to their employers or not" (American Medical Association 1991).

Susceptibility Screening

Susceptibility screening is used to identify workers who may be susceptible to toxic substances present in their working environment that may cause future disabilities (National Reference Center for Bioethics Literature 1993).

Types of Screening Organizations

Population Screening

Population screening is offered to groups of people through a coordinated program (Canadian Cancer Society 2004). The application of a screening test for early detection and treatment in large groups is called *population* or *mass* or *organized* screening. Screening programs are directed to entire populations or to large and easily identifiable groups within the population. For example, European breast cancer screening guidelines recommend that women between the ages of 50 and 69 have a mammogram every two years (Broeders et al. 2000).

Individual Preclinical Examination or Opportunistic Screening

Screening can also be offered outside an organized screening program, called *opportunistic* or *ad-hoc* screening (Canadian Cancer Society 2004). At the European level, opportunistic screening is considered to be ineffective (Arbyn et al. 2001). This is one of the conclusions of the consensus reached on the European recommendations for cancer screening at a conference organized by the European Commission with experts in research, health care, and cancer screening from all member states of the European Union (Vienna, November 1999), which only enforces the operation of organized screening. Despite this agreement, the corresponding political authorities have not yet officially validated the recommendations, and it is therefore anticipated that the lack of unified European policy will lead to a continuation of opportunistic screening.

The European Guidelines for Quality Assurance in Mammography Screening (Perry et al. 2001) recommend that "cancer screening be offered only in organised programmes with quality assurance at all levels, as well as good information about benefits and risks. Opportunistic screening activities should be discouraged as they may not achieve the potential benefits but result in negative side effects."

Rationale Supporting Cancer Screening Activities

Cancer is an important global health burden. According to recent WHO/IARC data, cancer incidence is estimated at 3.2 million new cancer cases in 2006 worldwide (compared to 2.9 million in 2004), of which nearly 2.3 million occurred in the 25 EU countries (Ferlay et al. 2007).

Cancer is the second most common cause of death in the EU, and its incidence as well as mortality, increase with age. Cancer is a disease usually having a long and detectable preclinical stage, thereby offering opportunities for early detection. In addition, treatment of occult disease offers advantages in many cases compared to treatment of symptomatic disease. So, if cancer is detected early by means of a screening test offered to the at-risk population, it is possible to prevent cancer progression and to improve survival.

As mentioned earlier, the preclinical phase is the part of the disease's natural history, during which the disease is potentially detectable, but asymptomatic. The interval between the time of disease detection through screening, and the time of presentation of disease symptoms or signs leading to diagnosis in the absence of screening, is called *lead time*. The lead time produced by a screening program for a given individual depends on the time of screening, in relation to the preclinical phase, and the actual duration of this phase. Furthermore, if the sensitivity of the screening test is low in combination with screening intervals, it may alter the duration of the lead time. The relative success of treatment for screen-detected diseases depends on how early the disease was detected (or the amount of lead time produced by screening). Some chronic diseases have relatively short preclinical phases (on average), without much variability between diseased individuals. Some others, such as most malignancies, have very long preclinical phases (on average), with large variability between diseased individuals. The distribution of lead times produced by a screening program depends on the durations of the preclinical phase, on the periodicity (or frequency) of screening, and on the sensitivity of the screening test.

Two important biases influence prognosis among screen-detected cases, even in the absence of any benefit from treatment:

- Lead-time bias—screen-detected cases experience lead time. Among screen-detected cases, lead time contributes to the duration of disease for those at risk of poor disease outcome at risk for poor outcome. Thus, even if screening does not change the time of death, screening will increase the proportion of screen-detected cases surviving beyond defined time intervals
- Length-biased sampling—intermittent screening preferentially detects cases with a long preclinical phase; that is, cases of less rapidly progressive disease. These persons would be expected to experience a relatively favorable outcome, even if allowed to progress to symptoms.

The effects of lead-time bias and length-biased sampling are difficult to separate from the effects of treatment. Therefore, prospective evaluations of the efficacy of screening must compare outcomes among all persons exposed to screening, with outcomes among all persons not exposed to screening.

Indicators of the Screening Test

In addition to sensitivity, several other indicators are used to evaluate the accuracy and reliability of a screening test. These include specificity, positive predictive value, and negative predictive value.

The *sensitivity* of a screening test is the proportion of persons who test positive during the screening process who indeed have the disease (at a preclinical or clinical stage). The *specificity* of the screening test is the proportion of persons who test negative during the screening who indeed do not have the disease.

The *Positive Predictive Value* (PPV) is the number of verified cases detected by a screening test as a proportion of the number of persons with a positive screening test result. PPV is directly and proportionately related to the prevalence of the pre-symptomatic disease for which the screening is performed, as well as to the specificity of the screening test. If the disease prevalence is very low (1%, as in the example of breast cancer) then the PPV of mammography screening will be very low. This should not, however, put the validity of the screening test in question. To the contrary, the only indicated measure to increase PPV is to limit the screened population to those groups with high prevalence—e.g., by age. In the case of the workplace setting, screening could be limited to groups at increased risk due to high corresponding occupational or environmental exposure.

The *Negative Predictive Value* (NPV) is the number of true negatives as a proportion of those who have had a negative screening test result. If NPV is close to 1, the test is accurate in detecting the absence of disease. Low NPV is the result of low sensitivity of the screening test.

Cancer Statistics

Looking at cancer mortality in the EU25 for 2006, lung cancer is the leading cause of cancer deaths in both sexes (19.7%), followed by the cancers of the colon and rectum and breast (Ferlay et al. 2007). Prostate and stomach cancers rank fourth and fifth, respectively. In female cancer mortality for 2006, breast cancer ranks first, followed by cancers of the colon and rectum and lung. Cancers of the pancreas, uterus, and stomach are in the fourth, fifth, and sixth places, accordingly.

Regarding cancer incidence for 2006 in EU25, breast cancer ranks first in new cases out of the total population (including both sexes), and (of course) for females only. Colorectal, uterine, lung, and ovarian cancers constitute a large proportion of female cancer incidence (Ferlay et al. 2007).

According to recent IARC data (Ferlay et al. 2007), breast cancer incidence rates have increased primarily because of better case detection at an earlier stage as a result of organized screening programs in the member states. The increase of new breast cancer cases is about 16 percent since 2004. As mentioned earlier, breast cancer has now become the most common cancer diagnosed in Europe (of men and women) consisting of 13.5 percent (429,000 new cases in 2006) of all cancer cases, followed by lung (12.9% or 412,900 new cases in 2006) and colorectal cancer (12.1% or 386,300 new cases in 2006). Considering the impact of occupational exposures in the development of several cancers, these rates may be substantially higher in some workplace settings, thus leading to the need for more intense screening in these environments.

These figures provide a clear general pattern of cancer in Europe facilitating the initiatives for cancer control. Screening programs have been initiated at the European level since the mid 1980s to control for cancers of the breast and uterus.

Trends in the Use of Cancer-screening Programs in the European Union

In 1987, the Europe Against Cancer program was launched by the European Commission, with the ambitious goal to reduce the expected number of deaths due to cancer by 15 percent (from 1,000,000 to 850,000) by the year 2000 (OJ-EU 1987). A recent review indicated that although this target was not met across the EU, a global 10 percent reduction in the number of expected deaths in men, and 8 percent in women, was achieved. Some countries achieved the 15 percent reduction in deaths (Austria and Finland), but Portugal and Greece had the poorest performance with *increases* in each gender group (Boyle et al. 2003). The report concludes that "renewed tobacco control efforts are clearly needed for women, and there is a strong case for the introduction of organized breast and cervix screening programs in all member states. Continuing to emphasize prevention within cancer control will help to promote the continuing decline in death rates in the future."

More recently, colorectal cancer mortality in the EU has increased by 1.8 percent since 2004, indicating the need for a public health intervention on two fronts: a) primary prevention through the adoption of a healthier lifestyle, and b) secondary prevention through the launch of organized screening programs throughout Europe (IARC Press Release No. 174, Feb 2007). National colorectal cancer screening programs have been launched in many European countries since the late 1990s, including Austria, the Czech Republic, Finland, France, Germany, Italy, Poland, Slovakia and (planned) in the United Kingdom (www.touchbriefings.com/pdf/1134/ACF1A8D.pdf).

Prostate cancer mortality has increased by 16 percent since 1995, partly because of the aging of the male population (IARC Press Release No.174, Feb 2007). Despite the existence of the prostate specific antigen (PSA) test, its efficacy as a screening test still needs to be evaluated, so no organized screening activity is presently suggested.

Despite its top ranking in cancer mortality, lung cancer screening is not yet used at the population level because the presently available tests have not been shown to effectively improve survival (http://health.msn.com). The screening tests used are the chest X-ray, sputum cytology, and a spiral CT scan. Clinical trials are under way to assess the efficacy of these tests (www.cancer.gov).

Ovarian cancer is another female cancer, claiming the lives of a substantial number of women every year in the EU. Randomized controlled trials (RCTs) are currently underway to test the efficiency of the proposed screening tests for the early detection of ovarian cancer—i.e., a blood test for the tumor marker CA125 and a transvaginal ultrasound. However, only about 85 percent of all women with ovarian cancer have raised CA125, only 50 percent of women with early-stage ovarian cancer have raised CA125, and women with other conditions can also have raised CA125—thus placing the validity of the screening test, as measured by specificity and PPV, in question. The ultrasound examination's diagnostic value is also questionable.

At present, only women at higher risk for ovarian cancer are invited to take these screening tests. Higher than average risk means having two or more relatives on the same side of the family diagnosed with ovarian cancer or breast cancer at a young age. One must bear in mind, however, that these screening tests have not been fully tested yet, and there is no guarantee that they will detect every case of early ovarian cancer. Women at a high risk are those from 35 years old onwards, and from 5 years before the age of diagnosis of the youngest relative who had the disease. Screening should be performed annually, and there is no upper age limit. (Cancer Research UK 2007).

Cancers of the lung and stomach may be prevented through primary prevention initiatives, such as smoking cessation, food preservation, better nutrition, and better control of infection from *helicobacter pylori*. Colorectal cancer may be prevented both through the adoption of a healthier lifestyle (e.g., balanced diet and uptake of physical exercise) and through the application of a screening test (colonoscopy, faecal occult blood test, and flexible sigmoidoscopy). For breast, cervical, and ovarian cancers, on the other hand, secondary prevention activities are the primary method of disease control.

Organized Cancer-screening Activities in the European Union

Following an EU Council Recommendation (2003), organized screening programs at the European level have been applied for the earlier detection of breast, cervical, and colorectal cancers.

Breast Cancer

Screening test: Mammogram every 2 years.
Target group: Women aged 50-69 years (in Europe, according to the EU Guidelines) Intervention studies conducted in the 1990s showed increase in the use of mammography (Meissner et al. 2004). Most EU member states operate organized screening programs at the national level.

Cervical Cancer

Screening test: Papanicolaou cervical smear every 3 years.
Target group: Women aged 20-30 years, no upper limit, but three consecutive negative smear tests from the age of 65 or older indicate cessation of cervical cancer screening. There is high participation primarily because the test is easy, safe, inexpensive, and well-accepted both by the women and physicians. Indirect evidence from observational studies shows that screening reduces cervical cancer incidence and mortality (Holmquist 2000). Similar to breast cancer, most EU member states have set up screening programs at the national or regional levels.

Colorectal Cancer

Screening test: Faecal occult blood test, flexible sigmoidoscopy, colonoscopy, at 5- and 10-year intervals.
Target group: Men and women aged 50-74 years.
There is low participation despite evidence from RCTs and case-control studies (Byers et al. 1997). A possible explanation might be the fact that the presence of more than one screening test hinders screening participation and creates confusion.

Evaluation of Cancer-screening Programs

The objective of screening is to reduce mortality and increase survival of the screened cancer by early detection. Provided all criteria to initiate a cancer-screening program are met, it is obvious that such programs require large human and financial resources. It is therefore fundamental to evaluate the efficacy of these screening programs and their cost effectiveness. If improved disease outcome and cost effectiveness cannot be demonstrated, the rationale for screening is eliminated. For this reason, a series of indicators have been developed that monitor screening performance and evaluate the impact on mortality, as well as on cost effectiveness. The indicators for assessing screening performance (also called short-term indicators) mostly assess the *quality* of the screening activities and should be collected and monitored at regular intervals. Such indicators include the participation rate, the recall rate, the rate of invasive investigations, sensitivity and specificity of the screening test, the surgical procedures performed, the time interval between screening test and test result, and many others.

The main indicator in assessing the impact of the screening program is mortality reduction, which in the case of cancer is long-term. For this reason, surrogate impact indicators have been developed that may predict the screening outcome, such as interval cancer rate, cancer detection rate (e.g., breast, cervical, colorectal), stage and size of screen-detected cancers at diagnosis, and so on. Interval cancers are cancers detected in the time after a screening test with a normal result and before the next scheduled screen. The interval cancer rate is the number of interval cancers diagnosed in a specified time period (usually the prespecified time interval during which the next screen is scheduled—e.g., two years for mammography screening or three years for a PAP test) since the last screening examination per 10,000 persons screened. In the case of breast cancer, a consistently low-interval cancer rate is correlated with a significant reduction in mortality in the screened population (Day et al. 1989, Tabar et al. 1992). Interval cancer rate is an indicator of the effectiveness of a screening program.

For the cancer screening programs implemented at the European level, specific European guidelines have been developed that regulate the operation and performance of these screening programs. These guidelines have been adopted by most EU member states and are adhered to in conjunction with national guidelines (where available).

Criteria for Initiating an Organized Program

Data on cancer incidence and mortality indicate the areas where control actions are needed, but in order to apply an organized screening program a series of criteria also have to be met (Wilson and Junger, 1968). In order to initiate a screening program, public health officials have to consider the following points:

- The disease in question must be an important public health problem in terms of seriousness of its consequences and/or frequency. In the case of occupational groups exposed to specific risk factors, this may be seriously modified, such as in the case of commercial female sex workers (screening for cervical cancer) or workers exposed to benzene and other polycyclic aromatic hydrocarbons (screening for leukemia or aplastic anemia).

- The natural history of the disease must be known. This is a prerequisite for the application of any screening program in order to identify the points at which the disease is potentially detectable by screening, and at which point intervention is likely to be effective—i.e., before any irreversible damage has been made. The natural history must also be known to enable the evaluation of the effects of any intervention. A common mistake is the inclusion of lead time when calculating the overall survival of the detected cases.
- The natural history of a disease is not the same in all people. For example, if it is likely that the interval between the first detectable presymptomatic phase and the appearance of symptoms is less than the time interval between screening tests, then cases will be missed. Persons with a long lead time (which might have better prognosis) are more likely to be detected than those with a short lead time. This variation is a critical feature when designing and evaluating a screening program.
- There must be an effective treatment for persons diagnosed early—which improves the prognosis compared with treatment at a later stage—otherwise, there is no point in detecting a disease early. Comparison of early treatment (following presymptomatic screening) with treatment at a later stage is performed by conducting clinical trials of the proposed intervention in groups with similar characteristics as the proposed target group for screening, thus allowing for controlling the effect of lead time.
- The facilities for treatment must be available, and the screening procedure acceptable by the patient, because a patient who believes that medical intervention will bring relief is more likely to accept treatment and even to endure some side effects.
- The screening test should be simple, quick, safe, and inexpensive, otherwise the success of the screening program will be jeopardized. The range of *normal* findings using the proposed screening test must be known. The test should be quick to use, because the goal is to test a large number of people. Screening is primarily a sorting process, which depends on the results of the single test. This test divides the screened people into two groups: those that tested positive and those that tested negative. It must be noted, however, that not all people with a positive test actually have the disease or condition for which the screening test was performed. Similarly, not all persons with a negative test are free from disease.
- The screening test must be widely accepted, because it primarily addresses symptom-free people who are less likely to undergo uncomfortable, time-consuming, and potentially dangerous investigations at regular intervals, than those who are seeking medical attention for a problem or potential problem.
- There must be a policy regarding the population to be screened. Ideally, all at-*risk* persons should be identified and invited for screening. Attention must be paid to the persons who respond to an open screening invitation, because these represent the more *health-conscious* people who often are at lower risk. Attention must also be paid, however, to those who respond because they have delayed in seeking medical advice about symptoms.

- The cost of screening should be as low as possible because health services resources of all types are not unlimited. For this reason, all direct and indirect costs involved in a screening program should be assessed prior to its introduction. Such costs involve manpower, consumables, the costs of any further investigations to identify false positives, and the total treatment costs of the false negatives. Benefits are considered the savings from the treatment of cases had they had not been identified and treated early. Additional costs for the screening program will result from the continuous training of the personnel involved.

Ideally, a screening test should be highly sensitive and highly specific, but this is rarely the case. All things being equal, the priority is usually to identify all those with early or asymptomatic disease at the expense of including some false positives. This way those with a negative screening test can be told with some confidence that they are not affected, and those who screen positive can be further investigated through a diagnostic test with higher sensitivity to exclude the false positives.

The predictive value (as described earlier) is determined by the sensitivity and the specificity of the test, as well as the prevalence of the disease in the tested population. The more specific the screening test is, the less likely it is for an individual tested positive to be free of the disease (false positive)—thus the greater the PPV. The more sensitive the test is, the less likely it is for an individual tested negative to have the disease (false negative), thus the greater negative predictive value.

In rare diseases, such as cancer, where the prevalence is generally low, the PPV of a screening test can be increased by targeting the groups at high risk of developing the disease by screening based on demographic factors, medical history, or occupation. Apart from achieving a high PPV by screening high risk individuals, the burden of screening to the population at low risk for the disease is minimized, but the information gained through the screening process also applies to the general population in terms of watching for symptoms, monitoring interval cancers, and false negatives.

Screening in the Workplace

Workplace screening is a fundamental strategy for optimizing employee health and can be applied to screen for occupational diseases, or diseases for which screening programs exist for certain populations and are not specifically related to the vast majority of workplaces, such as breast, cervical, and colorectal cancer.

Given the fact that most people of ages 25-65 years spend a minimum of eight hours a day, five days a week, 50 weeks a year at work, workplace environment offers the ideal setting to promote and assess health interventions. Despite the fact that workplaces have played a minor role in health monitoring so far, it is becoming notably clear in recent years that work is not only an activity to increase personal and community wealth, but also satisfaction and high self-esteem. Yet, it is an area that can have an adverse impact on human, and consequently *public* health to the point that it imposes substantial financial burden on the society at large.

In short, workplaces are ideal settings for promoting disease screening and to increasing effectiveness by applying effective health communication methodology. Health communication methodology has the potential to affect change in the workplace by taking advantage of the setting—i.e., the coexistence of a target group in a defined space for several hours per day. Another advantage of the workplace is the fact that the intervention may be offered at regular intervals, hereby strengthening the impact of the transmitted message and that it is possible to collaborate with peer groups such as labor unions (Allen et al. 2001).

Workplace Screening for Occupational Diseases

It is to the benefit of the employer, as well as of the employee, to regularly monitor the level of exposure to dangerous substances or factors present in the workplace and additionally apply screening programs that should be carried out in conjunction with environmental surveillance and biological monitoring. Such activities in the workplace are mostly referred to as health surveillance or health care programs, health examinations, or periodic examinations of workers (ILO 1998).

According to ILO (1998), any health surveillance program in the workplace must ensure: "a) professional independence and impartiality of the relevant health professionals, and b) workers' privacy and confidentiality of individual information."

Workplace exposures in some working environments may exert a carcinogenic effect on the worker or employee, and cancer may be the result of such hazardous exposures. For example, the International Agency for Research on Cancer has classified the evidence of carcinogenicity in humans as *sufficient* for several occupational exposures such as arsenic, asbestos, benzene, cadmium, formaldehyde, radiation (IARC 1987).

Example 1: Benzene Screening

Occupational exposure to benzene is a good example of workplace screening. Benzene may be inhaled or absorbed through the skin by exposed workers who may subsequently develop lymphohematopoietic abnormalities, such as pancytopenia and aplastic anemia through suppression of the hematopoietic system, or occupational cancer such as leukemia or lymphoma. Benzene exposure constitutes a good example of the application of a routine health surveillance program in the workplace (http://www.osha.gov).

Benzene has been used extensively in the chemical and petroleum industries, as well as in gas stations, painting, printing, and footwear manufacturing companies— areas that employ a substantial number of female workers (Hayes et al. 1996).

The Occupational Safety and Health Administration (OSHA) has issued specific hematology guidelines and diagnostic tests that the occupational health professionals should perform, and that constitute a routine screening of benzene-exposed workers (OSHA 2007).

Various biomarkers to identify level of exposure and potential toxicity of benzene are available to help identify high-risk groups of workers. Such biomarkers include measurement of blood benzene levels, urinary *trans*, *trans*muconic acids, DNA damage (by determining DNA strand breaks), and DNA repair capacity (Navasumrit et al. 2005). It is recommended that periodic examinations for benzene exposure at the workplace be performed annually, but there are special provisions for medical tests in the event of hematologic abnormalities. Symptoms and signs of benzene toxicity may be nonspecific, therefore a combination of detailed medical history and medical examinations must be available to the workers who are at risk of benzene exposure.

Exposure to benzene may also trigger adverse respiratory reactions or initiate dermatological problems. Such respiratory reactions occur after exposure to a sensitizing agent that causes hypersensitivity and may result in respiratory diseases such as occupational asthma.

Example 2: Occupational Asthma Screening

Another critical area for occupational disease screening is that of respiratory diseases. Asthma is the most common occupational respiratory disorder in industrialized countries, and its prevalence in women in specific occupations has been underestimated (Kogevinas et al. 1999). An average of 250 specific occupational exposures have been associated with asthma, involving several occupational categories such as farmers, agricultural workers, painters, cleaners, and chemical and textile workers, all of which are occupational sectors employing large numbers of females.

Asthma is a case that could be used as an example, where periodic assessments of exposed workers to sensitizing agents are recommended. Such assessments should be initiated six months after the beginning of work, and then on an annual basis, provided there are no predisposing health problems, such as emphysema, chronic bronchitis, or skin allergies. For the high risk groups, shorter intervals may apply. The periodic examinations should include examination of the skin for contact dermatitis, clinical examination of the lungs for disorders of any kind, testing for flow expiratory volume (FEV1) and forced vital capacity (FVC) for pulmonary function, along with an updated medical history for related symptoms or signs such as nose, throat, eye irritation, skin changes, coughing, wheezing, or dyspnea at work or at home (http://www.safetyline.wa.gov.au).

Example 3: Tuberculosis Screening

Another important area of workplace screening is that of infectious diseases. A classical example would be tuberculosis (TB)—a communicable disease caused by the mycobacterium tuberculosis which—constitutes a workplace issue because it affects workers and companies across the world (World Economic Forum 2006). TB is an occupational disease for several categories of employees, but persons at risk are also those who share the same environment with potentially TB-infected individuals for several hours a day, such as the workplace. It is estimated that eight million people are diagnosed with TB worldwide annually, and two million die from the disease, whereas if detected and treated early, 80 percent of the patients fully recover.

The occupational groups at high risk of contracting TB mostly include health care workers in hospital clinical wards, operating theaters, ambulatory services, nursing homes, homeless shelters, refugee centers, and detention centers. Nonoccupational exposure to TB is most frequent in co-workers, families, low-income people, homeless people, immigrants from countries where TB is present, prisoners, alcoholics and intravenous drug users, HIV-infected individuals, AIDS patients, and people with medical conditions such as diabetes, kidney disease, low body weight, or certain types of cancers.

Employers should recognize that TB in the workplace is an important factor in terms of increased labor costs and decreased productivity, and should therefore ensure the presence of mechanisms in the workplace to monitor the health of their employees through screening activities, either on their own initiative or integrated with relevant community programs.

The indicated screening test for TB is the purified protein derivative (PPD) test or *skin* test, which should be administered to all employees who have face-to-face contact with potentially infected persons. Once performed, the test should be read within 48 and 72 hours, and repeated annually. In the case of a positive skin test, a chest x-ray should follow to see whether or not the disease is active, and if so, the appropriate medication will be prescribed. The purpose of the screening test is to identify persons with latent tuberculosis infection (LTBI) so that they can be treated before they develop TB. Early identification and treatment of LTBI or TB improves disease outcome and reduces the risk of transmission. Companies who employ workers at high risk of developing TB, such as immigrants, low-income minorities, or immuno-suppressed persons, should apply prevention activities.

The employer should:

- Support TB awareness programs in the workplace through trained health professionals, and deliver education campaigns preferably by involving employees, as well. Especially in the case of immigrants, the identification of a leader-employee is of utmost importance, because it will help to overcome language and cultural barriers that hinder the success of health activities
- Ensure nondiscrimination of employees who tested positive
- Integrate community prevention programs whenever possible, and link workplace activities to TB control programs
- Ensure quality assurance in the diagnosis and proper treatment of TB (i.e., adhere to the available guidelines for TB control)
- Monitor and report results to the relevant health authorities
- Implement environmental measures to minimize infection of the other employees, such as proper ventilation, air disinfection, and installation of filter devices whenever possible

Workplace Screening for Nonoccupational Diseases

The main risk factors for the cancer sites for which organized screening activities exist at the general population level—namely, breast, cervical and colorectal—have rarely been associated with workplace exposures. Despite this, the working environment may be used to target populations at risk for each of these cancers and increase screening awareness as well as screening participation. It has been found that health interventions at multiple levels have succeeded in increasing participation in organized screening programs (Meissner et al. 2004). Such interventions may involve the individual directly, the health care providers, the worksite, the church, and other community groups (sports clubs, women's associations, etc.).

Design of Workplace Interventions

In the case of breast, cervical, and colorectal cancers, effective health communication development primarily uses the social marketing framework as a program planning system and a health belief model to promote individual behavior changes (e.g., to design media materials).

A series of theories and models affecting health behavior have been described, aiming at improving the effectiveness of health interventions. Most of the theories, as well as the models, overlap each other to a certain degree and it is almost impossible to identify one single theory and one single model that should be applied in a specific setting for a specific health topic. Responsibility rests solely with the health professional to possess good knowledge of existing theories and models and to identify the best fitting for the particular health behavior, population, and setting.

How to Design an Effective Health Communication Campaign in the Workplace

A. Define the goal—Describe the specific objectives of the campaign.
B. Identify the target group to whom to address the message—Consider creating subgroups to increase effectiveness, learn the target group (beliefs, current actions, social and physical environment, possible high prevalence of the presymptomatic stage of the targeted condition), learn about the workplace, and obtain employer cooperation.
C. Assess the group's needs with the specific health topic and identify of specific barriers or difficulties that hinder participation in organized screening programs (this may be done through a survey by means of administering specially designed questionnaires, or by personal interviews).
D. Identify female leaders from the target group who will act as effect multipliers for the target group, as well as a link to the health professionals.
E. Create effective health messages—identify channels and sources of communication appropriate for the target group, consider the best times to address the

target group, and work with the management. Design of the intervention, the approach, the health messages, and the communication methodology—such as posters in the workplace, dissemination of leaflets, educational videos, individual letters, health-related e-mails, group discussions with a facilitator, individual counseling, public service messages, and media campaigns.

F. Educate the leaders on the elements of the screening program, key issues they should be communicating to their peers, and basic scientific knowledge on issues relating to the specific health topic.

G. Pretest the health messages with a representative sample of the target group, and revise the messages accordingly.

H. Implement the campaign effectively by following the initial goals and plans—communicate with employers and other partners to ensure smooth running of the campaign, evaluate the campaign, and communicate results to employees and employers.

The choice of the appropriate method requires careful study of the target audience and the required behavioral change (U.S. Department of Health and Human Services 2003). The most critical and measurable issue is maximizing participation rates and following instructions for further assessment, if tested positive.

Breast and cervical cancers are the two major female cancers for which organized screening programs are available, and the main risk factors are not related to the workplace. There are occupational groups, however, where work-related exposures may constitute a substantial risk factor, such as ionizing radiation exposure of female radiologists, radiologic technologists, and nuclear industry workers; nonionizing radiation exposure (in the microwave range) of female police officers (through the use of radar guns for traffic enforcement), which has been related to breast cancer (American Cancer Society 2006; Ashmore et al. 1998); or HPV infection in female sex workers, which is an identified causal factor for the development of cervical cancer (Cancer Research UK 2007; WHO 2007).

In these cases, breast and cervical cancer should be considered occupational diseases; therefore, specific workplace-screening methodology (including modified screening intervals, if necessary) for these occupational groups should be applied. When using the workplace as a setting to increase breast and cervical cancer screening awareness and participation, the employer should involve health professionals in implementing specific intervention health communication methodology following the steps described earlier. Workplace interventions for these two cancers have been described in the literature and will be presented in detail in the next sections.

Another example of increasing screening awareness and participation in the workplace, is the case of colorectal cancer. Although both sexes are affected, most interventions published in the literature refer to male workers only, or make no distinction between sexes. Employers could take the following actions to reduce the risk of colorectal cancer among their workers:

- Educate employees about colorectal cancer risk factors and symptoms. Proposed ways are individual consultations with health professionals (such as occupational

doctors, nurses, social workers) and dissemination of promotional material, including information on primary prevention, awareness of colorectal cancer symptoms, and availability of screening options
- Make the working environment available to public awareness campaigns by facilitating circulation of informative material (e.g., posters, educational videos, pamphlets)
- Encourage learning family medical history and advocating for screening (i.e., awareness of the risks and benefits)
- Identify ways to cover the cost of screening, either fully or partially (e.g., through appropriate insurance plans), for employees over 50 years (the high risk group for colorectal cancer) and for younger individuals who are at increased risk (based on personal and family medical history)
- Set up worksite intervention programs that encourage healthy lifestyle habits
- Offer flexible work schedules to accommodate colorectal cancer screening

Special Issues in Female-orientated Workplace Screening

Intervention research has shown that the most important barriers for screening are lack of access to health care, lack of awareness, low educational level and low income (Calle et al. 1993; Glanz et al. 1992; Rimer et al. 2001). This, combined with the fact that breast and cervical cancers affect a substantial number of women in the workforce, adds weight to the application of intervention strategies to increase screening uptake for these cancers. Moreover, as a result of the horizontal and vertical segregation of female employment, women tend to be mostly employed in the service sector (also called tertiary sector, as opposed to the primary sector of agriculture and mining and the secondary sector of industrial production and manufacturing), to occupy less managerial job posts than men, to work more part-time, to be paid less than men, and to be under-represented in permanent job contracts, indicating a sexual division of the labor force with women being less privileged in receiving health interventions in comparison to men (Le Feuvre 1996).

Despite the fact that women constitute a large part of the workforce, the attribution of domestic responsibilities is almost exclusive to them, so women find themselves in a position of having to balance their professional life with their roles as mothers and wives. "Domestic work does not only involve a series of repetitive thankless tasks (Le Feuvre 1996) but also the ability to manage and coordinate specific needs and timetables of each member of the household," which, apart from the cost on the woman's time, also involves a substantial mental burden. In fact, lack of time due to balancing commitments at work and domestic responsibilities is an identified barrier for the participation of women in health promotion programs, and even more so in screening programs where time and cost is involved (Campbell et al. 2002).

Case Studies of Cancer-screening Interventions in the Workplace

Such interventions may consist of either promoting awareness of cancer screening to increase participation in organized screening programs, or the actual implementation of cancer screening activities in the workplace. A search of the existing literature has brought to surface several efforts of cancer-screening interventions in the workplace, the majority of which has been conducted in the United States, while there is a scarcity of such initiatives in European countries. Many studies addressing female employees, however, have been conducted to measure participation in *community* cancer-screening programs, as well as identification of screening barriers, but they cannot be considered workplace screening interventions. These studies use the advantages of the workplace to facilitate their study design.

Over the next few pages some workplace interventions regarding breast, cervical, and colorectal cancers will be presented.

Workplace Breast and Cervical Cancer Screening

The number of published studies in the literature focusing on interventions for breast and cervical cancer screening at the workplace is very limited. Most efforts have concentrated in community settings or in health care facilities.

Campbell et al. (2002) conducted a randomized health promotion intervention in female blue-collar workers (in North Carolina, United States) addressing several health behaviors (nutrition, smoking, physical exercise), including breast and cervical cancer screening. The intervention was based on the ecological model that links the individual health habits to broader social, community, and environmental influences (McLeroy et al. 1988). The planning of the intervention was based on the social cognitive theory (Bandura 1986), the transtheoretical stages of change (Prochaska & DiClemente 1982), and social marketing models (Andreason 1995). The goal of the study was to identify whether the intervention affected the health behavior of these women regarding increased cancer screening rates, better nutrition, and participation in physical exercise and smoking. A self-administered questionnaire identified health beliefs and attitudes before and after the intervention, which consisted of two strategies: a) individualized computer-tailored health messages, and b) the appointment of lay health advisors—i.e., women volunteers from the participating workplaces who were trained in promoting workplace health promotion activities and in disseminating information to their co-workers.

With regard to screening, women were asked whether they had had a PAP test during the previous 1-2 years, and for those aged 40 years or older, whether they had had a mammogram. Women were asked to prioritize the health behaviors targeted in the study so that discussion groups could be formed focusing on the specific health topics. A total of 859 women responded at baseline, 660 completed the six-month survey, and 650 completed the 18-month survey. The analysis was based on 538 women who completed all three surveys.

The majority of women reported having obtained breast and cervical cancer screening prior the initiation of the study, 85 percent reporting having had a PAP test, and 80 percent (of women aged 40 or over) had had a mammogram. After 18 months of the intervention, there were no significant differences in the screening rates between the two groups (i.e., those who received the intervention and those who did not). The low impact of the intervention may be due to the fact that this population generally had high rates of breast and cervical cancer screening to begin with, because these worksites provided health insurance coverage and over 80 percent of the employees reported having regular check-ups.

Allen et al. (2001) conducted a four-year RCT to evaluate the effectiveness of an intervention to promote breast and cervical cancer screening in the workplace in collaboration with a labor union. Overall, 26 worksites in the United States participated in the RCT, and the intervention focused on employee participation on the program planning and implementation phase. Volunteer advisory boards were formed, with the participation of employees and labor union representatives, that facilitated input from the employees in the program planning by selecting peer health advisors (PHAs). These advisors acted as role models in each worksite for screening practices, disseminated breast and cervical cancer information to their colleagues, and promoted a positive attitude towards screening. These employees received 16 hours of training on cancer epidemiology, screening principles and methods, and the availability of resources with regards to screening. The PHAs organized a series of six sessions addressing small groups of employees. One session addressed the topics of: "How to talk to your health care provider about screening" and "Setting goals for your health," following *social cognitive theory* (Bandura 1986). Another session focused on the identification of barriers for screening, and ways to overcome them following the *health belief* model (Rosenstock & Kirscht 1974). Events such as information campaigns, health fairs, and lectures by specialists targeting women employees at different levels of readiness for behavioral change according to the *transtheoretical stages of change* model (Prochaska & DiClemente 1982) were also organized. These activities were advertised by using newsletters, brochures, posters, and from one employee to another by word of mouth. Half of the worksites participating in the trial received the intervention, as opposed to the rest that did not. Randomization was done using random numbers.

A questionnaire on health habits was used to collect data, which was distributed to the employees at the worksite. Eligible subjects were women aged 40 years or older, working at least 15 hours a week on a permanent basis. Nonrespondents were contacted twice more, and incentives were given to the respondents. Apart from information on health habits, sociodemographic data were also included in the analysis, such as age, race, income, educational level, and job category. Evaluation of the intervention was based on adherence to the breast and cervical cancer screening guidelines for women aged 40 years or older, as set by the National Cancer Institute and the American Cancer Society—namely, receiving a mammogram within the previous one to two years, a clinical breast examination (CBE) within the previous year and a PAP smear test within the previous three years.

Mixed-model logistic regression analysis was used to test for comparability in the two intervention groups. Results showed that both groups (intervention and nonintervention) were comparable in terms of demographic characteristics. The percentage of women reporting having a recent mammogram, CBE, and recent PAP test increased from baseline to after implementing the intervention. After adjusting for worksite and age group, the degree of change observed was statistically significant only for the PAP smear tests. In detail, the odds ratio (OR) for the intervention effect for mammography was 1.14 (95% Confidence Interval [CI] 0.90-1.44), 1.19 for CBE (95% CI 0.96-1.49), and 1.28 for Pap-tests (95% CI 1.01-1.62). The confidence intervals for mammography and CBE indicate borderline significance of the findings.

Overall, the results indicate that the intervention had a weak positive effect. At present, the evaluative research of either breast or cervical cancer screening programs is limited, and is characterized by small, nonrandomized samples, low participation rates, and weak theoretical framework. Despite the modest impact of the intervention, the results indicate the need to further develop and deliver worksite interventions for breast and cervical cancer screening, provided they target specifically those individuals who have been unaffected by previous efforts. A key element for a successful health-related intervention is reinforcement, which will further increase the effect of the intervention, especially in the case of high initial interest.

Schrammel et al. (1998) conducted a U.S. study in Baltimore with the goal of identifying the costs of worksite breast cancer screening on the employer. During the course of the study, nearly 2,500 mammograms and 2,773 CBEs were performed, resulting in 292 referrals for further examinations. Of these referrals, 12 malignancies were found. After calculating the total costs including examinations, referral costs, and lost employee productivity, and comparing it with the corresponding costs in a community-based breast screening program, it was found that a substantial proportion of the cost was due to referrals resulting in benign or no disease. Overall, it was found that workplace screening is effective in the early detection of breast cancer compared to screening outside the workplace or the absence of screening.

Kurtz et al. (1994) organized an educational campaign addressing women employees at different worksites in the United States by distributing brochures discussing breast cancer epidemiology and introducing screening guidelines. The effect of the campaign was assessed by questionnaire before and after the dissemination of the material. Results showed that the material had a positive effect in terms of increasing perception of the importance of mammography and CBEs.

Mayer et al. (1993), delivered an education program on breast cancer addressing women aged 40 years or more in a state university (San Diego, California). The campaign consisted of distributing educational material, holding events, and organizing educational workshops. After one year of administering the campaign, the mammography rates were not significantly greater in the intervention group over the control group.

In late 1988, the organized cervical cancer screening program in Florence, Italy performed a workplace intervention in two local companies. All employees received educational lectures on the benefits of cervical cytology, and smear tests were performed. After linking the employee registers with that of the screening program, 26 women who had been previously screened were excluded and the remaining 286 were invited to have a PAP test at the workplace infirmary. The response rate was 52 percent, with no significant differences across the various age groups, indicating that workplace screening activities may help to increase screening compliance (Grazzini et al. 1989).

Aiming to improve interest in cervical cytology, the District Health Authority, the Women's National Cancer Control Campaign, and the South West Thames Regional Cancer Control Organization in London used a mobile unit to offer breast and cervical cancer screening examination to women at work aged 40 years or older (Thrornton & Chamberlain 1989). A total of 82 companies employing at least 25 women were approached, of which 39 participated. Of the eligible women identified through work registers, 91 percent visited the mobile clinic and had a smear test, as well as other examinations (such as CBE and gynecological examination). Workplace screening has the potential to improve screening coverage, provided the health authority participates in planning and organizing the activity.

Workplace Colorectal and Prostate Cancer Screening

A workplace colorectal cancer screening program was implemented in a large British industry employing 4,000 people (Hart et al. 2003). Overall, 1,828 male and female employees aged 41-65 years were invited in writing to participate. The program was also advertised with posters at the workplace and through the company's medical department. Each participant received a free Haemoccult test pack with instructions on how to perform the test. Those who tested positive were then invited to undergo colonoscopy and a complete physical examination. Compliance with this workplace screening program was 25 percent in men and 32 percent in women, with managers responding more than nonmanagers in both sexes. Overall, it was found that workplace screening initiatives are helpful in increasing interest in colorectal cancer screening, either independently or in conjunction with community programs, because it is easier to reach large numbers of people employed through health education campaigns.

A worksite randomized trial was conducted in an automobile industry in Houston, Texas, addressing employees (only men—no women employees were included) at increased risk for colorectal cancer (Tilley et al. 1999). Health interventions were applied to 5,042 workers in 28 worksites involving rectal examination, fecal occult blood test, and flexible sigmoidoscopy in the control group. In addition to this, an educational booklet and telephone call were added to the intervention group. Prior to the initiation of the study, 61 percent of the employees had been screened for colorectal cancer. After the completion of the study, there was a modest increase in screening compliance (OR=1.46, 95% CI 1.1-2.0) coverage in the intervention worksites (OR=1.33, 95% CI 1.1-1.6) leading to the conclusion that worksite interventions can promote employee participation in colorectal cancer screening programs.

This sample was analyzed further to examine associations between perceived risk for colorectal cancer and health-related behaviors, as well as correlates of risk perception (Vernon et al. 2001). Perceived risk was positively associated with family histories of polyps, family support for screening, and worry about colorectal cancer diagnosis, and was negatively associated with access to screening at the workplace (OR=0.6, 95% CI 0.4-0.9). Differences in the magnitude of perceived risk were found in men with and without history of polyps, indicating the need to consider the target group's characteristics and to provide tailored health messages.

As mentioned previously in this chapter, the effectiveness of screening for prostate cancer has not yet been established. A prostate cancer screening program has been applied in a screening setting in the United States, however, to identify the employer costs of the applied screening test, and of the referrals due to abnormal test results. A total of 385 men, aged 50 years or older and employed by a single employer, were given a digital rectal examination and prostate specific antigen (PSA) testing. After calculating all the emerging costs, it was found that prostate cancer screening in the workplace is efficient.

Available Resources

Two workplace resource kits for breast cancer screening are available that can be used as model tools for breast cancer screening interventions in different work settings.

BreastScreen Queensland Workplace Resource Kit[1]

This resource kit addresses employers, providing them with important information about breast cancer and breast cancer screening with the goal of educating working women about the importance of regular breast cancer screening. The resource kit contains some breast cancer statistics in the local area (Queensland), describes the local organized breast cancer screening program, and describes who is eligible to participate. It also refers to the reasons why women do not participate in organized breast screening programs, and indicates ways the employer can help. The proposed strategies include:

- Delivery of an education session
- Inclusion of a brochure or a message in the pay slip
- Use of the editorial in staff newsletters
- Sending e-mails about the importance of breast cancer screening
- Displaying posters and brochures in elevators, common rooms, foyers, lunch rooms, etc.
- Allowing women time off once every two years to attend screenings
- Displaying testimonials from staff members who have attended the program or who are breast cancer survivors

---

[1] Refer to *www.health.qld.gov.au/breastscreen/documents/21179.pdf*.

UCI Health Promotion Center: Workplace Health Promotion Information and Resource Kit—Helping You Help your Employees to Better Health[2]

This resource kit addresses owners and managers of small- to medium-sized companies with the goal of a) providing them with a basic understanding of workplace health promotion, especially in the context of their company, b) providing them with some realistic ideas on actions to improve the health of their employee(s) and c) indicating sources of free or low-cost information.

The resource kit addresses a series of health issues, such as lifestyle habits (nutrition, smoking, physical exercise), occupational health and safety, and cancer screening. It outlines the elements of a model health promotion program, indicates the dates of national health promotion activities, and provides a list of available relative resources.

References

Allen JD, Stoddard AM, Mays J, Sorensen G (2001) Promoting breast and cervical cancer screening at the workplace: results from the Woman to Woman study. *Am J Public Health*, 91, 584–590

American Cancer Society (2007) Radiation exposure and cancer. In: http://www.cancer.org /docroot/PED/content/PER_1_eX_Radiation_Exposure_and_Cancer.asp.

American College of Occupational and Environmental Medicine (1994) Code of ethical conduct. *J Occup Med*, 29, 28

American College of Occupational and Environmental Medicine: Genetic Screening in the workplace, http://www.acoem.org/guidelines

American Medical Association (1991) Council on Ethical and Judicial Affairs. Use of genetic testing by employers- *JAMA*, 226, 1827–30

Andreason A (1995) Marketing social change: Changing behaviour to promote health, social development and the environment. Jossey-Bass, San Francisco

Arbyn M, Van Oyen H, Lynge E, Mickshe M (2001) European Consensus on cancer screening should be applied urgently by health ministers. BMJ, 323, 396

Ashmore JP, Krewski D, Ziellinski JM, Jiang H, Semenciw R, Band PR (1998) First analysis and Occupational radiation exposure based on the National Dose Registry of Canada. *Am J Epidemiol* 148, 564–74

Bandura S (1986) Social foundations of thought and action: A social cognitive theory. Prentice-Hall, Engelwood Cliffs, NJ

British Medical Association (2005) Population screening and genetic resting, http://www.bma.org

Broeders M, Codd M, Nyström L, Ascunce N, Riza E (2000) Epidemiological guidelines for quality assurance in breast cancer screening. In: European guidelines for quality assurance in mammography screening. Luxembourg 3rd edition (ISBN 92-894-1145-7)

Byers T, Levin B, Rothenberger D, Dodd GD, Smith RA (1997) American Cancer Society Guidelines for screening and surveillance for early detection of colorectal polyps and cancer. *CA Cancer J Clin*, 112, 594–642

Calle EE, Flanders WD, Thun MJ, Martin LM (year?) Demographic predictors of mammography and Pap smear screening in U.S. women. *Am J Public Health* 1003, 83, 53–60.

---

[2] Refer to *www.healthpromotioncenter.uci.edu/InfoKit.pdf*.

Campbell M, Tessaro I, DeVellis B, Benedict S, Kelsey K, Belton L, Sanhuesa A (2002) Effects of a tailored health promotion program for female blue-collar workers: Health Works for Women. *Prev Med*, 34, 313–323

Canadian Cancer Society (2004), (http://info.cancer.ca/e/glossary/O/opportunistic_screening.htm)

Cancer Research UK (2007), http://www.cancerhelp.org.uk

Commission of the European Communities (2003) Proposal for a council recommendation on cancer screening, Brussels 5.5.2003 COM 2003/0093 (CNS), http://eur-lex.europa.eu/LexUriServ/site/en/com/2003/com2003_0230en01.pdf

Day NE, Williams DRR, Khaw KT (1989) Breast cancer screening programs: the development of a monitoring and evaluation system. *Br J Cancer* 59,954–58

Dos Santos Silva I (1999) Cancer epidemiology: Principles and methods. IARC Press, Lyon, France, pp. 355

European Commission-Public Health Overview of Health Policy - The state of women's health in the European Union, http://ec.europa.eu/health/ph_information/reporting/community_en.htm.

Ferlay I, Autier P, Boniol M, Heanue M, Colombet M, Boyle P (2007). Estimates of the cancer incidence and mortality in Europe in 2006. Annual Oncology 18, 581–592

Glanz K, Rimer BK, Lerman C, McGovern Gorchov P (1992) Factors influencing acceptance of mammography: implications for enhancing worksite cancer control. *Am J Health Promot*, 7(1), 28–36

Gochfeld M (1992) Medical surveillance and screening at the workplace: complementary preventive strategies. *Environ Res* 59, 67–80

Grazzini G, Cecchini S, Bartoli D, Ciatto S (1989) Pap smear screening at the workplace. *Am J Public Health*, 79(11), 1570–71

Halperin WE, Ratcliffe J, Frazier TM, Wilson L, Becker SP, Schulte PA. Medical screening in the workplace (1986) *J Occup Med*, 28,547–52

Hart AR, Glover N, Howick-Baker J, Mayberry JF (2003) An industry based approach to colorectal cancer screening in an asymptomatic population. *Postgrad Med*, 79, 646–649

Hayes RB, Yin SN, Dosemeci M, et al. (1996) Mortality among benzene-exposed workers in China. *Environ Health Persp* 104, 1349–52

Holmquist ND (2000) Revisiting the effect of the Pap test in cervical cancer. *Am J Public Health*, 90, 620–623

Hutchinson GB (1960) Evaluation of preventive services. *J Chron Dis*, 11, 497

International Agency for Research on Cancer (1987) *IARC Monographs on the Evaluation of the Carcinogenic Risk of Chemicals to Humans, Supplement 7. Overall evaluations of carcinogenicity: an updating of IARC monographs Vols 1 to 42*. IARC, Lyon

International Labour Organisation (1997) Protection of workers' personal data. An ILO code of practice. Geneva, Switzerland. International agency for Research on Cancer. Press Release No 174, 7 February 2007. New European cancer figures. World cancer agency says major efforts needed towards prevention in Europe, http://www.iarc.fc/ENG/Press_Releases/pr174a.html

International Labour Organisation (1998) Technical and Ethical Guidelines for Workers' Health Surveillance. Occupational Safety and Health Series No 72, Geneva, Switzerland

Kogevinas M, Maria Anto J, Sunyer J, Tobias A, Kromhaut H, Burney P (1999) Survey Study Group, European Community Respiratory Health. Occupational asthma in Europe and other industrialized areas: a population-based study. *Lancet* 353, 1750–54

Kurtz ME, Kurtz JC, Given B, Given CC (1994) Promotion of breast cancer screening in a worksite population. *Health Care Women Int*, 15, 31–42

Le Feuvre N (1996) Women, Work and Employment in Europe: Features of Women's Employment in Europe-Universite de Toulouse-Le Mirail-France; (http://www.helsinki.fi/science/xantippa/wee/wee22.html)

Mayer JA, Jones JA, Eckhart LE, Haliday J, Bartholomew S, Slymen DJ, Hovell MF (1993) Evaluation of a worksite mammography program. *Am J Prev-Med*, 9(4), 244–49

Meissner HI, Smith RA, Rimer BK, Wilson KM, Rakowski W, Vernon SW, Briss PA. Promoting cancer screening: learning from experience. Cancer Supplement 22 July 2004 (http://www/interscience.wiley.com)

National Institutes of Health - National Cancer Institute (2007), http://www.cancer.gov.

National Reference Center for Bioethics Literature (1993) Genetic Testing and Genetic Screening. Georgetown University, http://www.georgetown.edu/research/nrcbl/publications/scopenotes/nsn22.htm).

Navasumrit P, Chanvaivit S, Intarasunanont P, Arayasiri M, Lauhareungpanya N, Parnlob V, Settachan D, Ruchirawat M (2005) Environmental and occupational exposure to benzene in Thailand. *Chemico-Biological Interactions*, 153–154, 75–83

Official Journal of the European Union. (year?) Cancer Plan 1987–1989. C50, 26, 2

OSHA - Occupational Safety and Health Administration (2007) Medical surveillance guidelines for benzene. Standard Number 1910.1028 App C

Perry N, Broeders M, de Wolf C, Törnberg S, Schouten J (2001) European guidelines for quality assurance in mammography screening (3rd ed) Brussels European Commission

Prochaska JO, DiClemente CC (1982) Transtheoretical therapy: toward a more integrative model of change. *Psychother Theory Res Pract*, 19, 276–288

Rimer BK, Meissner H, Breen N, Legler J, Coyne CA (2001) Social and behavioral interventions to increase breast cancer screening. In Schneiderman N, Speers MA, Silva JM, Tomes H, Gentry JH (Eds.), Integrating behavioral and social sciences with public health (pp. 177–201). Washington, DC

Riza E, Linos A (2001) Introduction to screening In European Commission-DG for Education and Culture "Screening for data managers" (pp. 7–8) Educational manual from Leonardo da Vinci Program Vocational Training and Educational Tool Development for data managers in Screening Programmes (TRENDS). Project number DG XXII EL/98/2/05191/PI/II.1.1.a/ FPC (1999–2001)

Rosenstock I, Kirscht J (1974) The Health Belief Model and personal health behavior. *Health Educ Monogr,*2, 470–473

Schrammel P, Griffiths RI, Griffiths CB (1998) A workplace breast cancer screening program. Costs and components. *AAOHN J* 46(11), 523–29

Snyder C, Schrmmel PN, Griffiths CB, Griffiths RI (1998) Prostate cancer screening in the workplace. Employer costs. *AAOHN J*, 46(8), 379–84

Tabar L, Fagerberg G, Duffy SW Day NE, Gad A, Grontoft O (1992) Update on the Swedish two-country program of mammographic screening for breast cancer. *Radiol Clin North Am* 30,187–210

Thrornton J, Chamberlain J (1989) Cervical screening in the workplace. *J-Public-Health*, 11(4), 290–98

Tilley BC, Vernon SW, Myers R, Glanz K, Lu M, Hirst K, Kristal AR (1999) The Next Step Trial: impact of a worksite colorectal cancer screening promotion program. *Prev Med*, 28(3), 276–83

U.S. Department of Health and Human Services (1989, 2003). Making health communication programs work, NCI, NIH

Vernon SW, Myers RE, Tilley BC, Li S (2001) Factors associated with perceived risk in automotive employees at increased risk for colorectal cancer. *Cancer Epidemiol Biom Prev*, 10, 35–43

World Economic Forum (2006) New Toolkit protecting from tuberculosis. http://www.weforum.org

World Health Organization (2004) Gender, Health and Work. Geneva: Department of Gender, Women and Health (GWH), http://www.who.int/gender/documents/en/

World Health Organisation (2007) Initiative for Vaccine Research. Human Papillomavirus infection and cervical cancer, http://www.who.int/vaccine_research/diseases/hpv/en

World Health Organization (1968) Principles and practice of screening for disease. In Wilson JMG, Junger G (eds) Public Health papers 34. Geneva

PART III
WOMEN'S REPRODUCTIVE HEALTH ISSUES

Chapter 9
Workplace Health Promotion Aiming at Safe Working Environments for Pregnant Women

Alex Burdorf and Goedele Geuskens

Introduction

Women constitute a substantial part of the labor force in the European Union (EU). In 2004, about 56 percent of the women aged between 15 to 64 years had paid employment (at least one hour per week), which was a substantial increase from 51 percent in 1994. Fig. 9.1 presents the proportion of women employed in the various countries within the EU in 2004 (Eurostat 2005). The 15 most prevalent occupations are shown in Fig. 9.2 (ILO 2006). Approximately 56 percent of the women were employed in these 15 occupations, illustrating that most women worked as shop salespeople, domestic helpers, cleaners and launderers, clerks, and health care professionals.

Most women work during their reproductive years, and therefore, during the period in which pregnancy and breastfeeding occurs. On average in the EU, women give birth to 2.1 children (2004) at a mean age of 29.2 years (2002) (Eurostat 2005). With the increasing labor force participation among women in European countries, the likelihood that women will be exposed to a variety of chemical, physical, and psychosocial factors at work during pregnancy increases. Hazardous workplace conditions may have adverse effects on pregnancy outcomes and cause birth defects in offspring (Burdorf et al. 2006).

The purpose of this chapter is to describe the topics that workplace health promotion programs should address, to discuss the general content and pros and cons of introducing workplace health promotion programs, and to present implementation strategies and novel approaches in health promotion aimed at pregnant women. With respect to the first goal, a short review is presented on work-related risk factors for adverse pregnancy outcomes and fetal development. The second goal is addressed in the third section, describing the general contents of workplace health promotion programs and facilitators and barriers in implementation, and in the fourth section, outlining existing legislation that should be incorporated into health promotion programs. The third goal is addressed in the fifth section, which describes the essential conditions for a successful implementation of workplace health promotion programs, and in the last section, which reports on novel, promising approaches in health promotion directed at working women.

A. Linos, W. Kirch (eds), *Promoting Health for Working Women.*   243
© Springer 2008

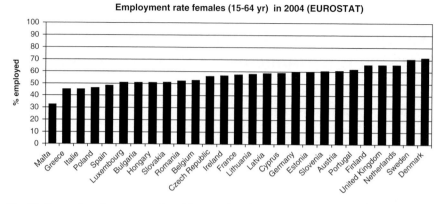

Fig. 9.1 Proportion of women employed in countries of the European Union as of 2004

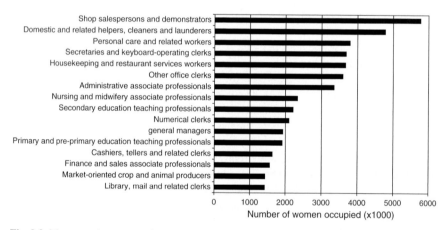

Fig. 9.2 Most prevalent occupations among women in the European Union (25 countries) in 2000

Risk Factors in the Working Environment for Adverse Pregnancy Outcomes and Fetal Development

Women may be exposed to a variety of chemical, physical, and psychosocial factors at work. These factors may directly affect the outcome of a pregnancy, such as spontaneous abortion, stillbirth, small-for-gestational age issues, and birth weight. Occupational exposure may also interact with fetal development, resulting in problems that range from birth defects, such as congenital malformations, to neurobehavioral disorders at a young age, and even to cancer at an older age (Burdorf et al. 2006).

It should be acknowledged that many adverse outcomes may be caused by multiple (work-related) factors, which makes it extremely difficult to attribute a particular outcome to a specific occupational exposure. In addition, adverse outcomes may be due to adverse effects of occupational exposure on both the female and male reproductive system. To complicate matters further, occupational exposure may only be relevant during a specific time window—for example, shortly before conception or during early pregnancy (Burdorf et al. 2006). Within the scope of this chapter, this section will be limited to maternal exposure to hazardous agents at work, because these agents will be targeted in the workplace health promotion programs for pregnant women.

Table 9.1 summarizes the main effects of maternal exposure at the workplace on pregnancy outcomes and fetal development (Burdorf et al., 2006; Figa-Talamanca 2006; Thulstrup et al. 2006). Four categories of risk factors can be distinguished—physical factors, chemical agents, psychosocial factors, and physical load. In all four categories, maternal exposure before or during pregnancy may lead to spontaneous abortion and, to a lesser extent, preterm birth and low-birth weight. The latter two outcome measures reflect an effect on intrauterine growth. The physical factor receiving the most attention in the literature is ionizing radiation

Table 9.1 Qualitative summary of the potentially adverse effects of occupational exposure on the female and male reproductive system

Occupational Risk Factor	Pregnancy Outcomes (maternal exposure)	Birth Defects (maternal exposure)
Physical factors		
Ionizing radiation	Spontaneous abortion	Congenital defects
Noise (> 90 dBA)	Spontaneous abortion	
	Low birth weight	
	Preterm birth	
Chemical agents		
Lead	Low birth weight	Neural tube defects
Mercury	Spontaneous abortion	
Organic solvents	Spontaneous abortion	Cleft lip/palate
Tetrachloroethylene	Spontaneous abortion	
Glycol ethers	Spontaneous abortion	Neural tube defects
		Cleft lip/palate
Dibromopropane	Menstrual disturbances	
Ethylene oxide	Spontaneous abortion	
	Preterm birth	
Aneasthetic gases	Spontaneous abortion	
Antineoplastic drugs	Spontaneous abortion	
Pesticides	Spontaneous abortion	Neural tube defects
		Cleft lip/palate
Psychosocial factors		
Irregular work hours	Spontaneous abortion	
Stress	Menstrual disturbances	
	Spontaneous abortion	
	Preterm birth	
Physical load:		
Heavy physical work (high energy expenditure)	Spontaneous abortion	
	Low birth weight	
	Preterm birth	
Frequent heavy lifting	Spontaneous abortion	
	Low birth weight	
	Preterm birth	
Prolonged standing	Spontaneous abortion	

among health care personnel—both before and during pregnancy—which has been consistently associated with spontaneous abortion and congenital defects. Chemical risk factors among health care personnel include anesthetic gases and antineoplastic drugs. As shown in Fig. 9.2, a substantial proportion of women in the EU work in health care organizations and may be partly exposed to these physical and chemical risk factors.

Various other chemical agents may also result in spontaneous abortion and low birth weight, and most notable is exposure to heavy metals (inorganic lead and mercury), pesticides, and organic solvents. Both latter types of exposures encompass a large range of specific chemicals, but most epidemiological studies are not specific enough to identify the particular solvents and pesticides that may lead to adverse pregnancy outcomes. Birth defects seem primarily related to exposure to lead, glycol ethers, organic solvents, and pesticides. Organic solvent exposure may occur with cleaners and pesticides among agricultural workers. Both occupations are among the most prevalent jobs held by women in the European Union (see Fig. 9.2).

Psychosocial factors have received less attention in epidemiological studies, but there is evidence that especially self-perceived stress has adverse effects on pregnancy outcomes. Work-related stress, most notably time pressure, has been reported in health care personnel, teaching professionals, and shop personnel.

With regard to physical load, women in jobs with a high energy expenditure and frequent manual materials handling are at risk, but it is difficult to distinguish between both risk factors because jobs with heavy physical loads are usually also those with frequent lifting of heavy loads. Fig. 9.2 demonstrates that several prevalent occupations among women in the EU are characterized by a high physical load—e.g., cleaners, housekeeping professionals, launderers, crop producers, restaurant service workers, and health care personnel.

In addition to pregnancy outcomes and adverse fetal development, fertility

Table 9.2 Qualitative summary of the potentially adverse effects of maternal and paternal occupational exposure on fertility

Occupational Risk Factor	Maternal Exposure	Paternal Exposure
Physical factors:		
Ionizing radiation	+	+
Heat	+	+
Chemical agents:		
Lead	+	+
Mercury	+	
Toluene	+	
Aliphatic hydrocarbons	+	
Aromatic hydrocarbons	+	
Tetrachloroethylene	+	
Glycol ethers	+	+
Ethylene oxide	+	
Anaesthetic gases	+	
Pesticides	+	+
Psychosocial factors:		
Irregular work hours	+	
Stress	+	

can also be affected by occupational exposure (see Table 9.2). Because time-to-pregnancy is the result of the reproductive ability of a couple, it is difficult to separate the specific contribution of occupational exposure of the woman from the role of occupational exposure of her male partner. However, both maternal and paternal occupational exposure to ionizing radiation and heat have been established as risk factors for fertility problems. Most chemical agents that are associated with adverse pregnancy outcomes and birth defects also seem to affect fertility, especially through the female-mediated pathway. The same observation holds true for the effects of stress and irregular work hours among women. The paternal exposures causing a reduced fertility have also been identified as occupational risk factors for reduced semen quality, indicating that the established effects of paternal exposures on fertility may find their origin in a male-mediated toxicity on semen.

It is important to bear in mind that this summary of the epidemiological evidence is based on studies from the 1970s onwards, spanning a 30-year period. A comprehensive evaluation of long-term trends in occupational exposure based on almost 700 sets of data showed that most chemical exposures declined at rates between –4 and –14 percent per year, with a median value of -8 percent per year. Hence, occupational exposures are generally lower today than they were years or decades ago (Symanski et al. 1998). Changes in the production process and control measures have had a noticeable impact on exposure levels. In addition, toxic substances may have been replaced by less toxic agents. Therefore, reproductive health effects observed in a particular industry years ago may no longer be a risk in the current workplace. Although several other studies in different industries have confirmed the downward trend in occupational exposure over time, one has to bear in mind that industries may have outsourced the most dirty jobs towards less developed countries or less well-protected small enterprises, resulting in hazardous workplaces that are usually not covered by occupational health care. A recent illustration can be found in the European study on occupational hazards of the male reproductive system, whereby blood lead levels dropped considerably during the period of 1965–1995 in several western European countries, but not in Poland (Burdorf et al. 2006). Thus, the results presented may not be generalizable across industries and across countries in the EU.

Considerations on Workplace Health Promotion Programs Aimed at Pregnant Women

In general, workplace health promotion programs should balance measures directed at ensuring safe working environments for pregnant women with other activities aimed at providing sound working conditions for all workers involved. The benefits and disadvantages of specific advices and measures should be considered. Barriers and facilitators of implementation of these proposed advices and interventions should be investigated to optimize the effectiveness of workplace health promotion programs.

Safe Working Environments

Workplace health promotion aimed at reducing adverse pregnancy outcomes and fetal developments requires the establishment of a safe working environment. The occupational hazards presented in Tables 9.1 and 9.2 should be considered for counseling and control measures targeting women and men trying to conceive. In general, the precautions to be taken for the protection of the reproductive health of both women and men will not differ from the safeguarding of all workers.

The evidence of occupational risk factors linked to adverse effects on the reproductive system is consistent for a limited number of risk factors, most notably exposure to lead, glycol ethers, organic solvents, pesticides, and ionizing radiation. It remains difficult, however, to arrive at sound conclusions on the level of exposure and the specific chemicals within the groups of glycol ethers, organic solvents, and pesticides that are associated with an increased risk. It is advised to inform women in relevant jobs on the potential effects of these occupational exposures on pregnancy and the health of their fetus. Easy accessible information should be available before conception because some women already start searching for information on occupational risk factors before pregnancy. In the communication on potential risks, it is a huge challenge to convey a risk-based assessment and avoid unnecessary concerns about levels of exposure that most certainly will not have any harmful effect whatsoever.

Given the large uncertainties in the type and level of exposure that constitutes a reproductive risk, it is advised to limit specific workplace control measures to those physical and chemical agents for which a formal risk assessment has identified the exposure situation as potentially harmful for the ability to conceive a child. Some companies have policies that offer women who intend to become pregnant the option of withdrawing from activities with exposure to specific chemicals, such as photoresistant solvents in the semiconductor industry, or antineoplastic drugs in health care organizations.

Several barriers exist in the implementation of appropriate workplace health promotion programs aimed at reproductive health. First, companies are faced with difficult questions regarding the necessary measures that need to be taken to ensure that negative effects on the reproductive system will not occur. These questions pertain to issues such as when to take action (which exposures constitute an unacceptable risk?) and the timing of the actual action (before or during pregnancy?). Companies and their occupational health professionals should use available guidelines on physical and chemical agents known to be harmful. The dilemma of when exactly to take action often will remain because the timing of the health promotion and subsequent action requires insight into the time-sensitive window when exposure constitutes an unacceptable risk. It is well-established that maternal exposure in the few months before conception is important for fertility, and that teratogenic effects may arise during the organogenesis phase (during the first 3-8 weeks of pregnancy). Long-term exposure may also be relevant, however, when the exposure of interest causes irreversible changes—for example, germline DNA modifications—or the agents are biopersistent and accumulate in body fat, such as several pesticides. For most occupational hazards, the appropriate windows of highest susceptibility are not well-established, which hampers clear advice as to when preventive measures should be undertaken. Precautions should definitely be taken in pregnant women, however, from the beginning of pregnancy onwards.

Women may not always report pregnancy during the first two trimesters, which limits the possibility of taking precautions. Underlying this phenomenon may be a lack of education, which could be prevented by informing employees of the risks of exposure in their job. Fearing to loose the job may also affect not reporting pregnancy—for example, in contract workers. Although these workers may be well aware of the risk, they may lack motivation—the ability and the opportunity for precautions. In these situations, a strong legal framework may assist women in the appropriate choices.

Finally, adverse pregnancy outcomes are the result of hazardous occupational exposure to both women and men. Although this does not form a barrier in the implementation of promotion programs directed at women, it makes clear that it is not possible to fully prevent adverse outcomes and fetal development by only focusing on women.

The Legal and Societal Context of Workplace Health Promotion

A specific EU directive targets the safety and health of pregnant workers at work, and workers who have recently given birth or are breastfeeding (Directive 92/85/EEC, Commission of the European Communities 1992). The directive also stipulates that an assessment must be made of the workplace of pregnant or breastfeeding women and women who have recently given birth. Should the assessment reveal a risk to health and safety, all reasonable steps must be taken to ensure that the risk is avoided. As a consequence, women should be allowed to go on paid leave if it is impossible to alter a woman's job or working conditions, to avoid any identified risk to health and safety.

For pregnant women, the directive presents detailed guidelines on the requirements with respect to physical, chemical and biological agents, and industrial conditions, including physical load, mental and physical fatigue, and physical and mental stress. These guidelines contain the mandatory provisions for pregnant women preparing antineoplastic drugs, or being exposed to lead, to be transferred to another job. In addition, women trying to conceive must be fully informed on the reproductive hazards of cytotoxic drugs, and women with reproductive capacity should be protected against blood-lead levels higher than $30\,\mu g/dl$ (Commission of the European Communities 1992; 2000). The guidelines also require that pregnant women should not work in a high-pressure atmosphere and should not be exposed to prolonged excessive heat or cold, manual materials handling involving risk of injury, working at heights, or working in awkward postures and movements, especially in confined spaces (Commission of the European Communities 2000).

Directive 92/85/EEC further states that the minimum length of maternity leave permitted under the Directive is 14 weeks. Importantly, the dismissal of a pregnant woman or a woman on maternity leave is prohibited, unless it is for reasons unconnected with the pregnancy (Commission of the European Communities, 2000).

Key Elements of Workplace Health Promotion

In the previous chapters, the actual content of a health promotion program aimed at providing safe working environments for pregnant women was outlined. This chapter focuses on the objectives and structure of the health promotion program and the consequences of a successful workplace health promotion program. Because there are no evidence-based examples described in the literature, this chapter applies general methods of health promotion at the workplace to the specific area of maternal health at work.

A first step in this process is to identify the individual and organizational needs and attitudes that must be addressed in the objectives of a health promotion program. An organization should start the development of a program with a needs assessment to determine what exactly is needed at the level of the individual woman and at the level of the organization. This needs assessment may reveal that information on the reproductive effects of potentially harmful working conditions should not only address women who are pregnant but also women wanting to conceive. Hence, the target population may be much larger, and different approaches may be needed, to address concerns in both groups. Table 9.3 provides an overview of possible items to be considered in the initial stage of program development.

The second step in program development is to consider various methods and strategies in designing and implementing the program. Table 9.4 presents some key elements and, again, this overview is only intended to demonstrate the type of areas that need to be addressed.

Table 9.3 Needs, attitudes, and objectives

Needs and Attitudes	Objective
Individual level	
Knowledge needs	
Attitudes & norms	Identify required information
Motivation	Present easy accessible information
	Provide necessary training when needed
	Identify attitudes towards specific precautions
	Identify potential barriers
	Identify motivation towards adjusting work during pregnancy
Organizational level	
Knowledge needs	Identify work conditions associated with potential reproductive effects
Attitudes & norms	Identify appropriate sources of information
Provisions	Identify target groups
Social support	Establish positive attitudes towards specific arrangements for
Enforcement	pregnant women
	Target personnel responsible for content and organization of program
	Establish resources
	Create organizational support for policy measures
	Recognize statutory requirements
	Identify appropriate enforcement measures
	Define standards of provisions

Table 9.4 Methods and strategies

Method	Strategy
Participative program design	Incorporate target group into design of the program
Public Relations advocacy	Involve company media (e.g. newsletter, intranet) to increase visibility of program
Peer participation	Create role models
	Recruit women with experience for support teams
Policy implementation	Provide training on program policies and guidelines
Policy enforcement	Develop an enforcement plan
	Monitor compliance with program

In the scientific literature, several approaches have been described for the development and implementation of health promotion programs. For programs aimed at providing safe working environments for pregnant women, the content of the program will be determined largely by the presence of specific hazardous working conditions, and the production and work processes. Thus, a flexible approach is needed. A suitable framework may be offered by the *intervention mapping* method that distinguishes five stages: 1) the definition of program objectives (often preceeded by a needs assessment) based on a thorough analyses of the health problem, 2) the selection of appropriate theories and methods to realize changes in the behavior of individuals and organizations, 3) the design of the intervention program, 4) the development of a structured plan for implementation, and 5) the evaluation of the implementation (Bartholomew et al. 2001). The application of the method may be time-consuming, but the structure and content of the approach dictates that the program is based on empirical evidence and theory, that the intervention is tailored to the relevant needs and characteristics of the target populations, and that the implementation takes into account the opportunities and possibilities of the people and organizations involved.

The third step is the evaluation of the impact of the health promotion program. In recent years, several evaluation strategies have been developed. A comprehensive approach is the Reach, Effectiveness, Adoption, Implementation, and Maintenance (RE-AIM) framework. This model includes an evaluation of the proportion of subjects in the target groups willing to participate (reach), an assessment of the impact of the program on targeted outcomes and quality of life (effectiveness), the agreement in the organization to deliver the program (adoption), the consistency and quality of delivery (implementation), and the extent to which the program is sustained over time (Glasgow 2005; Glasgow et al. 2006).

New Developments in Workplace Health Promotion

A new development in workplace health promotion is the extensive use of the Internet to provide computer-driven, tailored advice to individuals. Because the Internet is widely available in the EU and computer-tailored advice has been found to be effective in other domains of health promotion, the use of the Internet may be a very promising approach.

The Canadian website, Motherisk (Treating the Mother—Protecting the Unborn), provides evidence-based information and guidance about the safety or risk to the developing fetus or infant of maternal exposure to drugs, diseases, radiation, household chemicals, and environmental agents. It strives to provide authoritative information and guidance to both pregnant or lactating women and to health care professionals (Motherisk 2006). This initiative also provides a helpline for additional questions. A Motherisk workplace assessment program helps employers determine whether their chemical plant or laboratory exposes pregnant women to dangerous levels of hazardous chemicals. The Motherisk program is strongly linked to an extensive research program on the effects of various working conditions on reproductive health.

The Dutch ErfoCentrum promotes knowledge of genetic and nongenetic congenital disorders among the general public and healthcare providers. It has introduced two websites specifically aimed at women (and men) who are not pregnant yet, but intend to become pregnant. The website *ZwangerStraks.nl* provides information on pregnancy and also includes a section on occupations in which women could be exposed to risk factors for reproductive health effects (Zwangerstraks 2006). The website *ZwangerWijzer.nl* contains an online questionnaire providing insight into health risks before conception (Zwangerwijzer 2006). After filling in the questionnaire, feedback on health risks as a result of genetic predisposition, lack of folium acid, and lifestyle, for example, is provided. In some cases, the feedback includes a recommendation to discuss the outcome with a general practitioner or a midwife. The major strength of this website is that it provides people with tailored advice within a very short period of time before conception.

Conclusions

Workplace health promotion focusing on women who intend to become pregnant and pregnant women is important because occupational exposure may lead to adverse pregnancy outcomes and fetal development. Workplace health promotion should ensure a safe working environment for pregnant women. Although European legislation exists with respect to informing (pregnant) women on safe working environments, it remains difficult to determine the complete array of work-related exposures that may constitute an unacceptable risk. The timing of the intervention is another important challenge. It is advised to limit health promotion programs to risk factors that have consistently been identified. Precautions should then be taken from the earliest phase of pregnancy onwards.

References

Bartholomew LK, Parcel GS, Kok G, Gottlieb NH (2001) *Intervention Mapping: designing theory and evidence-based health promotion programs.* Mayfield, MountainView, CA

Burdorf A, Figa-Talamanca I, Kold Jensen T, Thulstrup A (2006) Effects of occupational exposure on the reproductive system: core evidence and practical implications. Occupational Medicine, 56, 516–520

Commission of the European Communities (1992) Council Directive 92/85/EEC concerning the implementation of measures to encourage improvements in the safety and health of pregnant workers, women workers who have recently given birth and women who are breastfeeding. *Official Journal L*, 348, Vol. 28.11.1992

Commission of the European Communities (2000) *COM (2000)-466 Communication from the commission on the guidelines on the assessment of the chemical, physical, and biological agents and industrial processes considered hazardous for the safety and health of pregnant workers and workers who have recently given birth or are breastfeeding (Council Directive 92/85/EEC)* Brussels

EUROSTAT (2005) http://epp.eurostat.cec.eu.int/portal/ (accessed Nov 2005)

Figà-Talamanca I (2006) Occupational risk factors and reproductive health of women. Occupational Medicine, 56, 521–531

Glasgow RE (2005) RE-AIM mode, http://www.re-aim.org (accessed Nov 2005)

Glasgow RE, Klesges LM, Dzewaltowski DA, Estabrooks PA, Vogt TM (2006) Evaluating the impact of health promotion programs: using the RE-AIM framework to form summary measures for decisiono making involvng complex issues. Health and Education Research, 21, 688–694

International Labor Organization (2006), http://www.ilo.org/ (accessed Nov 2006)

Khattak S, K-Moghtader G, McMartin K, Barrera M, Kennedy D, Koren G (1999) Pregnancy outcome following gestational exposure to organic solvents: a prospective controlled study. JAMA, 282, 1106–1109

Motherisk - Treating the mother - protecting the unborn, http://www.motherisk.org/index.jsp (accessed Nov 2005)

Symanski E, Kupper LL, Rappaport SM, (1998) Comprehensive evaluation of long-term trends in occupational exposure: Part 1. Description of the database. Occupational and Environmental Medicine 55, 300–309

Thulstrup AM, Bonde JP (2006) Maternal occupational exposures and risk of specific birth defects. Occupational Medicine, 56, 532–543

Zwangerstraks.nl - Information on aspects of pregnancy (aimed at fertile women), http://www.zwangerstraks.nl (accessed March 2006)

Zwangerwijzer.nl - Information for pregnant women (aimed at pregnant women and their partners), http://www.zwangerwijzer.nl (accessed March 2006)

Chapter 10
Workplace Health Promotion Aimed at Increasing Breastfeeding

Goedele Geuskens and Alex Burdorf

Introduction

Women constitute an increasing part of the labor force in the EU, with 56 percent of the women aged between 15 and 64 years employed in 2004 (Eurostat 2005). Most women work during their reproductive years, and many return to work after giving birth. Breastfeeding has many health benefits to both the mother and an infant. With the increasing labor force participation among women in European countries, however, the likelihood that employment and the workplace itself influence (the duration of) breastfeeding increases. Workplace health promotion directed at breastfeeding may therefore be of interest.

The purpose of this chapter is 1) to describe the topics that workplace health promotion programs aimed at increasing breastfeeding should address, 2) to discuss the general content and pros and cons of introducing these workplace health promotion programs, and 3) to present some examples of implementation strategies and novel approaches in health promotion. The first goal is addressed in the first and second sections, describing health benefits, the current performance of breastfeeding in the EU, and its determinants. The second goal is addressed in the fourth and fifth sections, in which the general contents of workplace health promotion programs, facilitators and barriers in implementation, and legislation and recommendations are described. The third goal on implementation strategies and promising approaches in health promotion is described in the last sections.

Benefits and Performance of Breastfeeding

Breastfeeding provides many health benefits to both the infant and the mother. Table 10.1 presents the wide array of health gains that have been associated with prolonged breastfeeding (WHO 2003).

Although the health benefits of breastfeeding are well-known, is seems difficult for most women to breastfeed for at least three months, let alone the often-advised period of six months. Figure 10.1 shows that, in many European countries, the proportion of babies still receiving breastfeeding after three months (exclusively,

A. Linos, W. Kirch (eds), *Promoting Health for Working Women.*
© Springer 2008

Table 10.1 Health benefits of breastfeeding to infant and mother

Benefits of Breastfeeding	
to infant	to mother
Reduced incidence and duration of diarrheal illnesses	Early initiation of breastfeeding after birth promotes maternal recovery from childbirth, accelerates uterine involution and reduces the risk of hemorrhaging, and preserves maternal hemoglobin stores through reduced blood loss, leading to improved iron status
Protection against respiratory infection	Prolonged period of postpartum infertility, leading to increased spacing between successive pregnancies if no contraceptives are used
Reduced occurrence of otitis and recurrent otitis	Possible accelerated weight loss and return to prepregnancy body weight
Possible protection against neonatal necrotizing enterocolitis, bacteraemia, meningitis, botulism and urinary tract infection	Reduced risk of premenopausal breast cancer
Possible reduced risk of auto-immune disease, such as diabetes mellitus type I and inflammatory bowel disease	Possible reduced risk of ovarian cancer
Possible reduced risk of sudden infant death syndrome	Possible improved bone mineralization and thereby decreased risk of postmenopausal hip fracture
Reduced risk of developing cow's milk allergy	
Possible reduced risk of adiposity later in childhood	
Improved visual acuity and psychomotor development, which may be caused by polyunsaturated fatty acids in the milk, particularly docosahexaenoic acid	
Higher IQ scores, which may be the result of factors present in milk or to greater stimulation	
Reduced malocclusion due to better jaw shape and development	

(Commission of the European Communities, 2000)

and in combination with formula feeding) is 70 percent or lower (HFA-DB 2005). The percentage of babies receiving breastfeeding after six months is shown in Fig. 10.2 (HFA-DB 2005). For the Netherlands, it has been reported that only about one in four mothers continues breastfeeding for six months (Nationaal Kompas Volksgezondheid 2005).

Legal and Societal Context of Workplace Health Promotion

The WHO's European region advocates that all infants be exclusively breastfed from birth to about six months of age, and at least during the first four months of life (WHO 2003). Clearly, many women in the EU do not follow this recommendation (Figure 10.2).

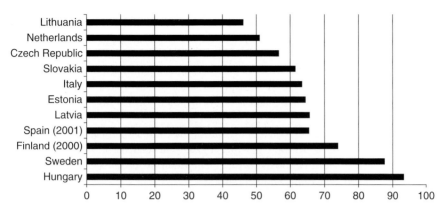

Fig. 10.1 Percentage of women breastfeeding for more than three months (both exclusive and non-exclusive, 2002) (European Commission, 2003)

A specific EU directive targets the safety and health at work of pregnant workers and workers who have recently given birth or are breastfeeding (Directive 92/85/EEC) (Commission of the European Communities 1992, 2000). The directive covers (among others) the assessment of risks to the health and safety of breastfeeding women in the workplace, a minimum maternity leave of 14 weeks, and protection against dismissal connected with pregnancy. The ILO standards for the protection and support of breastfeeding among mothers involve the provision of a minimum of 14 weeks of paid maternity leave (with at least two-thirds of previous earnings), job protection and non-discrimination for breastfeeding workers, and the entitlement of paid breastfeeding breaks (ILO 2000). Although the legislation in many EU countries goes beyond the provisions determined by the ILO, the standard regarding paid breastfeeding breaks during work time is not frequently met (European Commission 2003). In the Netherlands, this standard is met, with women being allowed to interrupt their work during the first nine months after pregnancy to

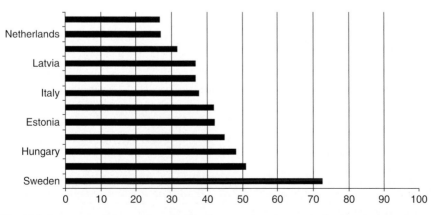

Fig. 10.2 Percentage of women breastfeeding for more than six months (both exclusive and non-exclusive, 2002 (European Commission, 2003)

breastfeed or express milk. This interruption may take up to a total of a quarter of their work time with maintenance of payment, and employers are obliged to provide adequate facilities. Many working mothers, however, are not protected by legislation even in countries where ILO standards are met, such as women employed for less than 6-12 months at the time of application for maternity leave, self-employed women, contract workers, irregular or illegal workers, and working students (European Commission 2003).

An EU project has developed a blueprint for the protection, promotion, and support of breastfeeding in Europe, and the legislation needed for working mothers that would further facilitate breastfeeding. The main measures are summarized in Table 10.2 (European Commission 2004b).

Table 10.2 Legislation for working mothers facilitating breastfeeding

Recommended Objectives	Responsibility	Outputs and Outcomes
To update national legislation where it does not meet ILO minimum standards	National and regional governments	Legislation upgraded
To ensure that sufficient legislative supports are in place to enable working mothers to exclusively breastfeed their infants for six months and to continue thereafter	National and regional governments	Effective legislative supports enacted, financial support approved
To extend maternity protection provisions to women who are not currently entitled to these: e.g. women with short term contracts, casual and part-time workers, students and immigrants	National and regional governments	Legislation extended
To ensure that employers, health care workers and the public are fully informed about maternity protection legislation and health and safety at work as related to pregnant and breastfeeding women	National and regional governments, employer organizations, trade unions	General awareness exists of maternity protection provisions
To inform employers of the benefits to them and their breastfeeding employees of facilitating breastfeeding following return to the workplace, and the facilities necessary to ensure that this is possible (flexible hours, time-off, and facilities for expressing and storing breast milk)	Relevant ministries, health and social authorities, employer organizations, trade unions	Employers informed of benefits and offering appropriate workplace supports

(EUROSTAT, 2005)

In addition to measures directly related to employment, more general initiatives to protect, promote, and support breastfeeding have been developed. In 1990, WHO and UNICEF released the Innocenti Declaration. In this declaration, four targets were outlined. First, an appropriate national breastfeeding coordinator should be appointed in every country. Second, the universal practice of the Baby Friendly Hospital Initiative was advocated. This initiative is formed by *10 steps to successful breastfeeding*, which summarize the maternity practices necessary to establish a supportive environment for women wishing to breastfeed, and thereby to bring about improvements in the incidence and duration of breastfeeding. Third, the Innocenti Declaration stated that the International Code of Marketing of Breastmilk Substitutes and subsequent relevant resolutions of the World Health Assembly had to be implemented. The aim of this Code is to contribute to the provision of safe and adequate nutrition for infants by the protecting and promoting breastfeeding, and by ensuring the proper use of breast milk substitutes, when necessary, on the basis of adequate information and through appropriate marketing and distribution (European Commission 2004a). The EU has adopted many provisions of the Code in its directive for the internal market of infant and follow-up formula (91/321/EEC) (European Commission 2003). Fourth, it is stated in the Innocenti Declaration that legislation to protect the breastfeeding rights of working women is necessary (European Commission 2004a).

Determinants of Breastfeeding

Many factors affect the choice of women to breastfeed their children and continue for a prolonged period. Some important examples of determinants and their potential positive and negative impact on breastfeeding are given in Table 10.3 (European Commission 2004a).

According to theories of planned behavior, the main determinants of breastfeeding are characterized by interrelationships between intentions, attitudes, and subjective norms, perceived behavioral control or self-efficacy, and environmental influences. Attitudes and social norms will be partly determined by socioeconomic status, as well as maternal education, on the advantages of breastfeeding. Self-efficacy will be influenced by practical skills in breastfeeding, the amount of milk available, and ready-on-hand breastmilk substitutes. Environmental influences include the opinions of family and friends, commercial pressure, traditional health care practices, and public health policies (WHO 2003; European Commission 2004a).

For working women, an important environmental influence is the paid employment and the workplace itself (WHO 2003). A relatively high proportion of employed females start breastfeeding compared with nonemployed females. Employed females quit relatively quickly, however, and the combination of work and breastfeeding is an important motive to stop (Nationaal Kompas Volksgezondheid 2005). For the protection of breastfeeding at the workplace, three factors seem to determine the decision to prolong breastfeeding practice: 1) longer maternity leave, 2) flexible working hours or part-time work, and 3) workplace breastfeeding

Table 10.3 Important examples of determinants of breastfeeding and their positive and negative impact

	Positive Association with Breastfeeding	Negative Association with Breastfeeding
Social and demographic determinants	Older age, high level of education of mother, small family	Younger age, lower level of education, single, urban, first child early return to work
Psychosocial determinants	Supportive family and peers, cultural acceptance, previous successful experience, positive maternal believes on breastfeeding and infant health	Low maternal confidence, shyness, mother not breastfed herself
Health care determinants and biomedical constraints	Early initiation of breastfeeding, prenatal class participation, skills training, apprenticeship	Premature birth, difficult labor, use of analgesics, sore nipples, maternity ward use of teats and bottles, ward distribution of free samples of breast milk substitutes
Community determinants	Consensus statements, media advocacy, workplace support, existence and acceptance of peer support groups, high level of community awareness and knowledge	Breastfeeding considered as indecent exposure, mis-beliefs, low level of community support and media advocacy
Public policies	Official recommendations, surveillance systems, maternity benefits including prolonged paid maternity leave, Baby Friendly Hospital Initiative (section 5), code of marketing of breast milk substitutes (section 5), inclusion in school curricula and in training staff	Short maternity leave, low priority of breastfeeding as a health concern, no supportive structure for breastfeeding issues

(EUROSTAT, 2005)

NOTE: European Commission, 2004b

or lactation breaks. Several specific workplace arrangements may also prolong the duration of breastfeeding among employed women. These include: 1) facilities for breastfeeding or lactation breaks (e.g., private accessible room with comfortable chair, hand washing facilities, fridge, access to electricity, and an electric pump to express and store breast milk), 2) paid time off during the working day, and 3) longer maternity leave (European Commission 2004a). In addition to flexibility within the job for lactation, and the presence of appropriate facilities, the social norm experienced at work is important (Nationaal Kompas Volksgezondheid 2005).

Support in the workplace, support through counseling on how to maintain lactation while working, and distribution of information kits in the workplace, increase both breastfeeding duration and exclusive breastfeeding rates.

Workplace Health Promotion Programs

Workplace health promotion programs should balance measures directed at ensuring safe working environments for pregnant women, described earlier, with measures that encourage breastfeeding after having given birth (in essence, taking into account the determinants described in the previous section). The benefits and disadvantages of specific advices and measures to promote breastfeeding should be considered. Barriers and facilitators of implementation of these proposed advices and interventions should be investigated to optimize the effectiveness of workplace health promotion programs.

Benefits and Disadvantages of Measures Promoting Breastfeeding to Health of Nursing Mother

Given the health benefits to both mother and child, workplace health promotion aimed at prolonging breastfeeding is warranted (see Table 10.1). It is of paramount importance, however, to pay attention to the concerns that may arise from potentially negative effects of mother's milk contaminated with hazardous agents. There is ample evidence that breastfeeding may expose infants to toxins such as PCBs and dioxins. These pollutants are quite common in the general environment with different exposure pathways, most notably through food. Because PCBs and dioxins are lipid-soluble compounds, they may be transferred from women to their infants through breast milk. There are indications that exposure to relatively high concentrations of PCBs and dioxins will result in neurodevelopmental effects, although most effects seem rather small (Vreugdenhill 2003). Although the presence of PCBs and dioxins has been of concern in the EU in the past decades, it is believed that their current presence does not warrant restrictions on breastfeeding because concentrations of dioxins in breast milk have decreased substantially in several European countries (Nationaal Kompas Volksgezondheid 2005).

In specific situations, mothers may be advised to refrain from breastfeeding, such as mothers with certain viruses (especially HIV), mothers under treatment with certain therapeutic drugs, or mothers with sensitivity to specific food allergens. Adequate screening and intervention, however, will prevent negative consequences for the infant (WHO 2003).

Workplace Health Promotion: Barriers and Facilitators

Health promotion programs aimed at initiating and prolonging breastfeeding are most effective when integrating several strategies and interventions. These programs are especially effective when they target initiation rates as well as duration and exclusivity of breastfeeding, using a combination of media campaigns, health education programs adapted to the local situation, comprehensive training of health professionals, and necessary changes in national, regional, and hospital policies. The effectiveness of these multifaceted programs seems to increase if peer counseling support is included, if interventions include the prenatal and postnatal periods—including the critical days around childbirth—and if information on breastfeeding is provided with extended face-to-face contact (European Commission 2004a).

The core of a workplace health promotion program should cover information for women, address the social norms among colleagues in companies with respect to breastfeeding, and address several important working arrangements, such as flexibility of working hours with (paid) lactation breaks and easy accessibility of facilities.

Several work-related barriers in the implementation of these programs may be encountered at both the company level and at the level of the employee. First, at the level of the individual employee, women need to be aware of the importance of breastfeeding and a sufficient duration of at least four months. There is evidence that further increase of duration of breastfeeding may have a positive impact on IQ development (Nationaal Kompas Volksgezondheid 2005). It has been shown that the use of printed material alone did not have an effect, and that information on the advantages on breastfeeding and required practical skills should be tailored to the individual characteristics of the woman. Some professionals have pointed out that the influence of health workers will be limited, because a woman's perceptions of infant feeding are often formed before they become pregnant or give birth (WHO 2003).

Second, at the level of the company, the experienced social norm with respect to breastfeeding is of importance. A positive social norm leads to a higher probability that breastfeeding will be continued. In addition, the continuation of breastfeeding implies (in most jobs) that employment is interrupted, which requires the approval and support of the employer. Approval and support of the employer is also needed to provide easily accessible facilities where women can express milk or breastfeed.

Implementation of Workplace Health Promotion at the Company Level

As stated in the previous section, health promotion programs in the workplace should focus on both personal health practices (individual), and the organization and the design of work (environment). According to the general model of Shain and Kramer [2004], several factors of success can be identified for the implementation of health promotion programs in the workplace. These characteristics most likely also apply to the promotion of breastfeeding in employed women. The factors of success include:

- Attention to the needs of individuals to set their own goals and approach them in a step-by-step incremental fashion, assessing the individuals' readiness to change. This refers to the principle of self-efficacy
- Attention to social support in planning and carrying out activities improving health outcome (e.g., support provided when a woman takes a lactation break, support through counseling on how to maintain lactation while working)
- Attention to the interactivity of health practices (e.g., the health promotion targeting pregnant women should be incorporated into general programs on creating a safe workplace and supporting a healthy lifestyle)
- The intervention should have a wide appeal, meeting the preferences, aptitudes, and requirements of a wide variety of women
- The intervention should be convenient and easily accessible
- Employees should participatie in the development of the program

In addition, two important environmental prerequisites are deemed essential—active management support, and a supportive management climate. Management support will usually include the provision of a physically safe working environment (e.g., for women providing breastfeeding), making some time available during working hours for health promotion activities (e.g., for taking lactation breaks), making resources available in the form of preferred health promotion programs in preferred modes of delivery (e.g., tailored advice given face-to-face or via the Internet on breastfeeding, fully equipped easily accessible lactation rooms), showing interest through requiring accountability from program coordinators on a regular basis, and providing a *family friendly* workplace through flexible work-time policies. A supportive management climate refers to the organization of work in ways that promote health and safety. This means keeping demands on time and energy within reasonable bounds, maximizing employee participation in the governance of their own work (including the maintenance of a physically safe environment), and providing adequate recognition and acknowledgement for the work done (Shain & Kramer 2004).

Developments in Workplace Health Promotion

It remains an interesting question whether the issues raised in the previous sections have been incorporated in campaigns where success has been shown in intervention studies. In the past few years several randomized controlled trials (RCT) have been conducted on the effectiveness of interventions to promote breastfeeding. Most trials have targeted women groups in general, and do not consider the workplace as a specific context. A comprehensive, systematic review of RCTs concluded that there was some evidence to suggest that health education and peer support can increase the initiation rates of breastfeeding (Fairbank et al. 2000). Another systematic review reported that professional support was effective in the duration of any breastfeeding, and that lay support was effective in promoting exclusive breastfeeding (Sikorski et al. 2002). Some trials, however, clearly show that effectiveness may be difficult to achieve in some settings. An RCT on peer support in a general practice in Scotland did not show any increase in breastfeeding (Muirhead et al. 2006), and another trial on a counseling session in the maternity ward of a Brasilian hospital did not improve the initiation rate or quality of breastfeeding techniques (Oliveira et al. 2006).

There is very limited evidence for the effectiveness of programs targeting working mothers. An illustrative example is an RCT with an intervention consisting of anticipatory counseling and monthly clinical follow-ups. This approach increased the proportion of infants exclusively fed with breastmilk at six months of life (53% vs 6%), and a key element in this success was the access to facilities to practice milk expression. Interestingly, all women in the intervention group stated that they would advise a friend to combine exclusive breastfeeding with work (Valdes et al. 2000).

A new development in workplace health promotion is the extensive use of the Internet to provide computer-tailored advice to individuals. Because the Internet is widely available in the EU, and computer-tailored advice has been found to be effective in other domains of health promotion, the use of the Internet may be a very promising approach. The international organization on breastfeeding, La Leche League International (LLL), helps mothers worldwide breastfeed through mother-to-mother support, encouragement, information, education, and a better understanding of breastfeeding. Its website offers information on breastfeeding, a mother-to-mother support forum, and the possibility of asking questions on breastfeeding (La Leche League International 2005).

Conclusions

Workplace health promotion that focuses on women breastfeeding their infant is of importance, because employment conditions may have an impact on the ability to start and continue breastfeeding.

Breastfeeding has clear health benefits to both mother and infant, but many women do not follow the recommendation of the WHO on breastfeeding for six months or more. Workplace interventions promoting breastfeeding could include information on the importance of breastfeeding to both mother and employer, improving social support at work for breastfeeding, introducing paid lactation breaks during working hours, and providing easy accessible lactation rooms. Because women often decide on breastfeeding before pregnancy, the early exposure to health promotion is important.

References

Commission of the European Communities (1992) Council Directive 92/85/EEC concerning the implementation of measures to encourage improvements in the safety and health of pregnant workers, women workers who have recently given birth and women who are breastfeeding. *Official Journal L*, 348, Vol. 28.11.1992

Commission of the European Communities (2000) *COM (2000)-466 Communication from the commision on the guidlines on the assessment of the chemical, physical, and biological agents and industrial processes considered hazardous for the safety and health of pregnant workers and workers who have recently given birth or are breastfeeding (Council Directive 92/85/EEC).* Brussels

European Commission (2003) EU project on promotion of breastfeeding in Europe. *Protection, promotion and support of breastfeeding in Europe: current situation.* Luxembourg: European commission, Directorate for Public Health. http://www.ilca.org/liasion/Current%20Situation%20PDF/Current%20English.pdf

European Commission (2004a) EU Project on Promotion of Breastfeeding in Europe. *Protection, promotion and support of breastfeeding in Europe: review of interventions.* Luxembourg: European Commission, Directorate Public Health and Risk Assessment, http://europa.eu.int/comm/health/ph_projects/2002/promotion/promotion _2002_18_en.htm

European Commission (2004b) EU Project on Promotion of Breastfeeding in Europe. *Protection, promotion and support of breastfeeding in Europe: a blueprint for action.* Luxembourg: European Commission, Directorate Public Health and Risk Assessment, http://www.iblce-europe.org/Download/Blueprint/Blueprint%20English.pdf

EUROSTAT (2005) http://epp.eurostat.cec.eu.int/portal/ (accessed Nov 2005)

Fairbank L, O'Meara S, Renfrew MJ, Woolridge M, Sowden AJ, Lister-Sharp D (2000) A systematic review to evaluate the effectiveness of interventions to promote the initiation of breastfeeding. *Health Technology Assessment,* 25, 1–171

HFA-DB (European Health for all database) (2005) http://data.euro.who.int/hfadb/ (accessed Nov 2005)

ILO (International Labour Organization) (2000) *Maternity Protection Convention C183.* Geneve: ILO, http://www.ilo.org/ilolex/cgi-lex/convde.pl?C183

La Leche League International (2005) *Happy mothers, breastfed babies.* http://www.lalecheleague.org. (accessed Nov 2005)

Muirhead PE, Butcher G, Rankin J, Munley A (2006) The effect of a programme of organised and supervised peer support on the initiation and duration of breastfeeding: a randomised trial. *British Journal of General Practice,* 56, 191–197

Nationaal Kompas Volksgezondheid (2005) http://www.rivm.nl/vtv/object_document/o4237n16906.html. (accessed Nov 2005)

Oliveira de LD, Giugliani ER, do Espirito Santo LC, Franca MC, Weigert EM, Kohler CV et al. (2006) Effect of intervention to improve breastfeeding technique on the frequency of exclusive breastfeeding and lactatioin-related problems. *Journal of Human Lactation,* 22, 315–321

Shain M, Kramer DM (2004) Health promotion in the workplace: framing the concept; reviewing the evidence. *Occupational and Environmental Medicine,* 61, 643–648

Sikorksi J, Renfrew MJ, Pindoria S, Wade A (2002) Support for breastfeeding mothers. *Cochrane Database of Systematic Reviews* 1, CD001141

Valdes V, Pugin E, Schooley J, Catalan S, Aravena R (2000) Clinical support can make the difference in exclusive breastfeeding success among working women. *Journal of Tropical Pediatrics,* 46, 149-154

Vreugdenhil H (2003) Neurodevelopmental effects of perinatal exposure to environmental levels of PCBs and dioxins in children at school age. Erasmus University, Rotterdam

WHO (World Health Organization) (2003) *Feeding and Nutrition of Infants and Young Children. Guidelines for the WHO European Region, with Emphasis on the Former Soviet Countries.* Copenhagen: WHO Regional Publications, European Series No. 87, http://www.euro.who.int/document/WS_115_2000FE.pdf

PART IV
LIFESTYLE DETERMINANTS

Chapter 11
Promoting Tobacco Awareness and Smoking Cessation for Working Women

Sherry Merkur

Introduction

This chapter will focus on workplace interventions for tobacco awareness and smoking cessation, with a particular focus on women. The first section of this chapter defines this public health problem; details the epidemiologic characteristics, socioeconomic impact, and future perspectives; and presents the institutional and legislative framework, including nonsmokers' rights, compliance with the law, health warnings, and smoking bans. The second section identifies the related risk factors, explaining why women tend to smoke, the population at risk, causal factors, and promoters, as well as preventable risk factors. Section three also looks at whether smoking is related to worksite factors, and how smoking may affect a woman's professional life. The role of working women as mothers, where they act as role models and convey healthy lifestyles to the family, is explored in the fourth section. The fifth section presents examples of prevention, such as best practice in promoting tobacco awareness and smoking cessation, avoidance of exposure, healthy lifestyles, and general guidelines. Available resources, including online and published material, is available in the sixth section. The chapter concludes with three case studies provided in Appendix 1.

Basic Concepts

Tobacco is the leading preventable cause of death in the world, with an estimated five million deaths per year, and is the fourth most common risk factor for disease worldwide (WHO 2006). Experience has shown that there are many cost-effective tobacco control measures that can be used in different settings and that can have a significant impact on tobacco consumption. According to the World Health Organization (WHO), the most cost-effective strategies are:

- Population-wide public policies—e.g., bans on direct and indirect tobacco advertising
- Tobacco taxes and price increases

A. Linos, W. Kirch (eds), *Promoting Health for Working Women.*
© Springer 2008

- Smoke-free environments in all public and workplaces
- Large, clear graphic health messages on tobacco packaging

In this chapter, we pay particular attention to the third strategy, as well as encouraging smoking cessation in the workplace.

Definition

There are over 4,000 chemicals in tobacco smoke. Quitting smoking is the single best thing one can do to improve his or her health and quality of life. The following diseases and medical conditions can be caused by smoking: lung cancer, chronic obstructive pulmonary disease (COPD), including emphysema, chronic bronchitis, eye problems, coronary heart disease, kidney cancer, stomach ulcers, aortic aneurysm, bladder cancer, impotence, and more.

Basic Epidemiologic Characteristics

The topic of smoking is relevant in every country. Statistics can be presented internationally, in Europe, or on a per-country basis.

Prevalence in the General Population

Tobacco is the second major cause of death in the world and is currently responsible for the death of one in ten adults worldwide, or about five million deaths each year. It is also the fourth most common risk factor for disease worldwide. If current smoking patterns continue, it will cause ten million deaths each year by 2020. Half the people that smoke today (about 650 million people) will eventually be killed by tobacco (WHO 2006).

A Special Eurobarometer survey showed a drop in smoking of European citizens, particularly in the United Kingdom, France, and Spain. On the other hand, Greeks, Cypriots, and Portuguese are the most enthusiastic smokers. Across the European Union (EU), only 27 percent of people in 2005 said they smoked, compared to 33 percent in 2002 when there were 15 EU countries[1] (DG Health and Consumer Protection 2006).

---

[1] The results of the survey carried out in 30 countries or territories in autumn 2005, including: Austria, Belgium, Bulgaria, Republic of Cyprus, Turkish Cypriot, Czech Republic, Denmark, Germany, Estonia, Spain, Greece, France, Hungary, Croatia, Ireland, Italy, Lithuania, Luxembourg, Latvia, Malta, Netherlands, Poland, Portugal, Romania, Slovenia, Slovakia, Finland, Sweden, Turkey, United Kingdom.

Frequency of Appearance Specifically in Women

In Europe overall, women (13.3 cigarettes a day) smoke less than men (16.2) and the level of their consumption has fallen more sharply than that of men. In fact, 57 percent of women state that they have never smoked compared with only 36 percent of men. Both women and young people smoke less and their consumption has fallen the most since 2002.

Women (45%) seem to be slightly more bothered than men (40%) by tobacco smoke in their daily life. The age of respondents, however, seems to be a significant factor in terms of difference in the reaction to tobacco smoke: the youngest respondents seem to be the most bothered by tobacco smoke in their daily life (53% in the 15-24 age group). Almost 95 percent of EU citizens seem to agree with the statement that smoking in the presence of a pregnant woman can be very dangerous for the baby (DG Health and Consumer Protection 2006). Unfortunately, society does not take the secondhand smoke exposure of babies and young children as seriously as tobacco use during pregnancy. This may be a reason why women resume smoking postpartum.

In Sweden, the Netherlands, and Belgium, only one citizen in five smokes cigarettes. A majority of Cypriots and Greeks smoke more than 20 cigarettes a day, while this percentage is less than 20 percent in Slovakia, Estonia, and Lithuania. Since 2002, the number of cigarettes per smoker per day has fallen in most countries, particularly in Belgium (-3.4), France (-2.2), and Luxembourg (-2.2) (DG Health and Consumer Protection 2006).

Examples for the United Kingdom:

- Around 25 percent of all adults in the United Kingdom smoke and most adult smokers want at some time to quit
- Most smokers start as teenagers, and the number of young girls taking up smoking is increasing
- It is becoming less socially acceptable to smoke and the number of adults is gradually going down
- Lung disease affects one person in seven, whether its mild asthma or lung cancer (British Lung Foundation 2006)
- Smoking kills 106,000 people in the United Kingdom every year and leads to unnecessary illness in many others ("The government" 2004).

Socioeconomic Impact and Future Perspectives

In Europe, unemployed people (45%) and manual workers (38%) have noticeably higher levels of tobacco consumption than the other socioprofessional categories (DG Health and Consumer Protection 2006). In addition to the high public health costs of treating tobacco-caused diseases, tobacco kills people at the height of their productivity, depriving families of breadwinners and nations of a healthy workforce. Tobacco users are also less productive while they are alive due to increased sickness.

A 1994 report estimated that the use of tobacco has resulted in an annual global net loss of US$200 billion, with two-thirds of this loss realized in developed countries (WHO 2006).

Institutional and Legislative Framework

This section will focus on nonsmokers' rights, compliance with the law, health warnings, and smoking bans.

Nonsmokers' Rights

There is a conflict between what some regard as the right to smoke, and what others regard as a right to clean air. This is an ethical judgment, but where there is a conflict, the right to clean air should come first. To uphold these rights, however, employers do have to actively manage smoking in the workplace. For some individuals, such as those with asthma or respiratory illnesses, a smoky workplace may actually be a barrier to their employment. A good smoking policy will uphold the employment rights of people who are particularly affected by smoke.

Compliance with the Law

In many jurisdictions, employers will have general duties to protect their staff and provide an environment suitable for them to undertake their contractual duties. If an employer does everything reasonable and practical to reduce employees' exposure to second-hand smoke, then the risks of litigation or employment disputes will be greatly reduced or eliminated. There may also be legislation concerning health, safety, and welfare in the workplace. Such laws may assign broad duties to employers. By having a good smoking policy, an employer can ensure compliance with any relevant legislation.

Health Warnings

Health warnings on tobacco packs have long been a method for informing smokers of the health risks associated with smoking. In 1991, 77 countries required some kind of health warning on tobacco products (World Bank 1999). The use of health warnings in European countries varied until an EEC labeling directive came into force in January 1992. This stated that all tobacco products should carry specified warnings but only required the warning to cover 4 to 8 percent of the pack.

Outside Europe, countries such as Canada and Australia have been making progress on the size and impact of health warnings. As early as 1985, Australian legislation required health warnings to take up 15 percent of a cigarette pack, while by 1994, 33 percent of the surface of all cigarette packs in Canada had to contain of a health warning (The ASPECT Consortium 2004).

The EU followed suit in its Directive 2001/37/EC (the *Labeling Directive*),[2] which stipulated that health warnings should cover 30 percent of the front and 40 percent of the back of tobacco packs, and be surrounded by a black border. The directive prescribed which health warnings had to be used: one of two general warnings on the front and one of fourteen more specific warnings on the back, with all of the warnings to be used regularly. It also carried a commitment that the European Commission would subsequently adopt rules for the use of color photographs or other illustrations to depict and explain the health consequences of smoking.

Since then, picture warnings have been introduced in Australia, Brazil, Canada, Singapore, and Thailand. European Commission Decisions containing rules on picture warnings and an image library of warnings were published in September 2003 and May 2005. The European Commission has developed 42 picture health warnings for countries in the European Union to use on tobacco packs. A public consultation in the United Kingdom was launched to address the picture warnings legislation that will apply to England, Scotland, Wales, and Northern Ireland. The consultation ran from May 27 to August 25, 2006 (see Department of Health 2006 for the new picture warnings).

Smoking Bans

A growing number of countries and regions around the world have implemented new smoking restrictions. Since 1998, several U.S. states and cities, including California and New York have restricted smoking in public places. In January 2004, the Netherlands banned smoking in many public places, while Norway imposed a national ban in restaurants, bars, and cafes in June 2004. Partial or total smoking bans in enclosed public places have been implemented in 2004 or 2005 in Ireland, Italy, Malta, and Sweden. In Spain, tobacco use fell by 12 percent in the month after a ban on smoking in public (apart from bars) was implemented in January 2006. In England, smoking is banned in all enclosed public spaces, including pubs, restaurants, offices and public transport beginning in the summer of 2007. Wales also announced a similar ban earlier that year. It is interesting to note that studies in Canada, the United States, and Australia report that smoke-free bylaws do not adversely affect restaurant and bar sales ("England to ban Smoking" 2006).

Risk Factors

Women tend to smoke for somewhat different reasons than men. They smoke as a coping strategy for feelings of stress and lack of control over their lives; as part of a daily routine to take a break from work and care-giving activities; as time to

---

[2] Directive 2001/37/EC of the European Parliament and of the Council of 5 June 2001 on the approximation of the laws, regulations and administrative provisions of the Member States concerning the manufacture, presentation and sale of tobacco products.

share intimacies with partners or friends; or in attempt to control negative emotions. Images of smoking as *cool* and a way to prevent weight gain have influenced many female teens and young girls who smoke. Many older women face barriers to quitting, including fear of weight gain, lack of confidence and lack of support, to overcome this addiction. Moreover, weight concerns are a major reason why women resume smoking in the postpartum period after having successfully quit during pregnancy (Levine et al. 2006).

Women are more likely than men to be employed in workplaces where there are few smoking restrictions. Small firms and service sector workplaces (e.g., food and beverage, hairdressing, and child care), where women are more likely to be employed, are less likely to have smoking policies than larger workplaces. Moreover, women in low-status jobs with little control over decision-making, and women with high effort-reward imbalance, are more likely to be smokers (Kouvonen et al. 2005). When workplace smoking is restricted, the desire to smoke and the actual amount smoked declines, and women become more interested in cessation.

Factors often associated with high smoking prevalence include unemployment, low-income or service-sector jobs, single-parent status, low levels of education, isolation and lack of social support, dual responsibilities of work and family, family violence, stress, and low self-esteem (Women's Health Bureau 1995). Women with multiple disadvantages or other addictions are more likely to smoke. Although social disadvantage affects men's smoking as well, the specific experiences of disadvantage often differ by gender—e.g., women are more likely to be low-income single parents or informal caregivers. These differences and the different types of stresses they entail need to be recognized in programming.

Many smokers believe that smoking is relaxing, but recent research indicates that smoking tends to increase a young woman's stress level rather than reducing it (Johnson et al. 2000). One reason is that smoking can impair respiration, which can contribute to panic attacks. Nicotine itself increases feelings of anxiety, but can trick the smoker into believing that smoking is relaxing. In fact, addiction to nicotine causes stress, which is then alleviated by smoking. Although anxiety temporarily increases when an individual stops smoking, a few weeks later her anxiety level will be lower than it was when she was smoking.

Women should be encouraged to quit smoking and respond to stress with healthy coping strategies. Healthier coping strategies include relaxation, physical exercise, communication, and social support. To manage stress effectively, a combination of these strategies is a good approach.

Smoking and the Workplace

Smoking and its Relationship to Worksite Factors

Exposure to other people's tobacco smoke causes a range of impacts from fatal or serious conditions, to irritation, sore eyes and throat, distraction, and smelly hair and clothes. Even though the latter are *minor* conditions, they may reduce productivity and create resentment among nonsmokers. At present, employers work to provide good working temperatures, adequate lighting, comfortable workstations, etc. The provision of clean air is a logical extension of any concern to improve working conditions.

The opportunity for employers to reduce the negative impact of smoking has never been greater, particularly as legislation on smoking in public places is being passed in many European countries (see more on smoking bans in the section on smoking bans). Awareness is growing of the costs to business of smoking, and of the health impact of second-hand tobacco smoke. In many EU member states, both large and small employers have access to smoking cessation services and advice on workplace smoking policies.

Providing a smoke-free working environment and restricting smoking breaks have been shown to (Faculty of Public Health & Faculty of Occupational Medicine 2006):

- Reduce the number of smokers within a workplace
- Help prevent relapses to smoking after a successful cessation attempt
- Reduce the number of cigarettes smoked by existing smokers during work time

Effects of Smoking on a Woman's Professional Life

Smoking Affects your Health

Quitting smoking is the single best thing you can do to improve your health and quality of life. Nonsmokers have a much lower risk of getting dozens of smoking-related diseases, such as lung cancer, heart disease, and COPD (including emphysema). The sooner you quit smoking, the less likely it is that your lungs and other organs will be damaged. Symptoms such as coughing can get better within days or weeks. If COPD has started to develop, quitting smoking will prevent further damage. Continuing to smoke causes a steady increase in shortness of breath. This limits your activity and increases the risks of lung and heart failure. It is never too late to think about quitting.

The risk of lung cancer increases the more you smoke, and the longer you smoke. Once you quit, the risk of lung cancer starts to go down. After ten years off cigarettes, the risk is halved compared to the risk if you had continued smoking. While some people go through life unaffected by smoking, millions do not. Too many people think "it will never happen to me," until they develop cancer or have their first heart attack.

Smoking Affects How you Look and Feel

Smoking also can harm a woman's appearance and mental health. Smokers have more facial wrinkles, gum disease, dental decay, and halitosis (bad breath). The

U.S. Surgeon General's Report (Office of the Surgeon General 2001), concluded that smokers are more likely to be depressed than nonsmokers, and that women with anxiety disorders are more likely to smoke.

Smoking and the Two-Fold Role of Working Women

Mothers as Role Models

Children brought up in nonsmoking homes are much less likely to take up smoking (British Lung Foundation 2006). Furthermore, both prenatal maternal smoking and children's exposure to secondhand smoke has been shown to decrease lung growth and increase rates of respiratory tract infections, otitis media, and childhood asthma—with increasing exposure leading to increasing severity (DiFranza et al. 2004). The harm that secondhand smoke does to children's lung development may result in respiratory symptoms and poorer lung function in adulthood (Svanes et al. 2004). The risk of sudden death in young children is also increased when their parents smoke. Furthermore, there is an increased risk of lung cancer in nonsmokers who are in close contact with smokers for a long time (Office of Surgeon General, 2001).

Passive smokers inhale the smoke breathed in and out by smokers. They also breathe in the smoke from the burning tips of cigarettes. This sidestream smoke contains more of the harmful chemicals than the mainstream smoke that has passed through the cigarette filter. Passive smoking often troubles nonsmokers, particularly if they have asthma or other lung problems.

Conveying Healthy Lifestyles in the Family

The costs of smoking are high, and well beyond the cost of purchasing cigarettes. Some of the less obvious costs—including physical, social and emotional—are detailed below.

Financial Costs

- At 2006 prices, a 20-a-day smoker (in the United Kingdom) will spend £31,025 over the next 20 years
- The cost of cigarettes could be spent on other things—holidays, savings, buying a home, or car, things for the children
- Smoking calculators can be accessed online to show smokers how much smoking is costing them financially (Department of Health 2007)
- There are also enormous indirect costs due to lost productivity from smoking-related illness (Rasmussen et al. 2004)

Physical Costs

- Wheezing, shortness of breath
- Lack of energy, poor concentration
- Dull skin, nicotine-stained fingers, premature wrinkling
- Reduced fertility, risky pregnancy, baby at risk
- Damaged taste buds, stained teeth
- Lung cancer, emphysema, stroke, heart attack, more health problems
- Damaged circulation, gangrene, amputation

Social Costs

- Polluting the air with carcinogens
- Children at higher risk of asthma, cot-death, and bronchitis
- Smoke gets in your eyes
- Dusty, stuffy home, nicotine-stained walls
- Spoiled clothes and furniture
- Increased risk of fire in the home

Emotional Costs

- Being a turn-off to potential partners and the possibility of missing out on relationships
- Feeling a slave to cigarettes
- Ever present, nagging sense of guilt that you should quit
- Disapproval and dislike, increasing pressure from a society that does not want to be subjected to smoke

Further Arguments in Favor of Smoking Cessation

Table 11.1 lists some good things that happen to your body once you stop smoking.

Workplace Considerations for the Family

Pregnant Women

Protecting pregnant workers from second-hand smoke, and encouraging pregnant women to stop smoking and remain nonsmokers after pregnancy should be a key objective for workplaces. Smoking during pregnancy is associated with significant medical complications for both mother and baby (British Medical Association 2004).

Table 11.1 The positive effects of quitting smoking

Within 8 hours	the carbon monoxide level drops in your body
	oxygen level in your blood increases to normal
Within 48 hours	your chances of having a heart attack start to go down
	your sense of smell and taste begin to improve
Within 72 hours	your bronchial tubes relax and make breathing easier
	your lung capacity increases
Within 2 weeks to 3 months	your blood circulation improves
	your lung functioning increases up to 30%
Within 6 months	your coughing, stuffy nose, tiredness and shortness of breath improve
Within 1 year	your risk of smokingrelated heart attack is cut in half
Within 10 years	your risk of dying from lung cancer is cut in half
Within 15 years	your risk of dying from a heart attack is the same as a person who never smoked
Other good reasons to quit	you'll set a good example for your children
	your smoking will no longer affect the health of people around you
	you'll have more money to save or to spend on other things
	you'll have more energy to do the things you love
	you'll pay lower life insurance premiums
	cigarettes will no longer control your life

Source: Tobacco Control Program, 2003

Children

Children are at particular risk from exposure to tobacco smoke, and workplaces that admit children have a particular responsibility to ensure that a smoke-free environment is maintained.

Prevention

This section will focus on examples of best practice, the stages of change model, five steps to help you quit, overcoming possible disadvantages, and organizational changes necessary to promote smoking cessation.

Examples of Best Practice

A combined plan of pharmacotherapy (such as nicotine or bupropion) with advice and behavioral support is the most effective method of helping smokers quit. In fact, the effects multiply rather than add together.

It is recommended that all health professionals should give simple brief advice regularly to all smokers whom they come across (Coleman 2004). Brief advice is defined as "verbal instructions to stop smoking with or without added information about the harmful effects of smoking" (Cochrane Tobacco Addiction Group 2006). A couple of minutes are necessary for effective brief advice to be delivered in routine consultations, which has been shown to achieve cessation in about 1 in 40 smokers, and is probably the most cost-effective clinical intervention. More intensive interventions, longer initial consultation time, inclusion of additional methods of reinforcing advice (such as self-help manuals, videos, and showing smokers' their exhaled carbon monoxide levels) and follow-up can increase success rates by about 1.4-fold.

Behavioral support can involve reviewing a patient's smoking history, their motivation to quit, recognizing situations where they may have a high risk of relapse, and developing problem-based strategies for dealing with these situations. Intensive behavioral support from appropriately trained smoking cessation counselors outside routine clinical care is the most effective nonpharmacological intervention. Individual counseling for smokers who are strongly motivated to quit has been shown to achieve cessation in about 1 in 13 smokers.

Nicotine replacement is the most common drug treatment to help smoking cessation, and increases the chances of quitting by about 1.7-fold (Srivastava, Currie & Britton 2006). Nicotine replacement therapy (NTR) is available in many different forms—gum, inhalator, nasal spray, lozenges, and transdermal patches—that deliver a lower total dose and deliver it to the brain more slowly than does a cigarette.

Bupropion is of similar efficacy as NRT in improving smoking cessation rates. It is an antidepressant, but its effect on smoking cessation seems to be independent of this property. Bupropion should be started one or two weeks before the quit date. There is no clear evidence that combining bupropion with nicotine replacement further improves quit rates, and it can lead to hypertension and insomnia (Srivastava, Currie & Britton 2006).

The effectiveness of workplace smoking cessation policies has been estimated at 20 to 30 percent (Katz & Showstack 1990), although this will depend upon many variables—e.g. the population being targeted, the smoking prevalence amongst this population, and the particular policy in question.

"Help 2 Quit" is a primary care intervention towards smoking cessation, where physicians try to identify each smoker's level of motivation for trying to quit. The primary objective of this method is to offer support to patients who are ready to quit and improve their chances of success (Coleman 2004). This method utilizes a simplified version of the *Stages of Change* model (see next section) to tailor the intervention to the smoker.

Applying the Stages of Change Model

Applying the *Stages of Change* model can increase the confidence and skills of women who are in the process of quitting smoking. This model views smoking cessation as a process rather than a single event. The model acknowledges the frequency with which relapse can occur in any of the stages, and that relapse needs to be seen as a natural occurrence that is to be expected when a smoker is trying to quit. The model identifies five stages of behavior change as a smoker gets ready to quit. These are:

1. Not thinking about quitting
2. Thinking about and deciding to quit
3. Getting ready to quit
4. Quitting
5. Remaining a nonsmoker

The *Stages of Change* model has many definitions of success within a program. Success can be defined as moving from one stage to another, becoming more aware of individual reasons for, and patterns of, smoking, and making a change in one's smoking behavior. Thus, the recognition of multiple definitions of success is an important part of woman-centered programming (see section on woman-centered programming).

An important outcome of expanding the use of cessation programs based on the *Stages of Change* model is that it makes the programs more attractive to a broader range of smokers. Support is no longer just for smokers who feel ready to quit soon, but it is also available for smokers who would just like to talk about smoking before making any decisions. Allowing for multiple definitions of success, according to each woman's degree of readiness or stage of change, can foster a sense of success as women achieve goals that are realistic for them. Creating feelings of success along the way contributes to confidence and self-esteem.

Five Steps to Help you Quit

It is generally a good idea to get ready to quit and fix a quit date, rather than gradually reducing your smoking. Tell people around you that you are going to quit, and try to get others at home or work to quit with you. This support network makes it easier when temptation arises. To help break the mental addiction to smoking, learn new skills and change your daily routine and habits to eliminate some of your smoking triggers. Avoid specific places or people with whom you are more likely to smoke. One concern for smokers is weight gain—smoking suppresses your appetite, so you can avoid gaining weight if you are aware of this and if you exercise and eat healthily. One idea is to have alternatives to smoking available, such as peppermints or carrot sticks. Furthermore, you may wish to discuss different medicines with your general practitioner. If you relapse, do not be too discouraged, because very few people quit successfully the first time. Instead, try to learn something about the methods that do and do not work for you. Also, be advised that people who switch from cigarettes to pipes or cigars gain very little benefit in terms of improved health—it is better to quit completely.

Research has shown that the five steps summarized below will help you quit for good (Patient pages 2003):

1. Get ready
2. Get support

3. Learn new skills and behaviors
4. Get medication and use it correctly
5. Be prepared for relapses or difficult situations

Overcoming Possible Disadvantages

Quitting smoking can be very difficult, but many smokers find it easier than expected. Many doctors, hospitals, and health authorities run support groups and courses to help. It should be recognized that many smokers would like to quit, and that smoking is driven primarily by addiction to nicotine. Most smokers are addicted to the nicotine in cigarettes and may have withdrawal symptoms, such as craving, irritability, depression, and loss of concentration. The severity of withdrawal symptoms can be reduced by using NRT. These can provide *clean* nicotine, and are much safer than smoking cigarettes. They should be used for about six weeks and then stopped, and are available from local pharmacists or by prescription from a general practitioner. Clinical trials have shown that using a nicotine replacement nearly doubles the chance of successfully stopping smoking (Nordenberg 1997).

New drugs are now available that help reduce the withdrawal symptoms of quitting. These are only available through prescription from a general practitioner, who may also advise that they be used alongside smoking cessation services. Despite the difficulties, more smokers are managing to stop every day. It can be done, and individuals will find very definite benefits in their health and quality of life.

A workplace smoking policy could include support for smokers who wish to quit by providing counseling and proven therapeutic products, such as NRT or drugs that aid smoking cessation.

Organizational Changes Necessary to Promote Smoking Cessation

Important Steps an Employer can Take

Develop a smoke-free policy in the workplace that applies to everyone. Put together a group of appropriate people, including employee representatives, to develop the policy. Ensure appropriate consultation with employees and unions, and the commitment of senior management (see section on creating a workplace smoking policy). Here are some guidelines for employers who wish to set up a smoke-free policy in the workplace:

- Give reasonable notice of the introduction of a smoke-free policy and set a date for your organization to become smoke-free
- Ensure that every employee is informed of the smoke-free policy and its implications, and include the policy in all recruitment and induction packets

- Find out what help or support is available from your local smoking cessation service and advertise it to employees
- If you have any designated smoking areas, make sure they are effectively screened so that smoke does not adversely affect other employees at work

Diversity with Workplace Smoking Policies

It is important to address the issue of smoking in the workplace in a professional and effective manner. The purpose of a smoking policy is to outline this practice. The main purpose will be to ensure that all parties (e.g., employers, employees, the public) have a clear understanding of their rights and obligations, that the workplace complies with relevant legislation, and that the employer handles this often controversial issue in a way that minimizes the negative impact of tobacco use on the business.

It is important to recognize that workplaces are diverse, including factories, offices, shops, public and government buildings, schools, bars, restaurants, prisons, hospitals and residential care, public transportation, and many others. Therefore, no single workplace smoking policy will accommodate all circumstances. In many cases, a complete ban on smoking will be possible and preferred—in others, an employer may choose to allow a smoking room. In some circumstances (where the law allows), smoking may continue, but measures can be taken to reduce employee exposure, such as banning smoking around a bar, or having improved ventilation in a restaurant (Action on Smoking and Health 2006).

Avoidance of Exposure to Risk Factors

This section will focus on creating a workplace smoking policy and opinions of smoking bans at work and elsewhere.

Creating a Workplace Smoking Policy

A workplace smoking policy should be designed to minimize, and if possible eliminate, exposure of employees and visitors to second-hand smoke. The policy should make allowance for the needs of smokers, while still achieving the primary objective. (Steps 1-6 are taken from Health Promotion Unit 2006).

Step 1: Preparation

1. The issue should be treated as a health and safety matter by stressing the positive rather than negative aspects.
2. Be informed by gathering as much information as possible on health risks and how other companies have dealt with the issue.

3. Assess the views of the workforce and ensure that employees are involved in how the policy is planned and implemented.
4. Prevent divisions in the workforce by ensuring that action on smoking is not seen as action against smokers.

Step 2: Consultation

Employers should consult with employees and their representatives to determine attitudes and views on how the policy should be structured. As the policy is developed, employees and their representatives should be further consulted. In larger workplaces, it may be useful to establish a smoking committee to collect and distribute information, and discuss, define and administer the policy. If a committee is established, it should include smokers, nonsmokers, employee representatives, and management. If it is not appropriate to set up a committee, then a person should be given responsibility for devising and implementing the policy. The manner and timing of the introduction of the policy should be discussed as part of the consultation process.

The recommended consultation steps of the committee (or person with responsibility) are:

1. Gathering of employee views by questionnaire or direct consultation with individuals, groups, or representatives. This will indicate employee attitudes towards smoking and preferences for the type of smoking policy. It will also ensure that employees are consulted and involved in the policy from an early stage. It is important that employees who may have specific problems with the policy are consulted, including asthmatics and heavy smokers.
2. Devise recommendations based on Step 1.
3. Recommendations sent to management for formulation of policy.

Step 3: Devising the Policy

The objective of a smoking policy is to establish a healthy environment for all employees. Supporting this goal is the general principle that the preference of both smokers and nonsmokers will be respected, but when these conflict, the preferences of the nonsmoker will prevail. The policy should be clear and inform both existing and new employees of why the action is being taken; how it is to be implemented, how it is to be reviewed, and what the penalties are for not obeying the policy.

When devising a smoking policy, the following issues should be considered:

1. Decide on the type of smoking policy to be introduced. Options include:

- Smoking bans in certain areas (e.g., factory floor, shared offices, meeting rooms, training rooms, corridors, lifts, canteens, reception areas, etc.)
- Partial smoking bans based on providing designated areas for smoking, or restricting smoking to certain times and certain areas

- Control of smoking in certain activities (e.g., smoking breaks for meetings and training courses)
- Provision for local agreement on smoking (e.g., all agree to allow smoking at a meeting)—a veto by an individual should be accepted
- Special provision for vulnerable persons (asthmatics or others with respiratory problems)
- A total ban on smoking

2. A complaint procedure for problems experienced with the policy by smokers or nonsmokers
3. A statement of the disciplinary policy governing breaches of the company policy on smoking
4. Appointment of a person with responsibility for advising and possibly arbitrating the details of the policy
5. A statement of the extent to which smoking may be banned for fire safety, hygiene, legal, or product image reasons
6. Adaptation of the workplace—e.g., ventilation of certain areas to minimize smoke nuisance

Step 4: Implementation

1. Timing—The development of the policy, including the assessment of employees' views, would typically take 12 weeks in a medium to large enterprise. A realistic period of time should be allowed for people to become accustomed to the new policy before the implementation date. This will also allow time to solve any *teething* problems that may arise. A reasonable time period would be 3 months to cater for smokers who may need to adjust their smoking pattern. Take advantage of any moves or redecoration of premises when setting the date. A decision needs to be made as to whether the policy is to be implemented in full from a certain date, or whether it is to be phased in.
2. The policy must be implemented evenly throughout the organization. A policy that is not implemented evenly is unlikely to succeed, because it will be perceived as being unfair.
3. Briefing employees—All personnel should be briefed on the policy and be given a copy of it. A two-way flow of information should be encouraged to facilitate monitoring. It is also important to ensure that smokers and nonsmokers both know where smoking is and is not permitted. If there is not going to be a complete ban on smoking, the provision of adequate facilities for smokers will also enhance the chances of the success of the policy.
4. It is often helpful to introduce a smoking policy in the light of an overall healthy lifestyle program rather than just dealing with smoking alone.
5. Because the introduction of a smoking policy may require smokers to change their smoking habits, consideration should also be given to providing services to help smokers who want to give up the habit. This may not only enhance the chances of the success of the policy, it may also result in more of the individuals in the organization becoming nonsmokers.

Step 5: Enforcement

To a large extent, smoking policies are enforced through self-enforcement by employees. The procedures to follow when breaches of the rules occur, however, should be clearly outlined in the policy. The normal company disciplinary procedures could be used.

Step 6: Evaluation

It is necessary to review the operation of the policy to ensure its continued success. The review should take place 6 to 12 months after the full introduction of the policy. It is a good idea to appoint a person specifically to monitor its effectiveness and encourage feedback from employees. This person could also be authorized to advise and arbitrate on the policy. Awkward problems should be referred to a meeting of the Smoking Policy Committee when one exists.

Please refer to Appendix 1 for examples of workplace experiences.

Opinions of Smoking Bans at Work and Elsewhere

Most Europeans are in favor of public bans on smoking. Four out of five EU citizens think smoking should be forbidden in offices, shops, and other indoor public spaces. The percentage of respondents to the Special Eurobarometer survey (DG Health and Consumer Protection 2006) who were totally or somewhat in favor of a ban were as follows:

- Office or indoor workplaces—86 percent
- Any indoor public space—84 percent
- Restaurants—77 percent
- Bars or pubs—61 percent

A strong majority of smokers in many European countries are in favor of banning smoking in offices and other indoor workplaces. Three-quarters of smokers and more than 90 percent of nonsmokers are in favor of banning smoking in offices and other indoor workplaces (see Fig. 11.1 for results by country).

Developing and Preserving Healthy Lifestyles

This section will focus on the benefits of workplace smoking policies and better health.

Benefits of Workplace Smoking Policies

Employers that introduce a smoking policy will have to address some of the consequences of employing smokers, such as increased absenteeism—smokers tend to

Q8.3 Are you in favour of smoking bans in the following places?
Answer: Offices, and other indoor workplaces

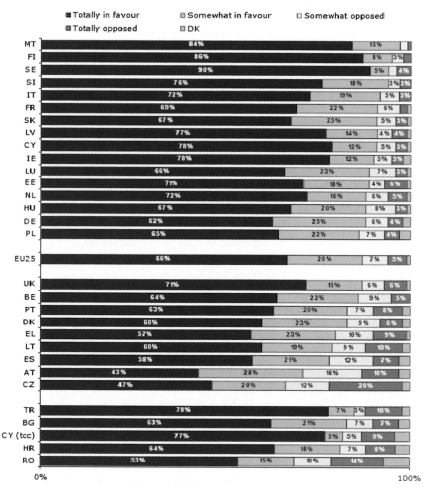

Fig. 11.1 Relevant results of the Special Eurobarometer Survey
Note: AT Austria, BE Belgium, BG Bulgaria, CY Republic of Cyprus, CY(tcc) Turkish Cypriot,
CZ Czech Republic, DK Denmark, DE Germany, EE Estonia, ES Spain, EL Greece, FR France,
HU Hungary, HR Croatia, IE Ireland, IT Italy, LT Lithuania, LU Luxembourg, LV Latvia, MT
Malta, NL Netherlands, PL Poland, PT Portugal, RO Romania, SI Slovenia, SK Slovakia, FI Fin-
land, SE Sweden, TR Turkey, UK United Kingdom.
Source: DG Health and Consumer Protection, 2006

be absent from work 33 to 45 percent more than nonsmokers (Royal College of
Physicians 1983)—decreased productivity, and increased life insurance. Employers
will also be in control of other costs such as cleaning and redecorating, providing
smoking rooms, fire risks, litigation risks, and insurance costs. The employer will
also have a means of controlling conflicts arising from smoking and be able to attract
new staff who increasingly expect no-smoking environments.

Better Health

Second-hand smoke is a toxic indoor air pollutant associated with a number of ill-nesses in those exposed. Among other health complications, these include:

- *A greatly increased risk of heart disease*—The increased heart disease risk for passive smoking is thought to be about one quarter that faced by an active smoker, even though exposure to cigarette smoke is only about 1 percent that of an active smoker
- *Lung cancer resulting from prolonged exposure*—A nonsmoker regularly exposed to second-hand smoke has a 20 to 30 percent increased risk of lung cancer compared to a nonsmoker that is not exposed to second-hand smoke. For nonsmokers who have been highly exposed to second-hand smoke at work, there is approximately a 100 percent increase in lung cancer risk (Stayner et al. 2007)
- *Aggravation of asthma*—Secondhand smoke can trigger asthma attacks or make these worse.
- *Chronic respiratory ailments*—Increased coughing, wheezing and phlegm, and aggravation of existing respiratory complaints
- *Ailments in children*—otitis media, more severe asthma, more acute respiratory infections, and impaired lung development

General Guidelines on Tobacco Smoking for Working Women

This section will focus on woman-centered approaches to tobacco awareness, as well as the role of feelings, social support, and adult education principles for women trying to quit smoking.

Woman-centered Approaches to Tobacco Awareness

Woman-centered approaches to tobacco awareness view women as experts on their own lives, recognize that individual *lifestyle* behaviors occur within a broader social context, address life stresses and barriers to change, allow for a range of success-ful outcomes depending on women's present needs and goals, integrate tobacco reduction with other concerns in women's lives, and recognize the importance many women place on social support (Kinnon & Hanvey 1995). A woman-centered approach also recognizes the barriers that women experience in making changes and addresses these barriers to ensure that programs are accessible to women.

Confidence, Control and Self-worth and Their Role in Cessation

Although feelings of confidence, control, and self-worth are important to anyone trying to quit smoking, such feelings may be especially important to women in dis-advantaged circumstances that often feel a lack control over their lives and may view smoking as something that is within their control. Smoking may provide them with feelings of independence and choice. When women decide that they can gain more control over their life by quitting smoking, but are then unable to reach that goal, their failed cessation attempts can undermine feelings of control and self-esteem. For women to change their smoking behavior, they must feel confident that they can achieve success and feel in control.

As a consequence, programs that allow for a range of goals, such as cutting back on the amount smoked, gaining the skills to be able to quit or quitting completely, and programs that tailor interventions to the circumstances of women, allow them to build feelings of confidence and self-worth as they experience success on their own terms. An evaluation by Holmberg-Schwartz (1997) found that the more confident women were about not smoking in a variety of situations, the fewer cigarettes they smoked per day. There is some evidence that women perceive more barriers associated with quitting, anticipate more negative consequences of quitting, and interpret their unsuccessful quitting attempts more harshly than men (Women's Health Bureau 1995).

The Role of Social Support for Women Who Try to Quit Smoking

Women appear to prefer a greater degree of social support when quitting than men. This support can take a number of forms, including group-based cessation programs. Group programs may be especially valuable when led by peers with previous smoking experience. Such groups allow women to benefit from others' experiences, share support and practical solutions, and build support networks.

Not all women wish to join group programs. Some prefer individual assistance from a health professional. Advice from health professionals, however, can be a barrier to cessation if it is delivered in an insensitive or judgmental way. Some women quit on their own, but desire the support of a partner, family, or friends. For example, women most likely to quit smoking are those with a nonsmoking partner or those who receive positive support from their partner (McBride 1998). Thus, support for smoking cessation programs directed at women entail making both group programs and individualized assistance accessible. In this context, accessibility means addressing financial, situational, physical, educational ,and emotional barriers.

Women's View of Adult Education Principles

The principles of personal empowerment and adult education may be useful in drawing out women's own beliefs and solutions. Messages to promote increased awareness of the negative consequences of smoking may be best achieved by asking women what they believe to be the drawbacks of smoking. By asking women what they could do for themselves to improve their health, they may raise the issue of quitting smoking on their own, rather than having a health professional impose it on them.

When smoking is addressed as part of routine service delivery, rather than being singled out as a problem, advice about quitting may be more acceptable. Moreover, messages encouraging women to quit smoking should not make women feel guilty or ashamed, because these strategies decrease self-esteem. Although some smokers may find negative messages motivating, positive messages might be more effective in reaching the smokers who are more resistant to change, such as those who have not begun to seriously consider quitting. These messages, combined with participatory adult education approaches, form a positive strategy for smoking reduction.

Available Resources

Useful Links and Websites with Educational Material

The increased attention to the special risks of smoking for women has resulted in a number of projects that focus on supporting tobacco cessation efforts specifically for women. These are marked below with **.

International Organizations

- **World Health Organization Tobacco Free Initiative (TFI)**
  (http://www.who.int/tobacco/en/)
  The Tobacco Free Initiative was established in July 1998 to focus international attention, resources, and action on the global tobacco epidemic. TFI's objective is to reduce the global burden of disease and death caused by tobacco, thereby protecting present and future generations from the devastating health, social, environmental, and economic consequences of tobacco consumption and exposure to tobacco smoke.
- **Tobacco.org**
  (http://www.tobacco.org/)
  Tobacco.org is a free international resource center that focuses on tobacco and smoking issues. It features tobacco news, information, assistance for smokers trying to quit, alerts on tobacco control issues, and more.

National Organizations (United Kingdom)

- **Smokefree** (http://www.gosmokefree.co.uk/)
  English National Health Service online resource.
  **Smoking and Pregnancy page:
  (http://www.gosmokefree.co.uk/whygosmokefree/smokingpregnancy/)

  Action on Smoking and Health
  (http://www.ash.org.uk/)
  Action on Smoking and Health (ASH) is a campaigning public health charity working to eliminate the harm caused by tobacco. They aim to be innovative and agenda setting with evidence-based policies, are committed to the efficient and effective use of resources, and work collaboratively with others to pursue their vision of a world free from the harm caused by tobacco.

British Lung Foundation
(http://www.britishlungfoundation.org)
The British Lung Foundation (BLF) supports people affected by lung disease through the individual challenges they face. Support is the focus of many activities, including the nationwide network of Breathe Easy patient support groups and Baby Breathe Easy parent support groups. They help people to understand their condition by providing comprehensive and clear information on paper, web, and telephone, and work for positive change in lung health by campaigning, raising awareness, and funding world-class research.

Centre for Tobacco Control Research
(http://www.ctcr.stir.ac.uk/index.htm)
The Centre for Tobacco Control Research (CTCR) was established by Cancer Research UK in 1999, and is part of the Institute for Social Marketing (University of Stirling and The Open University). CTCR goals are to develop and evaluate interventions designed to prevent smoking uptake and encourage cessation; investigate the processes and effects of the tobacco industry's marketing activities, and on the basis of this undertaking, determine the most effective ways to counter them; and evaluate specific tobacco control policies and identify those that successfully change smoking behavior.

National Organizations (North America):

- ****National Women's Law Center** released a study in September of 2003 entitled *Women and Smoking: A National and State-by-State Report Card*—the first comprehensive assessment of women's smoking-related health conditions and the policies that are proven to help reduce smoking among women and girls. The study grades and ranks each state, and the United States as a whole, on women's health status and evaluates the strength of state tobacco control policies. See http://www.nwlc.org/pdf/Women&SmokingReportCard2003.pdf
- ****National Organization for Women** created a public education campaign to raise awareness and take action against tobacco advertising. The Redefining Liberation campaign was funded by a grant from the Centers for Disease Control and Prevention (CDC). During the first phase of the campaign, the NOW Foundation and the California NOW chapter created the *Redefining Liberation* video. See http://www.nowfoundation.org/videos/libclips1.html
- ****National Center for Policy Research (CPR) for Women & Families** conducts the *Women and Smoking Public Education Project* to engage women's organizations in efforts to reduce smoking among women and girls. The goal of the project is to impact women's and girls' attitudes towards smoking as well as their tobacco-related behaviors. CPR seeks to educate women and their families about how smoking is especially harmful to girls and women. See www.center4policy.org
- ****Health Canada—Women and Tobacco Resource** provides details of a number of projects that have been initiated in Canada to enhance understanding of

the issue of women and tobacco, and to increase the level of action to reduce women's tobacco use. Addressing women's tobacco use became a priority following the initiation of the Canadian government's Tobacco Demand Reduction Strategy (TDRS) in early 1994. The goals of TDRS were to help nonsmokers stay smoke free, to encourage and help those who want to quit smoking to do so, and to protect the health and rights of nonsmokers. See http://www.hc-sc.gc.ca/hl-vs/pubs/tobac-tabac/women-femmes/index_e.html

- **Bridging the Visions** provides information on taking a health-determinants and woman-centered approach to health promotion activities intended to reduce tobacco use. It promotes the importance of adopting a community development approach designed specifically for women that involves collaboration among many different partners to reduce women's exposure to, and use of, tobacco. This publication is designed to be used by health organizations, women's groups, and other community groups committed to women's health and well-being (Marcelis, Moyer & Holmes 1996).

Relevant Published Material Available Online

References

ASH, Asthma UK, & Trades Union, Smoking in the Workplace (2005). London (September 2, 2006), http://www.ash.org.uk/html/workplace/html/workplace.html

Gray I, Willis K, Willmore I (2004) *Achieving Smoke Freedom Toolkit: A Guide for Local Decision Makers.* United Kingdom: Chartered Institute of Environmental Health & ASH, http://www.cieh.org/library/Knowledge/Public_health/Smoking_in_the_workplace/ManualA 0090.pdf (accessed March 7, 2007)

Griffiths J, Grieves K (2002) *Tobacco in the Workplace: Meeting the Challenges. A Handbook for Employers.* World Health Organization Regional Office for Europe, Copenhagen. Available at www.euro.who.int/document/e74819.pdf (accessed March 7, 2007)

Griffiths J, Grieves K (2002) *Why Smoking In The Workplace Matters: An Employer's Guide.* World Health Organization Regional Office for Europe, Copenhagen, www.euro.who.int/document/e74820.pdf (accessed March 7, 2007)

Health Promotion Unit, Working together for Cleaner Air (2000) Ireland (September 4, 2006), http://www.healthpromotion.ie/uploaded_docs/hput00079.pdf

Appendix 1: Case Studies

Case Study: Workplace Smoke-free Policy, Stadco (Faculty of Public Health & Faculty of Occupational Medicine 2006)   Stadco is a manufacturing employer with over 300 staff on site. It was approached in April 2004 by the Help 2 Quit @ Work service in Shropshire and Telford of the United Kingdom. Previously, the company had smoking rooms throughout their site and smoking was allowed on the shop floor.

Stadco sought to introduce a workplace policy on smoking. After considering all the relevant information provided by Help 2 Quit, they set up a working party consisting of a union representative, a representative from personnel, and a coordinator from Help 2 Quit. Posters were displayed throughout the site and emails were sent to all office-based employees informing them of the proposed changes to policy and the availability of a stop-smoking clinic. Employees who did not have access to email were given the information in team meetings. A survey was also carried out to find out how many people smoked and how many would be interested in stopping.

It was agreed that the company would pursue a smoke-free policy and that the Help 2 Quit @ Work service would be offered to employees at the same time as the policy was implemented. Following the policy consultation, a nurse was sent to the site to carry out two days of awareness-raising activity. It was agreed with the management that the company would pay for initial prescriptions for nicotine replacement therapy, to help increase the number of people taking up the scheme. The policy was implemented, although employees were told that it would not be *policed* until after the stop-smoking clinic had completed its 12-week course. Employees were asked to voluntarily abide by the policy during this implementation period.

About 40 people took up the offer of help with smoking cessation. Feedback from employees attending the clinic identified the change in smoking policy and availability of support at work as the prime motivating factors for stopping smoking.

Case Study: Smoke-free Workplaces and Public Places (Wanless 2004)

Measures that introduce more smoke-free workplaces and public places not only reduce exposure to second-hand smoke, but may also result in a fall in cigarette consumption—the harder it is to find somewhere to smoke, the more incentives there are to quit. Smoking restrictions in the workplace have been established in Australia, Canada, Hong Kong, and the United States.

California has been particularly vigilant and imposed a ban on the smoking of tobacco in all enclosed places of employment in 1995. Ireland also took stringent preventative measures and announced that smoking would be banned in all workplaces, including restaurants and pubs, in 2004. New York City has passed similar legislation.

Some studies estimate that a workplace smoking ban in England might reduce smoking prevalence by around 4 percent (Donaldson 2002). This is equivalent to a reduction from the present 27 percent prevalence rate to 23 percent, if a comprehensive workplace ban were introduced in this country. This could be an low estimate if it triggers a move to wider cessation or an high estimate if other measures are already impacting on the smoking prevalence rate.

Around half of the workplaces in England are not yet smoke-free. In the hospitality sector, the introduction of smoke-free policies on a voluntary basis has been particularly slow. Objections usually center on the perception that becoming smoke-free will result in a reduction in business. A recent study, however, which reviewed 97 published studies on the economic effect of smoke-free policies on the hospitality industry, concluded that "all the best designed studies report no impact or a positive impact of smoke-free restaurant and bar laws on sales or employment" (Scollo et al. 2003). This complements previous work, which estimated that introducing clean air policies actually increases productivity by 3 percent (Occupational Safety & Health Administration 1994).

In other countries, bans across individual cities or areas, such as implementation in California or New York, have served as a catalyst for wider change. If national restrictions are not introduced, an equivalent city or town in England could act as a champion for smoke-free public places across the country and make a real impact on the health of their population while piloting a ban on smoking in public places in England.

Working Together For Cleaner Air—The Workplace Experience in Ireland
Smoking control policies have already been introduced in many workplaces in Ireland. The experiences of some organizations that have developed smoke-free policies are available online (Health Promotion Unit 2006).

References

Action on Smoking and Health, Workplace smoking policies: why employers should act (2006) United Kingdom (September 7, 2006), http://www.ash.org.uk/html/workplace/html/why.html

British Lung Foundation (2006) London (June 15, 2006), http://www.britishlungfoundation.org

British Medical Association (2004) *Smoking and Reproductive Life: The Impact of Smoking on Sexual, Reproductive and Child Health*. British Medical Association, London

Cochrane Tobacco Addiction Group (2006) Oxford (September 1, 2006), http://www.dphpc.ox.ac.uk/cochrane_tobacco/

Coleman T (2004) ABC of smoking cessation. Use of simple advice and behavioural support. *British Medical Journal,* 328, 397–399

DG Health and Consumer Protection (2006) *Special Eurobarometer 293: Attitudes of Europeans towards tobacco.* European Commission, Brussels

Department of Health, Consultation on the Introduction of Picture Warnings on Tobacco Packs (2006) London (June 22, 2006), http://www.dh.gov.uk/assetRoot/04/13/54/96/04135496.pdf

Department of Health, Calculate the cost (2007) London (March 7, 2007); http://www.gosmokefree.co.uk/whygosmokefree/calculatethecost/

DiFranza JR, Aligne CA, Weitzman M (2004) Prenatal and postnatal environmental tobacco smoke exposure and children's health. *Pediatrics,* 113, (4 Suppl),1007–1105

Donaldson L (2002) Annual Report of the Chief Medical Officer 2002: Health Check - On the State of the Public Health. London: Department of Health

"England to ban smoking from mid-2007" News section. *Eurohealth*, 12, 1, 45–46.

Faculty of Public Health and Faculty of Occupational Medicine (2006) *Creating a healthy workplace.* Faculty of Public Health & Faculty of Occupational Medicine, London

Health Promotion Unit, Working together for Cleaner Air (2000). Ireland (September 4, 2006), http://www.healthpromotion.ie/uploaded_docs/hput00079.pdf

Holmberg-Schwartz DA (1997) *Catching our Breath: A journal about change for women who smoke.* Winnipeg: Women's Health Clinic

Johnson JG, Cohen P, Pine DS, Klein DF, Kasen S, Brook JS (2000) Association Between Cigarette Smoking and Anxiety Disorders During Adolescence and Early Adulthood. *Journal of the American Medical Association,* 284, 18, 2348–2351

Katz PP, Showstack JA (1990) Is it worth it? Evaluating the economic impact of worksite health promotion. *Occupational Medicine: State of the Art Reviews*, 5, 4, 837–850

Kinnon D, Hanvey L (1995) *Delivering Gender-sensitive Tobacco Reduction Programs: Issues and Approaches.* Ottawa: Health Canada

Kouvonen A. Kivimäki M, Virtanen M, Pentti J, Vahtera J (2005) Work stress, smoking status, and smoking intensity: an observational study of 46,190 employees. *Journal of Epidemiology and Community Health,* 59, 63–69

Levine MD, Marcus MD, Kalarchian MA, Weissfeld L, Qin L (2006) Weight concerns affect motivation to remain abstinent from smoking postpartum. *Annals of Behavioral Medicine*, 32, 2, 147–53

Marcelis, Moyer & Holmes (1996) *Bridging the visions: a guide to shared action about women and tobacco.* Ottawa: Health Canada

McBride CM, Curry SJ, Grothaus LC, Nelson JC, Lando H, Pirie PL (1998) Partner smoking status and pregnant smoker's perceptions of support for and likelihood of smoking cessation. *Health Psychology*, 17, 1, 63–9

Nordenberg T (1997) It's Quittin' Time: Smokers Need Not Rely on Willpower Alone. *FDA Consumer,* 31, 7

Occupational Safety & Health Administration (1994) *Indoor Air Quality.* United States Department of Labor, Washington D.C.

Office of the Surgeon General (2001) *Women and Smoking: a Report of the Surgeon General.* United States Department of Health and Human Services, Washington, D.C.

Patient pages (2003) Quitting Smoking. *A Cancer Journal for Clinicians*, 53, 372–375

Rasmussen SR, Prescott E, Sorensen TI, Sogaard J (2004) The total lifetime costs of smoking. *European Journal of Public Health,* 14, 1, 95–100

Royal College of Physicians (1983) *Health or smoking? Follow-up report of the Royal College of Physicians.* Pitman, London

Scollo M, Lal A, Hyland A, Glantz S (2003) Review of the Quality of Studies on the Economic Effects of Smoke Free Policies on the Hospitality Industry. *Tobacco Control,* 12, 13–20

Stayner L, Bena J, Sasco AJ, Smith R, Steenland K, Kreuzer M, Straif K (2007) Lung Cancer Risk and Workplace Exposure to Environmental Tobacco Smoke. *American Journal of Public Health*, 10.2105/AJPH.2004.061275

Srivastava P, Currie GP, Britton J (2006) Smoking cessation. *British Medical Journal,* 332, 1324–1326

Svanes C, Omenaas E, Jarvis D, Chinn S, Gulsvik A, Burney P (2004). Parental smoking in childhood and adult obstructive lung disease: results from the European Community Respiratory Health Survey. *Thorax,* 59, 4, 295–302

The ASPECT Consortium (2004) *Tobacco or health in the European Union: past, present and future.* Luxembourg: Office for Official Publications of the European Communities

"The government has published its long-awaited white paper on public health" (2004) November 16, 2004 BBC News, http://news.bbc.co.uk/1/hi/health/medical_notes/3756028.stm

Tobacco Control Program (2003) *On the Road to Quitting - Guide to Becoming a Non-Smoker.* Health Canada, Ottawa

Wanless D (2004) *Securing Good Health for the Whole Population*, Norwich, United Kingdom: HM Treasury

Women's Health Bureau (1995) *Women and Tobacco. A Framework for Action*. Health Canada, Ottawa

World Bank (1999) *Curbing the epidemic: Governments and the economics of tobacco control*. World Bank, Washington D.C.

World Health Organization (2006) Tobacco Free Initiative. (June 12, 2006), Geneva, http://www.who.int/tobacco/en/

Chapter 12
Women, Health, and Alcohol-related Harm

Kaisa Kauppinen and Tarita Tuomola

Gender Differences in Drinking Patterns

Alcohol use and drinking patterns differ significantly between women and men, age groups, ethnic and religious groups, cultures, and socioeconomic groups. In nearly every culture studied, men are more likely to drink than women, and drink more when they do. These gender gaps are greater for riskier behavior. Therefore, the burden of diseases attributable to alcohol use is higher in men than in women. Worldwide, it is estimated that among the 76.4 million people with alcohol use disorders, 63.7 are men and 12.7 million are women (M:W=5:1) (WHO, 2005).

Alcoholic beverages are consumed in various forms and used in various social contexts. Alcohol consumption is a lifestyle choice for many men and women, and is commonly associated with social situations such as eating, recreation, partying, and relaxation. The use of alcohol brings with it a number of pleasures. When people are asked about the effects of alcohol, more positive than negative answers are typically given. Stress reduction, mood elevation, increased sociability, and relaxation are the most common reported psychosocial benefits of drinking alcohol (Anderson & Baumberg 2006; http://ec.europa.eu/health-eu/news_alcohlineurope_en.htm).

However, alcohol consumption can have adverse health consequences through drunkenness (intoxication), alcohol dependence, or chronic heavy consumption. Throughout the EU, 55 million people are estimated to drink alcohol at hazardous levels. Altogether, 23 million Europeans (5% of men, 1% of women) are dependent on alcohol. The EU is characterized as the heaviest drinking region of the world. Alcohol is responsible for the premature death and disability of 12 percent of men and 2 percent of women in the EU (Anderson & Baumberg 2006).

Even the social context of drinking varies by gender, with women drinking relatively more often with meals than men and relatively less in public drinking places. Women also tend to prefer different beverages to men, drinking more wine and less beer, although this is less noticeable in the generally wine-drinking south of Europe. However, the countries differ in the size of gender gap in drinking due to cultural variation and the position of women in the society. (http://ec.europa.eu/health-eu/my_lifestyle/alcohol/index_en.htm).

A. Linos, W. Kirch (eds), *Promoting Health for Working Women.*
© Springer 2008

More Egalitarian Drinking Patterns

It has been suggested that there has been a convergence in drinking behavior between women and men over the past few decades, or that more *egalitarian drinking patterns* could be found in Europe (Anderson & Baumberg 2006). Recent trends in some European countries—like in the United Kingdom—fit this view, but such trends cannot be seen in some other countries, where only a limited evidence of convergence in levels of consumption and hazardous drinking can be found.

There is an expectation that women's drinking will more closely match that of men's in the EU (Euromonitor & just-drinks.com 2005). As a consequence, women are using more alcohol, and they are becoming increasingly more abusive of alcohol. "There still tends to be an impression that the abuse of alcohol and drugs by women is a marginal issue for women. But nothing could be further from the truth," reported the SafeWork program, which is managed by the International Labour Organization (ILO). The following factors explain the rise in alcohol use among women in most developed countries (ILO 2000):

- The growing independence of women in combination with the new trend towards starting a family later in life
- More women are working in professions where the stressful environments tend to lead to occasional and subsequent misuse of alcohol
- Working women are now facing many of the same frustrations, anxieties, and stress-inducing factors that have long pushed men into alcohol or drugs as a means of seeking escape or comfort, or merely coping with reality
- Many women work in medical professions, which tend to combine stress and the possibility of easy access to drugs to counter the demands of their job
- The social bonhomie associated with drinking after a hard day's work has extended to women as part of a climate of equality
- As a result of their increased purchasing power as women enter the labor market in larger numbers, marketers of alcoholic beverages have increasingly been targeting the glamorous aspects of women consuming alcohol in their advertising campaigns (www.ilo.org/public/english/protection/safework/drug/gender.htm).
- In addition, alcohol has become far more accessible to women through a range of outlets, such as supermarkets, restaurants, and wine bars. In the United Kingdom, pubs have generally ceased to be all-male drinking environments and have become more women-friendly (IAS Fact Sheet: Women and Alcohol; http://www.ias.org.uk)

An important additional stress factor for many working women is the juggling act that they have to perform between work and family responsibilities. The *superwoman syndrome* has led some women to over-extend themselves in trying to do it all—a successful career, marital harmony, well-adjusted children, caring for the elderly parents, and an active social life. Many women have burned out in the process, with some turning to alcohol or drugs.

Societal stereotypes and gender norms influence women's and men's alcohol drinking. In many cultures, drinking has been socially more acceptable for men than for women. Drinking among men has a strong masculine connotation—it is a means of maintaining friendships. Drinking is also considered to be a coping strategy for men when faced with difficult life events. In contrast, women face stricter social sanctions about alcohol, and experience more social or moral stigma related to alcohol use than men. In many cultures, women who consume alcohol freely are viewed as morally less integrated, and suffer stigmatization and discrimination. (WHO 2004).

Health Impact of Alcohol Use

The health effects of alcohol on the human body and the resulting disorders vary from person to person and from women to men, depending on a number of factors. These factors include how much and how quickly alcohol is being consumed, how long the person has been drinking; body size, age, general health, weight and nutritional status; whether alcohol is consumed with a meal, before driving or operating a machinery; and whether it is consumed on its own or together with other substances (WHO 2005).

Numerous surveys report that men drink more than women. Women are also less likely to drink alcohol frequently or heavily, or report drinking-related problems. Women are more often abstainers than men—e.g., in Austria 11 percent of the adult population are abstainers, of which three quarters are women (Anderson & Baumberg 2006).

Because of this, men have been much more likely than women to experience alcohol problems. In recent years, however, the gap between women and men has narrowed (at least to some extent) in relation to both consumption and problems. In the United Kingdom, there has been a particularly marked increase in heavy drinking in women (IAS Fact Sheet: Women and Alcohol; http://www.ias.org.uk).

Alcohol intoxication (or drunkenness) is the most common cause of acute adverse health consequences. It occurs when the amount of alcohol consumed by an individual leads to a temporary state of alteration of the person's perceptions, decision-making, judgement, emotions, and behavior (Anderson & Baumberg 2006).

A related term is *binge drinking*. Originally, the term *binge* has been used in its clinical sense to refer to periodic drinking, usually over a period of days. For research purposes, binge drinking is often defined as the consumption of more than a certain number of drinks over a short period of time—a single drinking session or, at least, a single day. Data for binge drinking in the EU are shown in Table 12.1. Even this definition has been criticized by some researchers. It has been suggested that a subjective, rather than a unit-based, definition should be used, with binge drinking defined as drinking that results in the drinker feeling at least partially drunk (IAS Fact Sheet: Binge Drinking; http://www.ias.org.uk).

Table 12.1 Proportion (%) of binge drinking to total number of drinking occasions (occasions past 12 months)

	Men	Women
Finland	29	17
France	9	5
Germany	14	7
Italy	13	11
Sweden	33	18
UK	40	22

Cited by IAS Fact sheet Binge Drinking; http://www.ias.org.uk.

Women's Vulnerability

Many adverse effects of alcohol are common to women and men. In some cases, women may be at greater risk, and there are some problems specific to women (IAS Fact Sheet: Women and Alcohol; http://www.ias.org.uk). Women tend, on average, to be physically smaller than men and therefore are affected to a greater extent than men by the same amount of alcohol. This is because women usually have lower body weight, smaller livers, and a higher proportion of fat to muscle (WHO 2004, 2005).

Women are at greater risk than men for developing alcohol-related health problems, and the risks to women's health start with lower amounts of alcohol. The culture of *thinness* and dieting that particularly affects young women also places them at an increased risk of the effects of alcohol (Australian Alcohol Guidelines: Health Risks and Benefits 2001).

Women react to alcohol differently than men in many ways. One of these is that women tend to get intoxicated quicker, even when taking into account the difference in body weight. According to a report by the National Institute on Alcohol Abuse and Alcoholism (NIAAA), women absorb and metabolize alcohol differently than men. Women who are heavy drinkers tend to develop liver disease more quickly than men. Heavy drinking is, therefore, more risky for women than it is for men. (Refer to http://pubs.niaaa.nih.gov/publications/brochurewomen/women.htm.)

According to research, alcohol plays a contributory role in the development of the following diseases:

- Breast cancer—moderate to heavy drinking of alcohol has been associated with the development of breast cancer in women
- Cardiovascular diseases—research shows that the use of alcohol is both a risk and a protective factor for cardiovascular diseases, but high levels of consumption tend to have long-term adverse effects
- Mental illness—alcohol-use disorders are associated with comorbid mental disorders that may include anxiety, depression, and other psychotic illnesses, such as schizophrenia. Studies show that depression is more common among male heavy drinkers and female ex-drinkers

- Consequences of alcohol use in pregnancy—a woman's consumption of alcohol during pregnancy can adversely affect her fetus. Women who drink during pregnancy are also at higher risk of miscarriage or premature delivery. (WHO 2005)

In addition, the social and economic consequences resulting from alcohol use affect women and men differently, and are partly related to societal gender roles. Women are more often affected by alcohol consumption by a partner or family member with negative social consequences. A woman whose husband drinks heavily is more likely than other women to drink too much. http://pubs.niaaa.nih.gov/publication/brochurewomen/women.htm

Indirect Social Harm of Alcohol on Women

Negative social consequences of alcohol use by other people's drinking are more commonly experienced by women than by men. This kind of indirect harm is referred to as environmental alcohol damage, which is caused by alcohol to people other than the drinker (Anderson & Baumberg 2006). Negative social harm from other people's drinking include such behaviors as being kept awake at night, harming home life, getting into a fight, being harassed, being insulted, being physically hurt, or having property damaged. These behaviors are reflected in other spheres of social life, including the workplace.

The indirect harm of alcohol on women is colossal according to the Safe-Work Program managed by the ILO. Violent and abusive behaviors are familiar problems to those women who are involved in relationships with heavy drinking partners (www.ilo.org/public/english/protection/safework/drug/gender.htm). A large number of studies on alcohol consumption and marital aggression have shown that a husband's heavy drinking increases the risk of marital violence (Anderson & Baumberg 2006). Alcohol is involved, in varying ways, in about 50 percent of domestic physical and sexual violence cases. (Australian Alcohol Guidelines: Health Risks and Benefits 2001).

Domestic violence and marital aggression can spill over into the workplace. The recipients may suffer either physical or psychological health problems, which may affect their work performance and result in time off from work. In addition, the threatening partner may make phone calls, send e-mails and text messages, and even visit the victim at the workplace. This will not only affect work performance, but the whole atmosphere of the workplace. It may also hurt the victim's reputation and professional image (Gender Issues in Safety and Health at Work 2003; www.agency.osha.eu.int).

It is typical for the affected persons, typically the women, to suffer their dysfunctional family situation silently and accept the shame and stigma associated with having an abusive partner. This stigma contributes to making it less likely for the victims to seek help for their alcohol-related problems, either caused by their own drinking, or indirectly by their partner's drinking. Therefore, treatment programs should be gender-specific to attend to the differing needs and problems of women and men.

In Finland, a program called *Silenced Womanhood* was started in 2004 to deal with women's violent and abusive behavior. The aim was to help women understand their own aggressive behavior. This has long been a silenced issue, and often connected with heavy drinking in women (www.vakivalta-apua.fi).

Alcohol-Related Harm, Reduced Work Performance, and Gender

The workplace is a significant channel for preventive actions, with the potential to reach a high proportion of people with alcohol problems. Several surveys have found that traditional *liquid lunches* are no longer a part of the working day for many work organizations, however, opposite views have also been presented (IAS Fact Sheet: Alcohol and the Workplace; http://www.ias.org.uk).

Alcohol abuse not only affects work performance in general, but also results in adverse health consequences, increased accidents, and deterioration in interpersonal relations—with all their related costs. Alcohol at work is an important health and safety issue in its own right (www.ilo.org/public/english/protection/safework/drug/impiss.htm).

Alcohol-related absenteeism, drinking during working hours, or working with a *hangover* all have a negative impact on work performance, and thereby on competitiveness and productivity (RAND 2006). One study by recruitment consultants in the United Kingdom estimated a 27 percent drop in productivity for each hangover day (http://ec.europa.eu/health/ph_determinants/life_style/alcohol_com_en.htm).

Studies show that harmful alcohol use and episodic heavy drinking increase the risk of arriving to work late and leaving work early, inappropriate behavior, disciplinary problems, theft, poor co-worker relations, low company morale, and damage to the reputation of the enterprise. One study conducted at 114 work sites showed an almost linear relationship between increasing average consumption and measure of job performance, finding strong associations between consumption and getting to work late, leaving early, and doing less work, but a weaker association with missing days of work (Anderson & Baumberg 2006).

One study in Denmark, Finland, Norway, and Sweden found that 3 to 6 percent of all men and 1 to 4 percent of all women have missed days of work at least once in the past year due to their drinking. Consequences of this type were much more common for 19- to 34-year olds than older ages for both women and men. In total, nearly 5 percent of drinking men and 2 percent of drinking women across the EU15 countries reported a negative impact on their work or studies in the past year. Young people were much more likely to report problems with work than other age groups, particularly young women (Anderson & Baumberg 2006).

Drinking during meals while at work can impair reaction time and have other adverse physical and psychological effects, thereby potentially leading to a hazardous situations or poor decision-making (ILO 1996). In some wine- and beer-producing countries, it is customary for the workers to drink wine or beer with their lunch, even in such hazardous industries as transport and construction (ILO 2000).

One of the problems in combating alcohol abuse in the workplace lies in the widespread acceptance of social consumption of alcohol. Alcohol plays a part in and around work as a way to socialize or network with clients and colleagues (IAS Fact Sheet: Alcohol and the Workplace; http://www.ias.org.uk). The difficulties lie in developing a distinction between social or moderate drinking with small quantities of alcohol, and the real dangers to health and safety of abusive drinking. Further research is needed to compare the impact of alcohol on the workplace in different EU countries.

Primarily Affected Work Sectors and Categories

The sectors that have been identified as being at special risk of alcohol abuse include the food and catering industry, transportation, the maritime sector, construction, military personnel, and recreation and entertainment services.

Several work characteristics have been recognized as being related to the increased use of alcohol and drugs. These include job stress, freedom from supervision, shift work, night work, occupational and co-worker norms, the availability of drugs and alcohol in the workplace, and long periods spent outside the family environment. The lifestyle imposed by a person's job may increase the risk of alcohol or drug abuse (www.ilo.org/public/english/protection/safework/drug/impiss.htm). Young people and men appear to be particularly vulnerable. For men, there may be a social pressure to drink on the job, during breaks and at work-related events, while refusing a drink can imply a lack of trust and a denial of mutual respect (WHO 2004).

Even women can be exposed to alcohol-related risks at work. A study in the International Archives of Occupational and Environmental Health identified several occupational risk factors for poor mental health among women—especially high alcohol consumption and sub-clinical depression. Occupational factors such as shift work, job strain, low occupational pride, poor stimulation at work, and poor social support were related to mental health problems (including high alcohol consumption) among the women (Bildt & Michélsen 2002)

A study published in the Journal of Applied Psychology (December 2000) concluded that where work problems interfered with family life, the affected workers were three times more likely to have mood disorders such as depression, 2.5 times more likely to have an anxiety disorder, and twice as likely to have a substance dependence disorder. In terms of practical implications, the results suggest that workplaces should not overlook conflict between work and family as a source of stress in the lives of employed women and men.

Work Stress and Alcohol Use—Three Paradigms

Stress is a common theme in women's lives. Research confirms that one of the reasons women drink is to help them cope with stress. It is not clear, however, just how stress may lead to problem drinking among women. Heavy drinking by itself causes stress in a job and in the family. How a woman handles stress, and the support she gets to manage it, also affect whether she uses alcohol in response to stress. Work qualities and work setting both play an important role (http://pubs.niaaa.nih.gov/publications/brochurewomen/women.htm).

The following three paradigms, developed by Professor Michael Frone (1999), offer a good picture of the relationships between work qualities, work stresses, and people's alcohol use:

- The *social control* paradigm suggests that alcohol use may be higher among employees who are not integrated into, or regulated by, the work organization Thus, two important risk factors in the social control paradigm are low levels of supervision and low visibility of work behavior
- The *cultural availability* paradigm suggests that work settings where alcohol is physically or socially available may promote alcohol use among employees. Physical availability of alcohol at work is defined as the ease with which alcohol can be obtained for consumption on the job, during breaks, and at work-related events. Social availability of alcohol at work is defined as the degree to which co-workers support drinking either off or on the job.
- The *work alienation or stress* paradigm suggests that employee alcohol use may be a response to the physical and psychosocial qualities of the work environment, such as work demands on an employee, an employee's level of boredom, lack of participation in decision-making, and interpersonal conflict with supervisors and co-workers

According to the stress paradigm, alcohol use is seen as a means of regulating negative emotions (e.g., depression, anxiety, or anger) or thoughts that result from aversive work environments. The paradigms are useful to better understand the reasons behind employee abusive drinking and to develop more effective ways of preventing problem drinking in the workforce.

The Management of Alcohol-Related Problems in the Workplace

Given that there are multiple causes of alcohol-related problems, there are consequently multiple approaches to research, prevention, and treatment of alcohol-related issues in the workplace.

The European Commission has adopted an EU strategy to support member states in reducing alcohol-related harm in Europe. One of its priorities is to prevent harm among adults and reduce the negative impact on the workplace. Therefore, workplace-based initiatives should be fostered. For all workplaces, there should be a policy to prevent alcohol-related harm—including information and education campaigns—and to provide help and specialized care for employees with alcohol-related problems (http://ec.europa.eu/health/ph_determinants/life_style/alcohol/alcohol_com_en.htm).

One example of preventive actions is *brief intervention* provided by the occupational health services (OHS). The purpose of brief intervention is to support the problem drinkers to break their harmful or hazardous drinking patterns. In mapping the problems and choosing the courses of positive action, attention must be focused on those work-related factors that predispose them to and maintain the problems—and also to those factors that can be used to solve them (Saarto 2006; http://www.paihdelinkki.fi/english/infobank/200_service_line/281e.htm).

Brief intervention has proved to be an effective treatment practice for ending excessive alcohol consumption before the development of dependency. Brief intervention helps in identifying hazardous drinking patterns and giving advice on how to change them (Anderson, Gual & Colom 2005). Brief intervention, as a well-defined preventive practice, makes it easier for occupational health professionals to encounter their clients and patients with alcohol problems. The purpose also is to sensitize occupational health professionals about alcohol-related problems within the occupational health settings (Heljälä, Jurvansuu & Kuokkanen 2007).

Gender Mainstreaming and Alcohol Preventive Programs

Preventive programs and action plans tend to be focused on men and often overlook the needs of women with alcohol-use disorders. There is a need for gender-specific preventive strategies, which consider how alcohol use and abuse affects women and men differently.

For prevention strategies and actions to be effective among women, priority should be given to the following issues (WHO 2005):

- Developing gender-specific data and adequate information
- Creating prevention programs with the participation of women
- Incorporating prevention activities in services that target women, such as family planning services or OSH services, if available
- Building capacity for health programmers and service providers (including health professionals within OSH) in identifying alcohol use and other related problems such as intimate partner violence
- Developing policies and services for women vulnerable to adverse health and social problems from the drinking behavior of their partners (indirect harm)

Treatment services (including OSH services) should be gender-specific so they are sensitive to the differing needs and problems of men and women. Health care professionals should be trained to detect alcohol-related problems among women. Constructive and nonjudgemental programs can improve health seeking behavior among women suffering from alcohol related problems—still taboo and silenced in many cultures and societies. Even brief intervention practices should be modified according to gender.

For the preventive practices to be effective, it is important to integrate gender in alcohol research—this will contribute to more focused research in the field. One must be careful not to overemphasize gender differences in harmful alcohol consumption in relation to other relevant factors such as ethnicity, culture, and social class, which also are important factors in those processes that produce health and illness. Stereotypical approaches should be avoided—male-female differences may sometimes be smaller than individual differences within gender (Kauppinen 2006; http://www.icohweb.org/newsletter/index.asp).

Two Cases of Preventive Actions

Preventive activities include education, arranging training for the staff, and providing services that support the moderate use of alcohol. The problem drinker herself has the main responsibility in finding solutions to her drinking. Alcohol-related problems in the workplace, however, are *personal* as well as *shared* problems.

CASE 1: AUDIT—Alcohol Use Disorders Identification Test

Practical Exercise: How Do You Know if You Have a Drinking Problem?

This case study is formed on the basis of the Alcohol Use Disorders Identification Test (AUDIT) developed by the WHO. It is widely used as a self-answer test and gives a quick answer about your drinking behavior. Answering the following questions can help you find out if you have a drinking problem. A score of 8 or greater may indicate the need for a more in-depth assessment of your drinking behavior. Even one Yes answer may suggest a possible alcohol problem. (WHO 2001; http://www.aa2.org/check_ups/audit.htm; http://whqlibdoc.who.int/hq/2001/WHO_MSD_MSB_01.6a.pdf).

For each question, select your answer and fill in the score given in brackets [ ] in the box.

One unit of alcohol is: a half pint of average-strength beer/lager OR one glass of wine OR one single measure of spirits (Note: A can of high-strength beer or lager may contain 3-4 units).

1. **How often do you have a drink containing alcohol?**
   [0] Never   [1] Monthly or less   [2] 2-4 times a month   ☐
   [3] 2-3 times a week   [4] 4 or more times a week
2. **How many units of alcohol do you drink on a typical day when you are drinking?**
   [0] 1 or 2   [1] 3 or 4   [2] 5 or 6   [3] 7, 8 or 9   ☐
   [4] 10 or more

3. **How often do you have six or more units of alcohol on one occasion?**
   [0] Never   [1] Less than monthly   [2] Monthly
   [3] Weekly   [4] Daily or almost daily   ☐
4. **How often during the last year have you found that you were not able to stop drinking once you had started?**
   [0] Never   [1] Less than monthly   [2] Monthly
   [3] Weekly   [4] Daily or almost daily   ☐
5. **How often during the last year have you failed to do what was normally expected from you because of drinking?**
   [0] Never   [1] Less than monthly [2] Monthly
   [3] Weekly   [4] Daily or almost daily   ☐
6. **How often during the last year have you needed a first drink in the morning to get yourself going after a heavy drinking session?**
   [0] Never   [1] Less than monthly [2] Monthly
   [3] Weekly   [4] Daily or almost daily   ☐
7. **How often during the last year have you had a feeling of guilt or remorse after drinking?**
   [0] Never   [1] Less than monthly [2] Monthly
   [3] Weekly   [4] Daily or almost daily   ☐
8. **How often during the last year have you been unable to remember what happened the night before because you had been drinking?**
   [0] Never   [1] Less than monthly [2] Monthly
   [3] Weekly   [4] Daily or almost daily   ☐
9. **Have you or someone else been injured as a result of your drinking?**
   [0] No   [2] Yes, but not in the last year
   [4] Yes, during the last year   ☐
10. **Has a relative or friend or doctor or another health worker been concerned about your drinking or suggested you cut down?**
    [0] No   [2] Yes, but not in the last year
    [4] Yes, during the last year   ☐

CASE 2: Project HUUGO in Finland

Project HUUGO (www.huugo.fi) is an educating and informative program that took place in Finland during 2005-2007. Its goal was to prevent alcohol-related harms in Finnish workplaces. It was operated by the Finnish Association for Healthy Lifestyles, in association with the Centre for Occupational Safety and all central trade unions and employers' associations as the main partners (http://www.elamantapaliitto.fi/english.html; http://www.tyoturva.fi/english/centre/).

The relationship between alcohol and work in Finland has complex roots in cultural history. The traditional Finnish problem—the use of alcohol while at work—has almost totally disappeared, but the work-related impacts of alcohol consumed during free time have increased. Alcohol is culturally considered both as a private matter and as a measure of masculinity.

With employers and OSH professionals often being quite far away from the viewpoint of a single employee, this has created a situation where preventive actions are often neglected and alcohol problems tackled only when they grow visible and severe. This, in turn, has encouraged the hiding of drinking problems in the workplace.

The need for preventive actions has become more and more urgent, with major cuts in alcohol taxation in 2004 that lowered the prices and dramatically increased consumption. Project HUUGO tried to provide answers for this need. Project "HUUGO" consisted of the following activities:

- Delivering information—Information on alcohol and its impacts was delivered to workplaces through multiple information channels, including the social partners' own effort and initiative
- Developing policies—Good preventive policies were collected and new ones developed in brainstorming sessions
- Providing tools for self-control—Leaflets, advice, and web pages with an easily accessible approach aimed at breaking the cultural taboos were produced
- Providing tools for carrying out development projects in the workplaces—A web portal consisting of relevant information for the key actors in the workplaces was opened
- Education—The key actors in workplaces were educated during the training courses and seminars to carry out preventive actions and tackle the multiple harms caused by abusive use of alcohol

Project HUUGO was primarily a preventive action—the idea could be characterized by the words "Always one step ahead." This means that the consumption of alcohol and its effects must be something that can be openly discussed before any problem emerges. Achieving this requires commitment from the whole staff of the organization for the common cause and employee well-being (Hytti 2006).

Selected Internet Resources

Alcohol and Health

- **About: Alcoholism and Substance Abuse (United States)**
  Articles and resources: Women and substance abuse, alcohol and women, health risks for women etc.
  http://alcoholism.about.com/od/women/Women_and_Substance_Abuse.htm
  Articles and resources on women's health issues: Alcohol and breast cancer, brain damage etc.
  http://alcoholism.about.com/od/whealth/Womens_Health_Issues.htm

- **Addiction Link—Päihdelinkki (Finland)**
  Information bank: Information line, service line, a-line.
  http://www.paihdelinkki.fi/english/

- **athealth.com: Alcohol, a Women's Health Issue (United States)**
  Women and drinking, moderate drinking, heavy drinking, safe drinking over a lifetime.
  http://www.athealth.com/Consumer/disorders/womenalcohol.html

- **Alcohol Policies Project (United States)**
  Fact sheet: women and alcohol.
  http://www.cspinet.org/booze/women.htm

- **Australian Government, The Department of Health and Ageing**
  Alcohol and Women's Health
  http://www.alcohol.gov.au/internet/alcohol/publishing.nsf/Content/fs-women

- **Eurocare—The European Alcohol Policy Alliance**
  WWW-pages thematic areas: alcohol policy, alcohol related harm, health forum, health working group.
  http://www.eurocare.org/

- **European Commission**
  Health Problems Related to Life Style, Alcohol.
  http://ec.europa.eu/health/ph_determinants/life_style/lifestyle_en.htm
  Health-EU - Public Health Thematic Portal
  http://ec.europa.eu/health-eu/my_lifestyle/alcohol/index_en.htm

- **Health A to Z**
  Alcoholism - overview: Short and long term physical effects, signs of alcohol abuse or dependence, blood alcohol levels, prognosis.
  https://www.healthatoz.com/healthatoz/Atoz/common/standard/transform.jsp?
  requestURI=/healthatoz/Atoz/dc/caz/suba/alco/alco_gen_ovw.jsp
  Alcohol hits women's health harder.
  https://www.healthatoz.com/healthatoz/Atoz/common/standard/transform.jsp?
  requestURI=/healthatoz/Atoz/dc/caz/
  suba/alco/alert01152002.jsp

- **Institute of Alcohol Studies**
  IAS Fact Sheet (2006). Binge Drinking. Nature, Prevalence and Causes. Institute of Alcohol Studies, December 2006.
  http://www.ias.org.uk/resources/factsheets/binge_drinking.pdf

- **International Society for Biomedical Research on Alcoholism (ISBRA)**
  Links to government organizations, journals and societies.
  http://www.isbra.com/

- **The Research Society on Alcoholism (United States)**
  Links to researches, virtual library on alcohol and drug problems.
  http://www.rsoa.org/

- **World Health Organization (Europe)**
  WHO Health Topics: Alcohol Drinking
  Programmes & projects, publications, press releases, fact sheets.
  http://www.who.dk/healthtopics/HT2ndLvlPage?HTCode=alcohol_drinking

Gender Perspectives

- **European Agency for Safety and Health at Work**
  Fact Sheet 42: Gender issues in safety and health at work. Summary of an Agency Report, 2003.
  http://osha.europa.eu/publications/factsheets/42/facts-42_en.pdf
  Fact Sheet 43: Including gender issues in risk assessment, 2003.
  http://osha.europa.eu/publications/factsheets/43/facts-43_en.pdf
  European Agency for Safety and Health at Work (2003). Gender issues in health and safety at work. A Review.
  http://osha.europa.eu/publications/reports/209/reportgenderen_en.pdf

- **Institute of Alcohol Studies**
  IAS Fact Sheet (2005). Women and Alcohol. Institute of Alcohol Studies, April 2005.
  http://www.ias.org.uk/resources/factsheets/women.pdf

- **International Labour Organization (ILO): Programme on Safety and Health at Work and the Environment (Safe Work)**
  Drug and alcohol abuse - a gender problem.
  http://www.ilo.org/public/english/protection/safework/drug/gender.htm
  Gender issues.
  http://www.ilo.org/public/english/protection/safework/gender/index.htm

- **United Nations: Office on Drugs and Crime**
  UN Office on drugs and crime (2004). Substance abuse treatment and care for women - Case studies and lessons learned. New York: United Nations.
  http://www.unodc.org/docs/treatment/Case_Studies_E.pdf

- **World Health Organization (Europe)**
  WHO (2004). Gender in Mental Health Research. Geneva: Department of Gender, Women and
  Health.http://www.who.int/gender/documents/en/mentalhealthlow.pdf

  WHO (2002). Gender and Mental Health. Gender and Health, June 2002. Geneva: Department of Gender, Women and Health.
  http://www.who.int/gender/other_health/en/genderMH.pdf

  WHO (2005). Gender, Health and Alcohol Use. Gender and Health, September 2005. Geneva: Department of Gender, Women and Health.
  http://www.who.int/gender/documents/Alcoholfinal.pdf

  WHO (2006). Gender Equality, Work and Health: A Review of the Evidence. Geneva: Department of Gender, Women and Health; Family and Community Health; Department of Public Health and Environment; Sustainable Development and Healthy Environments.
  http://www.who.int/gender/documents/Genderworkhealth.pdf

Intervention and Treatment

- AUDIT -test (Alcohol Use Disorders Identification Test) developed by World Health Organisation.
  www.aquarius.org.uk/pdf/Audit.pdf
- **Addiction Alternatives**
  WHO (1987). Alcohol Use Disorders Identification Test - AUDIT. Developed by the World Health Organization, AMETHYST Project, 1987.
  http://www.aa2.org/check_ups/audit.htm
- **American Medical Association**
  Bush et al. (1998). The AUDIT Alcohol Consumption Questions (AUDIT-C) - An Effective Brief Screening Test for Problem Drinking. Archives of Internal Medicine, vol 158, September.
  http://archinte.amaassn.org/cgi/content/abstract/158/16/1789
  https://afcrossroads.com/websites/corc_docs/SG_Toolkit/Bucket2/audit-c.pdf

  Aalto et al. (2000). Brief Intervention for Female Heavy Drinkers in Routine General Practice: A 3-Year Randomized, Controlled Study. Alcoholism: Clinical & Experimental Research. 24 (11), November 2000.
  http://www.alcoholism-cer.com/pt/re/alcoholism/abstract.00000374-20001100-000010.htm;jsessionid=FtQWBTshMlYFKvgTvvDflpLG3qnLQQTBJjnM51w-GbTdFpgTvDs8H!-1996709112!-949856145!8091!-1

- **Current Care Guidelines (Finland)**
  Finnish Society of Addiction Medicine (2006). Treatment of alcohol abuse. The Finnish Medical Society Duodecim.
  http://www.kaypahoito.fi/
- **Drug Alcohol Review**
  Aalto, M. & Pekuri, P & Seppä, K. (2003) Obstacles to carrying out brief intervention for heavy drinkers in primary health care: a focus group study. Abstract. Drug Alcohol Review, Jun; 22(2).
  http://www.ncbi.nlm.nih.gov/entrez/
  query.fcgi?cmd=Retrieve&db=PubMed&list_uids=12850903&dopt=Abstract
- **International Network on Brief Interventions of Alcohol Problems (INEBRIA)**
  INEBRIA's aim is to promote the implementation of brief interventions.
  http://146.219.26.6/pub/Du14/html/en/Du14/index.html
- **International Society for Biomedical Research on Alcoholism (ISBRA)**
  Heljälä & Jurvansuu & Kuokkanen & Seppä (2006). Brief Alcohol Intervention Trends in Finnish Occupational Health Services (OHS). Abstract for presentation at ISBRA 2006 World Congress on Alcohol Research.
  http://www.isbra2006.com/abstract/250.htm
- **Mental Help Net**
  Alcohol & substance abuse. AUDIT - alcohol screening test online.
  http://mentalhelp.net/poc/view_doc.php?type=doc&id=1860&cn=14

- **National Institutes of Health (NIH), U.S. Department of Health and Human Services**
  National Institute on Alcohol Abuse and Alcoholism (1999). Brief intervention for alcohol problems. No. 43, April.
  http://pubs.niaaa.nih.gov/publications/aa43.htm

- **Primary Health Care European Project on Alcohol (PHEPA)**
  Gual, A & Anderson, P., Segura, L. Colom, J. (2005). Alcohol and Primary Health Care: Training Programme on Identification and Brief Interventions. Barcelona: Department of the Government of Catalonia.
  http://www.phepa.net/units/phepa/pdf/tripa_training_ok.pdf
  Gual, A & Anderson, P., Segura, L. Colom, J. (2005). Alcohol and Primary Health Care: Clinical Guidelines on Identification and Brief Interventions. Barcelona: Department of the Government of Catalonia.
  http://www.phepa.net/units/phepa/pdf/cg_1.pdf

  PHEPA (2006) Disseminating Brief Interventions on Alcohol Problems Europe Wide, PHEPA II Luxembourg 21.03.06
  http://www.phepa.net/units/phepa/pdf/ecmeeting.pdf

- **The Research Society on Alcoholism (United States)**
  Babor & Higgins-Biddle & Saunders & Monteiro (2001). AUDIT - The Alcohol Use Disorders Identification Test Guidelines for Use in Primary Care. Second Edition. Department of Mental Health and Substance Dependence.
  http://whqlibdoc.who.int/hq/2001/WHO_MSD_MSB_01.6a.pdf

- **World Health Organization (Europe)**
  WHO Collaborative Project on Identification and Management of Alcohol-Related Problems in Primary Health Care
  http://www.who-alcohol-phaseiv.net/welcome.htm

  WHO (2003). Management of Substance Dependence - Screening and Brief Intervention, Fact Sheet. Geneva: World Health Organization.
  http://www.who.int/substance_abuse/publications/en/SBIFactSheet.pdf

  WHO (2006). Development of Country-Wide Strategies for Implementing Early Identification and Brief Intervention in Primary Health Care, Report on Phase IV.
  http://www.who.int/substance_abuse/publications/identification_management_alcoholproblems_phaseiv.pdf

Alcohol, Work, and Occupational Health

- **Finnish Institute of Occupational Health (FIOH)**
  Ahola, K. et al. (2006). Alcohol dependence in relation to burnout among the Finnish working population. Addiction, vol. 101, October 2006.
  http://www.blackwell-synergy.com/doi/abs/10.1111/j.1360-0443.2006.01539.x

- **GOHNET - The Global Occupational Health Network**
  Gohnet (2006). Psychosocial Factors and Mental Health at Work. Issue 10, 2006. Gohnet Newslette, World Health Organization.
  http://www.who.int/occupational_health/publications/newsletter/en/index.html

- **Hazards Magazine (United Kingdom)**
  Drug and alcohol testing. http://www.hazards.org/workstyle/
  Hazards Factsheet (2002). Drugs & alcohol. Working out sensible drugs and alcohol policy. Hazards Factsheet 77.
  http://www.hazards.org/haz77/drugsandalcohol.pdf

- **International Commission on Occupational Health (ICOH)**
  ICOH is an international non-governmental professional society whose aims are to foster the scientific progress, knowledge and development of occupational health and safety in all its aspects.
  http://www.icohweb.org/about.asp

- **Institute of Alcohol Studies**
  IAS Fact Sheet (2006). Alcohol and the Workplace. Institute of Alcohol Studies, December 2006.
  http://www.ias.org.uk/resources/factsheets/workplace.pdf

- **International Labour Organization (ILO): Programme on Safety and Health at Work and the Environment (Safe Work)**
  Workplace drug and alcohol prevention programmes.
  http://www.ilo.org/public/english/protection/safework/drug/index.htm
  International Labour Office (1996). Management of alcohol- and drug-related issues in the workplace. An ILO code of practice. Geneva: International Labour Office.
  http://www.ilo.org/public/english/protection/safework/cops/english/download/e970709.pdf

- **NIAAA - National Institute on Alcohol Abuse and Alcoholism (NIAAA) (United States)**
  Publications, research information, news and events, resources.
  http://www.niaaa.nih.gov/
  Frone, R. M. (1999). Work Stress and Alcohol Use. Alcohol Research & Health, Vol. 23 (4).
  http://pubs.niaaa.nih.gov/publications/arh23-4/284-291.pdf

- **Trade Union Congress (TUC) (United Kingdom)**
  Health & safety: Drugs and alcohol, e.g. testing at work.
  http://www.tuc.org.uk/h_and_s/index.cfm?mins=348

- **Health and Safety at Work (HSE)**
  A guide for employers on alcohol at work.
  http://www.hse.gov.uk/pubns/indg240.htm

Alcohol in Finland

- **Eurocare—The European Alcohol Policy Alliance**
  Alcohol Policy Network in the Context of a Larger Europe: Bridging the Gap
  2004-2006. Country reports, Finland:
  http://www.eurocare.org/btg/countryreports/finland/index.html

- **Finnish Centre for Health Promotion**
  General information of health promotion in Finland.
  http://www.health.fi/index_en.php

- **Ministry of Social Affairs and Health (Finland)**
  Ministry of Social Affairs and Health: Alcohol Programme 2004-2007.
  https://rtstm.teamware.com/Resource.phx/alkoholi/index.htx

- **National Public Health Institute, KTL & National Research and Development Centre for Welfare and Health, STAKES & Ministry of Social Affairs and Health (Finland)**
  Koskinen & Aromaa & Huttunen & Teperi eds. (2006). Health in Finland.
  Helsinki: National Public Health Institute, KTL; National Research and Development Centre for Welfare and Health, STAKES; Ministry of Social Affairs and Health.
  http://www.ktl.fi/hif/hif.pdf

- **National Public Health Institute (Finland)**
  Helakorpi S., Patja K., Prättälä R., Uutela A (2005). Health Behaviour and Health among the Finnish Adult Population. English Abstract. Helsinki: Publications of the National Public Health Institute.
  http://www.ktl.fi/attachments/suomi/julkaisut/julkaisusarja_b/2005/2005b18.pdf

- **Primary Health Care European Project on Alcohol (PHEPA)**
  Primary Health Care European Project on Alcohol - Implementation in countries: Finland.
  http://www.phepa.net/units/phepa/html/en/dir360/doc8875.html

  Anderson, P. A tool to assess the available services for the management of alcohol problems at the country or regional level, Finland.
  http://www.phepa.net/units/phepa/pdf/assessment_tool_finland.pdf

- **STAKES—National Research and Development Centre for Welfare and Health (Finland)**
  Social research on alcohol and drugs.
  http://www.stakes.fi/EN/Tutkimus/alueet/alcohol.htm

Alcohol in the EU

- **Alcohol In Moderation**
  Alcohol In Moderation (2005). Swings and Roundabouts - An Analysis of Consumption Trends 2005.
  http://www.aim-digest.com/gateway/pages/trends/articles/trends%202005.htm

- **Euromonitor International**
  Industries: Alcoholic Drinks. Euromonitor International's alcoholic drinks
  research provides a complete strategic picture of the beer, wine and spirits
  industries.
  http://www.euromonitor.com/Alcoholic_Drinks

- **Institute of Alcohol Studies (United Kingdom)**
  Anderson, P. & Baumberg, B. (2006) Alcohol in Europe. London: Institute of
  Alcohol Studies.
  http://ec.europa.eu/healtheu/news_alcoholineurope_en.htm

- **Just Drinks**
  Beverage industry and markets. http://www.just-drinks.com/

- **Primary Health Care European Project on Alcohol (PHEPA)**
  This European Project is aimed at integrating health promotion interventions for
  hazardous and harmful alcohol consumption into primary health care professionals' daily clinical work. It presents evidence-based information on the management of alcohol problems under different headings: The harm done by alcohol,
  identifying alcohol problems, intervening with patients, etc.
  http://www.phepa.net/units/phepa/html/en/Du9/index.html

- **World Health Organization (Europe)**
  WHO (2006). Framework for alcohol policy in the WHO European Region.
  http://www.euro.who.int/document/e88335.pdf

Alcohol Policies and Strategies

- **Australian Government, The Department of Health and Ageing**
  National alcohol strategy, Australian alcohol guidelines, resources and publications.
  http://www.alcohol.gov.au/internet/alcohol/publishing.nsf/Content/home

- **Eurocare—The European Alcohol Policy Alliance**
  Alcohol Policy Network in the Context of a Larger Europe: Bridging the Gap
  2004-2006. (E.g. country reports).
  http://www.eurocare.org/btg/index.html

- **European Commission**
  Press Release IP/06/1455: Commission adopts Communication on reducing alcohol related harm in Europe.
  http://europa.eu/rapid/pressReleasesAction.do?reference=IP/06/1455&format=
  HTML&aged=0&language=EN&guiLanguage=en

  Commission adopted Communication setting out a strategy to support Member
  States in reducing alcohol-related harm.
  http://ec.europa.eu/health/
  ph_determinants/life_style/alcohol/alcohol_com_en.htm

Commission of the European Communities (2006) An EU strategy to support
Member States in reducing alcohol related harm. Brussels: Commission of the
European Communities.
http://ec.europa.eu/health/ph_determinants/life_style/
alcohol/documents/alcohol_com_625_en.pdf

References

Anderson P, Baumberg B (2006) *Alcohol in Europe. A Public Health Perspective. A Report for the European Commission*. London: Institute of Alcohol Studies. Retrieved February 19, 2007 from http://ec.europa.eu/health-eu/news_alcoholineurope_en.htm

Bildt C, Michélsen H (2002) Gender differences in the effects from working conditions on mental health: a 4-year follow-up. *International Archives of Occupational and Environmental Health. 75 (4)*, 252–258

Commission of the European Communities (2006) *An EU strategy to support Member States in reducing alcohol related harm*. Brussels: Commission of the European Communities. Retrieved February 19, 2007 from http://ec.europa.eu/health/ph_determinants/life_style/alcohol/documents/alcohol_com_625_en.pdf

European Agency for Safety and Health at Work (2003) *Gender issues in health and safety at work. A Review*. Retrieved February 19, 2007 from http://osha.europa.eu/publications/reports/209/reportgenderen_en.pdf

European Commission (2006) *Health-EU - The Public Health Thematic Portal of the European Union*. Retrieved February 19, 2007 from http://ec.europa.eu/health-eu/my_lifestyle/alcohol/index_en.htm

Euromonitor (2006) *Alcoholic Drinks. Euromonitor International*. Retrieved 19.2.2007 from http://www.euromonitor.com/Alcoholic_Drinks

Frone MR (1999) Work Stress and Alcohol Use. *Alcohol Research and Health, 23 (4)*. Retrieved February 19, 2007 from http://pubs.niaaa.nih.gov/publications/arh23-4/284-291.pdf

Frone MR (2000) Work-family conflict and employee psychiatric disorders: The national comorbidity survey. *Journal of Applied Psychology 85 (6)*, 888–895

Gual A, Anderson P, Segura L, Colom J (2005) *Alcohol and Primary Health Care: Clinical Guidelines on Identification and Brief Interventions*. Barcelona: Department of the Government of Catalonia. Retrieved February 19, 2007 from http://www.phepa.net

Hazards (2002) Drugs & alcohol. *Working out sensible drugs and alcohol policy*. Hazards Factsheet 77. Retrieved 19.2.2007 from http://www.hazards.org/haz77/drugsandalcohol.pdf

Heljälä L, Jurvansuu H, Kuokkanen M (2006) *Alkoholin riskikäyttäjien mini-interventio työterveyshuollossa. (Brief alcohol intervention in occupational health services -guide for OHS to identify and counsel hazardous drinkers)*. Finnish Institute of Occupational Health, Helsinki

Horlings E, Scoggings A (2006) An economic analysis of the impact of alcohol on the economic development in EU. *The RAND Journal of Economics*. Retrieved 19.2.2007 from http://www.rje.org/

Hytti A (2006) *Project HUUGO*. Finnish Association for Healthy Lifestyles. Presentation in 'Addictive conduct and occupational risks in Europe, 20th October 2006, Paris

Institute of Alcohol Studies (2005) *Women and Alcohol*. IAS Fact Sheet, April. Retrieved 19.2.2007 from http://www.ias.org.uk/resources/factsheets/women.pdf

Institute of Alcohol Studies (2006) *Alcohol and the Workplace*. IAS Fact Sheet, December. Retrieved 19.2.2007 from http://www.ias.org.uk/resources/factsheets/workplace.pdf

Institute of Alcohol Studies (2006) *Binge Drinking. Nature, Prevalence and Causes*. IAS Fact Sheet, December 2006 http://www.ias.org.uk/resources/factsheets/binge_drinking.pdf

International Labour Office, ILO (1996) *Management of alcohol- and drug-related issues in the workplace. An ILO code of practice*. Geneva: International Labour Office.

Retrieved   19.2.2007   from   http://www.ilo.org/public/english/protection/safework/cops/
english/download/e970709.pdf

International Labour Organization, ILO (2000) *Drug and Alcohol Abuse - A Gender
Problem.* Programme on Safety and Health at Work and the Environment (Safe-
work). Retrieved February 19, 2007 from http://www.ilo.org./public/english/protection/
safework/drug/gender.htm

International Labour Organization, ILO (2000) *Drug and alcohol abuse - an important workplace issue.* Programme on Safety and Health at Work and the Environment
(Safework). Retrieved February 19, 2007 from http://www.ilo.org/public/english/protection/
safework/drug/impiss.htm

Just Drinks (2005) *Beverage industry and markets.* Retrieved February 19, 2007 from
http://www.just-drinks.com/

Kauppinen K (2006) Gender, *Health and Work - a women's perspective.* ICOH Newsletter 4 (3).
Retrieved February 19, 2007 from http://www.icohweb.org/newsletter/index.asp

National Health and Medical Research Council (2001) *Australian Alcohol Guidelines. HealthRisks
and Benefits. Alcohol and Women's Health.* Fact Sheet 1

National Institute on Alcohol Abuse and Alcoholism, NIAAA (2005) *Women and
Drinking.* Retrieved February 19, 2007 from http://pubs.niaaa.nih.gov/publications/
brochurewomen/Woman_En glish.pdf

Rehm J Room R Monteiro M, Gmel G, Graham K, Rehn N, Sempos CT, Frick U, Jernigan D
(2004) *Alcohol. Comparative quantification of health risks: Global and regional burden of
disease due to selected major risk factors.* Ezzatti M, Lopez AD, Rodgers A, Murray CJL (eds)
WHO, Geneva

Saarto A (2006) *What to do?* Addiction Link, Information Bank. Retrieved February 19, 2007 from
http://www.paihdelinkki.fi/english/infobank/200_service_line/281e.htm

Silenced womanhood (2006) (Väkivalta - apua, in Finnish) Retrieved February 19, 2007 from
http://www.vakivalta-apua.fi/index.shtml

World Health Organization, WHO (2001) *AUDIT - The Alcohol Use Disorders Identification Test.*
Retrieved February 19, 2007 from http://www.aa2.org/check_ups/audit.htm

World Health Organization, WHO (2002) *Preferences for alcoholic drinks in Europe.* Health for
all database. Retrieved 19.2.2007 from http://www.euro.who.int/hfadb

World Health Organization, WHO (2004) *Gender in Mental Health Research.* Geneva:
Department of Gender, Women and Health. Retrieved February 19, 2007 from
http://www.who.int/gender/documents/en/mentalhealthlow.pdf

World Health Organization, WHO (2005) Gender, Health and Alcohol Use. *Gender and Health*,
September. Geneva: Department of Gender, Women and Health. Retrieved February 19, 2007
from http://www.who.int/gender/documents/Alcoholfinal.pdf

World Health Organization, WHO (2006) *Framework for alcohol policy in the WHO European
Region.* Retrieved February 19, 2007 from http://www.euro.who.int/document/e88335.pdf

Chapter 13
Promoting Physical Activity and a Healthy Diet among Working Women

Gemma Janer and Manolis Kogevinas

Introduction

This chapter will focus on worksite interventions that aim to promote moderate physical activity and a healthy diet. Whenever data exist on working women, emphasis is put on the description of worksite health promotion interventions specifically for working women. This chapter is focused on the description of evidence from intervention trials on working women and men, in relation to physical activity and diet, and does not make an evaluation of other types of studies that do not include an intervention. Physical inactivity, inadequate diet, and their combination have long been recognized as risk factors for several chronic diseases, including cardiovascular diseases and cancer. These risk factors have been, together with tobacco, the most common targets of both community and worksite health promotion programs.

Nutrition, Physical Activity and Women's Health

Physical inactivity and its consequences are of major concern in Western society. Physical inactivity is associated with an increased risk of many chronic diseases, such as cardiovascular disease and some types of cancer, including female cancers such as breast cancer. Another consequence of physical inactivity is obesity. During the last few decades, the percentage of overweight and obese people has increased dramatically, and the consequences for public health, as well as the economic impact, are enormous. In Europe, obesity-related costs have been estimated at 1 to 5 percent of the total health care expenditure (Proper et al. 2004).

There is abundant evidence of the important role of nutrition on health status, and this evidence is continuously growing. Indeed, five of the leading causes of death in developed countries—heart disease, some types of cancer, stroke, diabetes, and atherosclerosis—are associated with poor dietary practices (Glanz et al. 1996). For instance, excessive consumption of dietary fat and low consumption of fiber-rich foods, fruit, and vegetables contribute to increased risk for chronic diseases—particularly cardiovascular disease and cancer. The association of nutrition and cardiovascular disease occurs principally through the role of diet in several primary and secondary risk factors, including high blood cholesterol levels, high blood pressure, obesity, and diabetes mellitus. Healthful eating patterns can reduce the risk of premature morbidity and mortality from these diseases, help many people avoid suffering and disability, and reduce the need for medical treatment. There is also increasing evidence on the importance of nutrition of pregnant mothers on the health of their offspring.

Current Situation

Despite the well-documented benefits of moderate physical activity, 40 percent percent of Europeans older than 15 years of age declared that they did not exercise or practice sports (Ministerio de Sanidad y Consumo 2005). A certain pattern between North and South can be observed in Fig. 13.1. Finland, Sweden, and Denmark are the countries with less inactive populations (4 to 17%), whereas Portugal, Hungary, Italy, and Greece (57 to 66%) showed the highest percentage of inactive population (Ministerio de Sanidad y Consumo 2005).

The geographic distribution of the caloric ingestion per person and day is shown in Fig. 13.1b. Apart from the total energy ingestion, the composition of this is also an indicator related to health. Figs. 13.1c and 13.1d show the distribution of the percentage of ingested calories that comes from fat and the consumption of fruits and vegetables. Differences between countries are important, and a clear North-South and East-West pattern exists. There exists little direct information on the effects of work on obesity—for example, obesogenic factors in the workplace—and even less data on this effect among working women.

Both physical inactivity and excess of energy intake are associated with the onset of obesity (WHO 2006). Obesity prevalence (body mass index (BMI) above $30 \, \text{kg/m}^2$) presents an extraordinary geographic variability (see Table 13.1). The percentage of adult population with a BMI above $30 \, \text{kg/m}^2$ ranges from 9.7 to 27.5 percent in men and from 9.9 to 38.1 percent in women in the 25 EU member states. Among women, the prevalence of obesity is highest in Greece (38%), Malta (35%), Portugal (26%), and the Czech Republic (26%). There exist no comparable population data across countries on obesity in working women.

Obesity in the Workplace

Physical activity might as well have direct consequences on work ability, especially in the older workforce. An adequate level of physical activity may be needed to maintain or promote work ability—in particular, among aging workers. The aging of the workforce will affect many industrialized European countries in forthcoming years. In order to prevent early retirement, for example, preventive promotion of health and work ability is needed.

(a)   (b)

(c)   (d)

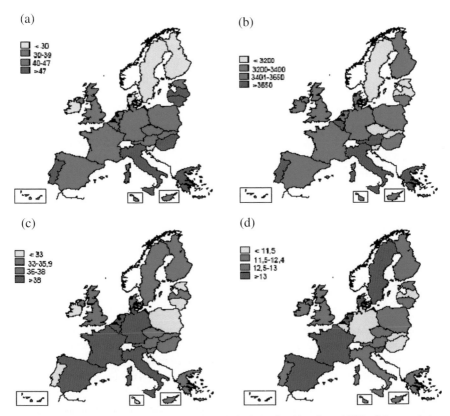

Fig. 13.1 Physical activity (data from 2004) and diet behavior (data from 2001) of the population in the EU member states A) Percentage of population over 15 years old that never exercises or practices sports; B) Average calorie consumption by person and day; C) Percentage of ingested calories from fat; D) Average consumption of fruits and vegetables per person and week.
Modified from Ministerio de Sanidad y Consumo (2005).

Table 13.1 Obesity prevalence (BMI $\geq$ 30 kg/m^2) in men and women of the European Union (1994–2002)

	Men	Women		Men	Women
Italy	9.5	9.9	Luxemburg	15.3	13.9
Latvia	9.5	17.4	Slovenia	16.5	13.8
Estonia	9.9	15.3	Slovakia	19.3	18.9
Austria	10.0	14.0	Finland	19.8	19.4
Sweden	10.0	11.9	Ireland	20.1	19.9
Poland	10.3	12.4	Hungary	21.0	21.2
Netherlands	10.4	10.1	Malta	22.0	35.0
France	11.4	11.3	United Kingdom	22.2	23.0
Lithuania	11.4	18.3	Germany	22.5	23.3
Denmark	12.5	11.3	Czech Republic	24.7	26.2
Spain	13.7	14.3	Cyprus	26.6	23.7
Portugal	13.9	26.1	Greece	27.5	38.1
Belgium	14.0	13.0			

The Two-fold Role of Working Women

The impact of obesity and physical inactivity can be evaluated on the woman herself, but also on the family. There is evidence on the effect of maternal work and childhood obesity, in terms of neglecting a healthy diet, but there exist no intervention trials on this issue. The role, however of work, in the onset of child obesity has not been adequately examined. There exists evidence on a social class gradient on child obesity, but this has been associated much more with wider socioeconomic factors rather than with the direct effect of work in women. In the following sections, reference is made to the potential effects of worksite interventions on the promotion of healthy eating in the family.

Intervention Trials—Prevention

Worksite vs Community Interventions

Worksites offer unique opportunities to encourage adults and their families to adopt healthy diets and increase levels of physical activity. Most adults spend half their waking hours at the workplace. Therefore, exposure to mass-reach approaches and behavioral interventions can be potentially more substantial than in many other community settings.

Worksite-based nutrition and cholesterol interventions also have several advantages in comparison with community-based interventions. They are accessible and convenient, they can be facilitated by support from co-workers and existing communication networks, and they are often less expensive than those offered elsewhere. The workplace also provides special opportunities for reinforcement and environmental supports for healthy eating through changes in cafeterias, vending machines, and catering policies. Last but not least, worksite populations can be enumerated by use of personnel records, and the opportunity for long-term follow-up is greater than in community-based programs, thus potentially improving the quality of program evaluations (Glanz et al. 1996).

Worksite Diet and Physical Activity Interventions

During the past 20 years, many corporations have implemented worksite physical activity and nutrition interventions. These interventions are expected to benefit workers—by promoting healthier lifestyles—but also have broader objectives, such as increasing productivity, reducing health care costs, reducing absenteeism, and decreasing stress.

Steps and Factors in Planning Diet and Physical Activity Interventions

The steps and factors to be considered when planning interventions towards diet and physical activity have generally been evaluated without making a distinction between women and men in the workplace.

Involvement of Management, Union Representatives, and Others

Obtaining the full support and, if possible, the involvement of the management and union representatives in the planning of the intervention is a crucial step for its success. In addition, the resources (time, space, and finances) granted will determine the type of the intervention to be offered.

Baseline Surveys and Recruitment of Participants

Baseline surveys—usually questionnaires, interviews, or medical examinations—are advisable ino identifying the needs of the target population and adapting interventions to them. In addition, baseline data are necessary to evaluate the results of the intervention.

Baseline surveys are also used to recruit workers for the interventions. When such surveys are not considered, recruitment of participants can be attempted by letters, e-mails, or phone calls, or actively through group leaders or union representatives.

It is important to actively recruit participants, particularly when facilities are offered. Otherwise, it is likely that the resources provided will be used by workers that already exercise, or already eat healthy—whereas, the program would not reach other workers that would potentially benefit more from it.

The Process (Contents) of the Interventions

Interventions can be classified into those aiming to: a) improve workers' knowledge and awareness of certain risk factors, b) help workers make behavioral changes, and c) create environments facilitating healthy lifestyles (see Table 13.2). The first strategy offers information such as an explanation of the relationship between physical activity and health. The second strategy offers persuasion and techniques to develop skills, such as learning to avoid tempting situations or identifying personal barriers towards the adherence to healthy behaviors. Environmental or structural interventions start changing the environment without requiring individual participation in educational activities, such as changing the available food in the office snack bar.

Programs can include components of three types of factors: awareness, behavioral, and environmental. In addition, flexible contents can be offered and tailored to each individual. One of the theoretical models that support this concept is the *Stages of Change* model. In this model, intervention messages are adapted to results obtained in baseline assessment. For example, workers could be classified at

Table 13.2 Examples of interventions on diet and physical activity

Diet	Physical Activity
Aiming to improve knowledge / awareness	
<ul><li>Food-based eating pattern messages; self-help booklets to adopt healthy diet</li><li>Nutrition classes</li><li>Healthy cooking demonstrations</li><li>Cholesterol values / cancer information</li></ul>	<ul><li>Educational programs: health benefits of physical activity</li><li>Classes on how to warm up and relax the muscles before and after exercising</li><li>Control of cardiac frequency</li></ul>
Environmental changes	
<ul><li>Changes in cafeteria, point-of-purchase</li></ul>	Provision of <ul><li>on site facilities (fitness centre, showers...)</li><li>Short exercise sessions</li><li>Leagues and competitions*</li></ul>

*Leagues and competitions should be carefully planned so that the risk of injuries is minimized.

the precontemplation stage if they did not intend to enroll in any physical activity program in the next six months; at a contemplation stage if they intended to enroll in a physical activity program in the next six months; and at a preparatory stage if they wanted to enroll in a physical activity program in the next month or if they had seriously attempted to follow a physical activity program during the last year. Workers then received different types of interventions depending on the stage they were in.

Delivering Modalities

Health promotion interventions can be directed to individuals, groups, or the whole workforce through environmental changes (e.g., changes in vending machine products). They can be offered by the workplace physician, by other workers, or by external experts. Apart from face-to-face contact, interventions can use letters, videos, posters, and phone calls.

Follow-up

Support over time can be offered to achieve better results in behavioral changes. Otherwise, the effect of sporadic interventions is likely to decrease with time.

Incentives

To achieve better results in behavioral changes, some interventions included competitions or provided financial incentives to the workers participating in the intervention.

Involvement of Workers in Planning and Implementation

Some interventions include workers in the planning and implementing of the health promotion program, although the effectiveness of this participation has not always been proven.

Evaluation of the Intervention Effects

The comparison of follow-up and baseline surveys can provide an estimate of the intervention effect. Nevertheless, observed changes might have occurred due to factors other than the intervention. Therefore, a reliable assessment of the effect of an intervention should include the comparison with a control group.

Targeting Women

Differences between men and women exist in the perception of risk and in the barriers and needs for changing risk behaviors. For instance, most women do not perceive heart disease as a high-priority health problem for themselves, yet heart disease affects one woman in ten between the ages of 45 and 65, and one in five over the age of 65 in the United States (Collins et al. 1997) and in many European countries.

In addition to differences in participation, or readiness to change health behaviors, the prevalence of health risk factors and disease differ between men and women. Women are especially susceptible to a series of health problems. For instance, rates of depression, urinary incontinence, arthritis, and anemia are higher in women than in men (Wollersheim 1993; Collins et al. 1997; Gopaldas 2002).

The particularities of health awareness and risk factors present in women need to be taken into account in planning the interventions. For example, diet interventions might include educational interventions focusing on iron intake to prevent anemia (Gopaldas et al. 2002).

Expected Effects of Worksite Interventions[2]

Worksite health promotion trials on diet focus on behavioral changes, particularly in increasing or reducing the consumption of specific food groups. Fruits, vegetables, and foods with a high proportion of fiber or fat have been the most common targets. Physiologic outcomes—including cholesterol levels, body fat, and blood pressure—have also been reported. Most trials observed changes in the treatment group in the

---

[2] Data presented in this section were obtained from reports in English, French, or Spanish of worksite health promotion trials published in peer-reviewed journals, having a control no-intervention group or evaluating in the same study different types of interventions, and including more than 100 subjects and a minimum of 50 in each study group.

Fig. 13.2 Effects of worksite interventions on fat, fiber, fruits, and vegetables intake Data from: Bauer et al., 1985; Kronenfeld et al., 1987; Hebert et al., 1993; Barrat et al., 1994; Glasgow et al., 1995; Sorensen et al., 1996; Reynolds et al., 1997; Glasgow et al., 1997; Buller et al., 1999; Sorensen et al., 1999; Tilley et al., 1999; Sasaki et al., 2000; Beresford et al., 2001; Campbell et al., 2002; Aldana et al., 2005.

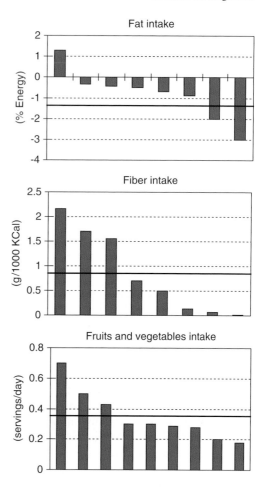

expected direction—i.e., decreases in the consumption of fat, and increases in the consumption of fruits, and vegetables, and fiber (see Fig. 13.2).

Programs targeting environmental changes, such as modifying the food offered in the company canteen and vending machines, were evaluated in six trials. All but one included some other kind of intervention. Results were similar to those obtained in trials not including environmental changes. French et al. [2001] showed, however, that environmental changes alone can also lead to significant changes in fat intake patterns. In particular, the percentage of price reduction and promotional material were associated with the percentage of low-fat snack sales. Some studies included more than one follow-up contact. The percentage of change maintained at 6 or 12 months following a program showed an intake increase or decrease that ranged from 30 to 65 percent.

The outcomes measured in the worksite health promotion programs on physical activity are variable, including the proportion of workers engaged in regular exer-

Table 13.3 Effects of worksite interventions on physical activity

	Outcome	Effects (I minus C)
Practice of Physical Activity	Proportion of workers engaged in regular exercise	10 - 12%
	Physical activity level in kcal/kg bodyweight/week (%)	8.06 (21%)
	Energy spent in intense physical activity	71%
	Vigorous physical activity (hours/week)	1.86
	MET (metabolic equivalent; e.g. 600 MET minutes per week is equivalent to 150 min of moderate activity weekly)	97
	Aerobic exercise (times per week)	0.3
	Strengthening/flexibility exercise (times per week)	0.49
	Blocks walked/day	5.77
	Flights of stairs up/day	0.4
	Total minutes walked/week (min)	27
	Scores ranging from 1 (never exercise) to 5 (three times or more a week) for different intervention groups	-0.5 to 0.01
Awareness	Progress through stages-of-change (% who progressed to action stage)	17.5%
	Progress through stages-of-change (number of stages progressed)	0.62
	Perception as more active	16%
	Better rates for social-cognitive variables (self-efficacy, pros, cons, intentions and behavior related to physical activity; scale 0-5)	0.04 to 0.20
Health Status	Aerobic capacity in V_{O2} max ml/Kg min	1-2
	Lack of fitness: Pulse rate greater than 120 beats/min after two minutes of stepping	4%
	Flexibility (cm)	2
	Reporting very much or rather much stress (%)	–5.5
	Total lifestyle score (range 0-6)	.33
	Total mortality (cumulative difference)	–17.5%
	Nonfatal myocardial infarction (cumulative difference)	–26%
	Cumulative sick leave (h) after the 15-month follow-up	22.5

Data from: Kornitzer et al., 1983; Bauer et al., 1985; Spilman et al., 1986; Kronenfeld et al., 1987; Shannon et al., 1987; Edye et al., 1989; Breslow et al., 1990; Shephard et al., 1992; Shpehard et al., 1992; Gomel et al., 1992; Heirich et al., 1993; Maes et al., 1998; Marcus et al., 1998; Emmons et al., 1999; Peterson and Aldana, 1999; Campbell et al., 2002; Nurminen et al., 2002; Purath et al., 2004; Plotnikoff et al , 2005.

cise, aerobic capacity, and body fat levels (see Table 13.3). Most studies reported positive findings, and significant changes were found in 10 of 17 studies.

Interventions in physical activity can be classified in two groups: a) those based on counseling and educational sessions, and b) those offering facilities, space, or time for the workers. Significant changes were reported in seven out of 12 trials using educational sessions and informative materials, and in three of five trials offering facilities, time, and space. One trial comparing both type of interventions found better results in educational activities that focused on behavioral changes, with 65 percent of at-risk employees exercising weekly, compared to 50 percent when offering facilities. Therefore, offering fitness facilities or classes by itself may not be

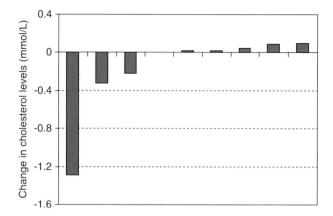

Fig. 13.3 Effects of worksite interventions on cholesterol levels
Data from: Cambien et al., 1981; Edye et al., 1989; Barratt et al., 1994; Glasgow et al., 1995; Glasgow et al., 1997; Reynolds et al., 1997; Aldana et al., 2002; Karlehagen et al., 2003; Proper et al., 2003; Aldana et al., 2005.

more successful than offering educational sessions. Therefore, resources allowing the combination of both components would be desirable.

Cholesterol levels were assessed in most studies that targeted behavioral changes in nutrition and physical activity. Part of the studies that aimed to reduce cardiovascular diseases also included interventions in other areas, such as tobacco control or stress management. The changes observed in cholesterol levels ranged from a 0.16 increase to a 1.29 mmol/L decrease (see Fig. 13.3), and only four out of 14 studies found a statistically significant intervention effect (note that some of these studies were not included in Fig. 13.2 because they did not report the magnitude of the effect). The noticeable variability in success among programs might be partially explained by the inclusion (or not) of a physical activity component in the intervention program. Thus, four out of nine studies that included interventions on physical activity reported a significant effect, while none of the five studies that did not include an intervention on physical activity reported a significant effect.

Figure 13.4 shows changes in body weight and BMI obtained in weight control interventions, and in programs that aim to reduce cardiovascular risks by offering interventions in nutrition or physical activity. Results varied among studies with the changes in body weight ranging from a 0.25 Kg increase to a 3.5 Kg decrease. Body fat reduction ranged from 0.45 percent to 2.0 percent, and BMI reduction ranged from 1.6 to -0.3. The changes achieved in programs that included elements of weight control that were evaluated after a short-term period were greater than those of studies reporting longer-term data. Nevertheless, maintenance of the intervention effect over time (six months to one year) was assessed in two studies without finding almost any reduction of the effect.

Fig. 13.4 Effects of worksite
interventions on body weight
Data from: Cambien
et al., 1981; Edye et al., 1989;
Erfurt et al., 1991; Jeffery
et al., 1993; Shannon
et al., 1993; Anderson
et al., 1993; Barratt
et al., 1994; Aldana
et al., 2002; Karlehagen
et al., 2003; Proper
et al., 2003; Aldana
et al., 2005.

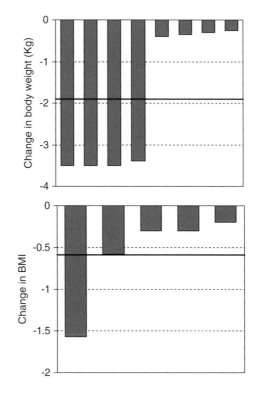

Problems and Barriers

Existing intervention trials in the workplace make little distinction on specific problems and barriers in working women as compared to working men.

Participation in Health Promotion Programs

One of the main problems that a health promotion intervention might face is low
employee participation rates. In a review of worksite health promotion programs,
participation in the health promotion activities ranged from 12 percent to 83 percent
(Janer et al. 2002).

There are limited data on whether and which baseline characteristics of the target
population are associated with participation rates. Factors that have been associated
with higher participation rates in program activities have been smaller worksites,
gender (female), and those who are younger, better educated, and actively employed
in a nutrition program. Several strategies have been used to recruit a high number
of participants and maintain low attrition rates—for example, involvement of workers in the planning and implementing of interventions, establishment of economic

incentives, or competitions intending to improve both participation rates and behavioral changes. However, evidence supporting the effect of such measures on the participation rates is weak.

Barriers

Women who are older, less educated, or of lower socioeconomic status are less likely than other women to engage in physical activity.

Many lower income and minority women are employed in blue-collar occupations in small- to medium-sized worksites, such as the manufacturing industry. These worksites, however, often lack comprehensive health promotion programs or resources, such as cafeterias or fitness facilities. Women working in blue-collar occupations in these companies tend to have elevated health risks due to a high prevalence of unhealthy behaviors and increased stress due to jobs with high demand and low control. Women also face unique barriers to participation in traditional workplace health promotion programs, including a lack of time due to balancing multiple roles and responsibilities.

References

Aldana SG, Greenlaw R, Diehl HA, Englert H, Jackson R. (2002) Impact of the coronary health improvement project (CHIP) on several employee populations. *J Occup Environ Med.* September 2002. 44(9):831–9

Aldana SG, Greenlaw RL, Diehl HA, Salberg A, Merrill RM, Ohmine S (2005) The effects of a worksite chronic disease prevention program. *J Occup Environ Med.* 47:558–564

Barratt A, Reznik R, Irwig L, Cuff A, Simpson JM, Oldenburg B et al. (1994) Work-site cholesterol screening and dietary intervention: the Staff Healthy Heart Project. Steering Committee. *Am J Public Health* 84(5):779–782

Bauer RL, Heller RF, Challah S (1985) United Kingdom Heart Disease Prevention Project: 12-year follow-up of risk factors. *Am J Epidemiol* 121(4):563–569

Beresford SA, Thompson B, Feng Z, Christianson A, McLerran D, Patrick DL (2001) Seattle 5 a Day worksite program to increase fruit and vegetable consumption. *Prev Med.* March. 32(3):230–8

Buller DB, Morrill C, Taren D, Aickin M, Sennott-Miller L, Buller MK, et al. (1999) Randomized trial testing the effect of peer education at increasing fruit and vegetable intake. *J Natl Cancer Inst* 91(17):1491–1500

Cambien F, Richard JL, Ducimetiere P, Warnet JM, Kahn J (1981) The Paris Cardiovascular Risk Factor Prevention Trial. Effects of two years of intervention in a population of young men. *J Epidemiol Community Health.* June 35(2):91–7.

Campbell MK, Tessaro I, DeVellis B, Benedict S, Kelsey K, Belton L, Sanhueza A (2002) Effects of a tailored health promotion program for female blue-collar workers: health works for women. *Prev Med.* March 34(3):313–23

Collins BS, Hollander RB, Koffman, DM, Reeve R, Seidler S (year?) Women, work and health: issues and implications for worksite health promotion. *Women and Health* 25(4): 3–38

Edye BV, Mandryk JA, Frommer MS, Healey S, Ferguson DA (1989) Evaluation of a worksite programme for the modification of cardiovascular risk factors. *Med J Aust* 150(10):574, 576–578, 581

Emmons KM, Linnan LA, Shadel WG, Marcus B, Abrams DB (1999) The Working Healthy Project: a worksite health-promotion trial targeting physical activity, diet, and smoking. *JOEM* 41(7):545–555

French SA, Jeffery RW, Story M, Breitlow KK, Baxter JS, Hannan P, Snyder MP (2001) Pricing and promotion effects on low-fat vending snack purchases: the CHIPS Study. *Am J Public Health.* January 91(1):112–7

Glanz K, Sorensen G, Farmer A (1996) The health impact of worksite nutrition and cholesterol intervention programs. *Am J Health Promot* 10(6):453–70

Glasgow RE, Terborg JR, Hollis JF, Severson HH, Boles SM (1995) Take heart: results from the initial phase of a work-site wellness program. *Am J Public Health* 85(2):209–216.

Glasgow RE, Terborg JR, Strycker LA, Boles SM, Hollis JF (1997) Take Heart II: replication of a worksite health promotion trial. *J Behav Med* 20(2):143–161

Gopaldas T (2002) Iron-deficiency anemia in young working women can be reduced by increasing the consumption of cereal-based fermented foods or gooseberry juice at the workplace. *Food Nutr Bull.* March 23(1):94–105

Hebert JR, Stoddard AM, Harris DR, Sorensen G, Hunt MK, Morris DH, et al. (1993) Measuring the effect of a worksite-based nutrition intervention on food consumption. *AEP* 3(6):629–635

Janer G, Sala M, Kogevinas M (year?) Health promotion trials at worksites and risk factors for cancer. *Scand J Work Environ Health* 28(3): 141–57

Karlehagen S, Ohlson CG (2003) Primary prevention of cardiovascular disease by an occupational health service. *Prev Med.* September 37(3):219–25

Kronenfeld JJ, Jackson K, Blair SN, Davis K, Gimarc JD, Salisbury Z, et al. (1987) Evaluating health promotion: a longitudinal quasi-experimental design. *Health Educ Q* 14(2): 123–139

Nurminen E, Malmivaara A, Ilmarinen J, Ylostalo P, Mutanen P, Ahonen G, Aro T (2002) Effectiveness of a worksite exercise program with respect to perceived work ability and sick leaves among women with physical work. *Scand J Work Environ Health.* April 28(2):85–93

Peterson TR, Aldana G (1999) Improving exercise behavior: an application of the stages of change model in a worksite setting. *Am J Health Promot* 13(4):229–232

Plotnikoff RC, McCargar LJ, Wilson PM, Loucaides CA (2005) Efficacy of an E-mail intervention for the promotion of physical activity and nutrition behavior in the workplace context. *Am J Health Promot.* Jul-Aug 19(6):422–9

Proper KI, Hildebrandt VH, Van der Beek AJ, Twisk JW, Van Mechelen W (2003) Effect of individual counseling on physical activity fitness and health: a randomized controlled trial in a workplace setting. *Am J Prev Med.* April 24(3):218–26

Proper KI, van der Beek AJ, Hildebrandt VH, Twisk JW, van Mechelen W (2004) Worksite health promotion using individual counselling and the effectiveness on sick leave; results of a randomised controlled trial. *Occup Environ Med.* March 61(3):275–9

Purath J, Miller AM, McCabe G, Wilbur J (2004) A brief intervention to increase physical activity in sedentary working women. *Can J Nurs Res.* Mar 36(1):76–91

Reynolds KD, Gillum JL, Hyman DJ, Byers T, Moore SA, Paradis G, et al. (1997) Comparing two strategies to modify dietary behavior and serum cholesterol. *Journal of Cardiovascular Risk* 4(1):1–5

Sasaki S, Ishikawa T, Yanagibori R, Amano K (2000) Change and 1-year maintenance of nutrient and food group intakes at a 12-week worksite dietary intervention trial for men at high risk of coronary heart disease. *J Nutr Sci Vitaminol* 46(1):15–22

Sedlak CA, Doheny MO, Estok PJ, Zeller RA (2005) Tailored interventions to enhance osteoporosis prevention in women. *Orthop Nurs.* Jul-Aug 24(4):270–6; quiz 277–8

Shephard RJ (1992) Twelve years experience of a fitness program for the salaried employees of a toronto life assurance company. *Am J Health Promot* 6(4):292–301

Sorensen G, Stoddard A, Peterson K, Cohen N, Hunt MK, Stein E, et al. (1999) Increasing fruit and vegetable consumption through worksites and families in the treatwell 5-a-day study. *Am J Public Health* 89(1):54–60

Sorensen G, Stoddard AM, LaMontagne AD, Emmons K, Hunt MK, Youngstrom R, McLellan D, Christiani DC (2003) A comprehensive worksite cancer prevention intervention: behavior change results from a randomized controlled trial (United States). *J Public Health Policy* 24(1):5–25

Sorensen G, Thompson B, Glanz K, Feng Z, Kinne S, DiClemente C, et al. (1996) Work site-based cancer prevention: primary results from the Working Well Trial. *Am J Public Health* 86(7):939–947

Tilley BC, Glanz K, Kristal AR, Hirst K, Li S, Vernon SW, et al. (1999) Nutrition intervention for high-risk auto workers: results of the Next Step Trial. *Prev Med* 28(3):284–292

Trends in Europe and North America (2003) The statistical yearbook of the economic commission for Europe 2003. Available at http://www.unece.org/stats/trend/trend_h.htm

WHO (2006) Global strategy on diet, physical activity and health. Available at www.who.int/

Wollersheim JP (1993) Depression, women, and the workplace. *Occup Med* 8(4):787–95

Yancey AK, McCarthy WJ, Taylor WC, Merlo A, Gewa C, Weber MD, Fielding JE (2004) The Los Angeles Lift Off: a sociocultural environmental change intervention to integrate physical activity into the workplace. *Prev Med.* June 38(6):848–56

Index

Printed in the United States of America